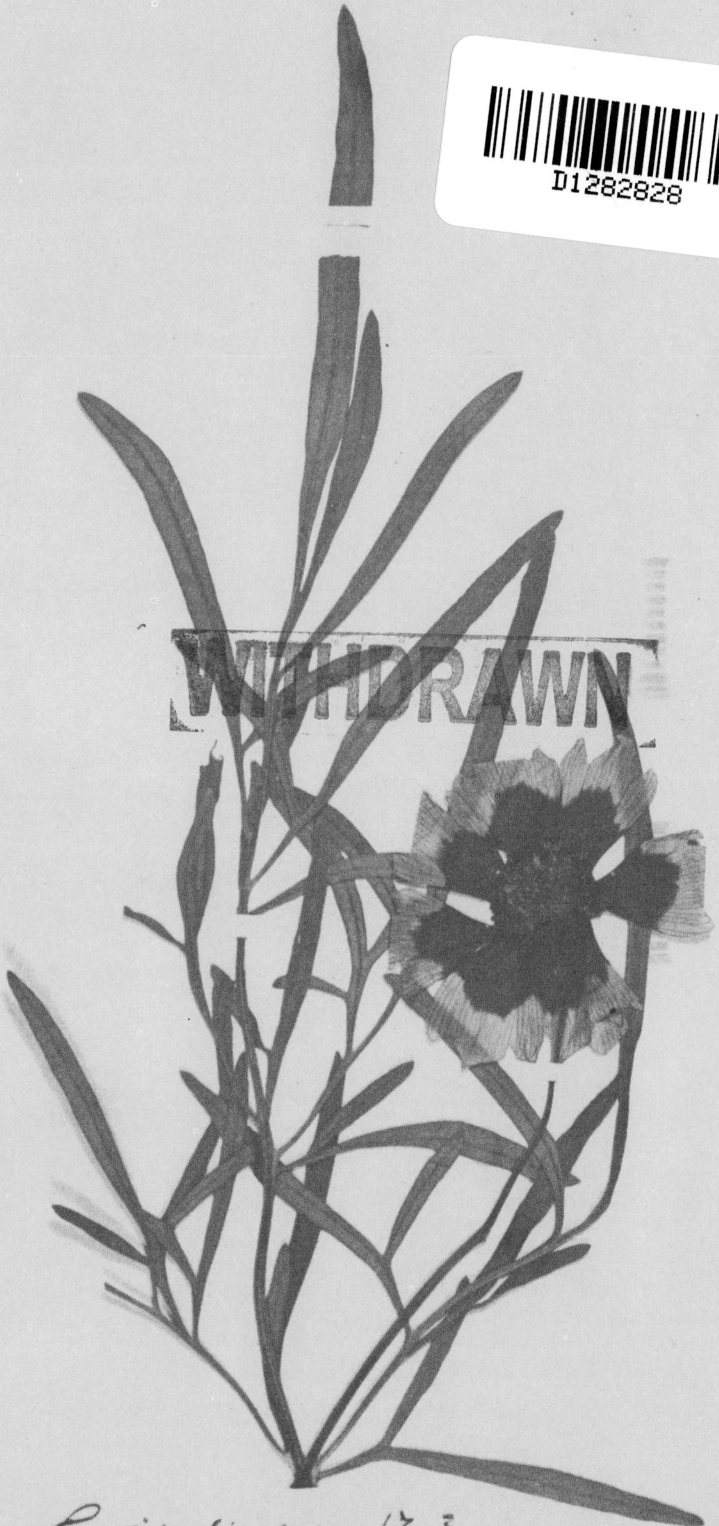

WITHDRAWN

Coreopsis. tinctoria. 17-3.

BK 928.1      D553S
LIFE OF EMILY DICKINSON          V1
1974           15.00  FV      /SEWALL, RI

3000 402719 30017
St. Louis Community College

928.1 D553S                v.1              EV
SEWALL
   THE LIFE OF EMILY DICKINSON
                  15.00

 St. Louis Community
College

Library

5801 Wilson Avenue
St. Louis, Missouri 63110

# THE LIFE OF

# *Emily Dickinson*

EMILY DICKINSON
From the daguerreotype taken at Mount Holyoke, December 1847 or early 1848

# THE LIFE OF
# EMILY
# DICKINSON

## VOLUME ONE

BY

# Richard B. Sewall

*Farrar, Straus and Giroux*

NEW YORK

*Copyright © 1974 by* RICHARD B. SEWALL

*All rights reserved*

*Second printing, 1975*

*Printed in the United States of America*

*Published simultaneously in Canada by Doubleday Canada Ltd., Toronto*


*Library of Congress Cataloging in Publication Data*


Sewall, Richard Benson.

*The Life of Emily Dickinson.*


*Bibliography: p.*

*1. Dickinson, Emily, 1830–1886—Biography.*

*I. Title.*

PS*1541*.Z5S42 *811′.4* [B] *74–8764*

To Til
*with love*

# Contents

# Contents

## VOLUME TWO

# Illustrations

## VOLUME ONE

# ILLUSTRATIONS

# Preface

G REAT POETS, like great dramatists, need great audiences. This is not to say that an audience, to be great, must be learned, or sophisticated, or heroic. The Athenians who went to the plays were average folk, and the Elizabethan groundlings were hardly noted for their high culture. Yet they were great audiences, attuned, receptive, expectant, bringing to the dramatic encounter shared traditions, fears and hopes, memories, passions, and mysteries. They were willing to submit them all to the artist's master humanity, as he unfolded essential truth before their eyes—to their amusement, or horror, or exaltation. They seem to have relished seeing the basic issues laid bare and to have shared with the artist (however vaguely) a sense of the ultimate issue, survival: what held the community together or tore it apart, what sustained the human psyche or worked for its destruction. We like to think they went away from the plays wiser, stronger, more humane.

My aim in this book is to help the reader into just such an experience with the poems and letters of Emily Dickinson. She, too, understood survival and its demands. She explored its limits with as probing an eye as any dramatist. She knew what horror was, and exaltation, and the power of humor. Only, her vision—dispersed and fragmented among the hundreds of short, tense lyrics that make up her canon—comes to us with none of the massive wholeness of the plays. It is not surprising that Sophocles and Shakespeare should be closer to us, have clearer shape in our minds, than our near-contemporary, the elusive poet of Amherst. With them, we know where we are—roughly, that is, and with the help of generations of scholarly and critical inquiry. With Emily Dickinson, the long process of assimilation has, relatively speaking, just begun. She is not yet *ours,* and she will not be until her hopes and fears and mysteries become as plain to us as Antigone's or Hamlet's are, and with much the same claim on us.

In my efforts toward this end, I have learned a number of things about the process. First, to work one's way, however partially, into the world of Emily Dickinson, the inner world and the outer, takes time, patience, care, and the sacrifice of many prejudices. The discerning reader can trace my path as vista after vista opened up. If the path seems long and the bypaths many, let me record my regret that it isn't longer and the bypaths so few. Henry James remarked that "the art of the biographer—a devilish art!— is somehow practically *thinning*. It simplifies even while seeking to enrich."

PREFACE

I hate the thought of having *thinned* Emily Dickinson. Even now, when I run through the poems and the letters again, I am appalled at what I left out: deft formulations that cut to the quick; revealing insights that, had I done them full justice, might even now qualify a generalization or a judgment; the seeming casual verse, or the chance remark in a letter that, apparently telling little, just might be telling all. As to the bypaths, there is no end. She is inexhaustible.

That I have come even this far is due in large part to those who opened the way. I think first of George Frisbie Whicher's pioneer biography in 1938 and of the work in the 1950s and 1960s by Thomas H. Johnson, Theodora Ward, Jay Leyda, and Millicent Todd Bingham which established the texts and expanded the area of relevant fact. No progress was possible until what they did was done. I have learned much, impossible to document completely, from the scholars and critics who, in the second wave of Dickinson studies, found new facts or (and here I learned to learn even as I disagreed) pressed old ones for what they would yield in theory or hypothesis. The dialectic has been kept alive and my understanding deepened by the work of Charles Anderson, Jack Capps, John Cody, Ralph Franklin, Albert Gelpi, David Higgins, Ruth Miller, Rebecca Patterson, David Porter, William Robert Sherwood. I have learned from scholars whose major manuscripts, unpublished as I write, will present, in still a third wave, new syntheses and open up new dimensions of the poetry: Joanne Diehl, Roland Hagenbüchle, Inder Nath Kher, Robert Lambert, Jr., Robert Weisbuch. From many of these, of both generations, I have benefited in conversation and conference; as they scan my chapters, they will hear echoes. To that indispensable group, those who typed, checked, indexed, read and criticized, my debt will be entirely clear—and infinite: Shirley Menn, Edith White, Helene Fineman, Wayland Schmidt, Leonard Conversi, Rosaline Schwartz, and Patricia Sierra. Gladys MacKenzie, Ruth Gay, and Polly Longsworth assisted my work with the Todd-Bingham Family Papers at Yale, and Carolyn Jakeman with the Dickinson Papers at Harvard. I have benefited throughout from the generous cooperation of Robert Giroux and the meticulous editing of Carmen Gomezplata.

It was in 1946, or shortly thereafter, that Mrs. Bingham first breathed to me the possibility of this work. Ten years later she gave me the first full view of its possible dimensions; and shortly after that her papers, indispensable to the project, came to Yale. She wanted, she said, "the whole story" of her mother's involvement told—but told in the setting of the larger story of Emily Dickinson. She tied no strings and asked for no prior commitments. She was unequivocal, and her aim was clear: through new documentation and the new insights it provided, to bring Emily Dickinson and her poetry closer to readers everywhere.

Finally, my deepest gratitude to Jay Leyda—scholar, critic, poet—who has been with this all the way.

*Bethany, Connecticut*                                                  R. B. S.
*May 19, 1974*

# Acknowledgments

I AM GRATEFUL FOR PERMISSION to quote manuscript materials, and materials under copyright, drawn from the following sources:

The Todd-Bingham Family Papers (herein called "Todd-Bingham Archive"), Yale University Library

The Dickinson Papers, The Houghton Library of the Harvard College Library

The Jones Library, Amherst, Mass.

The Amherst College Library

The University of Virginia Library

THE POEMS OF EMILY DICKINSON, *ed. Thomas H. Johnson, Cambridge, Mass.: The Belknap Press of Harvard University Press, copyright 1951, 1955 by The President and Fellows of Harvard College, reprinted by permission of the publishers and the Trustees of Amherst College. For poems originally published in* The Single Hound, *copyright 1914, 1942 by Martha Dickinson Bianchi; for poems originally published in* Further Poems, *copyright 1929, © 1957 by Mary L. Hampson; for poems originally published in* Unpublished Poems, *copyright 1935, © 1963 by Mary L. Hampson, reprinted by permission of Little, Brown and Company. For poems originally published in* Bolts of Melody, *edited by Mabel Loomis Todd and Millicent Todd Bingham, copyright 1945 by the Trustees of Amherst College, © renewed 1973 by Richard B. Sewall, reprinted by permission of Harper & Row, Publishers, Inc.*

THE LETTERS OF EMILY DICKINSON, *eds. Thomas H. Johnson and Theodora Ward, Cambridge, Mass.: The Belknap Press of Harvard University Press, copyright 1914, 1924, 1932 by Martha Dickinson Bianchi; copyright © 1958 by the President and Fellows of Harvard College, reprinted by permission of the publishers and the Trustees of Amherst College*

THE LYMAN LETTERS: NEW LIGHT ON EMILY DICKINSON AND HER FAMILY, *by Richard B. Sewall, Amherst, Mass.: The University of Massachusetts Press, copyright © 1965 by The Massachusetts Review, Inc.*

EMILY DICKINSON'S HOME, *by Millicent Todd Bingham, New York, Harper and Brothers, 1955*

THE YEARS AND HOURS OF EMILY DICKINSON, *by Jay Leyda, New Haven, Conn.: The Yale University Press, 1960*

The following abbreviations are used throughout:

P   *The Poems of Emily Dickinson,* ed. Thomas H. Johnson. Cambridge, Mass.: The Belknap Press of Harvard University Press, 1955.

L   *The Letters of Emily Dickinson,* ed. Thomas H. Johnson and Theodora Ward. Cambridge, Mass.: The Belknap Press of Harvard University Press, 1958.

YH   *The Years and Hours of Emily Dickinson,* by Jay Leyda. New Haven, Conn.: Yale University Press, 1960.

LL   *The Lyman Letters: New Light on Emily Dickinson and Her Family,* by Richard B. Sewall. Amherst, Mass.: University of Massachusetts Press, 1965.

AB   *Ancestors' Brocades,* by Millicent Todd Bingham. New York and London: Harper & Brothers, 1945.

*Home*   *Emily Dickinson's Home,* by Millicent Todd Bingham. New York: Harper & Brothers, 1955.

Quotations follow the original spelling, punctuation, and capitalization. The use of *sic* is reduced to a minimum.

*Unless otherwise indicated:*

Places mentioned, except for cities like New York, Philadelphia, etc., are in Massachusetts.

Ellipses are mine.

Dating of the poems and letters of Emily Dickinson follows the Harvard editions cited above.

The Harvard numbering of the poems is followed throughout. See also Index of First Lines.

# Chronology

| | |
|---|---|
| 1775 *October 9* | Samuel Fowler Dickinson, grandfather, born ("gentle and sensitive, and with more than ordinary mental gifts") |
| 1803 *January 1* | Edward Dickinson, father, born |
| 1804 *July 3* | Emily Norcross, mother, born |
| 1813 | Samuel Fowler Dickinson builds the Homestead, or "Mansion," on Main Street ("said to have been the first brick house in Amherst") |
| 1814 | Amherst Academy founded |
| 1821 | Amherst College founded |
| 1828 *May 6* | Edward Dickinson and Emily Norcross married |
| 1829 *April 16* | William Austin Dickinson, brother, born |
| 1830 *April 3* | Father buys half of Homestead from S. F. Dickinson |
| *October 15* | Helen Fiske Hunt Jackson ("H.H.") born ("she is quite inclined to question the authority of everything") |
| *December 10* | EMILY ELIZABETH DICKINSON born |
| *December 19* | Susan Huntington Gilbert born |
| 1833 *February 28* | Lavinia Norcross Dickinson, sister, born |
| *March* | Grandfather Dickinson sells his half of the Homestead to General David Mack and moves to Cincinnati, Ohio |
| *early May ?–* *June 10 ?* | Emily in Monson with Aunt Lavinia Norcross ("she is a very good child & but little trouble") |
| 1835 *August 4* | Father appointed treasurer of Amherst College ("he never . . . lost a dollar") |
| *September 7* | Emily begins four years at "Primary School" |
| 1838 *January* | Father's first term in Massachusetts General Court begins |
| *April 22* | Samuel Fowler Dickinson dies in Hudson, Ohio, "disillusioned, neglected, and forgotten" |
| 1840 *April* | Edward Dickinson sells his half of Homestead to General Mack and moves his family to house on North Pleasant St. |

| | |
|---|---|
| *September 7* | Emily and Lavinia begin their first year at Amherst Academy ("you know I am always in love with my teachers") |
| 1842 *April* | Austin at Williston Seminary; Emily's first extant letter (to Austin: "there was always such a Hurrah wherever you was") |
| 1844 *April 29* | Death of Sophia Holland, age fifteen ("then it seemed to me I should die too . . .") |
| *May* | Emily visits Aunt Lavinia in Boston |
| *June 4* | Emily visits Uncle William Dickinson in Worcester |
| *June* | Friendship with Abiah Root begins ("you were always dignified") |
| *December* | Religious revival in Amherst ("I attended none of the meetings") |
| 1845 *February* | Abiah Root leaves Amherst; first exchange of letters with Emily |
| *April 15* | Edward Hitchcock inaugurated president of Amherst College ("a large, noble looking man") |
| 1846 *spring* | Religious revival in Amherst ("the small circle who met for prayer missed me from their number") |
| *May 5* | Joel Norcross, grandfather, dies |
| *August 25* | Emily to Boston for health (to mid-September) |
| *August* | Austin enters Amherst College |
| *November 12* | Father chairman at Amherst Cattle Show |
| 1847 *August 4* | Frances Lavinia (Fanny) Norcross, cousin, born |
| *August 10* | Emily finishes seventh year at Academy |
| *August ?* | Abiah Root visits Amherst ("what delightful times we had") |
| *September 28* | Olivia M. Coleman dies, age twenty |
| *September 30* | Emily enters Mount Holyoke |
| *October 16* | Austin, Vinnie, and Abby Wood visit Emily at Mount Holyoke ("I watched you until you were out of sight Saturday evening") |
| *October 21* | To Austin: "Has the Mexican war terminated yet & how? Are we beat? Do you know of any nation about to besiege South Hadley?" [Treaty of Guadalupe-Hidalgo, Feb. 2, 1848] |
| *November 3* | Parents visit Emily at Mount Holyoke ("I danced & clapped my hands. . . . They wanted to surprise me") |
| *November 24–29* | Emily home for Thanksgiving ("never did Amherst look more lovely to me") |

| | |
|---|---|
| *December ?* | Emily sits for daguerreotype at Mount Holyoke |
| 1848 *January* | To Abiah: "I am now studying 'Silliman's Chemistry' & Cutter's Physiology, in both of which I am much interested" |
| *January 21–* *February 7* | Winter vacation ("my visit at home was happy, very happy, to me") |
| *March 25–* *May 11* | Spring vacation; Emily home ill ("Father is quite a hand to give medicine, especially if it is not desirable") |
| *May 11–* *August* | Last session at Mount Holyoke ("Father has decided not to send me to Holyoke another year") |
| *May 14* | Jacob Holt dies, age twenty-six |
| *August 3* | Abiah Root attends Commencement at Mount Holyoke ("what had sealed your lips toward me?") |
| *October 29* | Emily to Abiah: "If you dont want to be my friend any longer . . ." |
| *December 19* | Emily Brontë dies ("gigantic Emily Brontë") |
| 1849 *March 5* | Mary Lyon dies ("we may become almost what we will") |
| *May* | Longfellow's *Kavanagh* published (Austin brings it home) |
| *August* | Ben Newton leaves Amherst |
| *October 9* | Emily, Vinnie, and party climb Mt. Holyoke |
| *December 5* | Vinnie begins winter term at Ipswich ("they are not *Amherst girls,* yet some are pretty & fine scholars") |
| *December* | Austin finishes Hume's *History* amid "general uproar"; Emily returns *Jane Eyre* to Elbridge Bowdoin |
| 1850 *January* | Ben Newton sends Emerson's *Poems* (publ. 1847) to Emily |
| *late February* | Amherst College *Indicator* publishes Emily's "Magnum bonum" valentine (first mention of Emily's dog Carlo) |
| *March 4* | Emily sends valentine ("Awake ye muses") to Elbridge Bowdoin |
| *March–August* | Religious revival in Amherst ("I am standing alone in rebellion") |
| *May 5 ?* | Mother ill, Emily (as nurse) declines invitation to ride in the woods ("I told him I could not go") |
| *spring ?* | Susan-Austin courtship begins |
| *August 8* | Austin graduates from Amherst |
| *August 11* | Father and Susan Gilbert admitted to First Church by profession of faith |

| | |
|---|---|
| *August 14* | Father attends semicentennial celebration at Yale |
| *September* | Austin begins teaching at Sunderland |
| *September 20* | Richard Henry Dana begins Shakespeare lectures in Amherst |
| *October 14* | Emily and Vinnie plan to attend the lecture on *Hamlet* |
| *October 30* | Dickinsons attend First Annual Amherst Cattle Show |
| *November 3* | Vinnie admitted to First Church by profession of faith |
| *November 26* | Eclectic Society orations ("This night is long to be remembered. New things have happened") |
| *November 30* | Leonard Humphrey dies, age twenty-seven ("my master has gone to rest") |
| *December 31* | Emily to Abiah Root: "I love to buffet the sea. . . . I love the danger!" |
| | Published this year: Ik Marvel, *Reveries of a Bachelor;* Hawthorne, *The Scarlet Letter* |
| 1851 *January 1* | Vinnie begins diary |
| *March* | Joseph Lyman leaves for the South (Vinnie: "Joseph has gone, two years is a long time!") |
| *June 4* | Ben Newton marries |
| *June 7* | Austin begins teaching in Boston |
| *July 3* | Jenny Lind's recital in Northampton ("Father sat all the evening looking *mad,* and *silly*") |
| *July 26* | Serious fire in Amherst ("three cheers for Edward Dickinson, and three more for the Insurance Company!") |
| *August 14* | Commencement; honorary degree to J. G. Holland |
| *September 6–22* | Emily and Vinnie in Boston ("we were rich in disdain for Bostonians and Boston") |
| *September* | Susan takes up teaching post in Baltimore |
| *September 18* | Emily and Vinnie consult Dr. Wesselhoeft, homeopathic physician, in Boston |
| *September 29* | Father rings church bell for aurora borealis |
| | Published this year: *Moby-Dick* |
| 1852 *February 20* | *Springfield Republican* publishes Emily's "Sic transit" valentine |
| *June* | Father at Whig Convention in Baltimore; calls on Susan |
| *July 26* | Austin home from Boston, through with teaching |
| *December 17* | Father elected Representative to Congress from Tenth Massachusetts District |
| 1853 *March 9* | Austin enters Harvard Law School |

| | |
|---|---|
| *March 23* | Susan visits him in Boston (Revere House Hotel); engagement decided on |
| *March 24* | Ben Newton dies, age thirty-two ("The first of my own friends. Pace") |
| *March 27* | "Brother Pegasus" letter to Austin: "I've been in the habit *myself* of writing some few things . . ." |
| *May 9* | Amherst–Belchertown Railroad opens |
| *June 9* | "New London Day" on railroad: Father "like some old Roman General, upon a Triumph Day" |
| *July 28 ?* | Mother and Father at Yale reunion |
| *August 11* | Amherst Commencement; Austin receives M.A. |
| *early September* | Emily and Vinnie visit Hollands in Springfield |
| *October 7* | Father invited to Springfield Horse Show |
| *November 3* | Judge Otis Phillips Lord at Whig rally, Northampton |
| *December 5* | Father at 33rd Congress |
| *December 8* | Judge Lord elected Speaker of Massachusetts Legislature |
| 1854 *March 31* | Death of Charlotte Brontë |
| *April* | Family in Washington; Emily, Susan, and John Graves in Homestead |
| *July 19* | Rev. E. S. Dwight installed as pastor of First Church; Austin graduates from Harvard Law School |
| *September 19–20* | Emily and Vinnie's second visit to Hollands |
| *late September ?* | Emily to Susan Gilbert: "Sue – you can go or stay –" |
| *December* | Austin in Chicago with Susan |
| 1855 *early February ?* | Emily and Vinnie to Washington |
| *early March* | Emily and Vinnie visit Mount Vernon (". . . we reached the tomb of General George Washington . . . that marble story") |
| *March 4 ?* | Emily and Vinnie to Philadelphia, visiting Eliza Coleman; may have heard Rev. Charles Wadsworth preach |
| *April* | Father buys back the Homestead from General Mack |
| *August 8* | Emerson addresses Social Union at Amherst Commencement |
| *September 28* | Father appointed delegate to Whig Convention at Worcester |
| *October 2* | Judge Lord addresses the Convention |
| *October 29* | Father accepts Whig nomination for Congress; defeated Nov. 6 |

| | | |
|---|---|---|
| | *October 31* | Father and Austin form law partnership |
| | *mid-November* | Family moves to Homestead ("I cannot tell you how we moved. I had rather not remember . . . and still I cannot help laughing at my own catastrophe") |
| | *November 23* | Abby Wood and Daniel Bliss marry; move to Beirut, Syria, to found mission school (later, American University) |
| | *November* | Mother's long illness begins |
| | | Published this year: *Leaves of Grass* ("I never read his Book – but was told that he was disgraceful") |
| 1856 | *January 6* | Austin joins First Church by profession of faith |
| | *July 1* | Austin and Susan Gilbert married in Geneva, N.Y.; settle in the Evergreens |
| | *September* | Mother in Northampton Spa for water cure |
| | *October 17* | Emily's bread wins second prize at Agricultural Fair |
| | *October* | Norcross cousins visit (ED to Louise: ". . . you and I in the dining-room decided to be distinguished") |
| 1857 | *August 28* | Emily on Cattle Show committee (rye and Indian bread) |
| | *October 20* | Martha Gilbert and J. W. Smith marry and settle in Geneva, N.Y. |
| | *December 11* | Wendell Phillips lectures in Amherst on "Lost Arts" |
| | *December 16* | Emerson lectures on "The Beautiful in Rural Life" and is entertained at Evergreens ("as if he had come from where dreams are born") |
| 1858 | *spring?* | First (?) Master letter: "You asked me what my flowers said . . ." |
| | *October* | The Newman cousins (Clara and Anna) arrive at Evergreens as wards of Edward Dickinson; Austin has typhoid fever |
| 1859 | *January 4?* | First (?) letter to Louise Norcross: "You are one of the ones from whom I do not run away!" |
| | *mid-January?* | Catherine Scott Turner (Kate) visits Susan (Kate to Sue: ". . . those happy visits . . . those celestial evenings . . . *Emily – Austin* – the music – the rampant fun – the inextinguishable laughter . . .") |
| | *early February* | Vinnie to Boston to be with ailing Aunt Lavinia Norcross |
| | *February 18* | Chapman and Ware episode at Evergreens; Emily and Kate as "culprit mice" |
| | *March?* | Father escorts Emily home near midnight from "revel" at Evergreens |

| | |
|---|---|
| *May* | Judge Lord appointed to Massachusetts Superior Court |
| *May 27* | Father mentioned as candidate for governor |
| *August 10* | Emily meets Charles Wadsworth's friend, J. D. Clark (at the Dickinson Commencement Tea?) |
| | Published this year: Darwin's *Origin of Species* ("we thought Darwin had thrown 'the Redeemer' away") |
| 1860 *mid-March?* | Charles Wadsworth calls on Emily (" 'Why did you not tell me you were coming, so I could have it to hope for,' I said") |
| *April 17* | Aunt Lavinia Norcross dies |
| *June 9* | Judge and Mrs. Lord visit Amherst, call at Homestead |
| *August 12* | Major and Helen Fiske Hunt call at Homestead (Dickinson Commencement Tea?) |
| *September 2* | Rev. E. S. Dwight preaches farewell sermon |
| *September 18* | Father declines nomination for lieutenant governor |
| *October* | Emily and Vinnie visit Eliza Coleman in Middletown |
| 1861 *January?* | Second (?) Master letter: "If you saw a bullet hit a Bird . . ." |
| *May 4, 11* | *Springfield Republican* prints ED's poem "I taste a liquor never brewed," under title "The May-Wine" |
| *June 6* | Eliza Coleman and J. L. Dudley married in Monson |
| *June 19* | Austin and Susan's first child, Edward (Ned) Dickinson, born |
| *June 29* | Elizabeth Barrett Browning dies (ED to Bowles in Europe: ". . . if you touch her Grave, put one hand on the Head, for me – her unmentioned Mourner –") |
| *December?* | Exchange with Susan on the poem "Safe in their Alabaster Chambers" |
| 1862 *early 1862* | Third (?) Master letter: "Oh, did I offend it –" |
| *March 1* | *Republican* prints "Safe in their Alabaster Chambers" |
| *March 14* | Frazar Stearns killed in action |
| *April* | Thomas Wentworth Higginson's "Letter to a Young Contributor" appears in *Atlantic Monthly* |
| *April 15* | First letter (and four poems) to Higginson: "Are you too deeply occupied to say if my Verse is alive?" |
| *April 25* | Second letter (and three poems) to Higginson: "Thank you for the surgery –" |
| *May 1* | Charles Wadsworth and family sail for San Francisco |
| *May 6* | Death of Thoreau |
| *June 7* | Third letter to Higginson: ". . . will you be my Preceptor . . ." |
| *July 9* | Judge Lord delivers Amherst Commencement address |

| | |
|---|---|
| *mid-July* | Fourth letter (and four poems) to Higginson: "My Business is Circumference" |
| *late July ?* | To Hollands: *"My* business is to love" |
| *August* | Fifth letter (and two poems) to Higginson: "All men say 'What' to me . . ." |
| *November 16* | Bowles returns from Europe |
| *December 4* | Higginson made colonel of Negro regiment |
| 1863 *January 17* | Loring Norcross, uncle, dies; ED to the cousins: "Let Emily sing for you . . ." |
| *March ?* | Bowles to Austin: ". . . to the Queen Recluse my especial sympathy –" |
| *July 9* | Father awarded LL.D. at Amherst Commencement |
| *October 1* | Major E. B. Hunt killed in Brooklyn |
| 1864 *February 27* | Professor Edward Hitchcock dies |
| *March 12* | In New York, *Round Table* prints ED's poem "Some keep the Sabbath going to church" |
| *March 30* | *Republican* prints ED's poem "Blazing in gold, and quenching in purple" |
| *late April* | Emily to Boston for eye treatment (seven months); stays with Norcrosses in Cambridgeport ("Loo and Fanny take sweet care of me . . .") |
| *May 13* | Austin drafted, pays $500 for substitute |
| *May 19* | Death of Hawthorne |
| *November 28* | Emily returns from Cambridgeport |
| 1865 *April 1 ?* | Emily again to Boston for eye treatment |
| *October 17* | Emerson lectures in Amherst on "Social Aims" |
| 1866 *January 27* | ED's dog Carlo dies |
| *February 10* | "H.H." and Higginsons meet at Newport |
| *February 14, 17* | *Republican* prints ED's poem "A narrow fellow in the grass" (". . . it was robbed of me") |
| *April 27* | Samuel Bowles named Amherst trustee |
| *July 11–12* | Hollands visit Amherst for Commencement |
| *October 10* | Elisabeth Dickinson (aunt) and Augustus Currier, of Worcester, married (". . . the only male relative on the female side") |
| *November 29* | Austin and Susan's second child, Martha, born |
| 1868 *May 25* | Holland family off for two years in Europe |
| *September 23* | Father dedicates new church |
| 1869 *May 11* | Emily refuses Higginson's invitation to Boston ("I do not cross my Father's ground to any House or Town") |

| | |
|---|---|
| *June 11* | General and Mrs. George B. McClellan guests at Homestead |
| 1870 *August 16* | Higginson visits Amherst; first meeting with Emily (TWH to his wife: "I never was with any one who drained my nerve power so much") |
| *October* | First number of *Scribner's* issued, J. G. Holland, editor |
| *early December?* | *Verses,* by "H.H.," published in Boston |
| 1871 *June 3* | Eliza Coleman Dudley dies in Milwaukee, age thirty-nine |
| 1871–72 | Published this year: George Eliot's *Middlemarch* ("what do I think of glory –") |
| 1872 *January 27* | Joseph B. Lyman dies in Richmond Hill, Long Island, New York |
| *July 10* | Father resigns as treasurer of the college |
| *mid-October* | Emily Fowler Ford's *My Recreations* published in New York |
| 1873 *May 1* | Father: "I hereby give myself to God" |
| *May?* | Rev. Jenkins pronounces Emily theologically "sound"; Vinnie visits Hollands |
| *July 9* | Amherst Commencement: Bowles, Maria Whitney, Judge Lord attend |
| *August?* | Abby Bliss, back from Beirut, visits Emily |
| *November 5* | Father elected again to the General Court |
| *December 1* | Austin elected treasurer of the college |
| *December 3* | Higginson lectures in Amherst and calls on Emily (Mary Higginson to her husband: "Oh why do the insane so cling to you?") |
| 1874 *June 16* | Father dies in Boston ("His Heart was pure and terrible . . .") |
| 1875 *June 15* | Mother stricken with paralysis (". . . when she asks me the name of her sickness – I deceive for the first time") |
| *August 1* | Austin and Susan's third child, Thomas Gilbert (Gib) Dickinson, born |
| *October 22* | "H.H." and W. S. Jackson married at Wolfeboro, N.H. |
| *December* | Judge Lord elevated to Supreme Court of Massachusetts |
| 1876 *March 20* | From "H.H.": "You are a great poet – and it is a wrong . . . that you will not sing aloud" |
| *August 20* | "H.H." invites Emily to participate in Roberts Brothers' No Name Series |

| | | |
|---|---|---|
| | *October* | Judge and Mrs. Lord visit "a few days" |
| | *October–* | Austin ill with malaria |
| | *November* | |
| | *December 26* | Susan gives Emily *Of the Imitation of Christ* by Thomas à Kempis ("Emily with love") |
| 1877 | *June 28* | Bowles visits Emily ("Come down at once") |
| | *September 2* | Mary Higginson dies |
| | *October* | Bowles ill |
| | *December 10* | Mrs. Lord dies |
| 1878 | *January 16* | Samuel Bowles dies ("David's route was simple – 'I shall go to him'") |
| | *January 19* | Austin and Vinnie attend Bowles's funeral |
| | *April 29* | "H.H." again asks permission to publish Emily's poems |
| | *late June* | Mother breaks hip |
| | *July 25–31,* | "Saxe Holm" inquiry in *Republican* |
| | *August 3* | |
| | *September 10* | *A Masque of Poets* announced for No Name Series |
| | *October 24* | "H.H." and husband visit Emily |
| | *November 20* | *A Masque of Poets* prints ED's poem "Success is counted sweetest" |
| | *December 10* | "Success" attributed to Emerson |
| 1879 | *mid-January ?* | Emily receives *A Masque of Poets* from Thomas Niles of Roberts Brothers |
| | *March 19* | Emerson lectures again in Amherst |
| | *July 3–4* | Amherst's worst fire (Vinnie to Emily: "It is only the fourth of July") |
| 1880 | *March* | Austin ill with malaria |
| | *early August ?* | Wadsworth visits unexpectedly ("I am liable at any time to die") |
| | *August 23–30* | Austin's diary: "Judge Lord & Troupe arrived at Amherst House" |
| | *September 23* | Austin's diary: "Ev'ng Judge Lord in & his nieces" |
| | *September 26* | Austin's diary: "Judge Lord and the Farleys to tea and evening" |
| | *mid-November* | Emily asks Higginson's advice about "Hymns for a Charity" |
| | *December 24* | George Eliot dies ("the look of the words as they lay in the print I shall never forget") |
| | *December 25* | Judge Lord gives Emily *Complete Concordance to Shakspere;* Susan gives Emily ("whom not seeing I still love") Disraeli's *Endymion* |

| | | |
|---|---|---|
| 1881 | *March 15* | Judge Lord ill |
| | *April 4* | Another fire in Phoenix Row |
| | *April 17* | Judge Lord, recovered, guest at Evergreens |
| | *July 2* | President Garfield shot; dies September 19 ("when I look in the Morning Paper to see how the President is . . .") |
| | *August 31* | Professor and Mrs. David Peck Todd arrive in Amherst |
| | *October 12* | Dr. Holland dies ("Heaven is but a little way to one who gave it, here") |
| 1882 | *April 1* | Charles Wadsworth dies ("my closest earthly friend died in April –") |
| | *April 16* | Judge Lord visits ED |
| | *April 24* | Thomas Niles urges Emily to publish |
| | *April 27* | Emerson dies |
| | *May 1* | Judge Lord critically ill: "I ran to his [Tom's] Blue Jacket . . ." |
| | *July 15* | Emily does not receive Emily Fowler Ford ("Eheu! Emily Dickinson! . . .") |
| | *September 10* | Mabel Todd sings for Emily |
| | *September 11* | Mabel and Austin: "Rubicon" |
| | *September– October* | Mabel and Emily: Indian pipes–"Humming Bird" exchange |
| | *November 10* | David Todd leaves for California to observe transit of Venus |
| | *November 14* | Mother dies ("the dear Mother that could not walk, has *flown*") |
| 1883 | *January* | Mabel-Susan confrontation (". . . the old cordial, frank relations I am afraid can never be resumed") |
| | *August 8–9* | Dickinson family reunion in College Hall, 1,000 to 1,500 expected |
| | *September 8* | Austin's diary: "The Lords arrived this noon" |
| | *October 5* | Gilbert (nephew) dies, age eight ("No crescent was this Creature – He traveled from the Full – Such soar, but never set –") |
| | *October 7* | Austin has attack of malaria |
| | *October 12* | Vinnie ill |
| | *December 7* | Matthew Arnold lectures in Amherst |
| 1884 | *March 13* | Judge Lord dies ("I work to drive the awe away, yet awe impels the work") |
| | *June 14* | Emily has first attack of final illness ("revenge of the nerves") |

| | |
|---|---|
| *September 5* | "H.H." offers to be Emily's "literary legatee & executor" |
| 1885 *late March* | To "H.H.": "Pity me . . . I have finished Ramona" |
| *August 12* | Helen Hunt Jackson dies |
| *November* | George S. Merriam's *The Life and Times of Samuel Bowles* published |
| 1886 *January 12* | Mabel Todd's diary: "Emily Dickinson taken very ill in the afternoon" |
| *early spring* | Emily's last ( ? ) letter to the Hollands: "I hope the little heart is well. . . . Emily and Vinnie give the love greater every hour" |
| *spring* | To Higginson: "I have been very ill . . . bereft of Book and Thought" |
| *March 18* | Austin's diary: "Evening sat an hour with Emily . . ." |
| *March 24* | Austin's diary: ". . . sat with Emily a while" |
| *April 15* | Emily to Charles H. Clark: "The velocity of the ill . . . is like that of the snail" |
| *early May* | Last ( ? ) letter to the Norcrosses:<br>"Little Cousins,<br>   Called back.<br>     Emily." |
| *May 13* | Emily loses consciousness |
| *May 15* | Austin's diary: "The day was awful She ceased to breathe that terrible breathing just before the whistles sounded for six" |
| *May 19* | Emily's funeral; Higginson reads Emily Brontë's "Last Lines" ("No coward soul . . .") |
| 1890 *November 12* | *Poems* by Emily Dickinson, eds. Mabel Loomis Todd and T. W. Higginson (Roberts Brothers, Boston). Eleven editions by the end of 1892 |
| 1891 *November 9* | *Poems* by Emily Dickinson, second series, eds. T. W. Higginson and Mabel Loomis Todd (Roberts Brothers, Boston). Fifth edition, 1893 |
| 1894 *November 21* | *Letters of Emily Dickinson,* 2 vols., ed. Mabel Loomis Todd |
| 1895 *August 16* | Austin dies (Vinnie: "There is no landscape since Austin died") |
| 1896 *September 1* | *Poems* by Emily Dickinson, third series, ed. Mabel |

|  |  |
|---|---|
|  | Loomis Todd (Roberts Brothers, Boston). Second edition, 1896 |
| *November 16* | Vinnie files suit against Todds (decided in her favor, April 1898) |
| 1899 *August 31* | Vinnie dies |
| 1913 *May 12* | Susan dies (Mabel: "Poor old Susan died last night") |
| 1914 | *The Single Hound*, ed. Martha Dickinson Bianchi |
| 1924 | *The Life and Letters of Emily Dickinson*, ed. Martha Dickinson Bianchi |
|  | *The Complete Poems of Emily Dickinson*, eds. Martha Dickinson Bianchi and Alfred Leete Hampson |
| 1929 | *Further Poems of Emily Dickinson*, ed. Martha Dickinson Bianchi |
| 1931 | *Letters of Emily Dickinson*, ed. Mabel Loomis Todd |
| 1932 | *Emily Dickinson Face to Face: Unpublished Letters with Notes and Reminiscences*, Martha Dickinson Bianchi |
| *October 14* | Mabel Todd dies |
| 1935 | *Unpublished Poems of Emily Dickinson*, eds. Martha Dickinson Bianchi and Alfred Leete Hampson |
| 1937 | *Poems by Emily Dickinson*, eds. Martha Dickinson Bianchi and Alfred Leete Hampson |
| 1945 | *Bolts of Melody: New Poems of Emily Dickinson*, eds. Mabel Loomis Todd and Millicent Todd Bingham |
| 1951 | *Emily Dickinson's Letters to Dr. and Mrs. Josiah Gilbert Holland*, ed. Theodora Van Wagenen Ward |
| 1955 | *The Poems of Emily Dickinson*, 3 vols., "Including variant readings critically compared with all known manuscripts," ed. Thomas H. Johnson |
| 1958 | *The Letters of Emily Dickinson*, 3 vols., eds. Thomas H. Johnson and Theodora Ward |

# THE LIFE OF

## *Emily Dickinson*

# 1

## The Problem of the Biographer

ALMOST NOTHING to do with Emily Dickinson is simple and clear-cut. The reasons why this should be so are many and basic, and it is the delicate business of the biographer to explore and assess them all. Delicate, because, for one thing, she herself was almost no help. Seemingly with willful cunning and surely with an artist's skill, she avoided direct answers to the major questions that anyone interested in her as poet or person might have been moved to ask. With success seldom approached by one destined ultimately for literary fame, she kept her private life *private*. It is not that she said nothing about herself at any time; she said a great deal in nearly eighteen hundred poems and over a thousand letters. But it is as if she lived out the advice she gave in her famous lines: "Tell all the Truth but tell it slant – / Success in Circuit lies." She avoided specifics, dodged direct confrontations, reserved commitments. She told the truth, or an approximation of it, so metaphorically that nearly a hundred years after her death and after much painstaking research, scholars still grope for certainties.

It is virtually impossible to distinguish what was willful in her secretiveness from whatever there was in it which Emily Dickinson herself did not understand. Was it deliberate planning, or compulsive forces in her nature, that led to her withdrawal from society (almost complete by her late thirties) with never a reason that satisfied anybody?—anybody, that is, except those who knew her best, her immediate family, and they were inclined more to accept her choices than to ponder her motives. How much of her behavior was forced on her by circumstances? How much was arranged by herself because it suited certain purposes of her own or simply because she liked it that way?[1]

1. Emily Dickinson has in the last several decades been the subject of a number of suggestive psychoanalytic studies, some of them startling to those accustomed to conventional methods of literary biography or critical interpretation. To the literary

[ 3

At the outset, and knowing well how qualified it will have to be, I should like to emphasize the degree to which her way of life represented a conscious choice. I think we should at least walk into the mystery standing up. More than is true of almost any other poet in the tradition, her life, like the major vehicle of her poetry, was metaphoric; and as she grew older, it became more and more deliberately so. From girlhood on, she enjoyed that way of conveying truth, whether by word or action. In a lively valentine to an Amherst student when she was twenty, she wrote, "I am Judith the heroine of the Apocrypha, and you the orator of Ephesus. That's what they call a metaphor in our country. Don't be afraid of it, sir, it won't bite." Superficially, this led to not a little archness, posing, keeping the world at bay. She enjoyed riddles, apparently enjoyed being one, and was keenly aware of the dullness of the easy riddle: "The Riddle we can guess / We speedily despise –"

On a higher level, the "riddle" became metaphoric of cosmic questions that, though they haunted Emily Dickinson throughout her life, provided her very reason for being and for writing poetry.[2] "In a Life that stopped guessing," she wrote her sister-in-law, "you and I should not feel at home." But she grew up in a community and in an atmosphere in which the cosmic questions (at least officially) were all answered; "guessing"

---

and psychoanalytical biographer alike, however, a persuasive interpretation of her life must rest on the establishment of a common ground of fact. To this end, the present study seeks to broaden the factual context against which any theoretical interpretation might be measured. As new materials are found—lost letters, fresh contemporary testimony—some of the current psychoanalytical theories may find convincing factual basis; but as yet, in my opinion, they have not. Given what we know and do not know, it seems wise at this point to keep the possibilities open.

Much psychoanalytic interpretation of Emily Dickinson has, in justifiable reaction to brighter early biographies, stressed the darker side of the poet's life as seen through some of the agonized poems, the troubled letters, and the strange behavior of her later years. I have based my view on what seems to have been the figure most real to those closest to Emily Dickinson, and of most communicative value (to the rest of us) through hundreds of letters of wit and discernment and through hundreds of poems giving assurance not only of artistic mastery but of mastery and full acceptance of self. Those who wish to follow the development of the varying theories about the sources of Emily Dickinson's inner tensions (parental inadequacy, suppressed homosexuality, frustrated love) should consult Rebecca Patterson, *The Riddle of Emily Dickinson* (1951) and "Emily Dickinson's 'Double' Tim: Masculine Identification," *American Imago* XXVIII (Winter, 1971), 330–62; Anna Mary Wells, "Was Emily Dickinson Psychotic?" *American Imago* XIX (Winter, 1962), 309–21; Clark Griffith, *The Long Shadow: Emily Dickinson's Tragic Poetry* (1964); and especially John Cody, *After Great Pain: The Inner Life of Emily Dickinson* (1971). On this last, see below, Chapter 5, note 2.

2. In *Emily Dickinson and Riddle* (1969), Dolores Dyer Lucas relates ED's poetry to the ancient tradition of the riddle and shows how important a literary device it was for her "in a generation which did not permit her, without the ambiguity of the riddle to 'tell all the truth.' . . . she early learned that 'success in circuit lies'" (p. 138).

was out of order. A sentence in one of her letters to her spinster cousins would have sounded strange to orthodox Amherst ears (and perhaps to her cousins, had it not been buried in a whimsical context): "It is true that the unknown is the largest need of the intellect, though for it, no one thinks to thank God."

Thus, I think it can be said that Emily Dickinson's manner of life and her way of telling about her life were symptomatic of her sense of the mystery of things. Central to this mystery (certainly central to the biographer) was the mystery of herself. At nineteen, she wrote to a friend, "[I] pause, and ponder, and ponder, and pause, and do work without knowing why." I think she came to realize remarkably soon who she was and what she was intended for; but it was a mystery that, for the outside world, she would not profane by explication. "All men say 'What' to me," she wrote when she was thirty-one, "but I thought it a fashion – " and a fashion she dismissed. Twice, in reference to her way of life, she used the word "embarrass" in a revealing way. First, when she gave her reasons for " 'shunning Men and Women' ": "they talk of Hallowed things, aloud – and embarrass my Dog – "; and second, when for the third time she refused an invitation to mingle with the Boston literati: "My life has been too simple and stern to embarrass any." But this does not explain much, and one is thrown back on some such remark as Emerson's strikingly similar statement about Thoreau: "He had many reserves, an unwillingness to exhibit to profane eyes what was still sacred in his own, and knew well how to throw a poetic veil over his experience." Emily Dickinson at age twenty-two wrote to a friend (in her preferred spelling): "I find I need more vail."

That the prying eye of the biographer has long been baffled is a matter of early record. The two notes about "embarrassment" were sent (the first when she was thirty-one, the second when she was thirty-eight) to the courtly man of letters, Thomas Wentworth Higginson, who, trying his best to fit her into the mold of his conventions, gave up in dismay. "I have the greatest desire to see you," he replied, "always feeling that perhaps if I could once take you by the hand I might be something to you; but till then you only enshroud yourself in this fiery mist & I cannot reach you, but only rejoice in the rare sparkles of light." His insight into the degree of willfulness in her pose was true. The mist enshrouding her was partly of her own making, and one is reminded of the spies who tried in vain to pluck out the heart of Hamlet's mystery. Higginson was scarcely more successful. When he finally visited Amherst and "held her by the hand," at least figuratively, he found that it did not help much. "I never was with any one who drained my nerve power so much. Without touching her," he wrote his wife, "she drew from me. I am glad not to live near her." And twenty years later, in the *Atlantic Monthly,* he admitted his failure:

She was much too enigmatical a being for me to solve in an hour's interview, and an instinct told me that the slightest attempt at direct cross-examination would make her withdraw into her shell; I could only sit still and watch, as

[ 5

one does in the woods; I must name my bird without a gun, as recommended by Emerson.

His impression of her, he went on to say, was of an "excess of tension" and of "an abnormal life." He later called her, variously, "my eccentric poetess," "my partially cracked poetess at Amherst." His wife asked him, three years after his first visit, "Oh why do the insane so cling to you?"

Emily Dickinson had her own formulation for those who would thus dismiss her:

> Much Madness is divinest Sense –
> To a discerning Eye –
> Much Sense – the starkest Madness –
> 'Tis the Majority
> In this, as All, prevail –
> Assent – and you are sane –
> Demur – you're straightway dangerous –
> And handled with a Chain –     (#435, about 1862)

Clearly, Higginson and his wife were of the Majority, and just as clearly Emily Dickinson's defenses were up, both to Higginson and to the world he represented. She told him (mostly) the truth, but she told it so slant that he went away mystified. The trouble is, since he was one of the few men of letters who paid any attention to her as poet, and the only one to leave on record an extended contemporary account of his impressions of her, his mystification has blurred the biographical picture ever since. Later research has cleared up much of it, but its effect in polarizing attitudes toward her still lingers.

Another and more serious effect of Higginson's mystification may be seen (it has often been so argued) in Emily Dickinson's failure to publish. He was as much mystified by her poetry as he was by her person, and as a literary adviser he failed her completely. He thought her poems formless and "'spasmodic'" (at least this was the word she put in his mouth) and urged her not to publish them. Whether his advice was decisive or one of many causes is one of those delicate questions still to be answered definitively. Only seven of her poems found their way into print during her lifetime, all of them anonymous, most of them altered by others, and one of them, she later complained, was "robbed of me."[3] The great bulk of her poems was found in her room after her death. They were in a bewildering state. Some were in final form; there were many semifinal drafts, with variant readings undecided upon; there were hundreds of scraps and jottings; and there were almost no dates.

---

3. The seven are listed in *P* III, 1207. Each one has its own publication story. The "robbed" one ("The Snake," #986) was probably sent by ED's sister-in-law, Susan Dickinson, to their mutual friend, Samuel Bowles, who published it in the *Springfield Republican*, February 14, 1866.

## The Problem of the Biographer

The problem that this situation posed for the biographer (let alone the editor and critic) was enormous,[4] since Emily Dickinson's life, in a sense almost unique among poets, *was* her work. She left no hints as to the occasion or setting of any of the poems. Only a very few (twenty-four) had titles—and this in an age when it was the fashion to give titles to poems. Apparently Emily Dickinson had no notion that anyone at any future time would be curious about her poetic intention or development, or if she did, it was a curiosity she chose not to gratify. Fortunately, her handwriting, which varied greatly over the years and even from year to year, provided a chronological clue;[5] some poems could be dated approximately by internal evidence; and there were many she sent in letters either that she dated herself or that could be dated fairly accurately. All this evidence the editors of the first complete, scholarly edition of the poems (1955, sixty-nine years after her death) used in establishing at least a tentative chronological arrangement. But the date of almost every poem was prefaced by a qualifying "about," and subsequent research has shown how necessary that qualification was. Then, it was not until three years later (1958), that an edition of her letters brought together all the correspondence known to exist and added many new letters to the canon. Before this editing, the situation of the letters had been almost as bad as that of the poems. For scarcely more than a decade have students of her life been in a position to view the materials in approximate completeness.

As usual when such a vacuum exists, and especially with such an enigmatic figure as Emily Dickinson, whose tense and passionate writing is so at variance with her outwardly quiet and retired life, myth and legend rush in to fill it. The fictionists have written plays and stories on the flimsiest of evidence; biographers have indulged in the privileges of the novelist; the cultists and the gossips have always been with us; and most recently the methods of psychoanalysis have raised further possibilities. The difficulty for the biographer coming in the wake of all this is the impossibility of saying an absolute "no" to all but the wildest speculation—and even the wildest may have a grain of truth in it. Higginson, were he here today, would still have the right to be puzzled.

The three foci of legend—Lover, Father, Withdrawal—are closely

---

4. The difficulties were first described in detail by Millicent Todd Bingham, *Ancestors' Brocades: The Literary Debut of Emily Dickinson* (1945), and most recently by Ralph W. Franklin, *The Editing of Emily Dickinson: A Reconsideration* (1967).

5. Millicent Todd Bingham, in her introduction to *Bolts of Melody: New Poems of Emily Dickinson* (1945), was, again, the first to describe in detail the intricacies involved in deciphering the often difficult handwriting. Ten years later, the Introduction of the 1955 edition of the poems contained an invaluable section on "Characteristics of the Handwriting," indicating the criteria used in establishing the chronology adopted in that edition. All these editorial problems might have been cleared up, of course, had ED ever seen her poems through the press. As has often been pointed out, we are dealing with a poet's workshop—a life's work left for posterity to put in order and much of it defying the precision of modern editorship.

related, the first two serving to explain the third. Not that New England (or Amherst) had any reason to be surprised at eccentric and retiring spinsters. But Emily Dickinson was the Squire's daughter, known in her youth for her brilliance, her wit, even (to a small group) her literary talent. Something must have happened that could explain to concerned outsiders a withdrawal that by her late thirties was almost complete: "I do not cross my Father's ground to any House or Town," she wrote in refusing Higginson's invitation to come to Boston in 1869. In her later years, she conducted interviews (with the few friends permitted in the house) from the top of the stairs and behind half-closed doors. When the first thin volumes of her poems began to appear in the early 1890s (she died in 1886), the many poems of anguished passion and renunciation stirred rumors that had been circulating even before her death of a blighted romance that had cut her life in two. Then of course came the question: Who was the man? There have been many nominations (including both sexes) but as yet no firm, universally accepted choice.[6]

There is a legend that she renounced her lover at her father's command. Then, sensing her father's distrust, she committed herself to the narrow limits of his house and grounds, in order never to give him any further cause for suspicion. The story (again, it may contain an essential truth) has given rise to much speculation about Edward Dickinson's character and the nature of the home over which he presided. He has been variously described as a severe, latter-day Puritan, a power-minded tyrant, a Mr. Barrett of Wimpole Street; and Emily Dickinson's home depicted as a gloomy prison. Her fear and awe of him (it is said) dominated her life.[7] No doubt at times both these feelings entered into her attitude toward him; but, as with the hypothesis that it was one Love and one Lover for whom she renounced a so-called normal life and career, it is impossible in the light of what we now know to accept any such simple interpretation. Similarly, it is necessary to reassess her attitude toward her

---

6. My hope in this biography is, at the very least, to put this question, until recently overshadowing all others, into proper perspective. For now, let me warn the reader in the strongest terms against such a passage as the following from Martha Dickinson Bianchi (ED's niece), *The Life and Letters of Emily Dickinson* (1924), pp. 46–47:

> It was on a visit to this same Eliza [Coleman], in Philadelphia, that Emily met the fate [the Reverend Charles Wadsworth] she had instinctively shunned. . . .
> Certainly in that first witchery of an undreamed Southern springtime Emily was overtaken – doomed once and forever by her own heart. It was instantaneous, overwhelming, impossible. There is no doubt that two predestined souls were kept apart only by her high sense of duty, and the necessity for preserving love untarnished by the inevitable destruction of another woman's life.

As with so much in this mistitled book, this passage has little evidence to support it and much to call it in question. But its high romantic style and lofty sentiments have created an impression hard to dislodge. It must be seen in the light of the long and anguished story that will be the subject of later chapters.

7. This is Clark Griffith's thesis in *The Long Shadow*. But see below, Chapter 5, note 2, for John Cody's theory (in *After Great Pain*) about ED's mother.

home and the nature of its other inmates (besides her father)—her mother, her younger sister Lavinia, and especially her older brother Austin, perhaps the one human being who knew her and understood her best.[8]

Finally, was her withdrawal as complete as has been thought? Was its effect (as is often assumed) to detach her completely from the busy and expanding world of New England and from the great national events of her lifetime? Many accounts of her, especially the early ones, were so engrossed with her little world as to dissociate her entirely from the greater one. One would think that she saw no further than her own garden and had no thought but for her own private joys and sorrows. To allay such notions, the biographer must turn, among other things, to her friends, of whom she had a wide, varied, and distinguished circle. "My friends are my 'estate,' " she said, and she kept in touch with them—and with their doings in lands far and near—in thousands of letters (only a fraction of which survive)[9] to the end of her life. Although she boasted of seeing "New Englandly," there was nothing provincial in her interests. In recent years her friendships, sustained mostly by correspondence, have been the object of increasing study, but neither separately nor together have they yet yielded their whole truth.[10] (That among their number are several for whom the most detailed and vigorous claims have been made

---

8. Millicent Todd Bingham, *Emily Dickinson's Home* (1955), presented a wealth of new material concerning Edward Dickinson and his family. It is the unique source for many family letters and documents, the basis for a new estimate of her forebears, her surroundings, and her remarkable family. To see ED in solitary brilliance amidst mediocrity is to miss an important truth of her life. In *The Years and Hours of Emily Dickinson* (1960), Jay Leyda reduced to an almost daily chronology the existing materials concerning her life and the life of contemporary Amherst and added much of his own gleaning from journals, diaries, and local records of all sorts. Both these books, displacing legend and fancy with solid facts—the realities of daily existence—did much toward establishing a convincing continuity between ED's private life and the world she lived in. The present study draws heavily on both books; but even at its conclusion the reader should be aware of areas still incompletely explored—more convinced than ever, perhaps, that a "definitive" biography is an academic illusion.

9. See Appendix V ("A Note on the Missing Correspondences").

10. The decades of the 1950s and the 1960s saw many contributions in this area. The nature and depth of ED's friendship with Dr. and Mrs. Josiah Holland were unknown until the publication in 1951, by Theodora Ward, of sixty-four new letters from ED to Mrs. Holland. Mrs. Ward examined this relationship fully in *The Capsule of the Mind: Chapters in the Life of Emily Dickinson* (1961), where she also considers ED's relationships with Higginson and Samuel Bowles. Also in 1951, Rebecca Patterson's *The Riddle of Emily Dickinson* explored her friendship with Mrs. Kate Scott Anthon—a vigorous and significant one but hardly in itself the solution to the "riddle." Thomas H. Johnson's *Emily Dickinson: An Interpretive Biography* (1955), besides stressing the (at most) problematic relationship with Wadsworth, was the first to discuss in detail Higginson's importance in her literary career, as well as Helen Hunt Jackson's, another heretofore almost neglected figure. The discovery of the Lyman Archive (R. B. Sewall, *The Lyman Letters: New Light on Emily Dickinson and Her Family,* 1965) added another important name to the list of the friends of her youth and early maturity.

for the status and even the sex of the Lover makes the present undertaking all the more delicate—and precarious.)

Another way to allay the myth of her provincialism is to look more sharply, in both her letters and her poems, for her opinions on things temporal and concrete. She once wrote a friend, "So I conclude that space & time are things of the body & have little or nothing to do with our selves. My Country is Truth." Space and time may not have been her ultimate realities; but her reach for generalities, for essential truth, began with a very sharp perception of specifics. She was not reared in a household of lawyers and treasurers for nothing (both her father and her brother held long tenures as treasurers of Amherst College). Her animadversions upon a host of worldly matters, from the Civil War to the Stock Exchange, show acute understanding, however tersely or obliquely expressed. She was never discursive on these matters; sometimes she packed a whole complex of observation and insight into a single metaphor in a poem. But neither poem nor metaphor would have come into being had it not been for the original observation, sharp and shrewd.

A review of her cultural world, her schooling, her world of books, ideas, literary affinities, shows also a range and depth until recently denied her. Emily Dickinson did not dwell as far as many have thought from the main line of English and American literature. Again, she did not live in a college town for nothing. There were libraries, reading clubs, a good bookstore. She read widely and retentively throughout her lifetime; her letters stress again and again how necessary books were to her; and the more we know about her cultural resources, the less we are inclined to patronize them. Current research is making steady progress in all these matters, and its results must play a large part in any new synthesis.[11]

Jay Leyda, whose work has contributed much to this end, posed in 1955 the essential problem and stated the essential aim:

> Is it really possible that we can be shut away from the full work or real personality of so vital a poet? Can *any* false structure, no matter how buttressed by "family tradition" and scholarly authority, by poetical tributes and

---

11. The chapter, "Books and Reading," in George F. Whicher's pioneer biography *This Was a Poet* (1938) was the first treatment of the subject in any detail and is still a convenient summary. Subsequent studies have established more firmly many relationships and continuities; e.g., Judith Banzer, " 'Compound Manner': Emily Dickinson and the Metaphysical Poets," *American Literature* XXXII (1961), 417–33; Rebecca Patterson, "Elizabeth Browning and Emily Dickinson," *The Educational Leader* XX (1956), 21–48, and "Emily Dickinson's Debt to Günderode," *The Midwest Quarterly* VIII (1967), 331–54. Jack L. Capps, *Emily Dickinson's Reading* (1966), was the first full-length study; but it, too, is only a beginning. Two years later, Ruth Miller, *The Poetry of Emily Dickinson* (1968), added to it significantly, especially in her Appendix III, which lists the books found in the Dickinson library (now mostly in the Houghton Library at Harvard) and reprints relevant passages from them. John Evangelist Walsh, *The Hidden Life of Emily Dickinson* (1971), with its "whisper" of plagiarism (p. 108), argues mistakenly, I think, for her excessive dependence on books, old and new.

The daguerreotype, curls and ruff added, as it appeared in 1924
A stage in the developing Myth

Signatures, in ink, on back of envelope addressed,
in pencil, "Austin." Handwriting mid- to late 1870s

pilgrimages, by novels, plays, even two operas and a dance, forever obscure the real person who wrote those real poems? . . .

The worthiest aim for all Dickinson scholarship of the future is to make it easier for her poetry to speak directly and freshly to every reader.

His final words—"No pattern, please"—were a terse warning to the biographer. How to detach the real person from the stereotypes that have been imposed on her? How to bring her back alive? The word "pattern" is disturbing in all that it suggests of the preconceived, the rigid, the formulated. No human life, certainly not Emily Dickinson's, can be so reduced. But there is another sense in which the word may be legitimate. To question the old clichés—the Broken Heart, the Tyrant Father, the Recluse—is not to say that her life reveals no shape at all. Keats said of Byron that he "cuts a figure—but he is not figurative." Emily Dickinson cut no figure at all, but in a deeper sense her life was figurative, metaphoric.

As I have suggested, she was quite conscious of that deeper sense. The task of the biographer is to disclose what it was for the sake of which she *did* make certain renunciations. Emily Dickinson asked no favors from the world and granted it none. The truth seems to be that, like Thoreau, she had certain private affairs to transact that were more important to her. Thus the biographer must mediate between her and the world to which she refused so much, fill out the hints she dropped, be discursive where she was elliptical; give her a lineage, a background and foreground; a believable family, home, and friends; an education, culture, and (above all) a vocation. This must be done, I am convinced, *in the large,* in the richest possible profusion of detail. Only the "realest" context will suit the purpose for this perennially "unreal" figure. Goethe has been quoted in this connection with pertinent wisdom: "Nothing in nature is isolated; nothing is without reference to something else; nothing achieves meaning apart from that which neighbors it."

A word about plan and method. My approach to the problem is divided into two parts. Volume I concerns background. It involves, first, a look at what seems to me relevant in the culture of the Puritan New England Emily Dickinson was born into; as much about the Dickinson line as is salvageable from scanty records; and a sense of the Connecticut Valley and the town of Amherst, Massachusetts, where she was born. Then, when definable Dickinson traits begin to assert themselves, I have paused to deal in some detail with personality and personal history. I am aware that much remains still to be done. These Dickinsons were formidable people, especially the Dickinson men—Samuel Fowler, Emily's grandfather; Edward, her father; and William Austin, her brother. Each deserves, and I hope some day will receive, a full-length study. As for Emily's mother, if the word "formidable" hardly applies, the problem she presents to the biographer of the poet has a depth and complexity of its own.

Especially in the accounts of Emily's parents, of her brother Austin and his wife, and of her sister Lavinia, it should be noted that the chronological sequence of biography will be violated at every turn. Before taking Emily out into the world on her own (Volume II starts with the day of her birth), I shall take the members of the family, individually, through their lives and Emily with them. I shall try to show them as the world saw them, as Emily saw them, and as they saw Emily. This seems to me the truest way of presenting a figure upon whose biography no narrative structure can be imposed that is not to a degree arbitrary or fictitious. It is true that Emily Dickinson's life had a beginning, a middle, and an end. In Volume II we shall see her as she goes to school and college; as she makes her few, early sojourns abroad (to Washington and Boston); as she makes her early and futile gestures toward publishing her poems; as she confronts certain external, datable facts like the war and the deaths in her family; as she agonizes through her one documented (and late) love affair; and as she arrives at her final summing up in her last years. But the beginning, middle, and end are not articulated by any dramatic external events; her life can be divided only very roughly into periods. She can be known as a person not through what she *did* (excluding for the moment her poems and letters as forms of doing) so much as through her relationships with people, events, books, ideas—but mostly, being an intensely personal person, with people. Like Jamesian "reflectors," each relationship gives back a phase, or facet, of her character, her personality, and her literary purpose.

Volume I shows her in relationship with the people closest to her, her family. What we are after here is essence; and the essence is to be found not in actions but in character. Genevieve Taggard's insight was right:

> What has been called mystery is character; and character is the key to this extraordinary story—Dickinson family character and Emily's . . . under the pressure, the light and shade, of the moral climate of Amherst.[12]

This statement has particular bearing on the substance of the first volume.

The section "War between the Houses" (with its voluminous Appendix), on Austin Dickinson's marriage and his relations with Mrs. Mabel Loomis Todd, needs a word of explanation. Its size is dictated, simply, by its importance. Not only is it essential in the unfolding of Austin's character and of a situation that Emily lived with for thirty years, but it is the occasion for a fresh review of Emily's relations with Susan Gilbert Dickinson, Austin's wife, a relationship of crucial importance in Emily's life. Although ultimate clarity may still be far off, certain new

---

12. *The Life and Mind of Emily Dickinson* (1930), p. xii. It is worth noting that the family was to be the main focus of a biography of Emily Dickinson once projected by Amy Lowell. Millicent Todd Bingham (*Ancestors' Brocades,* p. 111) writes: "Miss Lowell had intended, as she told my mother, to write a life of Emily Dickinson in which analysis of her relationship to the members of her family would be the central theme."

materials, or materials at last made fully available, have shed light in many a dark corner: Austin and Mabel Todd's thirteen-year correspondence; Austin's diary; Mabel's diary and journal; and the materials represented in Appendix II.

The chapter on the Dickinson rhetoric (focusing on a theme suggested in the preceding chapters) shows the bearings of a family trait on Emily Dickinson's habits of expression and offers some suggestions, as we approach the narrative of her life, about a perennial problem: the Dickinson hyperbole. This is seen to lead to, and illuminate, the most basic problem of all: how *are* we to define the structure of this extraordinary life? In this final chapter of Volume I, I venture a prefigurement (in little) of this structure, thus pointing to the main concern of Volume II. To readers in haste to have her born and on the way, I can say only this: the more one knows about background, foreground, center, what's "above" and what's "below," the more real the poems become and the more awesome Emily Dickinson's achievement is seen to be.

# Forebears and Family

---

# *2*

# The New England Dickinsons

# and the Puritan Heritage

G ENIUS IS ULTIMATELY UNACCOUNTABLE, and none more so than Emily Dickinson's. One is reminded of the perennial question about Shakespeare: How did the humbly born, locally educated boy from Stratford write those plays? Even her niece, Martha Dickinson Bianchi, the most family-proud of biographers, found "nothing in the parentage or direct heredity of Emily Dickinson" to explain it. The Dickinson genealogy begins in this country with Nathaniel Dickinson, who came over with the Great Migration led by John Winthrop in 1630—not to be confused with the expedition of the more radical Separatists, who landed at Plymouth in 1620—and settled in Wethersfield, Connecticut. It was a sturdy stock, but its competence in worldly affairs, from founding and governing townships to fighting Indians and (later) the British, was unrelieved by any notable touch of the graces, at least until Emily's paternal grandfather; his daughter, Emily's versifying Aunt Elisabeth; and a lively Aunt Lavinia on her mother's side. The records show no Connecticut Valley Anne Bradstreets, or preachers famous for eloquence, or teachers with literary inclinations. The Dickinsons were men of affairs, and the affairs of the early generations were highly practical: farming, homesteading, problems of town and church. There was no time (or they made none) for poetry.

In 1659, because of a church split in Wethersfield, Nathaniel Dickinson led his family, with fifty-eight other men and their families, on another homesteading venture to establish the new plantation of Hadley, just east of Northampton in Massachusetts. He was a man of distinction in the community: the first recorder, an assessor, a town magistrate, and (initiating a Dickinson tradition still vigorous in Emily's generation) one of the first trustees of the Hopkins Grammar School of Hadley.[1] It is recorded that his grandson, Ebenezer Dickinson, fought with the Indians at Deerfield after the Massacre of 1704.[2] In 1745 Ebenezer's son, Nathan, with his son, Nathan Jr., made the move northeast from Hadley to the district that in 1759 was to become Amherst. Here the Dickinsons prospered as farmers, the tax rolls showing both father and (later) son near the top of the assessment list. Here, in 1775, Nathan Jr.'s son, Emily Dickinson's grandfather, Samuel Fowler Dickinson, was born. And here, in 1825, only five years before Emily's birth, Nathan Jr. died at the age of ninety.

This brief, and chilly, summary of six generations of human beings who hoped and feared and bled and died does scant justice to the humanity and the heroism of the founders of such a line. Actually, the Dickinsons could well be listed among "Americans of Royal Descent"—a title given to another famous Amherst family, the Boltwoods (whose name occurs frequently in the Dickinson annals), by a memorialist in 1905:

> It is a high honor to be able to trace one's line to the kings and queens who peacefully invaded New England, and, braving all odds, founded dynasties on the bleak sands of Cape Cod, amid the jagged rocks and tangled swamps of the Bay, or on the broad alluvial fields of the Connecticut Valley.

It was not until the generation of Emily's grandfather, Samuel Fowler Dickinson, that the Dickinson line, as far as the records show, produced qualities that foreshadow in any specific way Emily Dickinson's peculiar nature and, above all, her vocation as poet. Samuel Fowler left the "alluvial fields" for others to cultivate, and following his older brother Timothy, went on to higher education and became something of a man of

1. The fullest account of Nathaniel Dickinson is in Frederick Dickinson, *To the Descendants of Thomas Dickinson* (1897), pp. 13–18. Among other distinctions, he was one of the few who were privy to the secret hiding place (in the vicinity of Hadley) of the regicide generals Goffe and Whalley.
2. In "a list of names of those that fought In the Dearfield Medow on the last of Febewarey, 1703–4," the following Dickinsons (Dickesons) are recorded (George Sheldon, *A History of Deerfield, Massachusetts*, I, 1895, 298):

> Eben'r Dickeson
> Nathaniell Dickeson
> Samuell Dickeson

The annals of western Massachusetts fairly bristle with Dickinsons from the earliest years on. The patriarch Nathaniel had nine sons and two daughters (all his sons fought in King Philip's war). Families of nine or ten children were the rule. By the 1880s, a family historian records that the Dickinsons in the Amherst-Hadley area "threatened to choke out all other forms of vegetation." The Dickinsons are the largest family chronicled in E. W. Carpenter and C. F. Morehouse, *The History of the Town of Amherst, Massachusetts*, 1896, Chapter III, "Founders of Amherst Families." The *Boston Journal*, in its account of a Dickinson family reunion in Amherst on August 8, 1883, said that, even in the early years, "we may well doubt whether the Dickinsons belonged to Amherst or Amherst to the Dickinsons."

letters. Up to that time, the Dickinson heritage shows many of those massive traits of character we associate with New England and Puritanism, but little else.

A word about those "massive traits" before turning to their specific manifestations in the Dickinson forebears about whom there is detailed information. In an introductory note to his *The American Puritans,* Perry Miller wrote: "Without some understanding of Puritanism . . . there is no understanding of America," and (had it been within his purpose) he might have added that this is especially true, among its poets, of Emily Dickinson. Her relation to the Puritan tradition is the theme of a notable essay by Allen Tate. If, he argued, Hawthorne reconstituted in American fiction "the puritan drama of the soul" after Emerson had all but extinguished it, Emily Dickinson, with something of Emerson in her but more of Hawthorne, reconstituted it in her poetry. But she did so with sturdy independence, in itself one of the tradition's most massive traits.

One must not be misled by the fact that with her the drama was quite different in nature from the soul-torturings, the battles with sin and the Devil, recorded in Puritan literature. Indeed, her whole career may be regarded as a sustained, if muted, rebellion against this very inheritance. "I do not respect 'doctrines,' " she said at one point, and especially (she made clear) the Puritan doctrine of innate sin. Among her several rejections of this doctrine, perhaps the sharpest was a remark on a typical Amherst sermon: "While the Clergyman tells Father and Vinnie that 'this Corruptible shall put on Incorruption' – it has already done so and they go defrauded."

Emily Dickinson's sense of the past, certainly her New England past, could hardly be called vivid. She showed no interest in family lore as such. She left only one reference to her famous grandfather, Samuel Fowler, and that had more to do with her father than with him.[3] Nowhere in her surviving poems or letters did she cite any Dickinson accomplishment in the past. When in a letter of 1871 she used the phrase "Ancestors' Brocades" it was for an irrelevant metaphorical purpose: like Truth, they "stand alone." Yet she was very conscious of being an Amherst girl, and the line in her poem about seeing "New Englandly" is generally regarded as referring to herself. She knew what the massive Puritan traits were, saw them in her family and in herself, respected them, but was critical of them throughout her life. Speaking in large terms, Tate contended that Emily Dickinson came at the ideal time for a poet: when a once firm and mighty tradition was losing its vitality and opening for the poet new freedoms, some exalting, some terrifying. This is true; and it is the source of much of the anguish, as well as the ecstasy, in many of her poems. In the smaller, more intimate sphere, she saw the effects of the decaying

3. In a letter of about 1883 to her Aunt Catherine (Sweetser): "I have found and give it in love, but reluctant to entrust anything so sacred to my Father as my Grandfather's Bible to a public Messenger, will wait till Mr. Howard comes" (*L* III, 779).

tradition in, especially, the near-tragic lives of her father and brother and in the restricted life of the town—in the pettiness, the hypocrisy, and the narrow moral view that were the sad legacy of the tradition in many New England communities and a major reason, certainly, for her own alienation and withdrawal. Behind all the pages that follow, her New England, Puritan inheritance will be a sustained assumption. She could no more escape it, for better or for worse, than she could escape breathing the air of her native Amherst.

But what precisely was New England in Emily Dickinson's inheritance, and what Puritan? To start with the first, many of the qualities of these early generations in the northeastern part of the country are common to all folk who wrench their living from a grudging soil, in a climate of vivid extremes, and in pioneering conditions. They must be industrious or perish. The survival values, besides hard work, are practicality, shrewdness, stamina. "They were not easily discouraged" is still the definitive tribute to the early New Englanders. Living in tiny communities, often in widely separated farms, they became independent because they had to be. Existing close to the soil, with crops to raise and stock to keep alive, they were in daily contact with life and death, the creative and destructive forces of nature; and hence they were realists. Although life in mid-nineteenth-century Amherst was well beyond the primitive stage, the following passage is a good reminder of aspects of Amherst life in Emily Dickinson's time that would still seem crude to us:

> . . . the community was made up of self-sustaining homes in which the inhabitants were highly organized social units. At that time, Amherst's village green was still a rough pasture with birch trees and a frog pond, and the houses around it and along the few roads that led away from it were modified farms, provided with horses, cows, and chickens, vegetable gardens and orchards. Water was drawn by hand or by means of a pump from a well near the house. Many families owned their own woodlots, where the fuel was cut to supply their stoves and open hearths. No street lights brightened the paths along the unpaved roads. At night each house became a little island, where indoors the family gathered around an oil lamp after dark, and went to bed by the light of a tallow candle. . . .[4]

The forces of nature controlled much of the life in her own home and that of the village. Cold, heat, floods, and drought all had an immediate effect on everyday living.

4. In his essay, "Heating, Lighting, Plumbing, and Human Relations," *Landscape* (July 1971), Albert Eide Parr elaborates on the possible effect of such arrangements on family relationships "during the era of candles and kerosene." Because of fire hazard and the chore of tending wicks, cleaning sooty chimneys, and filling empty reservoirs, the number of lamps actually lit at any one time was kept to a minimum. The family's activities probably centered in one or two rooms and mostly in the living room, for reading, study, or conversation. This evening gathering "had a very strong effect upon the attitudes and personalities developed by the young members of the family during their formative years." Since reasonable quiet was essential to the family gathering, discipline among the children was more or less self-imposed:

This placed the parents in the favorable position of benevolent referees, rather than

## The New England Dickinsons and the Puritan Heritage

New Englanders were understandably frugal with everything, until frugality became a virtue which in later, more prosperous generations was cherished for its own sake, quite apart from need. Emily Dickinson wrote her poems, thriftily, on odds and ends of paper, on the back of recipes, invitations, shopping lists, clippings, while her father drove the finest horse in town. Although doubtless there were garrulous New Englanders —there certainly are—the habit of thrift extended to speech. They hated to waste words, a quality which became perhaps Emily Dickinson's most obvious New Englandism. Or they hoarded their words unless it was their bounden duty to do otherwise, as when their theologians wrote their mighty books, or their pastors worshipped God for hours on end in the pulpit, or their prominent men, like Emily's father, were called upon to address their fellows on state occasions. (The irony of Thomas Wentworth Higginson's description of Edward Dickinson as "thin dry & speechless" lay in the fact that Edward Dickinson was one of the most famous orators in Hampshire County.) And, like all people close to the soil, and by education overqualified for the often backbreaking work their livelihoods demanded, they developed a humor that was pithy and ironic.

All these qualities were true of the Dickinsons at least down to, and to a large extent including, Emily's generation. We see them, once she had set the bearings of her career, in her intensity of purpose, in her extraordinary capacity for work, in her often caustic wit and clipped phrasing. The extent to which she, and her brother Austin and sister Lavinia, departed from some of the more restrictive of them will also be one of our themes.

The specifically Puritan qualities in Emily Dickinson's heritage are more difficult to isolate and define. The genus Puritan subsumes many species, and the Dickinson species was a mixture of many paradoxical qualities. The religious motive that, at least in part, impelled the first Dickinson to New England does not recur overtly in Emily's direct line until Samuel Fowler Dickinson's generation, and even he gave up his

principal adversaries, on most minor issues of discipline and consideration for others. The ephemeral animosities of daily life were more likely to develop between siblings than between generations. Could it be pure accident that the generation gap does not seem to have been invented until after the invention of the electric light? Quiet, without complete silence, was naturally a condition particularly strongly insisted upon around the evening lamp, since you could close or turn your eyes, but not your ears.

With the coming of electricity and central heating, "bedchambers became studies and playrooms . . . and the family dispersed itself and its activities throughout the house at all hours . . . Parents became the principal ogres and disciplinarians of the household, and because they saw less of the brood under their command they had less opportunity to time and to design their parental intervention in filial affairs to best advantage."

To what extent such sociological generalization illuminates Dickinson family relationships is problematic. It is useful to keep in mind, at any rate, in attempting to picture Emily Dickinson in her contemporary surroundings and to judge their effect on her. It may tend to mitigate the harsh view of her isolation in her own family and of the stringency of the family discipline.

early inclination toward the ministry for a vigorous lay career. It was the work of *this* world that occupied the early Dickinsons, their otherworldly concerns manifesting themselves outwardly in community participation in the usual affairs of church and school. At least there is no record of an apostate Dickinson; Emily herself was the first avowed "pagan" (a term she applied to herself several times and not, it seems, entirely in jest). In the course of the generations, when Puritanism reached Emily as a part of her family tradition, it was a checkered affair, much Dickinsonized. What she got of the real thing, "pure" Puritanism, came from her reading, from the Amherst pulpit, from the hymns and prayers. It was her distinction that she perceived its central meaning in spite of the cloud of accretions that obscured it in mid-nineteenth-century America.

The major characteristics of this pristine Puritanism have achieved a near-mythical status in our consciousness, and we need pause only over those that seem most pertinent to Emily Dickinson and her poetry. In her intercourse with the world and with herself, they often appeared in action; and, as always, what posterity abstracts into concepts and doctrines must be qualified when it takes on the inevitable ambiguities of experience. Or, as Tate describes the peculiar tension she achieved between abstraction and sensation, the Puritan ideals ceased to be abstractions, so thoroughly fused did they become with her character and sensibility: "She did not reason about the world she saw; she merely saw it." That is, here as everywhere, she proceeded inductively, experimentally, putting all she encountered to the test of her own sensibility. An epigram in mid-career summed up her lifelong way:

> Experiment escorts us last –
> His pungent company
> Will not allow an Axiom
> An Opportunity          (#1770, about 1870)

What occurs to us first, perhaps, among the "axioms" that are distinctively Puritan are the virtues of simplicity, austerity, hard work, and denial of the flesh. These were ever-present disciplines in her life. Although her father saw to it that his family lived in a fashion far short of hardship, he might have served as a model for Perry Miller's note on the "Protestant ethic":

Man is put into this world, not to spend his life in profitless singing of hymns or in unfruitful monastic contemplation, but to do what the world requires, according to its terms. He must raise children, he must work at his calling. No activity is outside the holy purpose of the overarching covenant. Yet the Christian works not for the gain that may (or may not) result from his labor, but for the glory of God. . . . It was a razor's edge, and the true Puritan was required to walk it. No wonder that some Puritans fell off to one side, becoming visionary idealists, while some fell to the other side, becoming hypocrites.

## The New England Dickinsons and the Puritan Heritage

Emily Dickinson had a sharp eye for both idealists and hypocrites in pious, busy Amherst and caught occasional glimpses of her father teetering on the razor's edge. If she rejoiced in life, in the "ecstasy in living" (as she put it) in ways he would not have understood, the main outlines of her life were, like his, austere—"too simple and stern to embarrass any." But the sternness and simplicity had little to do with theological sanctions. Her experience taught her that these ways were best for her. Certainly she seems never to have undertaken them penitentially. " 'Consider the Lilies,' " she wrote a friend two years before she died, was "the only Commandment I ever obeyed."

Another phase of Puritan living and thinking that could be considered axiomatic became, after testing, a part of Emily Dickinson's way—if, again, for reasons of her own. To the true Puritan, denial and renunciation had meaning only as they made for the greater glory of God and the salvation of the soul. The Puritan lived in constant, fearful awareness of his soul, maintained continual vigilance, and took his spiritual measurements daily, even hourly. "Almost every Puritan kept a diary," wrote Perry Miller, "not so much because he was infatuated with himself but because he needed a strict account of God's dealings with him, so that at any moment, and above all at the moment of death, he could review the long transaction." Here, too, as with denial and renunciation, Emily Dickinson's need for a strict account may not have been entirely theological, but the fierce introspection and the diary keeping of the Puritans surely had a bearing on her mental habits. Her poems, some of which are couched in these very terms, were her way of keeping the long transaction in constant review. Miller's description of the Puritan's inner turmoil is strikingly close to what puzzles readers of Emily Dickinson's poems today, their extraordinary shifts and changes of mood, tone, and even belief: the Puritan "lives inwardly a life of incessant fluctuation, ecstatically elated this day, depressed into despair the next." It required clinical skill to narrate, in diary, journal, or autobiography, "these surgings and sinkings, all the time striving to keep the line of the story clear." Similarly, Emily Dickinson's poems often have that same breathless sense that all may be over at any moment, that the instant of reckoning may be at hand.

Further, the Puritan drama of the soul had its dialogue, where in diaries or, as in Anne Bradstreet's and Edward Taylor's formal verse or prose, the Soul addressed its God, or the Soul addressed the Self, or the Flesh addressed the Spirit. The Puritans talked a great deal to themselves—a way of thinking, of attacking one's inner problems, that Emily Dickinson was born to. If her communication with her God or her Soul is a good deal more informal, even chatty, than a true Puritan would have thought seemly, she never permanently lost hold of these spiritual realities, whatever the vicissitudes of her faith. She lived and moved, however restlessly, in the dimension prepared for her by the New England Puritans.

[ 23

To this general statement must be added one important particular: the peculiar quality of Connecticut Valley Puritanism. In the Great Revival in Northampton in 1740, Jonathan Edwards had given the drama of the soul a flaming immediacy for the people who came under the influence of his preaching. Always, as Miller noted, central to Puritan theology was the vision, the moment of inner light, the Augustinian revelation as opposed to the years of dialectical effort of Thomistic theology. The effort of Edwards was the continuation of the work of his grandfather, the great Solomon Stoddard, who in the "remote frontier fortress of Northampton" flailed away at the liberal tendencies he saw menacing the true faith. Stoddard had "made explicit that deep-seated reliance on the self which was from the beginning a hidden but irresistible thrust of the Puritan theology." It was this "spirit of sublime self-reliance" that Edwards preached as he reasserted in 1740 the primitive passion to the thousands who participated in the Revival.

The revival spirit, calling for deep individual soul-searching, confession of sin, and repentance, was very much alive in Emily Dickinson's time and caused her anguish. No fewer than eight revivals swept Amherst, college and town, during her formative years, roughly between 1840 and 1862. She could never see herself as a sinner in the hands of an angry God. She could never testify, as so many of her pious friends did, to that direct visitation of the Spirit which was essential to membership in the church. If she never became a "christian" (more often than not, she spelled the word with a small "c"), if her unique calling took her far from the ways of orthodoxy, it still was the Puritan in her that made her feel that the burden of proof was on her, and that the burden was a mighty one.[5] In

5. How continuously this sense of the burden was brought home to the community, especially to the young people, can be seen in this passage from Professor Edward Hitchcock's *Reminiscences of Amherst College* (1863), p. 162:

> Up to the present time, (July, 1863), the College has enjoyed marked seasons of special religious interest in the following years, viz.: 1823, 1827, 1828, 1834, 1835, 1839, 1842, 1846, 1850, 1853, 1855, 1857, 1858, and 1862. Besides these . . . prominent revivals, many other seasons of special interest have existed in the institution, which, though not dignified by the name of revivals, have yet been of unspeakable importance in raising the standard of practical piety. . . .

Theodora Ward, *Capsule of the Mind,* pp. 15–18, emphasizes the pressure these revivals put upon the young people, especially the recalcitrants. She quotes a little book, *Revival Conversations* (1844) by Dr. Heman Humphrey, Hitchcock's predecessor as president of the college. A troubled young man has come to his pastor for spiritual guidance.

> *Inquirer* O, you misunderstand me. I have not got so far. I have told you already that I am not even awakened yet, and how can I repent? I am somewhat troubled, to be sure, or I should not be here. But my feelings are all indefinite.
> *Pastor* Do you think your not having *got so far* is any valid excuse for not repenting, and giving your heart to God? The question is not, how far you have

the constant test of her own sublime self-reliance her only weapon was the moment of perception, or vision, that imparted to her such a different and unique message:

> On a Columnar Self –
> How ample to rely
> In Tumult – or Extremity –
> How good the Certainty
>
> That Lever cannot pry –
> And Wedge cannot divide
> Conviction – That Granitic Base –
> Though None be on our Side –
>
> Suffice Us – for a Crowd –
> Ourself – and Rectitude –
> And that Assembly – not far off
> From furthest Spirit – God –           (*#789, about 1863*)

Over, behind, and through it all, of course, were the Puritan conceptions of Divine immanence, providential history, the Whole Duty of Man; the sense of being Chosen, or Elected; the idea of Redemption. All these were at work, I think, in her complicated consciousness, if not as theological convictions, at least as fixed points in her spiritual navigation—sometimes vividly seen, more often suffused in fog or mist, sometimes lost in the blackness of night. She herself often used the metaphor of the voyage. "The shore is safer," she wrote, when she was twenty, to a pious young friend, "but I love to buffet the sea . . . I love the danger!"

---

advanced, but how far you *ought* to have advanced, – not how you feel, but how you *ought* to feel.
*Inquirer*  I do not feel anything. I have no sense of my sins, and how can I have? I wish I could feel as others do, but it is impossible.
*Pastor*  My dear young friend, do stop and think what you are saying. You do not feel! You have no sense of sinfulness! Astonishing! A sinner against a holy God, and under condemnation, and liable every moment to drop into a burning hopeless eternity – and yet cannot feel, cannot be alarmed, cannot "flee from the wrath to come." O, how stupid you must be!

What troubled the young "Inquirer" comes uncannily close to ED's often expressed spiritual worries, most dramatic at age nineteen: "I am standing alone in rebellion . . ." (*L* I, 94; to Jane Humphrey, April 3, 1850). In 1859, Humphrey reprinted *Revival Conversations* (of which the selection above is a tiny fragment) in a book entitled *Revival Sketches and Manual,* published in New York by the American Tract Society. (The last line quoted above reads, incidentally, "O, how dead you must be!", p. 427.) Evangelical clichés abound. A question by the Pastor (p. 473 in the 1859 volume) may have provided Emily with a phrase she used in a letter to Abiah Root (*L* I, 60; January 17, 1848): "*Pastor* . . . Whereas you was once blind, do you now see? The true question is, Are you *in* the ark of safety?"

The question of immortality—she called it "the Flood subject"—is seldom far distant from her poems and letters, even in their lighter moods. "The final direction of her poetry," writes Charles Anderson, "and the pressures that created it, can only be described as religious, using that word in its 'dimension of depth' "—the dimension, that is, of the ever-questing mind, not so much (in her case) rejecting the orthodoxies as pressing them for an assurance that continually eluded her. Although perhaps the most religious person in town, she had stopped going to church by the time she was thirty.

She was prepared to accept the loneliness of such a course, a loneliness endemic in the New England Puritan way and intensified by her own peculiar defections. A near-contemporary, Samuel G. Ward, the early Transcendentalist and writer for the *Dial,* sensed the Dickinson situation perceptively, even to Emily's relations with her family, in a letter to Higginson shortly after Higginson and Mabel Loomis Todd had brought out the first edition of *Poems:*

> MY DEAR MR. HIGGINSON,
> I am, with all the world, intensely interested in Emily Dickinson. No wonder six editions have been sold, every copy, I should think to a New Englander. She may become world famous, or she may never get out of New England. She is the quintessence of that element we all have who are of the Puritan descent *pur sang.* We came to this country to think our own thoughts with nobody to hinder. Ascetics of course, & this our Thebaid. We conversed with our own souls till we lost the art of communicating with other people. The typical family grew up strangers to each other, as in this case. It was *awfully* high, but awfully lonesome. Such prodigies of shyness do not exist elsewhere. We get it from the English, but the English were not alone in a corner of the world for a hundred & fifty years with no outside interest.

The following chapters will both confirm and qualify Mr. Ward's analysis. Higginson sent the letter to Mrs. Todd, calling it "the most remarkable criticism yet made on E.D."

All this grappling with the tradition she was born in, her debts and non-debts to her New England tradition and to Puritanism, will become more apparent when we follow Emily Dickinson in her lifelong struggle with her own attitudes and style. Confronting that tradition squarely, she appropriated its components selectively and shrewdly, revered it, but never capitulated to it. To quote Tate once more: "Unlike her contemporaries, she never succumbed to her ideas, to easy solutions, to her private desires. [In her poetry] there is no thought as such at all; nor is there feeling; there is that unique focus of experience which is at once neither and both." Her Columnar Self was founded solidly on the tradition, but its construction was her own work.

It is the tradition, however, that bears especially on this first part of our study, for the Dickinsons were pure stock, without even a wife in seven generations from outside New England. And the tensions inherent in

## The New England Dickinsons and the Puritan Heritage

New England Puritanism, especially in the period of its decline, contributed directly to the "Vesuvius at Home" in which Emily Dickinson lived and wrote. It may be true that nothing in her parentage or ancestry explains her genius, but the closer we look into them, the more we understand what went into that unique focus of experience where the "thought" of tradition is fused with the "feeling" of the individual to produce something new. Nothing is more applicable to Emily Dickinson than a fine remark of Erik Erikson's about those "who trust their origins" but have the "courage to emerge from them."

# 3

# Samuel Fowler Dickinson

S AMUEL FOWLER DICKINSON (1775–1838), the youngest son and seventh
of the eight children of Nathan and Esther (Fowler) Dickinson, is
the first of Emily Dickinson's forebears and the only one among the
grandparents on either side of the family about whom there is enough on
record to warrant examination. There is in fact a great deal, and to follow
it through in some detail is not only to learn much about the culture Emily
Dickinson was nurtured in—the town and the college—but to understand
better many of the tensions she had to live with in the Dickinson household and to cope with in her own person. Samuel Fowler's career, save for
its sad ending, was a model of the late-Puritan, New England way. Here
were all the elements: piety, work, singleness of purpose. It is essential
Amherst and essential Dickinson.

In 1896, Carpenter and Morehouse's fine old *History of Amherst* gave
the standard view of Samuel Fowler Dickinson:

> A descendant in direct line from Nathaniel Dickinson, who was among the
> original settlers of Hadley, he was the embodiment of those qualities and
> virtues that gave to New England strength and character from the earliest
> times.

One of the surest proofs that Emily was aware of these qualities in her
grandfather is that her brother Austin was. Seven years before the *History,* in 1889, Austin had paid him much the same tribute in an address
prepared for a celebration at the First Church in Amherst, the Dickinson
church.[1] Both tributes left out the sad ending, the shadow of which hung
over the family for years. In his all but fanatical work in the founding of

---

1. For Austin's tribute, see below, p. 41, and see Chapter 6 for a full account of
the address.

Amherst College, Dickinson ruined his health and his fortune, sold the Homestead,[2] and left Amherst when Emily was two.

His career started auspiciously. One of his daughters, probably Emily's Aunt Elisabeth, the family scribe, wrote of his early years:

He was trained by the same maternal hand as his brother [Timothy], and with like results of character and piety. Gentle and sensitive, and with more than ordinary mental gifts, he was one of the best beloved in his home by brothers and sisters, and was encouraged by his parents to follow his taste for study. After instruction by Judge Strong of Amherst, he entered Dartmouth College at sixteen, and maintaining high rank as a scholar, graduated . . . with the second honor, of Latin salutatorian.

He entered Dartmouth in 1791, six years after his brother Timothy had graduated. By the time he got there, the college, established some twenty years earlier for the education and conversion of Indians, offered a sound "classical curriculum" to all students, many of whom came from Massachusetts and Connecticut. Many of his thirty-one classmates went on to notable careers, especially in teaching and in law—not so many, be it noted, in the ministry. Though sufficiently pious, education at Dartmouth seems to have been less theologically strict than at some of its sister institutions like Yale and less evangelical than what Samuel Fowler later helped create at Amherst. At least, in 1772, a parent, sending his son to Dartmouth, wrote President Eleazar Wheelock: "The Education at Yale is not Liberal: they are too Contracted in their Principles and do not Encourage a Free Enquiry."[3]

Significant of this difference may have been Dickinson's Salutatory Address at the 1795 Commencement, still preserved in manuscript in the Dartmouth archives. There was little piety in it and much about this world and its affairs; its full title read: *De administrationis civilis et morum natura; atque momento eorum mutuae relationis,* or, "Nature of Civil government & manners; their mutual relation & influence in society." Only two years after his graduation, when he must have been a marked young man in his community, he turned the address into a sturdily patriotic oration for the Fourth of July festivities in nearby Belchertown. Here the title became *The Connection of Civil Government*

2. In her writings on ED, Martha Dickinson Bianchi regularly refers to the "Mansion." In *Home* it is the Homestead. In the deed of sale in 1833, it is called The Homestead. When Edward Dickinson repurchased the property in 1855, he was congratulated in the *Hampshire and Franklin Express* for bringing "The Old Homestead" back into the family. I have adopted this designation throughout. (See *Home,* pp. 9, 390, 523.)

3. Although, as Leon Burr Richardson, *History of Dartmouth College* (1932), I, 120, reminds the reader, Wheelock's purpose was still predominantly evangelical, the curriculum Samuel Fowler studied sounds "liberal" enough: the "learned languages" for three years; speaking and writing, mathematics, geography and logic; and (senior year) English and Latin composition, metaphysics and the "elements of natural and physical law." This was the same curriculum that faced Daniel Webster when he entered Dartmouth two years after Samuel Fowler graduated.

*with Manners and Taste.* It was published soon after in pamphlet form, in Northampton, its author announced on the title page as "Samuel F. Dickinson, A.B. Student at Law, Amherst."

The oration is more than a curiosity. Here at least are Learning and Letters (and apparently for the first time) among Emily Dickinson's hard-driving, workaday forebears. It is full of the cant of patriotism, but it has verve and sweep, from the opening sentence, "Everything, which respects the happiness of human society, is interesting," to the closing wish that all the world might enjoy America's freedom: "Then shall the morning stars, again, sing together, and all the sons of men shout for joy." In between, it traces the painful history of civil government from prehistoric savagery to the present state of moral order and refinement. Almost everything turns up that one would expect, and in predictable terms, the winnowings from a bright undergraduate's learning. We hear about the "profusion and luxury" of Babylon and Persia, the "dissipation" of Turkish despotism, the "jealous cruelties of the Venetian aristocrat," the "constant fidelity of a republican Swiss." We are taken through the fall of Rome, the Dark Ages, the rise of the Italian cities, and improvements in the arts and sciences. There is nothing about Sin and Redemption, little about God and His beneficence, and much about "the progress of reason and taste," about "the fitness of things" as ordained by Nature, about "rational inquiry," and how "science and a knowledge of things enlarge the mind."

A few passages from the oration show the enormous distance between Fowler's gift and Emily's; but it will be noted that his language is under control, sometimes by the same rhetorical devices that Emily herself was to use. There is a good sense of rhythm, construction, and cadence. Often the pose is crude and the rhetoric obvious:

> Were it needful, we might say, the virtues of American citizens would be strangers, in the gaudy realms of eastern monarchs, or in the dominions of European kings. Were it needful, we might say, the vices of those countries would be vagabonds in this free and independent commonwealth. But, modesty forbids.

An effusion on the delights of nature, couched in terms that might have come right out of the Enlightenment, has a more subtle balance:

> In the temperate climes, in which we live, nature seems to have combined her powers, to aggrandize the intellectual world, and to complete the circle of rational enjoyment. Here she has planted her garden, adorned with the richest fruits, and the finest flowers, which can either improve the taste, or please the fancy, of intelligent beings. And here she has prepared a *banquet for reason.*

This is refreshingly un-Puritan, but one looks in vain for a sense either of the peculiar beauty of the hilly New Hampshire setting where the speech originated, or of Fowler's own lovely Connecticut Valley. It remained for his granddaughter to get her eye on the object; but here, two generations back, was something of the same response to the beauty of this world that (as she put it) "holds – so – ."

A final burst of eloquence, this time in praise of General George Washington, then in his declining years, shows how near Fowler was, not only to the Enlightenment, but to the Revolution (there had been a score of Dickinsons among the Minutemen):

> I should do violence to original virtue, and to my own feelings, should I pass, in silence, the man, who has been our shield in war, our council in peace, George Washington, the illustrious patron of his country. The calm serenities of a pure unclouded mind shall *still* attend him, through the shadowy vale of declining age. The plaudits of an admiring world shall remain, a diadem to his memory, in the crown of hoary justice. The choir of guardian seraphs, who have protected him, through the perils of life, shall pitch their tents, in calm repose, around his venerable head, and softly tune their harps, to breathe his praise.

Again, here is no praise of a Divine Providence for sending the great man at the time of his country's need; and "the choir of guardian seraphs" have about as much theological significance as Emily's seraphs who swung their snowy hats "To see the little Tippler / Leaning against the – Sun – " There is not a fresh image in the passage, and its patriotic clichés are in the same vein as the clichés of the Revivalist preachers which were to fill Emily's letters when she was about Fowler's age. But the passage is well composed, and the last sentence, with its dying fall, has a rhythm perfectly suited to the declining state of the old general. Millicent Todd Bingham was the first to call attention to the interest "these stirring words – a kind of apotheosis of the living Washington – " might have for those "who search among the forebears of Emily Dickinson for intimations of genius." Unfortunately, we cannot be sure that Emily ever read the address.

In general, the slant of the oration is closer to Tom Paine than might have been considered seemly from a Connecticut Valley boy and closer to belles-lettres than might conventionally be expected from a boy descended from generations of farmers.[4] This is to say, of course, that the indepen-

---

4. Such latitude of thought gave considerable anxiety to the orthodox of the next generation. In 1859 Heman Humphrey's *Revival Sketches and Manual* included a brief history of revivals in New England (and abroad) from the earliest times. Commenting on the spirit of the period of the Revolution, Humphrey wrote (p. 99):

> The minds of the people were too much agitated and engrossed by conflicting political interests, to have much room for more than the ordinary routine of religious observances. . . . Zion languished. . . .
> In the mean time . . . *French Infidelity,* which our allies brought over with them, was sowed broadcast among our own officers and soldiers. Aided by Paine's "Age of Reason," Voltaire's assaults upon Christianity, Volney's Ruins, and other blasphemous publications, it spread rapidly, especially among the upper classes. . . . Instead of the Scriptures, French philosophy claimed to be the rule of faith

dence of thought and the cultural level of these so-called farmers should not be underestimated. If Samuel Fowler's lineage says nothing explicit about the origins of his tastes and abilities, and if it is condescending to call him the first literary Dickinson, at least it can be said with confidence that his descendants shared liberally in his qualities. His son Edward, Emily's father and the orator, wrote verses in his youth, read widely, and assembled a library of considerable diversity. Edward's sister Elisabeth was not only the chronicler but the bard of her generation. She once sent her young nephew Austin a rhymed letter of fifty stanzas on his tooth-ache, and she wrote a long verse history of the family for a Dickinson reunion in 1883. In the next generation, Emily's brother and sister were lively readers, enjoyed discussing what they read, and prided themselves on the style of their letters and their talk, often peppery and unconventional. They both at one time or another wrote verses. All this hardly accounts for Emily's gifts; but it makes her seem less isolated, less alone in a household usually regarded as insensitive to literary matters. It may explain, too, why the members of her family took for granted the occasional verses they knew she wrote (they seem to have had no idea how many). Such occupation was to be expected in all genteel families, especially among the daughters.[5] We can look back at Samuel Fowler's oration simply as one discernible landmark, the beginning of Dickinson literaria.

It is not surprising to learn that, during the year after his graduation, Fowler tried his hand at teaching (in New Salem, Massachusetts), perhaps to inspire his pupils in the cultivation of this same Reason he exalted in the oration. (Fifty-five years later, his grandson, Austin, was to experiment with teaching as a profession—and with the same results: they

---

and life, and ignoring all the "rights of God," was to usher in the glorious millennium of the "rights of man."

Seen in this light, Fowler's emendation, "and all the sons of *men* shout for joy," is significant. It took some time to restore a climate favorable to religious revivals. Humphrey was in the forefront of the movement. By Emily Dickinson's youth it was in full swing.

It is worth noting that Fowler's brother Timothy entered the ministry after graduating from Dartmouth and became pastor of the Congregational Church in Holliston, Massachusetts. In 1800 he preached an ordination sermon for the Reverend Drury Fairbank in Plymouth, New Hampshire. Printed that year in Concord, New Hampshire, the sermon is as rigidly orthodox as any Connecticut Valley conservative could wish. Compare Fowler's tone and attitude with this: "God's people are a peculiar people, by entering into covenant with the Lord, by joining themselves to the Church of Christ, and by separating themselves from sinners . . ." (Timothy Dickinson, *Sermon* . . . , Concord, 1800, p. 6).

5. In an unpublished study, "Emily Dickinson and the Practice of Poetry," Miriam Baker shows how widespread this practice was—and not only among daughters. Especially during the early decades of the century, the writing of verses for every occasion, or none, became almost a cultural status symbol; certainly it was the fashion. Many of the products spilled over into the journals and magazines. Edward Dickinson's, Austin's, and Lavinia's attempts will be discussed in the appropriate chapters.

each lasted a year.) It *is* surprising, in view of the sentiments in the oration, to learn that sometime during the year, and following an illness, Fowler was converted to Christianity and decided to be a minister. His calling was short-lived, however, and by 1797 we find him reading law in Amherst under the tutelage of Judge Simeon Strong, the leading barrister in the county. The law turned out to be his true vocation, and he very soon established himself as a leading citizen, a pillar of the church, and a distinguished lawyer.[6] He married Lucretia Gunn of Montague (some ten miles due north of Amherst) in 1802, had nine children, of whom Edward was the eldest, and in 1813 built an imposing house on Main Street, the first brick house in town, the Homestead, where Emily was born.

It was the founding of Amherst College during the next few years that was the triumph of Fowler's life, and also his tragedy. The challenge was extraordinary, and it brought out all his fine qualities, the "strength and character" that Carpenter and Morehouse praised. This was the heroic side of his involvement; the tragic lay in what can only be called an element of fanaticism, which, not so clear in the early stages of planning and discussion when he was at his best, is certainly apparent later, when all the resources of the town seemed for a time inadequate to achieve the purpose and he threw himself recklessly into the cause. It was here that Fowler (now "Squire Fowler") gave almost all he had, and gave too much. His practice—and his health—failed, he was near bankruptcy, and eventually he left town to take a job in the Midwest, where he died "disillusioned, neglected, and forgotten."

It is important, and worth a digression, to understand the nature of the new college for which Fowler Dickinson sacrificed himself. It both reflected and shaped the character of the community into which, nine years after the official opening of the college, Emily Dickinson was born. Not only was her grandfather a founder and member of the first Board of Trustees, but her father and then her brother were treasurers of the college for a span of sixty years, beginning when she was five. Its affairs and its people were daily in her consciousness. In her adult life, she could in turn be interested, inspired, repelled, or bored by the college and its people; but she was well aware of the distinction it brought to the town. It gave her something to match her spirit with, and sharpen her wits on, throughout her life.

From the beginning of the century, sentiment had been growing in the Connecticut Valley for an institution of higher learning somewhere in the vicinity of Amherst. Dartmouth, Williams, and Yale were too far away

6. His daughter Elisabeth testifies to his success in all these undertakings. "Accepting an invitation to become principal of the Academy at New Salem, he taught one year with marked success. . . ." At twenty-one he was elected deacon of the First Church and "for forty years 'filled the office well.'" As a lawyer, "his success was so great that it is said 'he *did* more business than *all* the lawyers in Hampshire County'" (*Reunion of the Dickinson Family at Amherst, Mass., 1883* [1884], p. 172).

for the indigent youth of the district, and Harvard too liberal in its theology for the pious. Various sites had been considered—Northampton, Hatfield, Hadley—and various proposals made. One of them was the addition of a professorship to the staff of Amherst Academy, in whose founding, in 1814, Fowler had also been deeply involved. It was he who insisted that such a step was inadequate, that only a separate collegiate institution would fill the need. In support of his conviction, he subscribed \$600[7] and was one of the signers of a \$15,000 bond.

The purpose of the new institution was clear and unequivocal: its "original object" was "civilizing and evangelizing the world by the classical education of indigent young men of piety and talents." And, it should be added, piety as the founders conceived it. Liberal Harvard was the enemy. When the Amherst leaders applied to the Massachusetts General Court for a charter for the college,[8] the Harvard Unitarians opposed it as "a priest factory,"[9] a sectarian tool. But the opposition merely strengthened the founding zeal, which grew into a flaming cause. The charter was eventually granted, and Amherst became a stronghold of orthodoxy, to remain so during Emily Dickinson's youth and early maturity; that is, until it could no longer hold out against the advancing secularism of the age, the unsettling influences of the Civil War, and the theological liberalism that inevitably spread from Boston and Cambridge.

It would be wrong, however, to represent the college as some sort of monolithic ogre or black theological cloud on Emily's bright young horizon. At least she never spoke of it in those terms. She saw it through the eyes of the faculty children with whom she was intimate, the students and young tutors who came to call, the graduates who read law in her father's office, and, above all, her father and (later) her brother, the treasurers, who were concerned mainly with its worldly affairs. She knew it through its public ceremonies and lectures, its Commencements, its receptions (some of which were held in her own house), its library,

7. This is the figure given in Carpenter and Morehouse, p. 159. He is said to have subscribed \$1,005 for the founding of Amherst Academy (H. F. West, "Forgotten Dartmouth Men: A Founder of Dartmouth College—Samuel F. Dickinson, 1795," *Dartmouth Alumni Magazine* XXVII, February 1935, p. 62).

8. One of those leaders was Fowler Dickinson. A letter from home to Edward at Yale catches him in the act:

Father left in the yellow gig for the Bay Road this morning. He has gone to Boston by coach to see about getting a charter for something they propose to call Amherst College. He looked so fine in his white beaver and new great coat.

This passage is reproduced in Professor West's "Forgotten Dartmouth Men," p. 62. Professor West attributes the letter to Fowler's "sister Lucretia," in error either for his wife or for his daughter, both named Lucretia.

9. Thomas Le Duc, *Piety and Intellect at Amherst College 1865–1912* (1946), p. 5. In Chapter I ("A College for Training Parsons") Le Duc gives a lively account of the founding of the college, stressing the involvement of the whole community in "a genuine folk movement, vigorous and creative" (p. 2). The hostility of the Cambridge Unitarians and the determination of the Connecticut Valley people to resist heretical influences from the East are main themes.

Lucretia Gunn Dickinson and Samuel Fowler Dickinson,
from silhouettes by William King, about 1828

"The birthplace of Samuel Fowler Dickinson Esq. Amherst Mass."
Charcoal drawing, date and artist unknown

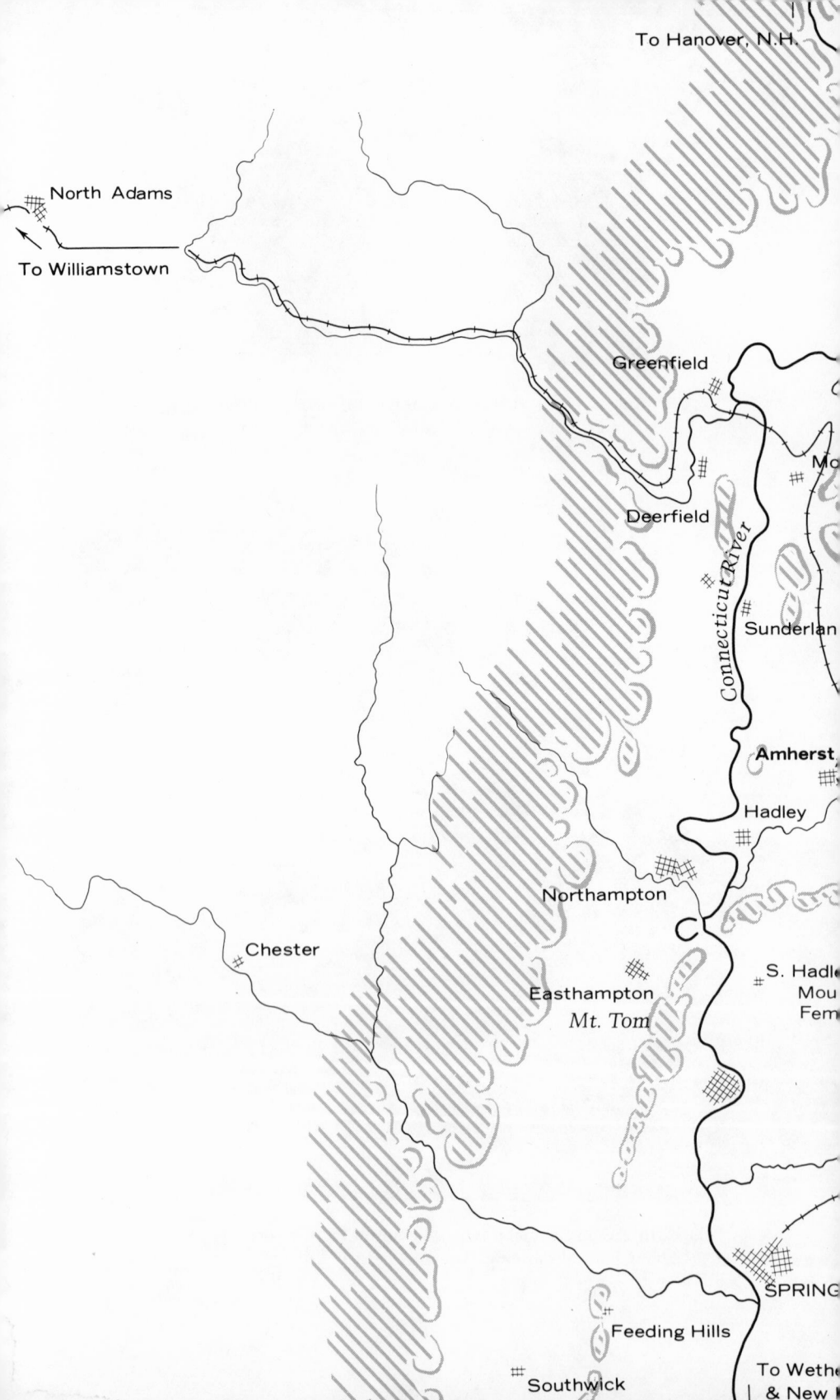

To Hanover, N.H.

North Adams

To Williamstown

Greenfield

Mo

Deerfield

Connecticut River

Sunderlan

Amherst

Hadley

Northampton

Chester

S. Hadl
Mou
Fem

Easthampton

Mt. Tom

SPRING

Feeding Hills

To Wethe
& New

Southwick

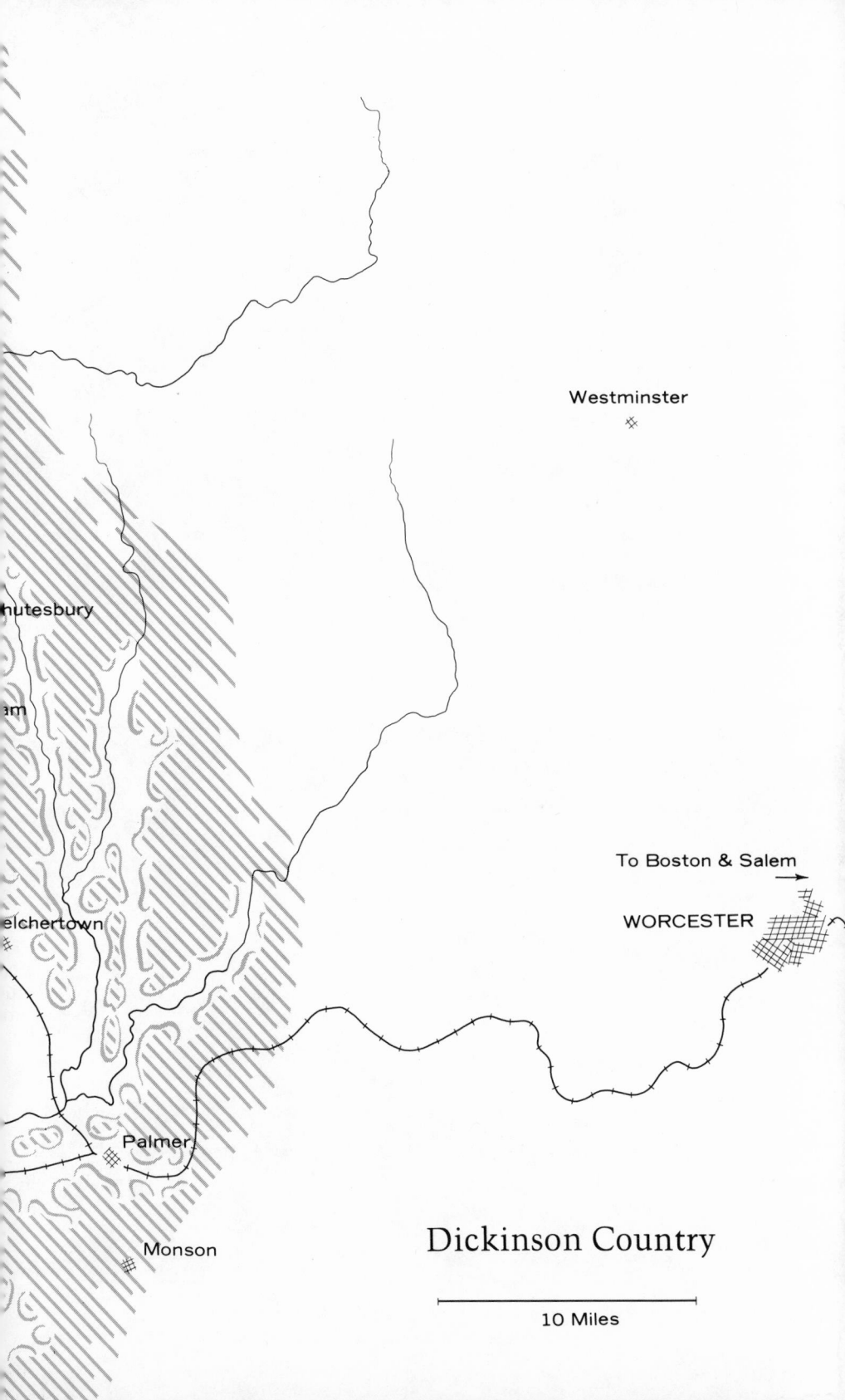

Westminster

hutesbury

am

elchertown

To Boston & Salem

WORCESTER

Palmer

Monson

Dickinson Country

10 Miles

The Dickinson Homestead, built by Samuel Fowler Dickinson, 1814
Lithograph by John Bachelder, 1858

Amherst College in 1848. Woods Cabinet and the College Observatory,
in center; built in 1847 at cost of $9,000

observatory, and "Cabinets" that housed the scientific and natural history displays. The atmosphere was not so theological as to overwhelm her. She surely benefited from the influence of Edward Hitchcock, who opened the eyes of a whole generation to the natural wonders of the Connecticut Valley and in the study of the natural sciences put Amherst far ahead of neighboring Williams, for instance, where Mark Hopkins was still resisting the geologists twenty years later. All this could go on, paradoxically, along with the periodic Revivals that upset Emily so and almost always had their start in the college—with Hitchcock himself, the pious scientist, in the forefront.

There was much of the revival spirit, certainly, in the founding of the college. Historians speak often of the crusading spirit of the founders. Rufus Graves, with Squire Fowler one of the two most prominent, was thought by his neighbors to be "beside himself." Fowler himself had apparently come a long way from the intellectual young Fourth of July orator, full of Reason and Nature and Scientific Inquiry. Hitchcock, who knew him well, later described him as "one of the most industrious and persevering men that I ever saw. . . . a man of very decided religious principles, and when once satisfied that he was in the path of duty, his face was as a flint, and he reminded one of the early Puritans." The cause to which he quite literally gave his life was a holy one, "urged by the command of our divine Saviour to preach the gospel to every creature."

There is a certain discrepancy in the early accounts of Squire Fowler's activities in the crusade, revealing a paradox in his character true of subsequent Dickinsons. On the one hand, he is the practical, judicious one, the "head" that guided Colonel Graves's impulsive "hand." As Hitchcock wrote: "Col. Graves was ardent and impulsive, and thought to be visionary, so that it needed the cooler and more practical judgment of Mr. Dickinson to prevent extravagance in opinion and give confidence to the public." Again, when the question of the location of the new college was being debated at a convention of delegates from thirty-seven Massachusetts towns, it was Dickinson's speech that won the day for Amherst. Tyler, the Amherst historian, called it "one of the most powerful and telling speeches which were made on this occasion." On the other hand, once the project was launched, his ardor was not only impractical but, for himself, ruinous. Tyler's *History,* which, published in 1873, was certainly available to Emily, describes her grandfather's sacrificial efforts. No modern summary covers the whole episode so movingly (the passage begins with a quotation from one of the participants) :

"A few will still remember how a few ministers came together often for prayer and consultation as to how the object could be accomplished. Nearly a whole week sometimes, would be thus spent. When it was decided to go forward and there were funds enough collected to begin the foundations of the first building, and the corner-stone was laid, the effort was only begun. As the work proceeded and they had used up all their available means, then he [Mr. Dickinson] would pledge his private property to the bank to obtain money that the work might go on. And when there was no money to pay for the teams to draw the brick or men to drive them, his own horses were sent for days and weeks till in one season two or three of them fell by the wayside. Sometimes his own laborers were sent to drive his horses, and in an emergency he went himself, rather than that the work should cease." At the same time, he boarded more or less of the workmen, and sometimes paid their wages out of his own pocket, while his wife and daughters toiled to board them. With all the zeal and efforts of numerous friends and benefactors, the work would often have stopped, had he not pledged his property till the money could be raised. His own means at last began to fail. His business which was so large as to require all his time and care, suffered from his devotion to the public. He became embarrassed and at length actually poor. And in his poverty he had the additional grief of feeling that his services were forgotten, like the poor wise man in the proverb who "by his wisdom delivered the city, yet no man remembered that same poor man."

Apparently the failure came on gradually and was more than merely financial. Local records show curious ups and downs in Squire Fowler's last years in Amherst. Only five years before he sold the Homestead and left town, he was elected Representative from Amherst to the Massachusetts General Court; and that same year (1828) he was "a prominent candidate" for the vacant office of Representative to Congress. He was not elected; but the *Hampshire Gazette* in a later tribute (November 7, 1838) said of his candidacy: "His native talents, his legal knowledge, his business habits, and his long experience in both branches of our State Legislature, would on the floor of Congress, have done honor to the district and the Commonwealth." And yet, also in 1828, there appeared in the *New-England Inquirer* (June 26) a curious proposal—curious, that is, for a man with a large and demanding law practice (if such it was), an active political life, and a consuming interest in the struggling young college:

> The subscriber proposes to open, at Amherst in the County of Hampshire, Massachusetts, a School for Instruction in the science and practice of the Law. . . . This Prospectus is issued *with extreme diffidence;* in as much as it promises only the efforts of *an humble individual* . . . Samuel F. Dickinson, Counsellor in the Supreme Judicial Court.

Diffidence and humility were hardly Dickinson traits—the italics are in the original—and do not square with the descriptions we have of Squire Fowler, the leader in community affairs.[10] A few weeks later (July 17), a sympathetic editorial in the *Inquirer* said perhaps more than it meant to say about the project and its initiator:

10. Professor West (*Dartmouth Alumni Magazine,* p. 62) quotes an unidentified source describing him at the time as

a tall, thin man, plain in his dress and appearance, of prodigious bodily and mental activity and energy, a famous walker, a ferocious worker, a born leader, a man of ideas and principles, of rare public spirit, strong religious faith and zeal, whose whole life was one of self-denial and self-sacrifice in the public service for education and religion, for the glory of God and the good of his fellow men.

We heartily wish [Samuel F. Dickinson] success in his undertaking. Mr. Dickinson has for some years been so unfortunately harrassed with cares and anxieties, that his attention has been considerably diverted from the business of his profession.

And in August the *Inquirer* again welcomed the project as a sign that Mr. Dickinson was about to return to his profession. Another heartening sign was a speech he gave before the Hampshire, Hampden and Franklin Agricultural Society in 1831, published that year in Northampton. He talked about education, his favorite theme, and even (an aspect not irrelevant to our purpose) about female education, of which he was very much in favor:

A good husbandman will also *educate well his daughters.* I distinguish the education of daughters from that of sons; because, Nature has designed them to occupy places, in family, and in society, altogether dissimilar.

Daughters should be *well instructed,* in the useful sciences; comprising a *good* English education: including a thorough knowledge of our own language, geography, history, mathematics and natural philosophy. The female mind, so sensitive, so susceptible of improvement, should not be neglected. . . . God hath designed nothing in vain.

Apparently, this was his swan song. Nothing permanent came of the law-school idea, and we hear no more of him as a public figure. By 1832 the college was in such serious financial straits that he saw the major work of his life threatened.

Shortly after this, and perhaps because of it, the low point of Fowler's career in Amherst was reached: the selling of the Homestead in March 1833. Next month, he left Amherst to take what must have seemed like an inferior position at Lane Theological Seminary in Cincinnati—the direction of the manual labor required of the students as part of the school's curriculum. (The job may have come to him through his Amherst associations with the Reverend Lyman Beecher, who had become Lane's first president in 1832.) His spirits steadily declined in the Western setting. Neither he nor his family adjusted well to the new environment. After three years he left Lane to become treasurer and supervisor of buildings in Western Reserve College in Hudson, Ohio, then referred to as in "the remote Ohio wilderness." Here his decline was rapid and complete. "His experience," writes a modern historian of Western Reserve, "was insufficient for the position and his health was poor. He died in the second year of service leaving his accounts in a sorry mess."

One is tempted to differ from this explanation of his failure. His experience was surely more than adequate. What he had suffered, apparently, was a general breakdown, the result of a gradual decline that had begun years earlier when he had overreached himself in his efforts for the college. Leaving Amherst had seemed like an exile. In May 1835 his daughter Catherine wrote from Cincinnati to her brother Edward in Amherst that their father's "spirits are completely broken down & probably will never rise again." The family letters following his death speak repeatedly of his last years as ones of "constant trouble," "gloomy apprehensions for the future," "anxiety & care & disappointment." Catherine wrote in April 1838 (a few days after he died) that "it seems as if his depression of spirits caused his sickness which terminated his life." This is hardly the same man whom President Hitchcock recalled as "one of the most industrious and persevering men that I ever saw," the man with the face of flint.[11]

The striking difference between Squire Fowler the Amherst leader and the miserable failure in the Midwest raises questions: Was his breakdown an isolated phenomenon or an aspect of the Dickinson heritage relevant to the next two generations? It is tempting to see in this experience—the intense dedication, the overreaching, the sense of exile, the collapse—a pattern that makes more understandable what seem on the surface to be the strange ways of the Dickinsons with whom we are directly concerned (Emily's, of course, being the "strangest" of all). We may well pause to examine a few of the clues embedded in this bit of family history.

To take one of the more obvious matters first, a problem around which much legend has accumulated and of especial relevance to Emily as recluse. If nothing else, Squire Fowler's sojourn in the West revealed a trait that became more extreme with each generation: home-centeredness. No Dickinson, at least in this branch of the family, flourished outside beloved Amherst. They did not transplant easily. They avoided travel whenever possible and were miserable when it was unavoidable. When daughter Catherine returned in 1835 from two years with her parents in Ohio, she wrote to them about her feelings in seeing Amherst again— "Everything looks beautifully here"—and included two sentences that might have been written by Emily herself: "I never saw any place half so beautiful as our own home. . . . I feel perfectly indifferent about going anywhere or seeing anybody." Once, to be sure, in the vigor of his young manhood, Emily's father Edward wrote his new wife from faraway New York that "I like travelling," and urged her on another occasion to see all

11. Nor does it sound like the man described in the memorial by his "loving daughter" (*Reunion*, p. 174):

He allowed himself but four hours of sleep, studying and reading till midnight, and rising at four o'clock he often walked to Pelham or some other town before breakfast. Going to court at Northampton, he would catch up his green bag and walk the whole seven miles. *"I cannot wait to ride,"* he would say to those who suggested that many horses in his stable would be idle, and outwalked the stage, with its four-in-hand, to Northampton. Bread, cheese and coffee, apples and old cider before breakfast were almost his sole diet. No man could outwork him, mentally or physically. He was ill but once in many years, till his last sickness of one week.

. . . I never saw him laugh but once, yet he was always cheerful and genial; always had the right word in the right place for every one, and could make himself agreeable to all classes of men, showing his appreciation of every effort.

the sights of the city (this time Boston) when she came. But from New York he added, "but *home* has charms for me, which I do not find abroad"; and the gist of his later letters from Boston or New York or Washington (he seldom got farther) is his longing for home. Also, there was a moment, at the time of his marriage, when Emily's brother Austin considered moving to Chicago, and another, only a few years before his death, when he thought of taking a job and starting a new life in Omaha. But the centripetal force was too strong. He never made the move and seldom traveled except on business. He took only one extended tour for pleasure (to the Midwest and South), with predictable results—he hated it.

This family peculiarity is all the more significant when viewed in the perspective of the times. One of mid-century America's greatest enthusiasms, it must be remembered, was the movement west and south. Even Amherst was on the move. "The world is full of people travelling *everywhere*," Emily wrote Austin in 1851. Lyman Beecher's move to Lane Seminary may have had something of the missionary motive in it, and (it has been suggested by those who would take the sting out of it) so might Squire Fowler's. Only a few years later Horace Greeley was to invite all young Americans to "go West and grow up with the country." Amherst men were investing in land in Michigan and Maine. In the other direction, European travel was becoming increasingly easy and fashionable. The Dickinsons, especially in Emily's generation, had many friends who traveled: Samuel Bowles of Springfield; Joseph Lyman, who left New England in 1850 to start his career in New Orleans, of which he wrote detailed accounts to the Dickinsons; Kate Scott Anthon, a frequent visitor in Austin's home and Emily's friend, who spent some eight of the years between 1864 and 1884 in prolonged travel in Europe and Great Britain; the cosmopolitan Thomas Wentworth Higginson; and others. Emily's girlhood friend, Abby Wood, married Daniel Bliss, a missionary, and moved to Beirut. Emily was very conscious of her friends in distant places, but her interest in travel remained utterly vicarious. In this she was true to family type.

Seen against this background, Emily's home-centeredness takes on less the aspect of some deep neurotic fear or psychological compulsion than of a family tendency carried to an extreme. Many times she was explicit on the subject. In 1851, when she went to Boston with sister Vinnie, they came back (she wrote Austin) "rich in disdain for Bostonians and Boston, and a coffer fuller of *scorn, pity, commisseration,* a miser hardly had." On her infrequent sojourns away from home, a recurrent theme of her letters is the superiority of Amherst to wherever she was. In Washington in 1855, she found that "all is jostle, here – scramble and confusion." Cambridge in 1864 was a "Wilderness," a "Jail"; she longed "to see the Grass, and hear the Wind blow the wide way in the Orchard." In 1870 Higginson asked her if she ever felt the need of something more than Amherst could offer her: "I never thought of conceiving that I could ever have the slightest approach to such a want in all future time," she answered. "I don't care for roving," she told him later; and again: "I do not go away, but the Grounds are ample – almost travel – ." Thoreau might have suggested some of this to her, he who traveled much in Concord—only, she went him one step farther: "To shut our eyes is Travel. The Seasons understand this." Here, too, may have been some of Emerson's self-reliance—and the Emerson who, home from a grueling trip to Europe, sighed with relief: "Back to myself." But mostly (although it is far from explaining her almost complete seclusion in the later years) in this most characteristic of family traits she was a Dickinson of the Dickinsons.

Another Dickinson tendency that certainly increased with the generations was the nervous instability (or whatever name medical science might give it) apparent in the nature of Squire Fowler's decline and collapse. He was the first complicated Dickinson—at least, the first whose complexities are a matter of record. Hitchcock's image of the face of flint missed some somber truth. Behind the bold front that both the succeeding male Dickinsons in Emily's family presented to the world were disquieting realities. Emily understood them well. She worried about her father's sad and lonely life. She worried about Austin, the most troubled of all, full of doubts, sensitivities, emotional conflicts, and (later) frustrations and wrecked hopes. Life was not easy for any of the Dickinsons, except perhaps Lavinia, though even she had a love affair that ended sadly, a temperament that was never placid, and eccentricities that in the end became extreme. How much of all this is foreshadowed in Squire Fowler's collapse no one can say, but there is something prophetic in the temperament that knew such extremes of enthusiasm and depression and that demonstrated for all to come that there was a Dickinson breaking point.

Compared with the rest of her family, Emily was one of the best composed of all, perhaps because she understood the problem better than any of them and through the discipline of her writing brought it under tolerable control. Nevertheless, the shifts in mood and tone in her poems, from despair to ecstasy, from a sense of the mastery of life to complete helplessness; the strange defenses that she eventually threw up to guard her privacy—the "fiery mist," as Higginson put it, with which she enshrouded herself; the behavior that even the most charitable could hardly call normal—all these signified, surely, an inner life that (to put it in the mildest terms) gave her a great deal of trouble. In this, too, she was very much a Dickinson.

The question is: How much did Emily know or think about her grandfather? (He died when she was seven.) The reference to the patriarchal Bible may tell much or little. There seems to have been a general reticence in the family about him, perhaps in itself a symptom. There are several bits of evidence. A dream that she recounted in a letter to Austin when she was sixteen may indicate how close to the family Squire Fowler's failure still was during her girlhood. She dreamed that her father had failed and that "our rye field . . . was mortgaged to Seth Nims" (the local postmaster and a political opponent of her father's). There is just a touch of panic in the passage; she seems to have wanted reassurance from Austin that all was well. The Dickinson family had once known failure and might know it again. Perhaps a hint of her grandfather's sacrificial career may be seen in her poems about noble failure and martyrdom, the saints of the earth who gave all for a cause.[12] But, to repeat, the surest evidence that Emily knew something about her grandfather is that Austin did. His 1889 memorial has the warmth of a family tradition:

> Samuel Fowler Dickinson; familiarly called Esq. Fowler; who stood in the forefront in the Amherst of his generation; a fine scholar; a lawyer of distinction and wide practice; a man of rare public spirit, the highest moral purpose, unflagging zeal; the leader in every local enterprise; holding many offices of trust, a dozen years and more a member of the Massachusetts Legislature, in both houses; of the most earnest and active religious faith and life, a deacon at twenty and for forty years thereafter, one of the leading founders of the college, sacrificing for it his property, time and professional opportunities, in the idea of getting the Gospel sooner to the ends of the earth.

Finally, of course, the work of Squire Fowler's hands was constantly around Emily from infancy on. *"Si monumentum requiris,"* wrote his "loving daughter" in her memorial, *"circumspice."* There was not only Amherst College but the house she was born in and (except for her years in the house on Pleasant Street, from 1840 to 1855) lived in all her life. Perhaps it was the sadness of his decline and the embarrassment of his financial failure that explained the family reticence, and hers.

This reticence, as I have suggested, seems to have been symptomatic. In Emily's family it extended to all things personal, certainly to the relations between parents and children. Indeed, it may have been at the heart of the family problem, which in turn may have been at the heart of the latter-day Puritan problem, when human nature, failing to meet the rigorous demands of the pristine discipline, began to hide its inadequacies behind smooth surfaces. Hence the much-maligned hypocrisy, the double lives, that have become almost synonymous with the tradition in its decline. In their eulogies of Samuel Fowler, neither his daughter Elisabeth nor Austin told the whole sad truth. Austin's father seems never to have talked freely with his children, and Austin in his maturity led one of the most grueling of double lives, all for the sake of appearances. No Dickinson, after Fowler, succeeded in bringing public and private life harmoniously together. Emily gave up the effort, developed a reticence of her own,

---

12. Such poems, for instance, as "Through the strait pass of suffering – / The Martyrs – even – trod" (#792, about 1863); "Each Life Converges to some Centre" (#680, about 1863); the theme of Moses denied Canaan (#597, about 1862, and #1201, about 1871) or the dying soldier in "Success is counted sweetest" (#67, about 1859), victory denied.

and resigned from public life. She dealt with the problem directly and without compromise.

In the light of such an analysis, there is something ironic about the following episode. The *Amherst Record* for August 30, 1871, recorded what a correspondent described as a "Beautiful Incident":

> In my walks about this beautiful town on the morning of the late Jubilee of Amherst College, I was attracted to the Cemetery. There I observed a Family gathering about the grave of the Hon. S. F. Dickinson. . . . All the daughters from their city homes with their husbands and children, and our friend Hon. E. Dickinson, were there. They came loaded with flowers.

This touching scene shows, among other things, the extent to which Squire Fowler, once a source of embarrassment to his children, was now revered by them. Speaking of the Squire's idealism that "outran his capacity to earn money," Jay Leyda says that it made him "a nobler figure to history than to those who lived beside him."[13] Yet here they were at his grave, thirty-three years after his death—with Edward, who had had to pay his debts and redeem the name of the family law practice, chief among the mourners. Perhaps there was a hint of expiation in this last gathering; there had been a general feeling in the family, following his death, that they had treated him shabbily in his declining years and had allowed him to die homeless. At any rate, here they were, with flowers.[14]

---

13. Apparently his difficulty lay not so much in earning money as in keeping it. He was overly generous—and not only to the college. His daughter writes:

> His large-heartedness and desire to help those in need sometimes overtaxed his judgment, and his name was often endorsed on notes to a large amount, which he was obliged to furnish the money for, while several men thus helped lived in affluence on his bounty, without recognizing the source.

She cites one final example of his civic-mindedness, a cause later to be espoused by his grandson Austin to the greater good of Amherst for generations to come: "His public spirit was shown in planting trees by the highway. When asked what benefit this would be to him, he would reply, 'Somebody will be benefited if not I' " (*Reunion,* pp. 172–74).

14. An even greater tribute came twelve years later at the Dickinson family reunion in Amherst in August 1883. Some five hundred persons attended, representing branches of the family from all over the country. This was the occasion of Elisabeth's verse history—in fifty-seven quatrains, with an introduction of forty-six lines in tetrameter couplets. It was printed in full in the Boston and Worcester papers. Samuel Fowler is the first Dickinson singled out for individual attention. After thirty-two stanzas in general praise of Dickinson qualities and achievements, he carries the poem for a full sixteen. A few samples will suffice:

> Of *Samuel Fowler,* Nathan's son,
> A townsman here, in Amherst born;
> We speak, of such as we've been told,
> And hope the venture not too bold.

> From Father, and from Mother, too,
> The love of knowledge straight he drew;

The only other comment about the scene is in the form of a question not hard to answer: Where was Emily?

---

So, youthful wish was gratified,
As with a College class he vied.

Old "Dartmouth" gave him his degree,
And second in his class was he;
To teaching, after, then he turned,
But for the *Law* his spirit yearned. . . .

Then follows the account of the founding of Amherst College and his sacrificial efforts:

His time, his infl'ence, and his prayers,
Despite his many worldly cares,
And all his gen'rous wealth, he gave
This College enterprise to save.

He sleeps, beneath the churchyard green,
Which from this place is plainly seen;
The words upon his marble plain –
"A man though dead, shall live again."

The only other Dickinson in Emily's branch of the family to be immortalized by Elisabeth's muse is *"Edward,* Samuel's eldest son, / An *honest Lawyer,* like his sire":

The College gave him, it appears,
Of College money – guardian care:
*And not one cent in forty years,*
But had its record full and fair.

Emily's letters of the period say nothing about the family reunion.

[ *43*

# 4

# Edward Dickinson

TRADITION HAS IT that Emily Dickinson's home was dominated by her father. Of recent years the picture has been getting darker as scholars have been opening up possibilities in the drama of the family that all but villainize Edward Dickinson and make him accountable for much of what is generally thought of as the tragedy of his daughter's life. It is from such studies—based, to be sure, on much in the record that gives them plausibility—that Edward emerges as a Mr. Barrett of Wimpole Street and Emily as the imposed-upon daughter, frustrated and forlorn. Edward had his dark side and was something of a mystery to his closest friends—even, at times, to Emily herself. No one close to him could escape completely the influence of his powerful personality. The possibilities must remain open. But the probabilities, taking the evidence all in all, are not so melodramatic. Like Melville's Ahab, he "had his humanities."[1]

Edward Dickinson (1803–1874) was, first of all, an ambitious and hardworking man and, from his early thirties, a public figure. From the evidence especially of his early letters, those written before his marriage in 1828, he seems to have started out, at least, less the dour Puritan of tradition than a typical success-oriented, work-oriented citizen of expansionist America and, in his emphasis on Reason, or what he called "rational happiness," and on the amelioration of the species through good works and the improvement of social institutions, a child of the Enlightenment not unlike his father in *his* younger days.

From what survives of his early correspondence—a few letters from his college classmates but mostly about seventy courtship letters to Emily

1. Clark Griffith, *The Long Shadow,* and John Cody, *After Great Pain,* dwell, often persuasively, on the dark side of Edward Dickinson's nature and its effect on Emily. We will never, of course, know the whole truth. Any estimate of the father-daughter relationship must be speculative. My own feeling is that she held a safe lead most of the way—until he died.

Edward Dickinson, dated variously 1853, 1860, 1874

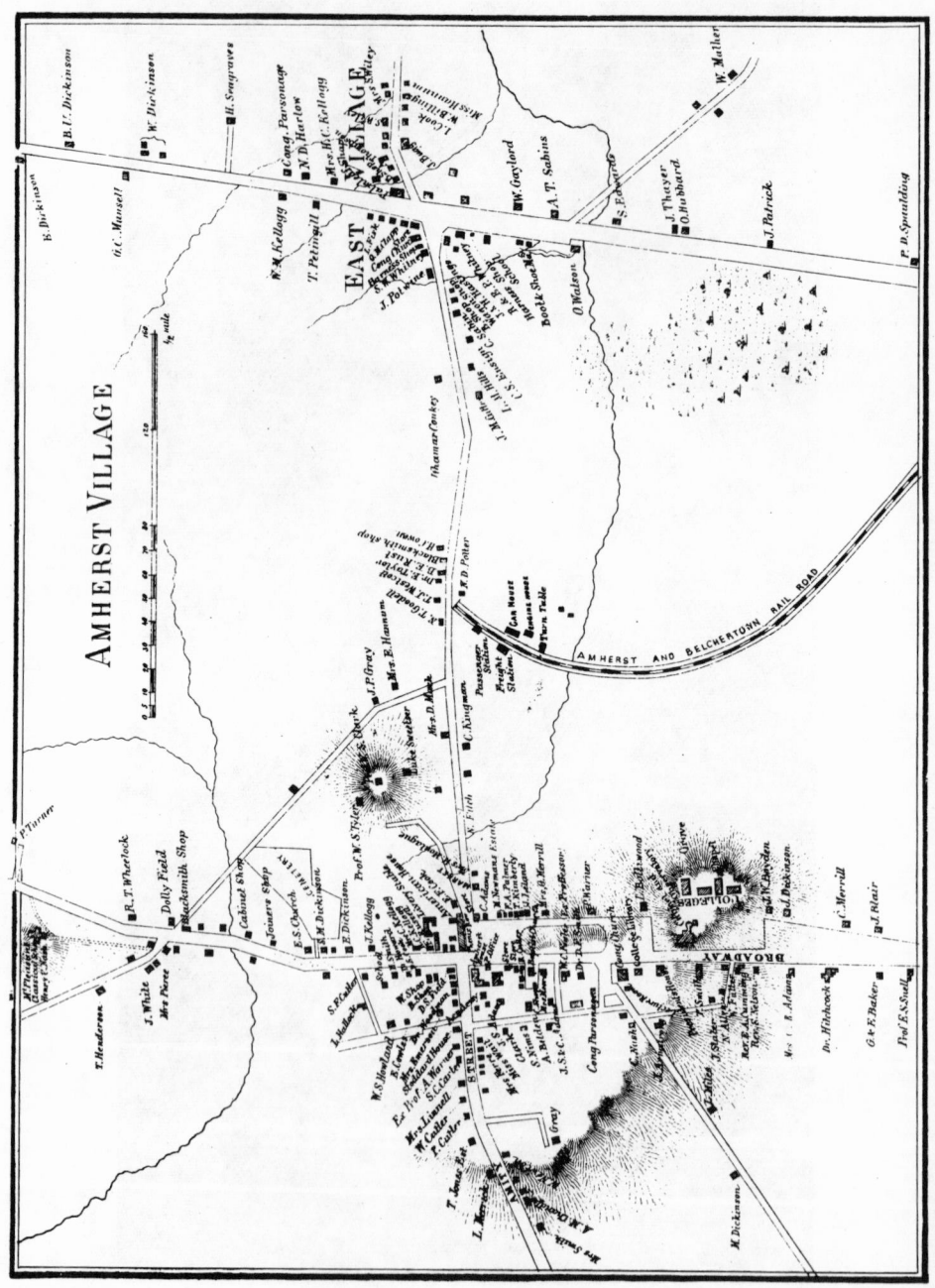

From "A Topographical Map of Hampshire County, Massachusetts," 1856. The
Homestead, just to left of center, was owned by Deacon Mack when the map
was drawn. The Edward Dickinsons were on North Pleasant Street, upper left

Norcross in Monson—the outlines of his character emerge sharp and clear, both as he quite frankly analyzes himself for Emily's benefit and from what can be inferred, at least, from the descriptions of his classmates. After schooling in Amherst Academy (which was to become a nursery of Dickinsons) and a year in Amherst College, he entered the class of 1823 at Yale. He seems to have been something of a figure. "To my Friend the Great Dickinson," begins a letter from a certain A. Thompson, Jr., written on June 24, 1820. The letters from his Yale friends—Osmyn Baker, George Ashmun, Talcott Bates—are breezy, cheerful, full of young ambition and high-flown rhetoric. "The Great Dickinson" becomes "Dick" and apparently a cherished member of a lively group. A letter from Baker (December 21, 1821), written perhaps during Edward's first Christmas vacation from Yale when he had to work off some academic requirements, sets the tone:

> How pass the heavy hours at the "Hill of Science?" Have you become reconciled to your situation or do you still savour [?] of better days? Does imagination travel back to Yale and dwell upon the scenes of friendship and good cheer which many a fireside within her walls, exhibit these long, cold evenings, and where many of your old friends tell stories of sophomore year and talk of Dick?

If many years later Higginson saw Edward Dickinson as "thin dry & speechless," he was anything but that to his friends at Yale.[2] But he had

2. Aside from such glimpses as this from Baker, the letters tell little about Edward's life at Yale, but we know that it resulted in a lifelong loyalty. (He attended his thirtieth reunion with his wife. *YH* I, 280; July 28 ?, 1853.) We can get a notion of its sources in some verses Edward contributed to a classbook, senior year. Apparently it was a custom to pass around among the seniors during the spring, when sentiment was running high, blank books, or albums, with a page reserved for each senior to record a thought or a bit of verse, his own or a quotation. Three such exist for the class of 1823. While most of his classmates quoted Burns or Shakespeare or Thomson, Edward Dickinson inscribed what appear to be his own compositions, even though each one is surrounded by quotation marks. Each is written in Edward's hand, dated, and signed.

> "With long farewell we leave the classic grove,
> Where science and the tuneful sisters rove,
> Abroad we wander, anxious to explore
> Antiquities of nations, now no more,
> To penetrate each distant realm unknown,
> And range excursive o'er the untravelled zone."

Yale College            Edward Dickinson
March 1st, 1823         Amherst, Mass.

> "One fatal remembrance – one sorrow that throws,
> Its bleak shade alike o'er our joys and our woes,
> To which life nothing darker nor brighter can bring,
> For which joy hath no balm – and affliction no sting."

Yale College            Edward Dickinson
March 21, 1823        Amherst, Mass.

moods. "Don't let your natural liveliness and universal good nature," wrote Baker about Edward's trouble with a certain tutor at Yale, "[receive] a tinge of sourness & discontent which will remain." The year after graduation, the moods deepened. Ashmun put his finger on at least one of the reasons in a lighthearted letter of December 23, 1823. He wrote enviously of the achievements of their classmates—two were already married, one had shot a man in a duel near New York, another had addressed a celebration at Plymouth Rock:

Dick can't we do something to signalize ourselves – I hate to be left so much in the rear. I wish you would take the subject into consideration & when you write again permit me to profit by your ideas on it.

Four months later, Baker, answering a gloomy letter from Edward, took the matter seriously. Edward was lonely, unhappy, and depressed over the meager opportunities in little Amherst:

I know well enough what a blackness of darkness that is which envelopes a young man in your situation. . . . "Act well your part," says Pope. . . . I don't see why you have not reason to go on your way rejoicing. Man is great only by comparison – and therefore I think it perfectly clear that you will not find it difficult to become and that shortly the greatest lawyer in A———t and that step being attained you will have nothing to do but step up another.

Talcott Bates echoed the refrain—perhaps as much a commonplace in the correspondence of young Americans of the era as sentimental effusion was in the letters of young ladies. But clearly in this instance Bates confirms a major insight into a fact of Edward's nature: ambition.

---

"When time who steals our years away,
Shall steal our pleasures, too,
The memory of the past will stay,
And half our joys renew.

Then talk no more of future gloom,
Our joys shall always last,
And Hope shall brighten days to come
And Memory gild the past." Farewell!

Yale College        Edward Dickinson
April 27, 1823      Amherst, Mass.

These may be cullings from the fugitive verse of the day; but the first has something of the genuine academic atmosphere and a young man's relish for it. Incidentally, Bingham, *Home*, p. 488, is mistaken in saying that Edward "was graduated as valedictorian of the class." The Order of Exercises for the 1823 Commencement reads: "Oration, 'On moral feeling,' with the Valedictory Address: By George Jones, York, Pa." L III, 937, also thrusts this honor upon him by having him graduated "at the head of his class."

I suppose [he wrote] that you are applying yourself to your studies most intensely and that the "welkin" ere long will resound with your praise. Well, be it so.

> "The fault, dear Brutus, is not in our stars,
> But in *ourselves,* if we are underlings."

Edward did not intend to be an underling. His letters to Emily Norcross, which begin on February 8, 1826, shortly after he had met her in Monson, make that clear. "My life," he wrote in the very letter in which he proposed marriage, "must be a life of business, of labor and application to the study of my profession." He talked about the profession of the Law in terms of the most enlightened humanism, as it may "enlarge & liberate & ennoble the mind," pry into "the causes of things – the origin and reasons for the changes which have taken place in Laws, manners, & customs," and lead the practitioner to "familiarity with the human character – acquaintance with science & literature. . . ." Although later, as the expenses of a growing family mounted, he complained bitterly of financial restrictions, he was no mere fortune hunter. Always he held up to Emily Norcross his high ideal for them both, a life in which their own happiness would be sanctioned only by their promoting "as far as in our power, the melioration of the condition of all about us."

He was an idealist like his father but better fitted for the battle of life, a metaphor he himself once used to describe for Miss Norcross's edification his thrill of victory in winning the acquittal of an Amherst student charged with drunkenness and burglary. He rejoiced "in having assisted in rescuing a young man of promise from the inevitable destruction which must have followed a conviction"; but what pleased him even more was the satisfaction of the full and successful use of his powers:

Let me be obliged to accomplish some important and difficult task, and I enjoy myself.

> "Man was made for action
> Action's his sphere, & for that sphere designed
> Eternal pleasures open on his mind."

An active life is my delight – I like the battle of business – tho' [and here he gives a design for living several times reiterated in subsequent letters] the retirement of study is also pleasant – but could I choose for myself I would confine myself to study one third of the time – spend a reasonable portion *in the bosom of my family* – and the residue in the most arduous and responsible duties of professional life.

(The italics are his.) Two months before the wedding, he came out even more emphatically:

Let us prepare for a life of rational happiness. I do not expect, neither do I desire a life of *pleasure,* as some call it – I anticipate pleasure from engaging with my whole soul in my business . . . and with my dearest friend. . . . May we be happy, useful & successful.

[ 47

At the very least, he seems never to have foreseen the presence of a poet in the family.

The lines of his character and of his proposed way of life come out not only clear but hard. We ask where in such a scheme a poet could possibly fit. But other phases of his character and interests appear in the letters and are somewhat more reassuring. He was deeply interested in education, especially for females. "Females, also," he wrote, as if discovering a great truth, "have a sphere of action, which, tho' different entirely in its kind from that of the other sex, is no less important." He lectured Emily Norcross on the subject many times and propounded his theories with the urgency of a reformer. He was deeply interested in Emily's cultural activities in Monson and sent her books (*The Spectator* in twelve volumes; Jane Porter's *Thaddeus of Warsaw;* a "new novel," *Hope Leslie,* by Catharine Maria Sedgwick, "which I presume you will find interesting – as the characters are drawn in a striking light, and innocence and villainy strongly contrasted"). He wrote her rhapsodically in the heat of many young enthusiasms. In a stirring letter on the Greek struggle for independence, then (the mid-1820s) at its height, he lingered over the ancient glories when Greece was "the dwelling place of beauty & elegance – & the abode of the 'gods & goddesses' – ":

> & in short the very name of Greece fills the mind with the idea of all that is beautiful & elegant – with all that can charm & please & animate – and the imagination delights to revel amid her shady bowers, her groves & caves & grottoes – to wander amid the classic retreats – to view the place where Homer sang – where Plato taught – & the eloquence of Demosthenes charmed & persuaded & convinced & delighted.

A year later (December 19, 1827) he was thrilled by the news of the success of the Powers in establishing the new Greece: "Let all the nations shout 'Hallilujah,' " he exclaimed, and assured Emily that, rather than be a slave, he would fight even against hopeless odds, kill as many of his oppressors as he could, then *"plant a dagger in my own breast."* The deaths of the ex-Presidents Adams and Jefferson on the same day (July 4, 1826) stirred him to similar rhapsodies on the glorious examples of these men, their valor, eloquence, devotion to liberty. Throughout, the letters are punctuated by lyric passages on the beauties of nature—spring in the Connecticut Valley; summer evenings in Amherst ("It is very late. . . . The evenings are now beautiful, and the brilliant moonlight ought not to pass unenjoyed"); and the fury of winter storms, when "the wind whistles and the trees crash." What little there is of religion comes in only in the latter months of the correspondence. Perhaps it was so much taken for granted that it needed no stressing. The piety seems sincere—and conventional: "and let our prayers ascend for each other, morning & evening, that we may individually experience that change which we believe must take place, before we can be rec'd into the abodes of the pure spirits who dwell in the presence of the Eternal!"

One further enthusiasm cannot pass unnoticed, if only for the high irony it contains for us, who a century and a half later can only wonder how a man of such convictions could have been blind to their living embodiment in his own daughter. In a letter of August 3, 1826, he wrote:

I passed Tuesday evening, of this week, in company with Miss Sedgwick, the Authoress of "Redwood" & "New England Tale", at a party at Judge Lyman's. She had an interesting countenance – an appearance of much thought, & rather masculine features. And I feel happy at having an opportunity of seeing a female who had done so much to give our works of taste so pure and delicate a character – and a conscious pride that women of our own country & our own state, too, are emulating not only the females but the men of England & France & Germany & Italy in works of literature – & we are warranted in presuming that, if they had opportunities equal to their talents, they would not be inferior to our own sex in improving the sciences.

To this unexceptionable statement he tied only one moral string:

Tho' I should be sorry to see another Mme. de Stael – especially if any one wished to make a partner of her for life. Different qualities are more desirable in a female who enters into domestic relations – and you have already had my opinions on that subject –

But the problem of another de Staël in his own family was surely not his. His failure was not so much one of conviction as of perception; or his own business and ambition came first. As his daughter Emily was to say later, "Father [is] too busy with his Briefs – to notice what we do." One is moved to remark only that, had Edward Dickinson noticed what his daughter was up to, had he nurtured her as his darling genius or tried to impose his will on her creativity, he might have spoiled her or destroyed her. As it was, she survived—and wrote. Perhaps it was just as well that he was too busy.

Whenever the subject of marriage comes up in the courtship letters, Edward is preeminently the man of reason and forethought. He urged Emily Norcross to view "the subject, as I always have, in a candid and rational light, and as one which ought to be treated with the most perfect plainness and frankness." He urged her to take her time (which she did, somewhat to his annoyance) in answering his proposal, to inquire into his character and prospects, to consult "Judge Howe, Mr. Mills . . . or almost any clergyman in the neighboring towns." Their life together must be one of "industry, frugality, application." The $20,000 failure of a law firm in Waterbury, Connecticut, is "a warning [he wrote] to all young men to be prudent and industrious." "Preserve your health," he urged her several times (although Emily's health seems at that time to have been excellent), and once delivered a little lecture on the whole duty of woman:

Continue in the path of innocence and virtue and fidelity – continue to cultivate those graces which are the charm of your sex and let that sincere desire for that pure and unsullied reputation which are the pride of both sexes incite us to avoid the appearance of evil – and let our conduct be marked by that correctness which shall insure our happiness and may an approving conscience be our reward.

One of the steps in his rational approach to marriage (although it came a little late, only two months before the wedding) was a frank assessment of what he called their "dispositions." In previous letters his personal talk concerned mostly his work and ambitions; here he becomes introspective—he wants Emily to be clear about his virtues and defects, and about her own:

> I will plainly tell you what I think of my own disposition, and what I think of yours. I am naturally quick & ardent in my feelings, easily excited, tho' not so easily provoked – decided in my opinions – determined in accomplishing whatever I undertake – hard to be persuaded that I am wrong when I have once formed my opinion upon reflection – sometimes unyielding and obstinate – rather particular – like to have everything in the right place & done at the right time – have a little personal irritability in my constitution – am rather high-spirited, at times – tho generally moderate – like to have things go pretty smoothly, have business enough to keep me occupied. And now I come to you. I think you are resolute – decided – rather particular – want to see everything go on well – & see everybody happy. I think your disposition to be good – that you are kind – benevolent – patient in trouble – able to endure sickness – that you will deprive yourself of comfort & repose to render a friend more comfortable – and I think, too, that your feelings are somewhat easily excited, & that your vivacity might, in case of emergency, approach to spirit – Is this a correct picture? Of the many good qualities which I think you to possess, it may not be proper here to speak. I do not flatter, My Dear, when I say that I find in you just what I have long wished to find a lady to possess.

His analysis of his "dearest friend" will concern us later. She must have been pleased. As to himself, the "quick & ardent" feelings may come as a surprise. Actually, they should not, even though in later years Edward gave a very different impression to the world. His daughters were to report certain mild domestic explosions; but he was eminently the man of conviction, not feeling. As for the rest of his self-analysis, it was all too prophetic. At twenty-five he set his course, and he never deviated. Again, we cannot help looking to the future with foreboding. It was just as well that at a certain point his daughter Emily geared her life, not to happiness, but to a purpose and meaning of her own.

Only a few times in the letters does he talk tenderly, as on those moonlit nights and, in gentler mood than usual, when he contemplates coming home "after the business of the day is finished" to share confidences with "my friend" (twice he called them "secrets"). His rhetoric is always formal and restrained—the very opposite of the youthful letters of the next Dickinson generation—and we can only hope that Emily Nor-

*Edward Dickinson*

cross saw in it depths of feeling not apparent to us. Here is a typical valediction:

> And now, My Dear Emily, I must leave you, let me join with you in the wish that we could press the parting hand, & give the parting ———s, but while that is denied, let me hope that ere long we shall enjoy each other's society constantly, & experience the true happiness which kindred spirits (are not ours such?) are fitted to produce. ˋ

Actually, there is more feeling in later letters when he scolds her for refusing his many invitations to visit Amherst; for her failure to write—to his daily letters she answers but once a month; and finally when he all but loses patience over their delayed wedding plans: "I have already waited a year longer than I ever intended to wait." But he respected her deliberateness, insisting again and again that her happiness came first. He threw himself enthusiastically into the work of preparing their first home. He wanted to have everything right. He arranged for the carpenters, the painters, the cleaners, and oversaw every detail—always, be it said, asking for Emily's opinion on colors and arrangements. He may not have been a passionate lover, but he was persistent, considerate, and always practical. He wrote her a special note to say that the new stove drew beautifully.

This is the young man, who, after deciding against several opportunities to practice elsewhere, hung out his shingle in Amherst on September 27, 1826, started business that very afternoon, and went straight for the top, as Osmyn Baker predicted. The thrill of success often enlivens the early letters, and his marriage on May 6, 1828, provided further purpose and drive. Although he never said as much, either in the early letters or later, a part of that purpose may have been the restoration of the family name after his father's collapse. Edward was the eldest son and the only one of the children who stayed in Amherst.[3] At any rate, he soon estab-

3. After Squire Fowler's failure and the breakup of the family in 1833, the children scattered widely. William, the next eldest son, had left for Boston several years earlier. In 1829 he settled in Worcester, Massachusetts, where he became a successful industrialist and later insurance executive and director of companies. He died in 1887. Samuel Fowler, Jr., went to New York and then entered business in Savannah, Georgia. Timothy also went south; he died in Griffin, Georgia, in 1852. Frederick stayed with his brother Edward's family until he graduated from Amherst College in 1837, when he went west to join his parents in Ohio. Lucretia, the eldest daughter, married Asa Bullard (Amherst '28) and settled in Cambridge, Massachusetts. Mary married Mark Haskell Newman (Bowdoin '25) in 1828. They lived in New York City, where Newman founded a publishing house. Catherine married Joseph A. Sweetser in 1835, who had moved to New York City from Amherst in 1833. Elisabeth, the youngest child, lived variously in Amherst and Worcester, where she kept house for her brother William when his wife died in 1851. In 1866 she married Augustus N. Currier of Worcester. Together, these aunts and uncles presented ED with thirty-two cousins. Except for Edward, William was the most successful of Fowler's sons, kept on close terms with Edward, and with him bore the brunt of their father's failure. Of the daughters, Elisabeth, the family bard, was the most striking—"a large, tall

lished himself firmly and successfully in the areas of his father's main concern.

It is well first to follow, if only in outline, his long career of service to the town, the college, and the state. His career shows no such dramatic rise and fall as his father's. The year his father left for the Midwest, he became Moderator of the Town Meeting, a post to which he was elected, off and on, for the next sixteen years. In 1835 he undertook the work for the college his father had had to abandon and served it as treasurer for thirty-seven years. No accounts of *his,* it should be said, were ever "in a mess." Tyler reports:

> The best financier in the Corporation has publicly announced, as the result of careful examination for many successive years, that, as Treasurer of Amherst College, he has never lost a dollar. And one of the sharpest and shrewdest of the Board of Overseers declares that after the most prolonged and patient scrutiny of his books and accounts, only a single error of less than a hundred dollars could be detected, and that error was *against* himself.

He was zealous in good causes, even fanatically so. His passion for bringing the railroad to Amherst became almost as much of a cause with him as the college had been to his father. But he was better balanced and kept his family, his fortune, and his position in Amherst intact. Tyler, speaking from firsthand observation, wrote of his "unbending firmness of purpose and his great freedom and boldness of speech under excitement." Of all the brothers, Edward was most like his father, and here is perhaps the surest link between Squire Fowler's intellectual, literary turn and Emily's. At any rate, there can be no doubt that these qualities of firmness and dedication, and his power as a speaker, brought Edward Dickinson to a position of prominence, especially when his achievements in state and national politics are added to all he did for the town and college of Amherst, unapproached by any Dickinson and hardly equalled by any Amherst figure of his generation.

Edward's first major recognition outside Amherst came when he was elected Representative to the General Court of Massachusetts in 1838. He was twice elected State Senator (1842 and 1843), became president of the newly formed Henry Clay Club in Amherst in 1844, and in the mid-1840s was a member of the Governor's executive council and major in the militia. In 1852 he was delegate to the National Whig Convention in Baltimore and (the peak of his political career) was elected later that year to the Congress of the United States as Representative from the Tenth Massachusetts District. In 1854 he was admitted to practice before the Supreme Court. He was considered as a possible candidate for governor of

woman, rather distinguished in appearance"—and determined: "the only male relative," as ED described her, "on the female side." Many days after one of her visits, ED wrote, "its flavor of court-martial still sets my spirit tingling" (*L* II, 561; to Mrs. Holland, August 1876). (*Home,* pp. 486–87 and passim, is the best single source of information on the relatives.)

Massachusetts in 1859 and was offered the opportunity to run for lieutenant governor in 1861, which he refused. He received an LL.D. from Amherst College in 1863 (much, so it is recorded, to his surprise); and in 1873 (the year before he died) he was for the second time elected to the General Court of Massachusetts.

On the local scene, he became a commanding figure, not only as the leading lawyer in Amherst, a pillar of the church and a trusted town father, but as the close and valued associate of three presidents of Amherst College. He was the man of the hour on many occasions requiring more than sober judgment and learned counsel. Of a bad fire in the village in July 1851, which threatened a whole street, Emily wrote to Austin (with a touch of her usual satire at her father's expense):

> Father and Mr. Frink took charge of the fire, or rather of the *water,* since fire *usually* takes care of *itself.* The men all worked like heroes, and after the fire was out Father gave commands to have them march to Howe's [Hotel] where an entertainment was provided for them – after the whole was over, they gave "three cheers for Edward Dickinson, and three more for the Insurance Company"!

Of similar nature is the famous anecdote of his ringing the church bell to summon the town to witness an unusually fine display of northern lights. He was an inveterate speaker on patriotic holidays, at dedications and the laying of cornerstones. His speeches were variously described as "bold," "eloquent," "spirited."[4] For all his alleged austerity and dourness, he and

4. These are comments from the local scene. For samples of Edward Dickinson's oratory as a Congressman, see *Home,* Appendix IV, where his arguments against the civilian management of the national armories, a matter which concerned the House of Representatives during the session of 1854, are printed in full. He was one of the two members of the committee on the problem who dissented from the majority report. His hour-long speech was described as "blunt, stubborn, and forthright" (*Home,* p. 532). He was moved at one point to a flight of oratory (p. 544) that recalls the heroics of the youthful Samuel Fowler Dickinson's Fourth of July oration.

> It is said, too, that the military system discourages enterprise, paralyzes inventive genius, is an insult to the mechanics of the country, and weakens their attachment to our republican institutions. Sir, the mechanics of this country are above the need of any eulogium from me – their reputation for skill is world-wide; and if I believed the charge to be true, I should be found among the foremost in my efforts to put an end to a system which produces such results. Not believing the charge to be true, the obvious answer to it is, that while our mechanics, as a body, are superior to those of any other country in intelligence, skill, and mental power, and while the instances are numerous of those who have made the most brilliant discoveries, and signalized themselves by the highest scientific and literary attainments, and been conscious that no circumstances could control or diminish the power of the "Divinity that stirs within them" – while we are proud, as American citizens, of the honor they have earned for us as a nation, and while they are acquiring wealth and power by the force of their own talents, they need not the feeble aid which we can render them in placing them in responsible positions – they need not our praise to make them conscious of their own deserts. They are entitled to receive, and will ever receive from every intelligent man, the respect due

his wife were acknowledged social leaders in Amherst, not only for their famous Commencement receptions but for the stream of visitors, many of them famous or near-famous, who enjoyed their hospitality. He had many warm friends of high degree who came often to Amherst to see him— Judge Lord of Salem, Samuel Bowles of Springfield, the Hollands of Springfield and New York. On June 17, 1869, the *Amherst Record* printed the following item:

> Gen. and Mrs. Geo. B. McClellan were in town last Friday. . . . Among those who received calls from the distinguished personages were Profs. Warner and Crowell, Mrs. Jones, and Hon. Edward Dickinson.

(It is interesting to note, however, that as early as 1857 the social center of gravity had begun to shift. When Emerson and Wendell Phillips visited Amherst that year, they stayed with Susan and Austin Dickinson, who had been married and had moved next door into the Evergreens only the year before. As Sue triumphantly wrote many years later, "both were our royal guests.")

There was hardly a civic project in Amherst, from the founding of Massachusetts Agricultural College to the establishment of the local water works, in which Edward Dickinson was not a central figure. He not only brought the railroad to Amherst but became president of it—the Amherst & Belchertown Rail Road. He helped bring the telegraph to Amherst. He was a life director of the Home Mission Society and in 1859 was appointed by Governor Banks trustee of the lunatic hospital in Northampton. He led the pallbearers at President Hitchcock's funeral; he had a locomotive named for him; and during his own funeral the shops in Amherst were closed and all business was suspended in his honor.

Even this partial list of Edward's accomplishments shows how deserved his public image was. But, like most images, it has hardened into a cliché. Higginson's peremptory summing up is typical. Indeed, Emily's father seems to have attracted stereotyping—including the image of the ogre father—about as readily as Emily herself, suggesting a quality of these Dickinsons, from Edward on down and most certainly including her brother and sister, that stimulated legends. Another description by

---

to them for their mental and moral qualities, and for their manly virtues; and will ever look above all distinctions of class or caste, and render to every man according to his desert, and cordially adopt the noble sentiment of the poet:

> "Honor and shame from no condition rise;
> Act well your part, there all the honor lies"
> [Pope, *An Essay on Man*, IV, 193]

(Pope's "Act well your part" stuck with him since Osmyn Baker's letter.) Two years earlier (July 26, 1852), Dickinson's speech at a Whig meeting in Northampton to ratify the nomination of General Scott was received (so the *Springfield Republican* reported the next day) with "great applause." The speech was "sensible, strong, practical and effective" (*YH* I, 254).

*54* ]

Tyler shows the legendary Mr. Dickinson as he stood in the community, the embodiment of all those public virtues his daughter found a little tedious.

At the age of threescore years and ten Mr. Dickinson still stands erect, perpendicular, with his senses of seeing and hearing unimpaired, with his natural force and fire chastened and subdued but scarcely abated, one of the firmest pillars of society, education, order, morality and every good cause in our community.

There is a touch of the legendary, too, in an account of Edward Dickinson in the *Boston Journal* (later reprinted in the *Springfield Republican*) eight months before he died. Here he was said to recall the patriarchs of the Connecticut Valley—the Hopkinses, the Stoddards, the Hookers of ancient fame:

He is a man of sterling personal character and integrity, always manifesting the keenest interest in public affairs, especially in town affairs. He is a type of the men once known as the "River Gods."

"Although slow and conservative," the article concluded, "[he] will prove a valuable man in the [Massachusetts] House," to which, on November 10, 1873, he was elected on an independent ticket. When he died in harness the following spring—arguing in the House for more appropriations for the Massachusetts Central Railroad—he went out of public life as he came in, a model citizen, respected by all.

His inner life was another matter. For all his worldly success, his many good works, and his brilliant family, he was a lonely and somber man. The exclusiveness of his early ambitions took its toll. Two very different observers saw him as "remote." He had his humanities; but he shared another quality with Melville's Ahab; he lacked "the low, enjoying power"; or, as his daughter Emily put it (in a remark that will need some qualification), ". . . he never played, and the straightest engine has its leaning hour." Emily, it seems, saw him more clearly than did any of his intimates, but in a moment of bafflement even she said, "I am not very well acquainted with father," a view that many others shared most of the time. Once, at the height of his career, Emily said how happy she was for him in Washington "among men who sympathize with him, and know what he really is," but it may be doubted that they understood him any better in Washington than they did in Amherst. A public eulogy after his death—by Samuel Bowles in the *Republican*—even suggested that he had failed to "understand himself."

We come, in him, to another stage in the increasingly complicated inner life of the Dickinsons. As to its origins, we can only speculate: excessive ambition thwarted in the small town of Amherst; a tendency toward melancholy like his father's; or a too stern devotion to duty. Or it may have been a sense, only partly understood and never expressed (as Emily could express it), of the inadequacy of an ethic which had come to

[ 55

stress the public virtues of respectability and achievement at the expense of the private requirements of friendship and parenthood—warmth and play and easy availability. Emily understood this paradox of public success and private failure, and her understanding illuminates and warms her mixed, sometimes caustic, remarks on him during the long years of their life together. But, in essence, her understanding seems to have grown steadily in depth and humanity.

Although Emily was proud of her father, the public image of him was not a matter of importance to her. He might march perpendicular at the forefront of town affairs or be the last of the River Gods to the State of Massachusetts; but what struck her, in her youth, was the slightly comic aspect of it all. Early in 1852 when the decision (mostly her father's work) was made to construct the Amherst & Belchertown Rail Road, there was general rejoicing in the community. Emily's comment to Austin about their father was a nice combination of detachment, love, and humor: "Father is really *sober* from excessive satisfaction, and bears his honors with a most becoming air." And in June of 1853, on the day of his greatest local triumph—the celebration of the road's completion—she described him as "marching around the town with New London at his heels like some old Roman General, upon a Triumph Day." It is good to be reminded that the tone of these remarks is typical of some ninety percent of her recorded comments on him, a tone that does not noticeably change until after his death. In 1851 in a letter to Austin, she described his going forth on an errand with "his pantaloons tucked in his boots. . . . I don't think 'neglige' quite becoming to so mighty a man." "Father steps like Cromwell when he gets the kindlings," she wrote her Norcross cousins in 1870. He makes "the Barn sound like the Bible." During the real-estate boom in Amherst in the early 1850s, "Father [she wrote Austin] looks very grand, and carries his hands in his pockets in case he should meet a *Northampton man.*" Indeed, about this time Emily (age twenty) confided to Austin that "we young ones . . . think he is rather crazy."

It was not that Emily failed to take her father seriously; she took him very seriously indeed, if more acutely after she lost him than during his life. But by the time she was twenty she recognized the profound differences between them and began to carve out for herself a separate domain in which she could live her own life intact—a domain from which she could emerge to give her father the kindnesses and attentions that naturally flowed from her fondness for him but to which she could repair whenever she chose. Her comment in a letter to Austin in 1851 marks the beginning, or near it, of this conscious effort to establish her own world within the world of the family. Lamenting Austin's absence, she writes:

> When I know of anything funny, I am just as apt to cry, far *more* so than to *laugh*, for I know who *loves jokes best*, and who is not here to enjoy them. We don't *have* many jokes tho' *now*, it is pretty much all sobriety, and we do not have much poetry, father having made up his mind that its pretty

Edward Dickinson

much all *real life*. Fathers real life and *mine* sometimes come into collision, but as yet, escape unhurt!

Edward Dickinson's household has been described as a dictatorship, a prison, a "world of parental tyrannies" where "a little girl [Emily] suffered silently and stubbornly." Such a view needs qualifying, at least as it applies to the children's formative years. There may have been minor eruptions, but the real "Vesuvius at Home" came later. Like all sensitive, individualistic children, Emily must have had moments of feeling trapped and rebellious and at times, perhaps, ignored. She could complain about father and his "Briefs," but in the next sentence comes her acknowledgment that "He buys me many Books – but begs me not to read them – because he fears they joggle the Mind." There is ample evidence that, by the standards of his day—long before the era of permissiveness and child-oriented households—he was a good father. For better or worse, children demanded less then, and expected less. A passage from one of Emily's early letters to Austin has been used as evidence of Edward's absolute authority in the household:

We're rejoiced that you're coming home – the first thing we said to father, when he got out of the stage, was to ask if you were coming. I was sure you would all the while, for father said "of course you would," he should "consent to no other arrangement," and as you say, Austin, what father *says*, "he means."

Millicent Todd Bingham took the episode quite seriously (although she may be partly right about Edward's authority in the family):

No one openly opposed his decisions, least of all his family. He knew what was right and what was wrong and that was the end of it. As his daughter Emily remarked, "What Father says he means."

But Emily's concluding remark seems, in context, quite clearly the focus of a little family joke at father's expense, as if saying to Austin, "You and I know how he carries on."

Even against what I take to be Edward's mild authoritarianism, the children developed adequate defenses. One of them surely was humor, especially between Emily and Austin. They enjoyed making fun of him. The question is: Was it always behind his back? They clearly saw through the lawyer's manner and were not in the least awed by it. Emily recounted to Austin a minor domestic crisis of a few months back (June 8, 1851), involving a head-on collision between her father's "real life" and hers. The episode, like the one just cited, has been regarded as another example of parental tyranny. But note how blithely she tells it:

Tutor Howland [sister Vinnie's suitor of the moment] was here *as usual,* during the afternoon – after tea I went to see Sue – had a nice little visit with her – then went to see Emily Fowler, and arrived home at 9 – found Father in great agitation at my protracted stay – and mother and Vinnie in tears, for fear that he would kill me.

[ 57

She gives an equally bland account of another episode of the next year, when her friend Martha Gilbert (several years her senior) was visiting:

Mat came home from meeting with us last Sunday, was here Saturday afternoon when father came, and at her special request, was secreted by me in the *entry,* until he was fairly in the house, when she escaped, *unharmed.*

The episode is sandwiched into a happy letter, with no comment.[5]

The household seems to have been less a dictatorship than a confederation of independent states. It was certainly not a prison. Vinnie is reported as saying that they all lived "like friendly and absolute monarchs, each in his own domain." Higginson in 1870 described the household as one "where each member runs his or her own selves"; and Emily said later, perhaps with oblique reference to household management, "We have no statutes here, but each does as it will, which is the sweetest jurisprudence."

It is important to note that Edward himself encouraged this independence. Although the town of Amherst presented excellent educational facilities, he sent each of the children away to school—Austin to Williston Seminary in Easthampton, Lavinia to Ipswich Female Seminary, Emily to Mount Holyoke (in this case, of course, Amherst did not offer the equivalent). They each had a chance, that is, to see life on their own and to shape their destinies, should they have so chosen, apart from parental influences. That they all came back to center their lives in Amherst and in their home may have been due less to any authoritarian pressure by Edward than to their own peculiar natures. They had an excellent home, and they knew it.

To Joseph Lyman, the country cousin and Austin's schoolboy friend at Williston who visited him for some months in the 1840s in the house on North Pleasant Street, the Dickinson household was sheer delight; he called it "that charming second home of mine in Amherst," and a dozen years later he was still retailing its delights in his letters to his fiancée. A letter to Lyman from Austin, written during an Amherst vacation (Austin graduated in 1850), gives a sense of how well the young people functioned, for all the alleged repressiveness of the Dickinson home. To be sure, the atmosphere is perhaps more than usually relaxed: mother and father—"the ancient people"—are off on a trip to Monson:

Now you have got enough of momentary description [the books, the crackling fire], to go a little fa[r]ther back, I go[t] up at 5: o.clock, fed the horse, then eat my breakfast. At 6: o.clock, I led the horse, attached to the buggy[,] to the front steps, and in the space of two or three minutes, perceived two mysterious forms emerging from the front door, apparently a male and female, which, upon raising my lantern, proved to be those of my father and mother, who immediately seated themselves in the wagon and drove off to

5. Mrs. Bingham (*Home,* p. 289) takes this as an example of Martha's timidity in contrast to her sister Susan's cool self-possession. But Martha was no child (she was nearing her mid-twenties) and she may have determined, for any one of a number of reasons, to avoid a meeting with Edward Dickinson that afternoon.

Edward Dickinson

Monson, bidding us "good morning", as they went, expecting to return tomorrow – . . . . [Vinnie being away] Emily and I are left, lord and lady of
the "mansion", "with none to molest or make us afraid". We are anticipating
a fine time in the absence of the ancient people. Wish you were here to help
us laugh – I think there is a chance for our having some company tonight.

Emily spoke often and fully on this subject. Her love of home was
intense and her loyalty complete. During her first months at Mount
Holyoke, her letters (although she loved her studies, her teachers, and her
friends) are filled with longings for home—my "very dear home," "my
*own* DEAR HOME"—and on her first return the very sight of Amherst
filled her with ecstasy:

We rode swiftly along & soon the Colleges & the spire of our venerable
Meeting House, rose to my delighted vision. Never did Amherst look more
lovely to me & gratitude rose in my heart to God, for granting me such a
safe return.

South Hadley, it should be noted, is all of ten miles from Amherst.

Once out of Mount Holyoke and well settled in her home (a spell of
ill health had something to do with her leaving college after three terms),
she did all she could to lure back the wandering Austin, who was then
teaching school in Boston. "Come home," she said in a dozen different
ways—come back "to freedom and the sunshine here at home. . . . Duty
is black and brown – home is bright and shining." She even felt slightly
guilty in loving her home so much, with Austin away and miserable in
Boston. "I am so sorry for you," she wrote. "I do wish it was *me,* that you
might be well and happy, for I have no profession, and have such a snug,
warm home that I had as lief suffer some, a great deal rather than not,
that by doing so, you were exempted from it." A few months later she
confessed to her friend Jane Humphrey, "I'm afraid I'm growing *selfish*
in my dear home, but I do love it so, and when some pleasant friend
invites me to pass a week with her, I look at my father and mother and
Vinnie, and all my friends, and I say no – no, cant leave them, what if
they die when I'm gone." In her finer flights, her rhetoric becomes more
exalted: "Home is the definition of God." "Home is a holy thing – nothing of doubt or distrust can enter it's blessed portals. . . . here seems
indeed to be a bit of Eden." And many years later she wrote to a friend
about the "Infinite power of Home."

The legend of the dismal home and the tyrannical father comes from
the later years. Its source may be traced mainly to Lavinia in her embit-
tered state, when she unbosomed herself to two late entrants upon the
Dickinson scene, Mrs. Mabel Loomis Todd and Miss Mary Lee Hall.
Although Vinnie's reminiscences are unquestionably part of the record
and must remain so, they must be read in the context of her character and
situation. They slip too neatly into stereotypes of the times (and of
Edward Dickinson) that must be seen in connection not only with what
Emily herself said about her home, her father, and her early social doings

[ 59

but with the prevailingly cheerful tone of Vinnie's own contemporary letters and diary, with several of Austin's comments, and with the warm recollections of such visitors as the Newman cousins (Edward's wards),[6] and Joseph Lyman. Mrs. Todd describes a conversation with Vinnie in the summer of 1893:

> Went to Vinnie's to tea, and had an interesting talk with her & Austin on the peculiarities of their bringing up. It must have been a stiff, Puritanical and trying home. Some of Vinnie's stories were appalling – of the way they were watched and guarded for fear some young man might wish to marry one of them. It made me indignant.

Such stories lost nothing in the telling, nor did they lose anything in the retelling. Vinnie had the Dickinson sense of the dramatic and the family gift for rhetoric; and there were many reasons why Mabel Todd, at that

6. Clara and Anna Newman, daughters of Edward's sister Mary, who became his wards when they were orphaned in 1852, lived next door in the Evergreens with Austin and Sue Dickinson for several years, beginning in 1858. Clara later recorded her impressions of the Dickinsons (both families) in a document entitled "My Personal Acquaintance with Emily Dickinson" (see Appendix II, 3). The two Newman girls, then in their teens, much preferred the Homestead. They took their troubles to Edward and to Emily, and were in and out of the house continually. They "never wavered in their love and loyalty to their Uncle Edward," writes Mrs. Clara Newman Pearl (Clara's niece), who says in her comments on her Aunt Clara's document:

In my childhood recollections he [Edward Dickinson] is far from the stern, unapproachable person which he is represented in some of the recent biographies of Emily Dickinson. It only needed Edward Dickinson's "Very pleasantly impressed," in his most dignified manner, after my father had been presented to him at a cousin's home in Cambridge, to make my mother feel that she had chosen her husband wisely. Another anecdote of Edward Dickinson. When the circus came to town the young people wanted to go, but circuses were much frowned upon in those days. They were not quite respectable. My mother was appointed a committee of one to interview Uncle Edward. His advice, "Go and make it respectable," is still quoted in our family.

The following passage from the document itself recounts a revealing episode:

[Edward Dickinson] was a grand type of a class now extinct – An Old-School-Gentleman-Whig! His bearing was almost stern in its dignity and nobility, but his nature was as beautiful, and sympathetic, and tender as a mother's. . . . As a child I feared him, until I found him out when trouble and difficulty came, and my Guardian became my strong, and tender, and lovingly-revered Friend. To show you a little glimpse of him – As I left the door of his son's house [the Evergreens] after my wedding [October 14, 1869], he turned to my husband with this remark, "If she makes you as little trouble as she has me, you will be much happier than most men." Not fulsome flattery, surely, but coming from this man, and crowned, as it was, with the beautiful and rare smile we all felt it a success to win, it was a benediction on my new life.

Perhaps Edward Dickinson was more successful with his nieces than with his own children. But the rare smile that Anna remembered is something of a benediction on the Homestead, too. Emily worried about him because he did not smile enough. But had the household been entirely without the spirit Anna here records, Emily's delight in her home, expressed again and again, would hardly be credible.

time, was especially impressed with the pathos of the Dickinson story. She later reported other gleanings from Vinnie's conversation, all pointing in the same direction, all open to question, and some simply contrary to fact. She summarized her impressions of Vinnie's talk as follows:

The father was terrific. If he had married a different woman, he wouldn't have been such an overbearing man. He kept the girls down in a little valley in his mind. . . .

He did not like to have students come to see the girls. . . .

[Emily] was repressed, and had nothing to do with young men. Vinnie was pert and flirted if she wanted to. The father and mother would not let young men come [to the house] for fear they would marry. They [Mr. Dickinson and Austin] were men that could manage the world if they wanted to, and wouldn't have any foreigners in their family. They didn't want a strange young man in the family. Austin always admired his father very much, but he'd bang you if anything went wrong. The father never knew fine intellectual women. He needed to know about them.

Of a piece with this is the story, coming from Lavinia, of Edward Dickinson's refusal to let Emily receive the attentions of a young suitor—a refusal that (according to Vinnie) resulted in her lifelong withdrawal.[7] Miss Hall reported that "Miss Vinnie told me many times that she and Emily *feared* their father as long as he lived, and loved him after his death." Another story, again from Miss Hall, would seem to clinch the matter. Bending over his father's coffin, Austin kissed him on the forehead and is reported to have said, "There, father, I never dared do that while you were living."

In spite of such testimony, I cannot look upon the Dickinson household as fear-ridden. The children may have been reluctant to interrupt or impose upon their hard-working father; but this may have been more from disciplined respect than from fear. Austin's remark at his father's coffin may simply be another example of the almost pathological undemonstrativeness of this late-Puritan, New England family. An early letter of Austin's to Sue speaks of the lack of tenderness in his life: "I have never *before* received *any* – from any *body* – I never *would*." Emily's attitude toward her father, even as we have seen it so far, was compounded of many elements incompatible with fear. It developed early into an amused tolerance, a touch of condescension arising from an entirely justified sense of intellectual superiority, a tender devotion that made her delight in serving him in many ways (baking his bread, mending his

---

7. The suitor was George Gould, Amherst '50, and a close friend of Austin's. The story comes to us circuitously: from Lavinia, who told it to Mrs. Aurelia Davis (an Amherst neighbor), who told it to Mary Lee Hall, who told it to Genevieve Taggard, who made Gould the lost lover in her biography of ED. (See *YH* I, 177–78, entry of August 1850; and *YH* I, l, where Leyda urges that the dramatic details of the story be read "with some skepticism." Vinnie later made it clear that she thought Emily's withdrawal was due more to basic inclination and the family situation than to any such personal disaster.)

slippers, playing music for him), and later on into a deep, pervasive pity for his lonely and austere life. It was a complex and delicate relationship, changing and maturing with the years. Vinnie's, Miss Hall's, and Mrs. Todd's versions seem, in the light of all we know, oversimplified and static.

Not that life in the Dickinson household was one long idyl of prolonged though muted harmony. The place bristled with personalities, and there were frequent clashes. "Vesuvius at Home," even in a whimsical, lighthearted sense, was an apt metaphor; Vinnie used a similar one when, early in July 1853, she warned Austin against bringing home too many guests over Commencement: "You know home has not *altered* in your absence & sometimes the *fire kindles suddenly!*" This may refer to her father's temper, or it may mean simply that at Commencement time, when (as Vinnie wrote) "every thing is always so confused," the household was inclined to be on edge. Edward was not in fact notorious for his temper; he kept his "quick & ardent" feelings under control. Perhaps a remark of Emily's to Austin a few months earlier throws some light. It shows how Dickinson wills could clash—but against a background of mutual respect and affection. Speaking of Austin's letters home, she described them as

> very funny indeed. . . . Father takes great delight in your remarks to him—puts on his spectacles and reads them o'er and o'er as if it was a blessing to have an only son. . . .
> I do think it's so funny – you and father do nothing but 'fisticuff' all the while you're at home, and the minute you are separated, you become such devoted friends; but this is a checkered life.
> I believe at this moment, Austin, that there's no body living for whom father has such respect as for you, and yet your conduct together is quite peculiar indeed.

Emily was clearly more adroit than her brother in managing their father, perhaps because she understood better than Austin that he needed managing. Her letters speak often of the little compromises she daily made—like joining in family prayers every morning while he addressed "an Eclipse" and she thought her own thoughts. When their ideas of real life collided, she contrived ways of stating her position that would avoid any serious rupture. There is an anecdote about a chipped plate. Mrs. Bingham used it to illustrate Edward's "standard of good workmanship," his insistence that everyone in the household live up to the same standard he set himself. But it also shows Emily as a master strategist, replying to his imperiousness with a humor and dispatch he could not have missed:

> One day, sitting down at the dinner table, he inquired whether a certain nicked plate must always be placed before him. Emily took the hint. She carried the plate to the garden and pulverized it on a stone, "just to remind" her, she said, not to give it to her father again.

62 ]

And "just to remind" him, I suggest, that two could play at the game of temperament as well as one.

There is record of only one real blowup between father and daughter, with tempers up and voices raised. Vinnie recounted it in a letter to Austin—but with enough whimsey to make one wonder how serious she was, and with no hint of how the situation was resolved:

> Oh! dear! Father is killing the horse. I wish you'd come quick if you want to see him alive. He is whipping him because he didn't look quite *"umble"* enough this morning. Oh! Austin, it makes me so angry to see that 'noble creature' so abused. Emilie is screaming to the top of her voice. She's so vexed about it.

Aside from the reassuring revelation that Emily could scream, it is not clear (again) precisely what this means about the father-daughter relationship. It may suggest that Emily, for all her usual tone of tolerant understanding, could match him, temper for temper.

Edward was never famous for gentleness, at least among his children. Vinnie said, "Father was the only one to say 'damn.' Someone in every family ought to say damn of course." He was "quite a hand to give medicine," said Emily, "especially if it is not desirable to the patient." When she returned from her eye treatments in Boston in 1864, she said that Father was "as gentle as he knows how."

There is something very touching about this and many similar remarks by Emily about her father. For all the humor and gentle satire with which she usually spoke of him, what in the end impressed her most was the pathos of his life, its austerity, its rigor, and its loneliness, even in the family. As the years went on, she saw the gap widen between him and his children. Although Edward as a young father had been protective and solicitous about his family's welfare, his early letters, peppered with do's and don'ts, were more admonitory and didactic than affectionate. He was devoted to his family and dependent upon them; but he seems to have been quite without the ability to say so. Even Vinnie, not so quick as Emily in these matters, sensed his remoteness. When she was twenty, she wrote Austin:

> Father was *thoughtful* enough to spend last evening with us *socially* & as he seemed rather dull, I endeavoured to entertain him by reading spicey passages from Fern leaves, where upon he brightened up sufficiently to correct me as I went along. . . . Father has seemed quite pensive & exhibited much of the martyr spirit since you went away. . . . I think Father is perfectly home sick with out you. What will he do when *we* are *all* gone?

As his family slipped away from him, whether geographically, intellectually, or emotionally, Edward showed his disappointment, or grief, not in words whose effect might have been restorative, but in what seems to have been a general moroseness and anxiety, the pensiveness that Vinnie noted. Emily refused invitations because father was "in the habit of me";

she felt he would miss her, would want something in her absence. Once she reminded Austin that "this is a lonely house, when we are not all here." Eventually, of course, they all stayed in Amherst—Emily and Lavinia in the Homestead; Austin, with his wife, next door—partly, perhaps, out of loyalty to this lonely, hard-working, melancholic, and dedicated man.

On one hand, Emily could poke fun at her father's Puritan streak, as when she described his reading "the letters of suspected gentlemen . . . [in] our family library . . . with a mixture of fun and perseverence, which is quite diabolical"; or, a different slant, perusing (with Mother, in the sitting room) "such papers only, as they are well assured have nothing carnal in them"; or leading family prayers with his "militant Accent"; or (perhaps her best vignette of him) sitting out, in Puritan impatience, Jenny Lind's recital in Northampton:

> Father [she wrote Austin] sat all the evening looking *mad,* and *silly,* and yet so much amused you would have *died* a laughing – when the performers bowed, he said "Good evening Sir" – and when they retired, "very well – that will do," it was'nt *sarcasm* exactly, nor it was'nt *disdain,* it was infinitely funnier than either of those virtues, as if old Abraham had come to see the show, and thought it was all very well, but a little excess of *Monkey!*

But she penetrated beneath the comic to the lonely figure who lacked the "low, enjoying power." And this for Emily, who was geared to "ecstasy" (a favorite word with her and apparently unknown to her father) as few human beings have ever been, was the saddest of losses. "He never played." Like old Abraham at the show, he kept his distance.[8]

8. Again we must qualify this generally dour picture. He could, on occasion, "play." Here he was, at least, at Jenny's concert, however skeptical he seems to have been of the whole performance. And there is other evidence. He took his wife and children on walks and rides. In August 1837 he and his wife ascended Mt. Holyoke (*YH* I, 34). In Boston, in 1838, he "attended a concert at the Odeon, last evening, of the Boston Academy of Music, and was delighted with it" (*YH* I, 49; April 5). Next year he went to the theater but (it must be admitted) "would not be hired to go again" (*YH* I, 52; January 13). In Amherst he did his share, with his wife, of calling and receiving calls. He apparently was something of a mimic and could take off important people. He chortled over Austin's letters home. The Dickinson teas were annual features of Commencement Week, and he went to his Yale reunion. Perhaps the one luxury he allowed himself was fine horses, an interest that (probably through Samuel Bowles) was known outside of Amherst. On October 11, 1853, the *Springfield Republican* printed the following letter, dated October 7, 1853:

GENTLEMEN, –
Your letter, inviting me to attend the "grand Agricultural Banquet during the progress of the National Horse Exhibition at Springfield on the 19th inst." has been received, and should have received an immediate answer. . . . I was much pleased with the first published suggestion of the project; and have watched, with the liveliest interest, the readiness with which the people, in all parts of the country, have seized upon it, to show their regard for the noblest of all irrational animals.
The occasion cannot fail to afford a fitting opportunity for the dissemination of

Thomas Wentworth Higginson, whose first impression of Emily's father was so far from the whole truth, in another remark came much closer. "Her father [he wrote] was not severe I should think but remote." Perhaps the distance between the two generations was no greater than in most families; but in spite of Emily's insistence on the solidarity of the family—"We are having a pleasant summer [she wrote Austin in July 1851] – without one of the five it is yet a *lonely* one"—communication never seems to have been good. The story of her father's trying to teach her to tell time, how she was too frightened to learn and too afraid to tell him or anyone else for years afterward, may indicate a real failure on Mr. Dickinson's part, although I cannot regard it as the traumatic experience of Emily's childhood that shut her off from her father forever.[9] Her humor about him may have been in part protective, according to her own theory of mirth as "the Mail of Anguish." Certainly she practiced minor evasions. She spoke of reading books he didn't approve of; of hesitating to read in his presence the "poetic" parts of Austin's letters to her; of the "kitchen meetings," when she and Austin (and Vinnie?) could talk freely.

> I dont love to read your letters all out loud to father – it would be like opening the kitchen door when we get home from meeting Sunday, and are sitting down by the stove saying just what we're a mind to, and having father hear. I don't know why it is, but it gives me a dreadful feeling.

Things went better when "the ancient people" were away.

The most poignant expression we have of Emily's sense of her father's remoteness comes in a letter to Joseph Lyman, written probably in the

---

useful information, and the cultivation of those kindly and generous feelings which make all the participants happier and better; while it produces a liberality and nationality of views, and stimulates a laudable emulation in all to excel.

. . . I am sure it must be a glorious affair; and leave indelible "horse tracks" in the valley of the Connecticut, to mark an "epoch" in the "natural history" of the race, for a continent.

My love of fine horses, would, of itself, be sufficient to attract me to the exhibition; but the expectation of meeting and exchanging congratulations with gentlemen of the highest standing and character, from different sections of the country, all interested in promoting its welfare, will render it, in the highest degree, pleasant and profitable to be there. . . .

Yours very truly<br>EDWARD DICKINSON

The letter should be read, surely, in conjunction with Vinnie's story of his beating the horse. And finally, there is a legend that Edward, sitting for his picture, was asked by the town photographer to "smile, a little," please: "To which the Squire thundered back, 'I *yam* smiling.'" (See *AB*, p. 232.)

9. See Clark Griffith, *The Long Shadow*, pp. 278 ff., who finds "no reason to disbelieve this remarkable story." For the origin of the story (Higginson's gleanings from ED's conversation as he passed them on to his wife), see *L* II, 475. I find it hard to believe for many reasons, among them ED's careful scientific training in Amherst Academy. Either she willfully exaggerated to Higginson, or his reporting was faulty.

mid-1860s. It is also another example of what Emily complained of when she said, "All men say 'What' to me"—including, we now see, her father. It gives her mature sense of the pathos of his life:

> My father seems to me often the oldest and the oddest sort of a foreigner. Sometimes I say something and he stares in a curious sort of bewilderment though I speak a thought quite as old as his daughter. . . .
> Father says in fugitive moments when he forgets the barrister & lapses into the man, says that his life has been passed in a wilderness or on an island – of late he says on an island. And so it is, for in the morning I hear his voice and methinks it comes from afar & has a sea tone & there is a hum of hoarseness about [it] & a suggestion of remoteness as far as the isle of Juan Fernandez.

Apparently Edward Dickinson did "lapse into the man" occasionally and speak his heart. But here he is, a foreigner in his own family, bewildered by his daughter and as far from her as "the isle of Juan Fernandez." The picture is of a piece with what others said: the perpendicular stance, the failure of his fellows to understand him thoroughly, Higginson's impression of his remoteness.

It coincides, too, with another comment on him, this one having to do with another kind of isolation, or apartness, with which Emily was herself familiar. The story is recorded by Emily's supposed suitor, George Gould, who in September 1877 entered in his notebook the following description of Edward's religious conversion, which had taken place during the Revival in Amherst in 1850:

> While Hon. E. D. of Amherst was converted – who had been long under conviction – His pastor said to him in his study – "You want to come to Christ as a *lawyer* – but you must come to him as a *poor sinner* – get down on your knees & let me pray for you, & then pray for yourself."

It was not easy for Dickinsons to get down on their knees and pray before others—or to be demonstrative even before God. Although Edward had supported the church and attended its services for years, he was forty-seven before this episode occurred. It seems typical of the man as he faced the world. Emily, too, held out; she "paused and pondered and pondered and paused," and resisted the efforts of her friends to get her to accept Christ. "I am standing alone in rebellion," she said in 1850, the year of the Revival that led Edward into the church. The doctrine of the "poor sinner" was congenial to neither father nor daughter. Here surely was an element of Dickinson pride, a sense of self-sufficiency, of being able to get along without the spiritual support that others found necessary—"the ark of safety," Emily called it when she was seventeen. With Edward, if we are to believe Gould's anecdote, it seems to have been a stubborn unwillingness to humble himself completely. It was said of him that he thought himself imperishable; others might sicken and die but not he. Lawyer that he was, he left no will. He could have "managed the world" if he'd wanted to, said Mrs. Todd (who never saw him). Emily, with her intense love of nature and infinite pride in human capacities (not necessarily Dickinson capacities), sublimated this stubbornness and touch of imperiousness into her own personal theology, in which the World and Man and God were all but coordinate. This opened up relationships unknown, apparently, to her father. He was left with his public duties and dedications, while she at least—when things were going well—could be chatty with the Deity, her "Old Neighbor – God – " and, with the poets, make a summer that "lasts a Solid Year –." It is tempting to speculate how much of her attitude she derived from her father—and transformed.

Edward Dickinson died in Boston on June 16, 1874. That morning, "a cruelly hot day," he had felt faint while giving a speech before the General Court and was forced to stop. He repaired to his hotel, summoned a doctor, and died after (and perhaps because of) a dose of morphine. Though his fatigue had been noted, nothing like this sudden end had been expected. The House was adjourned and a Resolution (later published in the legislative *Journal*) was immediately prepared. The news appeared in papers across the state and was the occasion of much obituary comment. Here the note of perplexity comes in, the same that made Emily wonder about how "well acquainted" she was with her father. The *Amherst Record* for June 17 predicted that Edward Dickinson would be "even more respected and honored" when "his character is more fully understood." Samuel Bowles, writing in the *Springfield Republican* for that same day, turned the matter inward:

> He was, indeed, a New England Chevalier Bayard, without fear and without reproach. He was a Puritan out of time for kinship and appreciation, but exactly in time for example and warning. His failing was he did not understand himself; consequently his misfortune was that others did not understand him. . . . he possessed and exhibited that rarest and yet most needed of all qualities in these days of cowardly conformity and base complaisance, *the courage of his convictions*. This was the essence of his life – this is his noblest bequest to his community and his state.

The second Sunday after the funeral, Reverend Jonathan L. Jenkins, strong friend of the Dickinsons and much cherished by Emily, preached a sermon on Edward Dickinson. Here, too, the stress was on his failure to be understood and on the gentleness he never successfully communicated. Jenkins compared him to the prophet Samuel:

> It is a condition of human life that men are not known by contemporaries. . . . Here influences that warp and distort judgements are many and strong. Here occasions for conflict, for misunderstandings, for alienations are so frequent that perfect concord is impossible. . . .
> It is said that in the apparition in which [Samuel] was evoked after death, there was something terrific, and yet this man whom a whole village feared, in whose appearance there was that which terrified, was gentle in na-

ture, and no more gentle in nature, than our friend and father whom we mourn to-day. . . . Aye there was yet a finer fibre in the gentleness which was in him, but which he so carefully, and may I say, so unwisely, concealed. Had he the Puritan notion that sentiment betrayed weakness, or was it his training in that elder school whose primal precept was repression . . . ?[10]

10. The sermon, in holograph among the Dickinson Papers, Houghton Library, Harvard, combines conventional funeral rhetoric with intimate personal insights. We can only speculate on how precisely Jenkins meant this description of Samuel to apply to Edward Dickinson:

Not since Moses who died four hundred years before, had there been in Israel so great a man as Samuel. In troublesome times he preserved order, administered justice. He consolidated the nation, founded schools, faithfully served the state for thirty years in high offices.

His external appearance was rough, he repelled men, inspired fear. He lived in extreme simplicity, his whole career was so just that learned Grotius gave him the name of the Jewish Aristides.

Although such, his countrymen grew weary of him, preferred in his place the brilliant, fickle, incompetent Saul, practically forced him into retirement before, as Matthew Henry says, he was super-annuated.

At last he died, and then from neglect and rejection, he passed at once to most generous appreciation and homage.

It is hard to understand Jenkins' emphasis on Samuel's rejection. Edward may have been losing touch with the town, but not, it would seem, to that extent. The rest of the sermon is a fine tribute to his character and to his influence, "intrinsically so beautiful," on Amherst. Jenkins commended him for having dedicated his life to one place:

Not all men who are born in a place, and stay in it, love it. The fact of being born in it, often seems to create a dislike of it, an unwillingness to serve it. It has been said Amherst was Mr Dickinson's passion. I believe it was. . . . His right hand would sooner forget its cunning, than he forget Amherst.

Jenkins touched perceptively on other qualities, his gentleness, his taciturnity, his religion. The theme of the misunderstood man recurs several times.

His was a deep-seated gentleness, working in and sweetening the secret fountains, not a gentleness that expended itself in pleasant speeches and manners assumed for effect, but a gentleness that felt others' pains and losses, and excited efforts for relief. . . . was it a native delicacy of soul that kept covered the choice bright feelings that too often like rare perfumes are ruined by exposure? . . .

He had no great faith in ceremonies, in formulas of doctrine. He was free in his speech about religion, most unconventional in his practices. His religion was however most excellent and genuine. . . .

Our friend and father was a silent man. If any must judge his religion this must be taken into account. . . . At one time he read much upon the subject of religion, read theological works, was always an attendant upon Sabbath worship, and a most generous supporter of the Parish. . . .

I have had from the Rev Mr Colton an account so far as they were known to him of the steps by which Mr. Dickinson was led to a Christian profession [on the 11th of August 1850]. . . . The man who instinctively avoided all mention of himself would be pained at any publicity given to what he experiences at such a crisis. And I who loved him with something of a son's partial affection, could not by any possibility do it, and yet my love is so strong that since he suffered himself so often to be misjudged I would at any sacrifice have him known as he was, not as he seemed, by all christian men and women. Years after his connec-

The effect of her father's death on Emily was devastating. She remained in her room during the funeral and apparently did not attend the memorial service, if we can judge from a neighbor's letter to a friend: "Memorial service at our church today, lots of laurel & other white flowers. I think Austin & Wife, Vinnie & her mother were all at church. . . ." Emily was shocked to find how shocked she was: "I cannot recall myself [she wrote to her Norcross cousins]. I thought I was strongly built, but this stronger has undermined me. . . . Though it is many nights, my mind never comes home."

Emily now saw her father's life in a wholly new perspective. She seems not to have realized what she had in him until too late. The playfulness and the whimsey disappear entirely from her remarks about him. A letter she wrote Higginson during the month following her father's death touches the tragic, a tone from which she never departed. It begins with a description of one of the very few moments on record of complete rapport between Emily and her father:

> The last Afternoon that my Father lived, though with no premonition –
> I preferred to be with him, and invented an absence for Mother, Vinnie
> being asleep. He seemed peculiarly pleased as I oftenest stayed with myself,
> and remarked as the Afternoon withdrew, he "would like it to not end."
>
> His pleasure almost embarrassed me and my Brother coming – I suggested they walk. Next morning I woke him for the train [to Boston] – and saw him no more.

And then (in her next sentence) the new vision of this strange and remote man: "His Heart was pure and terrible and I think no other like it exists."

This is the figure that haunted her for a long time. Two years later she told her Norcross cousins: "I dream about father every night, always a different dream, and forget what I am doing daytimes, wondering where he is." Three years after his death she avoided a family reunion because "accustomed to all [the relatives] through Father, they remind me too deeply of him for Peace."

Her father grew and grew in her imagination. He is no longer "Cromwell with the kindlings" but a figure around whom revolve the great questions that had harassed her for years, now brought intensely home. Every death among her relatives and friends (and there had been many) had come as a peculiar shock to her; she adjusted slowly; but this was the first in her immediate family and the first of the "mighty" deaths that wracked her so in the decade of the 1870s and in the early 1880s. A

---

tion with the church while a member of Congress he wrote to Mr Colton from Washington these words, "I am even while I write, melted to tears at the remembrance of what we saw and felt at the working of God's spirit among us in 1850." In the same letter he wrote "I hope that I may never cease to have your prayers that I may illustrate the principles of Christianity in my life."

quatrain of the late period could apply to any of the deaths, certainly to her father's:

> Lives he in any other world
> My faith cannot reply
> Before it was imperative
> Twas all distinct to me –          (#1557, about 1882)

If the matter of faith—"wondering where he is"—became suddenly imperative, his death (or any death) forced a readjustment of her sense of time:

> The vastest earthly Day
> Is chastened small
> By one heroic Face
> Behind a Pall –[11]          (#1328, about 1874)

Perhaps (she reasoned in another poem), if we understood time—which is to say eternity—we would not be so shocked at its sudden intrusion:

> The Infinite a sudden Guest
> Has been assumed to be –
> But how can that stupendous come
> Which never went away?          (#1309, about 1874)

Several of her tiny epitaphs—the form her thoughts about her father seemed inevitably to take—point to personal qualities she had grumbled about during his lifetime. The sense of duty that had kept him from his children now becomes a mark of triumph over fate:

> To his simplicity
> To die – was little Fate –
> If Duty live – contented
> But her Confederate.          (#1352, about 1876)

"Old Abraham" at the show, keeping his skeptical distance from the entertainers, now becomes a figure of awe and glory:

> Gathered into the Earth,
> And out of story –
> Gathered to that strange Fame –
> That lonesome Glory
> That hath no omen here – but Awe –          (#1370, about 1876)

11. In the light of the elegiac quatrain sent to Higginson ("Lay this Laurel on the One") and discussed below, ED's variants—"chastened" for "shrunken" in line 2 and "heroic" for "Defaulting" in line 3—seem applicable to her father.

The stiffness that amused her in his "Roman General" bearing now has the dignity of a tall cedar:

> To break so vast a Heart
> Required a Blow as vast –
> No Zephyr felled this Cedar straight –
> 'Twas undeserved Blast –       (#*1312, about 1874*)

If she chafed under his discipline around the house or smiled at his sometimes highhanded way in village affairs, now he is the departed king of subjects who love him all the more:

> From his slim Palace in the Dust
> He relegates the Realm,
> More loyal for the exody
> That has befallen him.       (#*1300, about 1874*)

Two poems explicitly about her father (the above can only be assumed to be) sum up her view of him most poignantly. Both were sent to Higginson, one about two years after Edward's death, the other near the third anniversary of it. In the first, a comment she had made about a poem sent earlier to Higginson on immortality suggested her father:

> When I think of my Father's lonely Life and his lonelier
> Death, there is this redress –

> Take all away –
> The only thing worth larceny
> Is left – the Immortality –       [#*1365*]

From what she wrote to Lyman, it is clear that, for all her joking, she had been keenly aware of her father's remoteness and what it meant in sadness to him as well as for the family. The poem at least shows her faith as by now more "certain."

The second poem to Higginson is a remarkable distillation of the thought and feeling, attitude and appraisal, that her ultimate view of her father became. The occasion needs some comment. Three years before, she had been much moved by Higginson's poem "Decoration," which had appeared in *Scribner's Monthly* for June 1874, the month her father died. Its seven lilting stanzas—in tribute to an unsung hero in a lonely and uncared-for grave—is in the standard Memorial Day tradition. Emily thanked Higginson for his "beautiful Hymn": "was it not prophetic? It has assisted that Pause of Space which I call 'Father' – ." Then in 1877, she sent Higginson her own version, of which he later said, when he was editing the poems with Mabel Loomis Todd, "She wrote it after re-reading my 'Decoration.' It is the condensed essence of that & so far finer."

Emily's redaction is a model of a poetic procedure she followed many times. In Higginson's poem the speaker has gone to decorate the graves of the fallen heroes:

> Mid the flower-wreath'd tombs I stand
> Bearing lilies in my hand.
> Comrades! in what soldier-grave
> Sleeps the bravest of the brave?

Not, it seems, where his comrades think, in a grave surrounded by mourning friends and wreathed with flowers—"Garlands veil it; ask not mine." The speaker then turns to "one low grave," untended and unnoticed, where the true hero lies:

> One low grave, yon tree beneath,
> Bears no roses, wears no wreath;
> Yet no heart more high and warm
> Ever dared the battle-storm,
>
> Never gleamed a prouder eye
> In the front of victory,
> Never foot had firmer tread
> On the field where hope lay dead,
>
> Than are hid within this tomb,
> Where the untended grasses bloom;
> And no stone, with feign'd distress,
> Mocks the sacred loneliness.
>
> Youth and beauty, dauntless will,
> Dreams that life could ne'er fulfill,
> Here lie buried; here in peace
> Wrongs and woes have found release.
>
> Turning from my comrades' eyes,
> Kneeling where a woman lies,
> I strew lilies on the grave
> Of the bravest of the brave.

There was much here to suggest her father to her: his lonely death, especially; the world's failure to recognize his true virtues and to understand him; the peace after a life of dedication and self-sacrifice. Three years after his death, she may have felt that she was the last and lonely mourner, like the woman in Higginson's poem. So she changed the lilies to laurel and put it where it would redeem the world's failure:

*Edward Dickinson*

Lay this Laurel on the One
Too intrinsic for Renown –
Laurel – vail your deathless tree –
Him you chasten, that is He![12]                    (#*1393*)


This lonely and angular man will continue to move in and out of these pages. When we take up Emily's life from the beginning, he will appear as the young husband and father, worried about his family, chafing under financial limitations and looking to the mid-century land boom for his fortune. His concern about his children's education and his own worldliness will come out in some revealing letters to his wife and one to all three children. I have chosen to leave these matters to later chapters, when they become of more immediate concern to Emily's early years. That he figured less and less in her life as she set out on her own lonely path is part of the pathos of their relationship. Her remark about her father's being too busy to notice his children is, like many of her remarks on her parents, a little quick and cruel. I think he noticed more than her remark implies. But there can be little doubt that at an early stage he began to lose touch. Such letters as we have from him to Austin are businesslike and terse. Emily could have helped him more than she did, a delinquency she realized only after he died. Such a failure, on both sides, is usually attributed to New England reticence or reserve. It is characteristic that, as she described her last day with him, she recalled her own "embarrassment" at his pleasure in her company and extricated herself by suggesting that he and Austin take a walk. To this extent, the failure of the relationship can be attributed less to his heartlessness or a willful desire to control than to the inhibiting effect of a tradition that put duty and diligence over love. "*My* business," Emily concluded as in her early thirties she faced the world on her own, "is to love." The emphasis is hers.

12. The explanatory note in *Poems* gives an account of the episode, the full text of Higginson's poem, and the existing MS. redactions of ED's poem. As the editor points out, the poem may well have been of eight lines, whether of two stanzas or one "it is impossible to know." The first four lines slip into Higginson's military rhetoric ("triumphed," "Victor"). The last four are more appropriate to her father:

> Lay this Laurel on the one
> Triumphed and remained unknown –
> Laurel – fell your futile Tree –
> Such a Victor could not be –
> Lay this Laurel on the one
> Too intrinsic for Renown –
> Laurel – vail your deathless Tree –
> Him you chasten – that is he –

# 5

# Emily Norcross Dickinson

THERE IS A LEGEND that, on the day Emily Dickinson was born, Mrs. Dickinson, against her husband's express wishes, had her bedroom papered. If true, it is one of her few willful, assertive acts on record—one of the reasons, surely, she obtrudes so little into the annals of her family, at least compared with "Father," who appears on almost every page.[1] In character and temperament, Emily was a Dickinson; it has been said that all she inherited from her mother was her first name. Emily herself did much to establish this notion of her mother's nonentity in two remarks to Higginson, one in conversation in 1870 and the other in a letter in 1874. Both are often quoted: "I never had a mother. I suppose a mother is one to whom you hurry when you are troubled." "I always ran Home to Awe when a child, if anything befell me. He was an awful Mother, but I liked him better than none."

Both of these remarks require looking into. They must be seen in the

---

1. The source of the legend (it is probably little more than that but may contain a grain of truth) is a letter from Mary Adèle Allen (whose *Around a Village Green*, 1939, contains much Amherst lore) to Orton Clark, February 14, 1944: "[Lafayette Stebbins] was a painter and paper hanger in Amherst. . . . [his daughter] says that at the time Emily Dickinson was expected that Mrs. Dickinson wanted to have her bedroom painted but the Hon. Edward Dickinson would not allow her to have it done – nevertheless she went secretly to the paper hanger and asked him to come and paper her bedroom. This he did, while Emily was being born" (*YH* I, 16). To give Mrs. Dickinson her due, another instance of her willfulness, if it can be called that, should be recorded. Lavinia wrote Austin on March 23, 1853: "Father is so outraged towards parson Cooke [a temporary supply in the First Church] that he would not let Emilie or me go to church all day last Sunday. Mother would go part of the day though he preferred she should not" (*Home*, p. 268). It should be said, also, that the young lady of Edward's courtship letters seems much more spirited and assertive than the self-effacing figure of later years.

context of Emily's situation at the time and of the heightened, aphoristic rhetoric she habitually used with Higginson. It was her brother Austin's opinion that she "posed" in her letters to Higginson, as she certainly did in her conversations with him. She was turning forty in 1870 and was in the summing-up mood—only a few years earlier she had summed up her father, though more gently, to Joseph Lyman. The Dickinson family was nothing if not critical, of each other as well as everybody else. They had moods and, especially the younger generation, enjoyed hyperbole. Even her usually buoyant friend Samuel Bowles recognized this in Emily. In 1863 he wrote Austin: "I have been in a savage, turbulent state for some time – indulging in a sort of disgust at everything & everybody – I guess a good deal as Emily feels." It may have been that Emily was firmly convinced that her mother had been no mother at all and that she bore her a lifelong grudge. But the main outlines of the relationship as seen over the years tend to put in question her acerbic remarks to Higginson. At any rate, of first importance is what she made of the relationship. And even if we accept the notion that her mother's failure placed her under severe handicaps, it makes of her life with her mother even more of a triumph of self-discipline, humor, patience, and (however belated) love.[2]

2. Mrs. Dickinson's dark role in Emily Dickinson's life is the theme of Dr. John Cody's *After Great Pain*. Millicent Todd Bingham noted a potentially destructive trait in Mrs. Dickinson's character, her "tremulous fear of death" (*Home*, p. 4). Dr. Cody pressed this clue much further. He sees Mrs. Dickinson as a lifelong hypochondriac who must have communicated her fears to her children; an abjectly dependent wife; a fussily compulsive housekeeper; a failure as a mother, especially of her most sensitive child, Emily, whose "voracious love-hunger" (p. 101) was never satisfied. Emily interpreted this failure (so the theory goes) as a "cruel rejection" (p. 2) and grew up in repressed bitterness toward her mother; resented being female; tried to be unlike her mother by defying her father; rebelled against religious submission; read voraciously; and sublimated her "love needs" in her writing. Hence the persistent themes of death, anxiety, suffering in the poems and letters; the withdrawal, self-immolation, and exorbitant concern for every member of her family that became characteristic of her mode of life. All these are interpreted as symptoms of repressed guilt at her deep sense of hostility and alienation, at her unconscious wish to have all her friends and relatives dead, all of whom failed her in one way or another. And the principal failure was her mother's.

In such a diagnosis, everything becomes symptomatic, even (or perhaps especially) the poems, and all is woven into a seamless web. Motives are deduced from scanty evidence—widely scattered poems and remarks in letters that can be read in contradictory ways. To open up the possibility of the truth of other readings is not to deny the possibility that Dr. Cody's hypothesis may also contain an element of truth. He likens it to the "plaster bone" (p. 2) used by archaeologists in reconstructing the fossil skeleton. But the bone is still plaster; ". . . there exists no record," Dr. Cody admits, "of any concrete instance in which Mrs. Dickinson took such an attitude toward her daughter" (p. 2). But if it is permissible to question Dr. Cody's diagnosis, one must insist with him that the old sentimental view—of Emily's lovely, harmonious home and her own normal "blossoming"—is gone forever. Nor is it to slip into any biographical conspiracy to stress the positive side of her relations with her mother. As Dr. Cody himself says, "If I appear to be concentrating on the gloomy side of Emily Dickinson's childhood it is because the brighter side is overstressed by most biographers" (p. 83).

Emily Norcross Dickinson (1804–1882) was born in Monson, Massachusetts (about twenty miles south of Amherst), the daughter of Joel and Betsy Fay Norcross. Like the Dickinsons until Squire Fowler's generation, the Norcrosses were farmers.[3] They also read books and believed in education. Daughter Emily was the third child among her six brothers and two sisters. A baby brother died when she was seven, and her sister Lavinia was born the next year. Her girlhood seems to have been undistinguished,[4] but at least her family thought enough of her to send her to boarding school in New Haven, where she wrote to Lavinia the one letter we have from her girlhood, dated "New Haven July 1823." The letter is sweet and sisterly, full of affection and misspellings. She says she is happy, in good health, and longs for her *"dear dear* home." There is of course no mention of Edward, then in his senior year at Yale.

Whatever she may have become as wife of an exacting husband, Emily Norcross was no nonentity when Edward started courting her three years later in Monson. As he said again and again in the courtship letters, she embodied all the qualities of his ideal woman—"amiable disposition," "modest and unassuming manners," "thorough knowledge of every aspect of domestic economy," "good taste – cultivated & improved by a moderate acquaintance with a few of the most select works of taste" and by association with "refined society." Years later, her daughter Emily was to speak condescendingly of her "unobtrusive faculties," hardly up to the Amherst intellectual level. But one of Edward's letters shows Emily Norcross busy in local cultural programs equal to Amherst at its liveliest. Here is Edward, himself a bit condescending, speaking from the intellectual heights of his college town but obviously impressed by Monson's resources:

I suppose you are now wading in the snow to or from some meeting and you have something to lead you from home every evening! – I would like to examine you on the subjects to which your attention is so much called, of late – perhaps I could judge of your proficiency and I might possibly give you some useful hints as to the best course to be pursued in making so many studies profitable, at the same time. Let us examine a little – singing school – Chemical Lectures, historical Lectures – Bible Class – Concerts – Missionary, Charitable, & Female Bible Associations – Cent [?] and Tract Society – and

3. Joel Norcross was one of the most substantial farmers in Monson. He kept in close touch with his married daughter in Amherst and at one point advised his son-in-law about building a new house. Relations seem to have been cordial. Emily made only one reference to him (he died when she was sixteen; his wife died the year before Emily was born): "We expect Grandpa Norcross . . . up here this week –" (*L* I, 5; to Austin, May 1, 1842). Her Norcross uncles, aunts, and cousins were another matter; to some of them Emily became devoted.
4. Unless a little yellow certificate, "treasured among the daughter's most cherished papers," be considered a mark of distinction (Martha Dickinson Bianchi, *The Life and Letters of Emily Dickinson,* p. 10):
Miss Emily Norcross, for punctual attendance, close application, good acquirements, and discreet behavior merits the approbation of her preceptress.

Edward and Emily Norcross Dickinson,
from portraits by O. A. Bullard, 1840

Fishing Party. Water color by Emily Norcross, 1827

others of a name and description which do not now occur to me. Let me say in a word, My Dear Emily, that while I think that all these combined will not produce so much solid good as a much less number, with more time to reflect upon them will produce, still I would have you act your pleasure entirely, in regard to your attendance upon any or all of them – only preserve your health.

Two days later, when he warned her again about taking too many courses, he was confident that "your good sense will guide you right." As to belles-lettres, he himself saw that she was well supplied with the latest novels and with such cultural staples as the *Spectator,* in twelve volumes.

His assurance that she should "act her pleasure" about the evening events is one of many such remarks in his letters, both before the marriage and after.[5] He may have meant exactly the opposite of what he said, of course, but at least he gave her a nominally free rein. And in several ways during the courtship she asserted her independence. She answered his letters at her leisure. She braved his annoyance by refusing his many insistences that she come to Amherst to visit ("invitations without number," as he put it). She disregarded his impatience about the date of the wedding. He finally gave up: "I find that my arguments are without much weight, and I shall not press them against so decided an expression of your will in relation to it." As the date drew near, she was clear about the disposal of her things, which were soon to be sent from Monson by oxcart: "All I wish of you is to lay them in your part of the house and let them rest untill I come." And she was very clear about the arrangements for the ceremony itself, which he had left entirely to her: "I think it best that we stand up alone as I do not wish for company."

Apparently at one point during the courtship, *she* lectured him. In spite of the lofty tone of his response, he seems to have been both impressed and pleased by her show of spirit.

> I was much pleased with the *moral* part [of her letter] and shall endeavor to profit by the good advice which you gave in a few words . . . – I am happy to receive useful hints from any quarter but they come with a peculiar force from you – and will doubtless have a salutary effect – tho' I must confess I was rather amused at the decision of character . . . the air of *authority* & *independence* which you assumed – and I am sure that I have nothing

5. At least in the early years of the marriage, Mrs. Dickinson made frequent trips to see her family in Monson and her brother Joel in Boston. In July 1836 she visited in Springfield. A letter from Edward written (September 11, 1835) during one of her visits to Boston, again insists that she act her pleasure and includes a heart-warming domestic moment:

> Your letter was rec'd last evening, & Loring's this evening – and found us all well – and gave us much pleasure to hear that you were enjoying yourself so well in Boston – that you had concluded not to go to Portland – As to this, I would have you do exactly as you please – I want you to spend as much time & go as far as you desire to now you have got started – tho' I should not object to your coming home as soon as you wish to – . . . Austin enquired very anxiously when he awoke in the night, & found me in bed with him, & I told him I had rec'd a letter

to fear from the exercise of a freedom & frank avowal of sentiment which the fact that "we are not strangers" induced you to speak.

Edward may have been condescending, but he was no antifeminist, at least in principle. He was not only a strenuous advocate of female education, but he knew who set the tone in any household: "A woman, you know [he wrote Emily], gives a character to her house & family, if possible, more than her husband, and when she is what she should be, amiable, virtuous, prudent & intelligent & benevolent, she can hardly fail to draw blessings on herself and on her household."

Edward, as here, seldom resisted the temptation to itemize the qualities of the perfect wife, as if he thought Emily needed constant reminding. At least he included himself in similar reminders, which multiplied as the wedding approached. He outlined the qualities of the perfect married couple.

> May we be virtuous, intelligent, industrious and by the exercise of every virtue, & the cultivation of every excellence, be esteemed & respected & beloved by all – We must determine to do our duty to each other, & to all our friends, and let others do as they may.

Obviously these two young people looked upon marriage less as romantic fulfillment than as a contractual agreement to fulfill together certain social and religious aims and obligations. Tenderness was almost always subordinate to a loftier purpose, whether immediate or eternal. Sometimes Edward seems too tired or preoccupied. "My Dear," he wrote three weeks before the wedding, "my heart is with you, and you are constantly in mind – I can only give you the parting hand, this morning, & leave the expression of a more ardent attachment till another time." There is a wisp of sentiment, and perhaps trepidation, in one of Emily's remarks three days later: "I have many friends call upon me as they say to make their farewell visit. How do you suppose this sounds in my ear. But my dear it is to go and live with you." And Edward, just a week before the ceremony: "The time is short, My Dear, and we shall probably soon have occasion to enter upon the serious duties of life – Are we prepared? But I am too tired to 'moralize.' "

If all this sounds ominous to modern ears, it was pure New England— or at least pure Amherst and pure Dickinson—and seems to have been taken quite for granted by Emily Norcross. She grew into an eminently conventional woman and was probably so as a girl. (It was her spirited sister Lavinia who was the unconventional one, marrying her cousin against family opposition and, we are told, for love.) She apparently fitted without friction into the traditional pattern of dominant husband and sweet submissive wife, with both recognizing a still higher authority, Duty—to each other, their children, their community, and God. Just how dominant Edward became and whether his wife's submissiveness became

---

from his mother, whether *she said anything about* losing her luggage! We all want to see you. . . .

so abject as to degrade her in the eyes of the children (especially Emily's) are questions that must still, I think, remain open. There is little to indicate that the Dickinson domestic situation, at least in its beginnings, was anything but conventional, which is the way the new bride, apparently, liked it.

When, finally, she came to Amherst as Edward's bride, they settled in half of the Widow Jemima Montague's house, painstakingly prepared by Edward. The first year apparently went smoothly, Edward's business growing steadily and Emily adjusting to her new life, "situated pleasently," as her sister Lavinia described her, and only a touch homesick. There was a question of taking in a student boarder, partly for economy, partly as a protection for Emily during Edward's absences. From Court in Northampton, Edward wrote:

> The Hon. Mr. Bliss of Springfield has spoken to me to-day, about boarding his son. . . . You know my opinion respecting it, and I leave it entirely with you to manage as you think best. The work, you know, comes upon you, and it is wholly immaterial with me, what you conclude. . . .

The first child, William Austin, was born on April 16, 1829. (Sister Lavinia's comment during the pregnancy: "It is enough to make any-one discouraged to see what all the married folks are coming to.") A year later, Edward bought from his father one half of the brick Homestead on Main Street, a sign of his growing prosperity as it was of his father's decline. It was here that Emily Elizabeth was born in December, with or without benefit of paper hanger. The following June, Mrs. Dickinson wrote one of her infrequent letters to her husband, then in Boston on business. So far, the auspices were bright.

> I have retired to my chamber for a little space to converse with you, with my little companion on the bed asleep. I have as yet had the pleasure of heareing from you every day which has given me much support. . . . Little Austin often speaks of you. When the bell rings he thinks you are comeing and opens the door to welcome you. Sister Lavinia has not come yet, but I look for her evry day. . . . I must leave you my deare to resume my usual employment which you may well suppose.

The auspices may have been bright, but there is still the problem of Emily Norcross Dickinson as "nonentity" and her influence on her daughter Emily's character and career. Here again there is the baffling fact of Dickinson reticence, in the face of which one must proceed largely by inference. Emily, for instance, spoke once of her mother's "grieved life," but she was never precise about causes and only occasionally about symptoms, notably on matters of the ill health that plagued Mrs. Dickinson periodically from the early 1850s on. Much has been made of Mrs. Dickinson's tendency toward hypochondria, her "tremulous fear of death" (Mrs. Bingham's phrase), and the degree to which she communicated these fears to her children. The cause here is thought to be the early deaths in her immediate family—the baby brother, and two brothers in their twenties, one of them, and her mother, dying the year Austin was born. Surely these events were saddening, but the Norcross losses were not exceptional among the large families of the day. Edward recognized his wife's tendency to worry, especially when the children were young, and he did a good deal of worrying himself. In view of the precarious state of medicine at that time, their anxiety is hardly surprising. But nothing in the Dickinson annals suggests Mrs. Dickinson as the source of such anxieties in any of her children. If the recurrent theme of death in Emily's poems and letters was neurotic in origin, at least there was nothing tremulous about it, and what occupied her as mature artist and thinker was death as an existential phenomenon and as the central religious mystery, to be probed and pondered with the objectivity, almost, of the clinician and the philosopher. Whatever damaging effect, if any, her mother's nervous disabilities had on Emily can only be guessed at. Vinnie seems to have escaped entirely. Austin, even in his maturity, was shocked and stunned by deaths in his immediate circle, but there is no evidence that his fear of death was a constant neurotic disability.

It is well, however, to look for a moment into what *is* known about Mrs. Dickinson's ill health, which after a point was a more or less constant source of worry to the family and was of undoubted importance, good and bad, in Emily's life. It is known that her recovery from Lavinia's birth was much longer than it should have been; and the fact that she had no more children is notable in view of the large families (nine children in each) from which she and her husband came. There are indications that Emily began to worry about her in the mid-1850s. Then, and later when she suffered a stroke in 1875, the sisters spent a good deal of time nursing her and taking care of the house when she was incapacitated. For the last four years of her life she required constant attention.[6]

6. Here is a brief survey of Mrs. Dickinson's illnesses, in so far as they can be traced in the annals:

The trouble following Lavinia's birth in 1834 lasted, apparently, for some months. Mrs. Dickinson seems to have been in good health for the next dozen years or so. "We are sick hardly ever at home," ED wrote Abiah Root on May 7, 1850, reporting her dismay at a sudden illness of her mother's. On the seventeenth, she wrote, "Mother is still an invalid tho' a partially restored one. . . . [In her absence from the kitchen] I am yet the Queen of the court" (L I, 97, 99). On May 10, 1852, she wrote Austin that "[Mother] was attacked Friday, with a difficulty in her face, similar to the one you have, and with which you suffer so much once or twice in a year. . . . Vinnie and I have had to work pretty hard on account of her sickness" (L I, 204). Edward added a note: "Mother has been severely afflicted with the Neuralgia arising from her front tooth . . . it was lanced . . . & she is now relieved" (YH I, 248). In January 1856, ED wrote Mrs. Holland that "Mother has been an invalid since we came *home,* and Vinnie and I 'regulated,' and Vinnie and I 'got settled,' and still we keep our father's house, and mother lies upon the lounge, or sits in her easy chair. I don't know what her sickness is . . . (L II, 324). In September 1856, a letter from Jane Hitchcock to a friend outside Amherst speaks of "Mrs. D's health" as "poor": "she is at the

Certainly one of the influences that kept Emily at home and contributed to her secluded life was her mother's health and the extra work it entailed. Vinnie once called it the decisive one. Perhaps it was simple physical inadequacy that kept Mrs. Dickinson from the vigorous fulfillment of all her motherly duties. Emily spoke once of her weariness. Perhaps it was this kind of inadequacy, among others, that she had in mind in those two remarks to Higginson. But it is at least worth noting that we have no bitter complaints from either daughter—a hint of fatigue now and then, and preoccupation, but no resentment. A note of Emily's to the Norcross cousins in 1880 is typical:

> I have only a moment, exiles, but you shall have the largest half. Mother's dear little wants so engross the time, – to read to her, to fan her, to tell her health will come tomorrow, to explain to her *why* the grasshopper is a burden, because he is not so new a grasshopper as he was, – this is so ensuing, I hardly have said "Good-morning, mother," when I hear myself saying "Mother, good-night."

Apparently, the tedious duties, undertaken with discipline and imagination, became even pleasant. Emily enjoyed at least something of what she called, when her mother was helpless, "a holier demand." After her mother's death she wrote a friend:

> Only the night before she died, she was happy and hungry and ate a little Supper I made her with such enthusiasm, I laughed with delight, and told her she was as hungry as Dick.

One need not be a sentimentalist to see in Emily's ultimate feeling for both her mother and father a tenderness and humane understanding that redeem, if they do not contradict, her earlier posturings.

The picture brightens a bit, too, as we look beyond the family. Mrs. Dickinson was not quite the nonentity in the community she has been pictured. One commentator, more generous than most, has given an appealing account of her function both within the family and outside:

> The habit that grew up among the Dickinson children of lampooning their neighbors may have had its origin in the characterizations formed by their father's keen and critical mind. Through their mother they were more directly connected with the joys and the calamities in the families of Amherst, rich and poor.

---

water-cure in N. Hampton" (*YH* I, 344). Her illness "was a condition that lasted for several years and caused the family much anxiety" (*L* II, 324 n.). Leyda (*YH* I, lxxvii) thinks her "nervous illness at that time" (*ca.* January 1858) may have prompted ED to write the Reverend Charles Wadsworth of Philadelphia for advice. ED wrote Mrs. Haven that summer: "Mother is much as usual. I know not what to hope of her" (*L* II, 337). But on July 12, 1863, a neighbor wrote a friend: "Mrs. Edward Dickinson sent [Dr. Stearns, president of the college] a most elegant Boquet . . . she . . . admires him, & is now quite herself" (*YH* II, 81). Nothing of importance is recorded from then until the stroke she suffered on June 15, 1875, from which she never fully recovered. It was from this time on that she required ED's and Lavinia's constant care, made all the more difficult when she broke her hip in June 1878.

Emily once caught her in a characteristic project: "Mother drives with
Tim [the stableman] to carry pears to settlers." We hear of her sending
apples to Samuel Bowles and a bouquet to President Stearns of the
college. She seems to have been much more chatty and sociable than the
mousy figure of tradition, loving her friends and her calls—Emily called
them "rambles." We hear of her going to parties at "Prof. Warner's" and
"Prof. Haven's." She loved gossip. Once, when her mother was sick,
Emily wrote a friend: "Mother pines for you, and says you were 'so
social.' Mother misses power to ramble to her Neighbors – and the stale
inflation of the minor News." As to what her friends thought of her, the
records are meager. The words "fluttering," "anxious," "timid," "meek"
come mostly from those who knew her in her later years. Those who
knew her at her best speak of her as "pleasant" and "sweet," though
"plaintive." Edward, who was always conscious of family status, seems
never to have wavered in his loyalty to her.[7]

Though hardly a leader, Mrs. Dickinson was active in the community
in many ways that must have made Edward proud of her. In one of his
courtship letters, he wrote enthusiastically from Northampton about the
Cattle Show then on display:

> There are a great variety of fine specimens of domestic industry & skill
> which it would be creditable to any lady to imitate – and I consider it as an
> honor to any female to have her name publicly announced as having obtained
> a premium for her excellence in any branch of domestic economy.

The Amherst Cattle Show was no less an event, and Mrs. Dickinson contributed to it annually. She served on committees and won premiums for

7. Martha Dickinson Bianchi described her grandmother as the "fluttering little
mother, always timorous, always anxious" (*Life and Letters*, p. 10). Martha was only
sixteen when Mrs. Dickinson died, and hence knew only her invalid days. Mabel
Loomis Todd, who hardly knew her at all, dismissed her as "a meek little thing"
(*AB*, 232). Her immediate contemporaries, though sometimes agreeing, seem to
have sensed other qualities. A caller in the early days found her "as usual full of
plaintive talk" (*YH* I, 81, September 15, 1843), but another described her as "very
pleasant" (*YH* I, 282, August 31, 1853). As for Edward, his letters home from his
business trips during their early married years have been considered condescending,
but I see no reason why remarks like the following cannot be taken at face value.
After ten years of married life he could say of her letters: "I find you always have
something to say, & it is very easy for you to say it" (*YH* I, 40, January 9, 1838). On
his trips, he continually longs to be back home. (Cody, pp. 69, 87, sees him as protest-
ing too much and as secretly wishing to be rid of his family.) As he became more
and more involved in public affairs and as responsibilities mounted, he may have become increasingly aloof from her as he did from the children. Her ill health was obviously a burden. But his early respect and affection for her never seem to have
diminished. When she died, she was among the "great losses" Mrs. Boltwood described to Mrs. Ford: ". . . Mr. & Mrs. Sweetser & now dear Mrs Edward Dickinson
. . ." (*YH* II, 385, November 25, 1882). The opinion of those who knew her best in
the later years seems to have been close to Emily's: she "achieved in sweetness what
she lost in strength" (*L* III, 771, spring 1883).

her cooking and produce. She was the hostess, however anxious and fluttery, at the famous Dickinson receptions at Commencement time, a sign at least of some social talent. She joined the First Church, whether from tremulous fear or positive commitment we do not know, nineteen years before her husband, and was active in its work.

Her few ventures into the intellectual life of the college, it seems clear, were of mixed success. One lecture was said to have "interested" her, but she was apparently swamped by another on Adam Smith; it was this latter that she confessed (as Emily phrased it to Austin) to be "too high for her unobtrusive faculties." "My Mother," Emily later told Higginson, "does not care for thought." But that she was incapable of thought, or intellectually illiterate, is another matter. Her cultural activities in Monson before her marriage gave her at least a start on higher education. There are signs that she pursued it, however intermittently. Her brother William gave her three volumes of Cowper's poems for a wedding present; and in 1855 Edward's colleague in the General Court, Charles Sumner, the famous orator who had spoken at the Amherst Commencement in 1847 and had probably been entertained at the Dickinsons', sent her a copy of Lydia Child's biography of the Quaker, Isaac T. Hopper, just off the press. Emily gives us a glimpse of her reading "uncarnal" books in the family circle, and once spoke of her "reading a little" during her later years of illness. What little we have of her correspondence shows her as no ardent letter writer and a rather graceless one at that. She usually protested that she was too busy for letters, a tendency that started early and became a family joke. In 1836 her sister-in-law, Lucretia, writing to Edward, asked that she at least "write her *name*" in Edward's next letter, "so as not [to] forget how to write." Years later, when the family was well established, Emily wrote Austin, "Mother was much amused at the feebleness of your hopes of hearing from her – She got so far last week once, as to take a pen and paper and carry them into the kitchen." Once she sent him a lock of her hair in a letter of Emily's, who transmitted her message: "to put you in mind of your affectionate mother." This epistolary reticence is, of course, one of the reasons we know so little about her. Such a gap may have profound implications about her inadequacies; but one simple explanation may be that she enjoyed other ways of expressing herself, like sending flowers, or fruit, or locks of hair. Like her daughter Vinnie, she was a doer. Her literary deficiency, especially when Austin was away, gave Emily her chance. Emily's letters to him are sisterly and motherly at once, a function Mrs. Dickinson once used as an excuse for not writing herself.

One wonders how often Mrs. Dickinson joined in the family humor that Emily spoke of often and happily. It is reassuring to hear that she could be "much amused" by Austin's complaint about her not writing him; and Emily, once describing a family scene in which her "rheumatic sire" behaved badly toward some visitors, found her mother and Vinnie in the kitchen "making most desperate efforts to control themselves," presumably their mirth. In a family that enjoyed quoting one another, her voice is heard less than most and much less than her husband's. Sometimes she is quoted straight. Vinnie wrote Austin that "Mother had a nice time in Boston & told fine stories of your fame among Bostonians," and once, when he had not written for some time, "Mother says it seems as though you had been struck out of existance." When Mrs. Dickinson came home from the funeral of her brother-in-law, Loring Norcross, Emily wrote her cousins: "Mother tells how gently he looked on all who looked at him – how he held his bouquet sweet, as he were a guest in a friend's parlor and must still do honor. The meek, mild gentleman who thought no harm, but peace toward all"—a good description, probably, of Mrs. Dickinson herself; and if the simile of the first sentence is her own and not her daughter's, we must revise our notion of Mrs. Dickinson's lack of imagination. Apparently she was good at funerals. When Mrs. Hitchcock died, Emily wrote the Norcrosses:

> Jennie Hitchcock's mother was buried yesterday, so there is one orphan more, and her father is very sick besides. My father and mother went to the service, and mother said while the minister prayed, a hen with her chickens came up, and tried to fly into the window. I suppose the dead lady used to feed them, and they wanted to bid her good-by.

(The final thought, however, was probably Emily's.) Mostly, when Emily quoted her mother, it was to poke fun at her motherly anxieties—about Austin's clothes when he was in Boston teaching school; his safety ("and mother – oh she thought the bears in the wood had devoured you, or if you were not eaten up, you were such a monster of thoughtlessness and neglect!" for not writing); or the fierceness of his discipline in school: "Mother feels quite troubled about those little boys – fears you will kill one sometime when you are punishing him – for *her sake* be careful!" Sometimes she seems to be making fun of her mother's commonplace thought or language, as when Mrs. Dickinson hoped her grandson Ned "would be a very good Boy." "Not very dood," Emily has him say; and adds: "Obtuse ambition of Grandmamas!" Twice Emily quoted her mother condescendingly. Austin had sent her a bonnet: "Mother wants me to thank you for all your pains and trouble, and says you 'are very kind to do so much for your mother.'" And again about one of Mrs. Dickinson's simple pleasures: "The horse is doing nicely, he travels 'like a bird,' to use a favorite phrase of your delighted mother's."

A family scene in the spring of 1851, described for Austin's benefit, puts both mother and father under the same gentle fire and brings up the whole problem of Emily's humor toward her parents, and, indeed, her use of humor in general. Was her mirth protective—the "Mail of Anguish," her way of concealing bitter resentment or fear? Or was it carefree, unambiguous, lighthearted? How much of it was the exercise of wit, in this instance, on slightly vulnerable subjects?

Mother is warming her feet, which she assures me confidently are "just as cold as ice.["] I tell her I fear there is danger of icification, or ossification – I dont know certainly which! Father is reading the Bible – I take it for *consolation,* judging from outward things. He and mother take great delight in dwelling upon your character, and reviewing your many virtues, and Father's prayers for you at our morning devotions are enough to break one's heart – it is really very touching; surely "our blessings brighten" the farther off they fly! Mother wipes her eyes with the end of her linen apron, and consoles herself by thinking of several future places "where congregations ne'er break up," and Austins have no end!

Whatever the verdict on Emily's humor—what was going on subconsciously must remain a mystery—its part in her achievement, both personal and artistic, was powerful. It seldom left her for long. Through it she could maintain, or regain, her poise. What her moods were like when she was not writing we have no way of knowing; but her wits—and her wit—seldom failed her when she put pen to paper. She could even pun in her remark to Higginson about coming home to "Awe": "He was an awful Mother, but I liked him better than none."

The remarks got tenderer as time went on. A letter to the Norcrosses in the early spring of 1870 says that "Mother went rambling, and came in with a burdock on her shawl, so we know that the snow has perished from the earth. Noah would have liked mother." A little of the old bite, perhaps, came in a remark to Mrs. Holland three years later, thanking her for kindnesses to Vinnie (this was a year before her father's death and two before her mother's stroke): "She [Vinnie] has no Father and Mother but me and I have no Parents but her." The remark is an isolated one, and there is no bill of complaints. If Mrs. Holland was shocked, there is no record of it; apparently Emily felt she would make the proper discount. When Dr. Holland showed signs of failing strength in 1881, Emily described to Mrs. Holland, with unconcealed surprise and delight, one of her mother's finest moments:

I ask Mother "what message" she sends – She says, "Tell them I wish I could take them both in my Arms and carry them –"
I never before have heard her speak so – those were the very words –

And later that year, when Dr. Holland died, Emily reported her mother's earlier comment on Edward Dickinson's death: "I loved him so." Emily added: "Had he a tenderer eulogy?"

In the history of the Dickinson complexities—that is, the tendency, from Samuel Fowler on down, toward introversion and a highly developed inner life—Mrs. Dickinson hardly figures at all. There is no indication that she was admitted to the secret discontents of her husband, or her troubled son, or her two independent daughters. She seems to have had little idea of what Emily was up to. She found her, as one contemporary said, "a mystery and a constant surprise"—and sometimes a shock. Emily recorded one such incident in a letter to Mrs. Holland in July 1880:

Austin and I were talking the other Night about the Extension of Consciousness, after Death and Mother told Vinnie, afterward, she thought it
was "very improper."
She forgets that we are past "Correction in Righteousness –"
I dont know what she would think if she knew that Austin told me
confidentially "there was no such person as Elijah."

Indeed, it is hard to imagine what she would have thought had she
known a fraction of the rebellious notions that crowded Emily's mind.
Except for this attempt (certainly a futile one), there is no record that she
ever interfered with Emily's inner life. But perhaps in this very way she
contributed to it most. Whether intentionally or out of sheer bewilderment, she made herself dispensable. Emily had enough to contend with in
her father; a prying or domineering mother would have made life intolerable.

Mrs. Dickinson seems to have been important in Emily's life both for
what she did and for what she was. On the practical side, there is ample
evidence that, as far as her strength permitted, she was a loving and
attentive mother and did all she could to anticipate and meet the wants of
her family. "Mother makes nicer pies with reference to your coming,"
Emily wrote Austin, then teaching in Boston. She had certain positive
interests and skills that Emily shared. The herbarium that Emily kept as a
girl must have owed something to the encouragement and guidance of
her mother,[8] who loved flowers and kept a fine garden. One of Emily's
abiding concerns, horticulture, may have had this simple, obvious source.
Emily described her once, when the family was away, as never busier
" – what with fruit, and plants, and chickens, and sympathizing friends."

In another practical way, Mrs. Dickinson contributed to her daughter's
life. When Emily came home in the fall of 1864 from the months in
Boston, where she had gone for treatments for her eyes, she was incapacitated for anything but housework. "Mother and Margaret [O'Brien] are
so kind," she wrote her cousin.

They say I am a "help." Partly because it is true, I suppose, and the rest
applause. . . . For the first few weeks I did nothing but comfort my plants.
. . . I chop the chicken centres when we have roast fowl. . . . Then I make
the yellow to the pies, and bang the spice for cake, and knit the soles to the
stockings I knit the bodies to last June.

8. Now in the Dickinson Room of the Houghton Library, Harvard, the herbarium
shows a fine sense of composition, as well as a concern for precise Latin nomencla-
ture which she probably did *not* get from her mother. (Botany was one of her important studies at school.) Nor did her mother help her much in the matter of clothes;
"for you may not remember," Emily wrote Joseph Lyman, "that our amiable mother
never taught us tayloring and I am amused to remember those clothes, or rather
those apologies made up from dry goods with which she covered us in nursery
times . . ." (*LL*, p. 70). For samples of ED's herbarium, see the endpapers of this
volume.

That she could do the work was due to her mother's training. Emily enjoyed cooking and was good at it. We have some of her recipes,[9] and Higginson reported that her father would eat no bread except that baked by her.

It is in this regard that the one bit of unqualified praise of Mrs. Dickinson has come down to us. Among the glowing memories of Joseph Lyman, that schoolboy visitor in the Dickinson home during the 1840s, none glowed more brightly than that of Mrs. Dickinson's cooking: "Vinnie's mother was a rare and delicate cook in such matters as crullers and custards and she taught the girls all those housewifely accomplishments." (Lyman was a sharp observer and saw enough, incidentally, to reverse the stock notion of the role of the two sisters in the household: "Em is an excellent housekeeper – Vinnie is sometimes afraid of soiling her little fat hands but can do very well when she chooses.") Later on, Lyman became something of an authority on domestic affairs, even to the point of writing a book on the subject, *The Philosophy of Housekeeping*, which had considerable currency in the late 1860s. It is clear from the many references in his early letters that he learned the first principles from his observations of Mrs. Dickinson's household.

Besides the domestic skills (although she hated the cleaning and

---

9. Here, for instance, are her recipes for gingerbread and black cake.

GINGERBREAD
1 Quart Flour,
½ Cup Butter,
½ Cup Cream,
1 Table Spoon Ginger,
1 Tea Spoon Soda,
1 Salt
Make up with Molasses – (L II, 493)

BLACK CAKE –
2 pounds Flour –
2 Sugar –
2 Butter –
19 Eggs –
5 pounds Raisins –
1½ Currants –
1½ Citron –
½ pint Brandy –
½ – Molasses –
2 Nutmegs –
5 teaspoons
Cloves – Mace – Cinnamon –
2 teaspoons Soda –
Beat Butter and Sugar together –
Add Eggs without beating – and beat the mixture again –
Bake 2½ or three hours, in Cake pans, or 5 to 6 hours in
Milk pan, if full – (L III, 783–84)

[ 87

dusting, which she called "a prickly art"[10]), Emily learned from her what was perhaps more valuable than anything a brilliant mother could have given her: some lessons in simple, devoted humanity, important for a precocious girl not disinclined to the Dickinson snobbery and the satiric Dickinson wit. She may have condescended to her mother's unobtrusive faculties, but she could hardly doubt her tender heart or love. Here is the scene as Emily described it at her first homecoming from Mount Holyoke.

Soon the carriage stopped in front of our own house & all were at the door to welcome the returned one, from Mother with tears in her eyes down to Pussy who tried to look as gracious as was becoming her dignity.

When Austin, on a similar occasion a few years later, failed to show up, she scolded him on her mother's account:

Mother got a great dinner yesterday, thinking in her kind heart that you would be so hungry after your *long ride,* and the table was set for you, and nobody moved your chair, but there it stood at the table, until dinner was all done, a melancholy emblem of the blasted hopes of the world. And we had new custard pie, too, which is a rarity in days when hens dont lay, but mother knew you loved it, and when noon really got here, and you really did not come, then a big piece was saved in case you should come at night.

A deeper tenderness and a fuller understanding came when Emily had outgrown her youthful condescension. A late reminiscence sums up what she learned from her mother:

Two things I have lost with Childhood – the rapture of losing my shoe in the Mud and going Home barefoot, wading for Cardinal flowers and the mothers reproof which was more for my sake than her weary own for she frowned with a smile [–] now Mother and Cardinal flower are parts of a closed world –

When Mrs. Dickinson died on November 14, 1882, after the long illness that demanded so much of her daughters, Emily's letters contain no sigh of relief, only shock and loss and an enlarged sense of what her mother was and what she meant to her. "I hoped to write you before," she wrote the Norcross cousins in Monson a few days after the event, "but mother's dying almost stunned my spirit. . . . She was scarcely the aunt you knew. The great mission of pain had been ratified – cultivated to tenderness by persistent sorrow, so that a larger mother died than had she died before." A few weeks later, she was still trying to rally her forces: "Blow has followed blow, till the wondering terror of the Mind clutches what is left, helpless of an accent." The metaphor and cadence of one of

---

10. *L* III, 827 (to the Norcrosses, early August 1884). This is in line with her earlier remark, "God keep me from what they call *households* . . ." *L* I, 99 (to Abiah Root, May 17, 1850). She liked the creative part—"making things"—but routine maintenance bored her. Nor did she ever show Vinnie's tendency to take charge.

her early poems came back to her: "Her dying feels to me like many kinds of Cold – at times electric, at times benumbing – then a trackless waste" (recall the last lines of "After great pain": "As Freezing persons, recollect the Snow – / First – Chill – then Stupor – then the letting go –"). Then came a summing up quite different from the aphoristic sentences to Higginson and Mrs. Holland:

> We were never intimate Mother and Children while she was our Mother – but Mines in the same Ground meet by tunneling and when she became our Child, the Affection came – When we were children and she journeyed, she always brought us something. Now, would she bring us but herself, what an only Gift – Memory is a strange Bell – Jubilee, and Knell.

There is reason enough, even here, for Emily's notion of her mother's "grieved life." Life for these late-Puritan parents was real and earnest, and it would seem especially so for Mrs. Dickinson, with an overworked husband and with children she had difficulty understanding. As in many New England homes, the parents did not cultivate intimacy with their children. Emily's admission of the belated affection is a striking one; we can guess that often in such households the affection did not come at all. It came, too, with Vinnie, who (in a letter to Mrs. Todd) composed her mother's tenderest eulogy:

> The days are beautiful but so sorrowful without my sweet Mother. I'm so glad you saw her dear face & *she* heard your bird voice. She was so fond of every bird & flower & so full of pity for every grief. Keep fast hold of your parents, for the world will always be strange & homesick without their affection.

Or, as Emily later wrote a friend who had lost her mother: "To have *had* a Mother – how mighty!"

Oddly enough, although it is seldom seen this way, the greatest tribute that Emily paid her mother lay perhaps in the fact that she never wanted to leave the home that Mrs. Dickinson helped create. There were many and more complicated reasons for her staying at home, but the fact that she stayed suggests strongly that she felt freest at home—free to live the kind of life and do the kind of work that suited her. Although Mrs. Dickinson may not have nurtured her daughter's genius with wise talk and literary encouragement, she was a central figure in establishing the milieu in which her genius came into its own. That Emily never wanted to leave it can, I suppose, be regarded as an unfortunate eccentricity or as a symptom of profound psychic fear. The undeniable facts are that she stayed home, wrote her poetry and letters, and learned to love her mother.

Though the love came late, there was nothing mawkish about it. Emily found a poem (probably more than one) in her mother as she had in her father—something awesome and fathomless in the life and death even of this fluttery, timid woman whom latterly she had to care for like a child. Some months after Mrs. Dickinson died, she wrote:

[ 89

All is faint indeed without our vanished mother, who achieved in sweetness what she lost in strength, though grief of wonder at her fate made the winter short, and each night I reach finds my lungs more breathless, seeking what it means.

> To the bright east she flies
> Brothers of Paradise
> Remit her home,
> Without a change of wings,
> Or Love's convenient things,
> Enticed to come.
>
> Fashioning what she is,
> Fathoming what she was,
> We deem we dream –
> And that dissolves the days
> Through which existence strays
> Homeless at home.                     [#*1573*]

But again we will let Vinnie have the last word: "Father believed," she said in her later years, "and mother loved."

# 6

# William Austin Dickinson

T HE DEEPER WE GET into Dickinson complexities, the more grueling they become. And none are more so than those surrounding Emily's brother, Austin (1829–1895)—his character, his career, his establishment next door with his wife, Susan, and all that this tangled relationship meant to Emily, for better and for worse. Austin's story is the most harrowing and, in its innumerable relevancies to Emily, the most immediate to our purpose. Of all the family, he was closest to Emily in temperament, taste, sense of self and of the world. He had something of the philosopher and the poet in him, without the talent for either. From early manhood, he was a soul in trouble. His letters reveal, in groping but sometimes impressive prose, many of the inner problems and anxieties Emily worked out in her poems. The two of them had the same sense of humor and often talked as if they were the only Dickinsons who counted. Their sister Lavinia was indispensable, but in another way. It was Austin and Emily against the world, a relationship of infinite importance to both. What that "world" was, especially that aspect of it which pressed in on them both, daily, in the Dickinson enclave on Main Street, must be explored fully.

It has been said of Mrs. Dickinson that "she served chiefly as a carrier of Dickinson traits." In this humble function she served Austin as well as Emily, so at the outset it is proper to consider him in the light of the line we have traced from his grandfather. By the time he came to maturity, the family name and fortune were fully restored, to the point of acknowledged leadership in the town and some prominence in the state. The Dickinsons had acquired an aura of superiority in Amherst, even a snobbishness that some townsfolk found hard to forgive. There is a legend that they preempted the sidewalk in front of the two mansions—that lesser citizens gave way when members of the family walked abroad. Austin had a brusque and blunt way that made enemies in a fashion not recorded of his father. It was said he looked down on almost everyone—except his sister Emily. As treasurer of the college for twenty-two years, he (like his father before him) instructed Amherst presidents in their duties; as the saying went, "Presidents come and go but Dickinsons go on forever."

Nevertheless, Austin also had warmer friends, perhaps, than any recorded of his father. Henry Hills, a local businessman whom Austin helped in difficulty, wrote his wife, "Austin is the same royal friend in adversity as in prosperity and I declare life is worth something to have such a friend." Mabel Loomis Todd records Austin's fondness for taking Amherst ladies to drive—and "proud" they were to be asked. But like his father he had a sharp tongue. Once, Leander Skinner, postmaster and prominent citizen, complained bitterly of Austin, who had chided him on the station platform for leaving for vacation while others were working. Skinner wrote his wife: "Then Dickinson blated out in his rough way loud enough to be heard half a mile. . . . It seemed to me quite uncalled for in this bitter sort of way and so much in public." Earlier Skinner had spoken of Austin's "enemies," who, blaming him for increased expenses in the church that year, had kept him from being elected to the Parish Committee. "This," wrote Skinner, "is a little hard on Austin, should consider it so if it was me."

Austin was a more colorful and assertive figure than his father, with a temperament that pointed toward the future rather than the past—that is, away from the latter-day Puritanism that seems to have been at the core of his father's lonely and rigorous life. He developed tastes and a style that his father would not have understood. His flamboyant dress is a part of Amherst history: he "had about him a picturesque quality, as he appeared in his light-colored driving coat, his yellow wide-brimmed planter's hat, and his orange-wood cane."[1] As a youth he was described as tall and straight, "with a head of unruly reddish hair."[2] He had a deep love of nature and carried on a tradition started by his grandfather (but, as far as we know, neglected by his father) for beautifying Amherst with trees and shrubs. He often combed the countryside for the right specimen for a special purpose and was the leader in a movement from which the town

1. Claude M. Fuess, *Amherst: The Story of a New England College* (1935), p. 185. At least Fuess's description is part of Amherst legend. He calls him "high-strung, lavish, born to lead." Millicent Todd Bingham quotes Miss Vryling Buffum, friend of Vinnie's and principal of a girls' school in Amherst, as saying that Austin "used to preside over town meetings in lavender trousers and a Prince Albert coat" (record of conversation of November 2, 1934; Todd-Bingham Archive, Yale).

2. *Home*, p. 5. Mrs. Bingham (p. 293 n.) scouts the rumor that Austin in his later years wore a *green* wig. (Stanley King, *A History of the Endowment of Amherst College*, 1950, p. 104): "Following an attack of fever [malaria] after his visit to the Philadelphia Centennial in 1876, he wore a wig – a reddish wig." She continues: "As a child . . . I do remember wondering why his hair was so long. And I vividly recall the coppery glint of it and the shining highlights." King, like Fuess, makes much of Austin's unorthodox qualities: "he permitted himself more personal eccentricities than is usual with a college treasurer" (p. 104).

William Austin Dickinson, about 1890

North Pleasant Street. The Dickinson house was on the right, about a block down

Main Street. The Dickinson houses (the Homestead and the Evergreens) are on the left, the First Congregational Church (the Dickinsons' church) on the right

still benefits. He was passionately fond of art. His wife once described him as he returned from a trip to New York "in a feverish excitement over pictures – utterly worn out with his passion – The real fact of the matter is his desire and half plan for three of the Dusseldorf collection – He is fascinated with the longing, and I advise him to get them." On July 5, 1884, he noted in his diary, "bought a water color of some one at the door this P M for $20.00"—an extravagance his father would not have dreamed of.[3]

Austin was more sociable than his father, read widely, and was fond of giving advice (especially to his lady friends) on what to read. In his early years he was known among his friends as a budding Transcendentalist; at least, this is the implication of the long verse letter sent him in 1850 by his Aunt Elisabeth.[4] His letters show a conscious attention to the epistolary

3. Barton L. St. Armand, currently engaged in a study of Austin's art collection, finds his preference to have been for foreign genre scenes of the French and German schools.

4. The letter (dated "winter 1850"), now in the Dickinson archive in the Frost Library, Amherst College, is the fifty rhyming stanzas already referred to. *YH* I, 184, prints only the two and a half having to do with Austin's facial ailment and Emily's owing Aunt Elisabeth a letter. The stanzas about Austin's Transcendental tendencies are:

> Transcendentalism tis said,
> By one who's well and ably read,
> Is moonshine, shavings, dust, and fog
> And does some noble footsteps dog.

> Forgive me, if I tell you, "dear,"
> *Your* feet are dogged by it, I fear,
> And do you ask – "pray, tell me why"?
> Ah yes! I'll tell you by and by.

Whether Emily's footsteps were similarly dogged is a question. Perhaps so, in her youth. At any rate, Emily seems to have been more on Elisabeth's side when she chided Austin for being her "romantic Brother" (*L* I, 115, June 22, 1851). The racy stanza in her valentine of 1852 (*P* #3) shows no particular respect for Transcendentalism:

> I climb the "Hill of Science,"
> I "view the landscape o'er;"
> Such transcendental prospect,
> I ne'er beheld before!

But whatever his intellectual leanings, Austin's advice about this time to Susan Gilbert on what to read was conservative. "For myself," he writes, "I take most pleasure in looking over *old* books, what little time I have for reading – books that I have read before – piled on my shelf & scattered over my table are Bachelor's Reveries – Dana's Prose & Poems – The Bible – 'Grantley Manor,' 'Shirley' Pollok's Course of Time – Coleridge's Table Talk – Kent's Commentaries – &c &c &c and Mosses from an old Manse – I have been reading your Adam & Eve article & like it – I cant the moment think of anything among the things you havent read that will interest you more than Irving's 'Life of Columbus' " (*YH* I, 218, October 11 ?, 1851). Since all three of the young people exchanged literary gossip during these years, most likely this same kind of advice went to Emily. A year and a half later, he tells Susan in great detail

art in an age that made much of it. Emily found them "much funnier –
much funnier" than *Punch,* and praised their *"descriptive* merits." Her
father called them, so she told Austin, "altogether before Shakespeare."[5]
He was deeply stirred by the theater at its best.[6] One of his enthusiasms

why he advised against her reading Georgiana Fullerton's *Lady Bird:* it is "un-
healthy," "disease laden," "full of only wretchedness & misery. . . . a story of deeper
suffering than many ever know – that it's best *any should* know till they are
obliged to . . ." (*YH* I, 275). But Sue had read it anyway.

5. *L* I, 233, 113, 122. A letter from Austin to Joseph Lyman written when they
both were in college (Austin in Amherst, Lyman at Yale) shows how these young
people cultivated the art of letter writing. This, of course, was a conscious and lifelong concern also of ED's, to the extent, as Robert Lambert, Jr., shows in his forth-
coming study, "The Prose of a Poet: A Critical Study of Emily Dickinson's Letters,"
that many of her letters can be compared with her poems as organic, coherent works
of art. Austin's letter begins (*LL,* pp. 11–13):

FRIEND JO.
   Pardon me for not having before answered your letter. The reasons have been
various. In the first place, when studying constantly, as we must in term time, I
feel but little in the mood of writing to anyone, and, consequently, am extremely
dillatory, and even impolite about writing or answering letters, during term. –
Secondly, (in order, not importance) in answer to your production, I hardly knew
whether you expected me to criticize your essay on letter writing, to enter into an
argument with you on the subjects of Epistles, or, strictly to follow the rules, so
nicely and perspicuously laid down. I have, however, concluded, after much consideration and reflection, influenced somewhat by not being able to find your
letter, just at present, to (this time) write what I please, in my own way. Before
I write you again, I shall look up your letter, (which I believe is in my college
room, and we are not allowed access to them in vacation) and receiving an
answer to this, shall carefully compare the two, to see how well your practice ac-
cords with your theory. I will (by the way) mention here that, I liked you[r]
idears on the subject, very well; and think that to be well followed, *your,* as well
as all *other* rules on the subject should be speedily forgotten – for in attempting to
follow rules for being easy, a person will be almost sure to be stiff – Dont you think
so? – Well, Jo – whether you do, or not, – to dispense with your letter for the
present, perhaps I cannot do better, as I feel rather dull, and egotism is allowable
in letters, than to tell you just where and how I am at the present moment – then,
something, of myself, family, and affairs in Amherst, generally –

There follows one of the nicest descriptions we have of life in the Dickinson household, with the fire crackling in the stove, the kitchen table littered with books (the
list begins with "Webster's big Dictionary"), Emily going on a mysterious errand,
and preparations being made for festivities in the absence of "the ancient people"
(Father and Mother) who have gone to Monson to see the relatives. Austin is at his
best, easy and relaxed. His letters were cherished by all the family, especially Father.
That Austin valued Emily's letters and expected much of them is clear both from the
fact that he preserved them carefully (while destroying his wife Susan's) and from
such a comment as this from Emily: "John Emerson just went away from here – he
has been spending the evening, and I'm so tired now, that I write just as it happens,
so you must'nt expect any style" (*L* I, 296, early June 1854).

   6. His diary for April 11, 1883, notes the following: "Evng went to the Museum
[Boston] to hear Salvini and Clara Morris as Othello and Desdemona, a revelation to
me of human power" (*YH* II, 396). The diary contains many other references to plays
and musical events, especially during his trips to Boston (e.g., "Faust at the Globe,"
November 9, 1880; Sarah Bernhardt in *Camille,* December 13, 1880, and in *Frou Frou*

came down from father to son: he kept fine horses and was very proud of them.

In such ways, more than any Dickinson before him, Austin cut a figure. The style of life in the Evergreens, once he and his wife were well established, outshone anything the Homestead had known. His service to the community, the church, and the college was in the good Dickinson tradition, but unlike his grandfather and father he never became involved in politics outside Amherst. Respected like them, he was more of an eccentric than either, less inclined to restrain his moods and inclinations. He was disturbed early by religious doubts and cosmic anxieties that they either never knew or never expressed. His youth was much stormier than theirs appear to have been. And later, under heavy domestic pressures, he chafed sadly against the confining life and ethos of Amherst.

Emily appears most frequently in his early years, since all her letters to him cover that span. His youthful problems, as he broods over them in the scraps of correspondence that survive from that period, provide insights into much that may have been troubling her. But what for her became the stuff of poetry meant frustration, sadness, and tragedy for him. His development from exuberant if puzzled youth, toward melancholy and introversion, and finally to the harrowing complexities of his later relationships, is a continuous revelation of what Emily called "that Campaign inscrutable / Of the Interior."

Emily's first letter to Austin, the first of hers we have to anybody, was written when she was eleven. This was long before the clouds began to gather. He was away at school, and she missed him:

> As Father was going to Northampton and thought of coming over to see you [at Williston Seminary in nearby Easthampton] I thought I would improve the opportunity and write you a few lines – We miss you very much indeed you cannot think how odd it seems without you there was always such a Hurrah wherever you was.

Nearly ten years later she wrote in the same vein, though more moderately: "I long so to see you Austin, and hear your happy voice, it will do

---

the next evening; "Took half an hour of Oscar Wilde standing," January 31, 1882; "Went to see Black Crook," May 1, 1882; "Went to hear and see Mrs. [Lily] Langtry [at New York] in evening," November 21, 1882, etc.). At least once (and probably many more times) he shared his enthusiasm with Emily, who commented on his experience at *Othello:* "Austin heard Salvini before his Idol died, and the size of that manifestation even the Grave has not foreclosed –" (*L* III, 811; to Mrs. Holland, early 1884). A note suggests that Austin had seen Salvini in *Othello* in the winter of 1873–74, before the death of Salvini's wife, "his Idol." Some months later, autumn 1884, Emily wrote to Maria Whitney: "Austin brought me the picture of Salvini when he was last in Boston" (*L* III, 847). Henry James also heard Salvini (in 1883) and commented much as Austin did on this "revelation . . . of human power": ". . . the depth, the nobleness, the consistency, the passion, the visible, audible beauty of [his performance] are beyond praise" (*Notes on Acting and the Scenic Drama,* Rutgers University Press, 1948, p. 171).

us all more good than any other medicine." Again and again, she begged him to come home and bring the fun that, apparently, he alone could provide. Their Aunt Elisabeth, the poet, and only six years older than Austin, shared Emily's enthusiasm (and rhetoric): "We are very lonesome without you – one reason as Emily says, is 'because you always make such a hurra.'" Emily spoke repeatedly of the "uproar," "the famous stir" that his presence brought to the house—so quiet, she said, in his absence, with "nobody to laugh with – talk with, nobody down in the morning to make the fun for me!"

In a household in which it was pretty much all "real life," Austin's presence was tonic. Emily relished the release of spirit he could provide, his wits to match her own against, the joy of life which only he could share on something approaching her level. When he was away, she missed not only the fun but their long talks "upon the *kitchen stone hearth,* when the just are fast asleep." They developed a little language, a rapport which, though desperately exclusive, had survival value. Austin's side of the dialogue must be inferred from Emily's many and long letters to him.

Only two letters from him to her have survived, and one is a draft. (All of Emily's correspondence was destroyed by Lavinia after Emily's death, by Emily's direction.) Mrs. Bingham recounts all that is known about the drafted note, which was found in a little package among Austin's things. There were several drafts of it, the shortest addressed to "Dear Sister Emily." Evidently he had worked hard on this effusion, an elaborate fantasy on their youth in the Homestead. The allegory is far from clear, but the reference to early rising and "vigorous children" has obvious bearing on Father and domestic discipline. It is worth reproducing in full as an example of the play of wit Emily and Austin enjoyed together, the only two in the household who shared the taste or skill for it. (That Emily excelled in the same vein we know from the harum-scarum verse valentines that now grace the opening pages of her collected poems and from a certain glorious fantasy—a dream allegory—sent to her Uncle Joel Norcross when she was nineteen.) It begins with a nice genre piece on the Dickinson domestic scene.

From half past ten oclock of last evening until eleven of the same, your fathers house was the scene of great commotion. About the time first mentioned, as mother Lavinia & myself were seated around a bright blazing fire in the sitting room, each one attentive to his or her own peculiar duties, we were all of a sudden aroused by *loud shouts,* & huzza's followed by peals of laughter, and various strange sounds which seemed the effect of unbounded Joy. Quite startled by such a tumult at that time of night, in the quiet little village of Amherst, we all immediately rushed to the window, and from thence, I to the door from the outside of which I beheld a thing, from a hole in whose head, the noise seemed to proceed, dressed in man's attire and running at the top of its speed, in a moment it stoped short, turned sumerset, then rising up it leaped and danced, and shouted and gestured and performed the strangest evolutions, and oddest pranks imaginable. As the image drew near me I perceived that it was a man, who in his hand held an open letter which he seemed to be trying to read and at the sentiments and expressions of which he seemed to be almost transported out of himself. He was so intent on his letter that he evidently took no notice of any body or thing although a great number of people, both male and female, of all ages, ranks, and conditions, attracted by the disturbance had collected together and completely lined the street on both sides for a considerable distance, as he came nearer I distinctly heard him read these words, "I told her you were not afraid of her being too strict with me, and she replied, Tell him I am much obliged to him." After he had uttered of this word of this quotation, he presently swelled to such a prodigious size, and grew so lofty in stature that it verily seemed as if he would burst the bonds of nature, and strutting about he reared his sublime eye almost to the clouds, with these movements and a few haughty gesticulations he resumed the reading of his letter. The next sentence was this "and when I told her how gratified you were at our early rising she said Tell him that is the only way to make vigorous children," before he had quite finished this sentence it was apparent to all that the ineffable delight inspired by the answer would cause him to make some mighty effort to free himself from the steam which was pent up within, and had come well nigh exploding him when his eyes had read the last word of the former sentence. And well did he prove that the previous indications had not been deceitful, for while the word "children" was even on his lips he roared out in such a *terrific, great, coarse horse-laugh* that the whole welkin rang, and the distant forests echoed back the awful din, then in his great vehemence, he drew up his monstrous foot and stamped the earth with the most terrible force, so great powerful was the concussion that the whole firmament was shaken, the whole planetary system was deranged, the stars twinkled, and the clouds fell from the heavens strewing the earth with a white feathery substance.

This was probably the *"imaginative* note" that Emily thanked him for in her letter of May 29, 1848. She was "highly edified . . . & think your flights of fancy indeed wonderful at your age!!"

"I think we miss each other more every day that we grow older," Emily wrote in 1853, when Austin was at the Harvard Law School, "for we're all unlike most everyone, and are therefore more dependent on each other for delight." Speaking of the Newman cousins whom her father (to add to his burdens) had just taken under his wing, she wrote Austin: "The Newmans seem very pleasant, but they are not *like us*. What makes a few of us so different from others? It's a question I often ask myself." And the few were very few indeed. Even Lavinia, according to Joseph Lyman, was not "inside the ring." Until Austin married and moved into the house next door (he was twenty-seven then and Emily twenty-five), he seems to have been her chief support, as her girl friends, like Jane Hitchcock, Abby Wood, Jane Humphrey, and Sophia Holland, married, or left town, or died. Her troubled relations with Susan Gilbert, to whom Austin became engaged in 1853, will concern us later.

Austin had the usual Amherst schooling (which meant, of course,

Amherst Academy) until his thirteenth year, when his father sent him to boarding school at Williston Seminary (now Williston Academy).[7] He was there for the term April–August 1842, and again for the year 1844–45. It was during the latter period, apparently, that he formed his warm friendship with Joseph Lyman, the distant cousin from Chester. They both were entered in the classical course for that year. In 1846 Austin entered Amherst College and, unlike his father, went through the full four-year course, graduating Phi Beta Kappa in the class of 1850.[8] He was a Commencement speaker, sharing that honor with his two close friends, George Howland and George Gould, frequent visitors at the Dickinson house and special friends of his sisters. The topic of his address (the title alone survives) was "Elements of Our National Literature," a long stretch from the post-Revolutionary fervor of Samuel Fowler's oration at Dartmouth, and an indication perhaps of the kind of subject that occupied these young people at least some of the time in their conversation. Since Emily shared his interest—she kept a sharp eye on literary developments and often shared books with him—she probably heard his speech.

Whether it was his literary inclinations or his loyalty to his grandfather's and father's concern for education, Austin tried teaching after graduation, first in Sunderland, a village ten miles north of Amherst, for a few months and subsequently in Boston for about a year (1851–52). The periods of teaching were interspersed with several months of reading law in his father's office (between Thanksgiving 1850 and June 1851). That he tried teaching again after such exposure to his father's training and influence is fairly good evidence of his ability to get out from under his father's wing when he wanted to. But he was not a born teacher: the routine bored him, and the problem of discipline irked him. From Sunderland he wrote to Susan Gilbert a characteristically unenthusiastic note, with a touch of Dickinson homesickness and an indication, perhaps, of why he stayed out of politics:

> Of a dozen compositions to decipher and correct – of an hour or two a day spent in declamation – of a colloquy on my hands to prepare for exhibi-

7. He was sent there, Edward writes Austin on April 14, 1842, "to improve." His solicitude about his son's education is impressive and specific: "I want to have you improve in writing, as much as you can – If Mr. Wright thinks it best for you to study English Grammar, or Arithmetic, you may do it. I think you had better spend the most of your time, in studying Caesar. I want to have you very particular to be thorough in every thing you study – It is not much matter how little you go over, if you understand it well – learn all about every word you study.

"Take pains to read distinctly – and give every little word its full sound – and the correct emphasis" (*YH* I, 74). Emily and Lavinia were probably getting the same advice, or would when they were ready for it. (Emily, clearly, took it to heart.) Austin became a good Latinist. On the program of the Spring Exhibition of Amherst College, April 18, 1848, appears the following: "1. Translation. From Longinus on the Sublime. Austin Dickinson, Amherst" (*YH* I, 142).

8. At the Commencement three years later (August 11, 1853) Austin was awarded the degree of Master of Arts.

tion – of all the hard sums brought to me for solution – of the time occupied with scholars and others, who call at my room to interrogate me on literary and scientific points – of my being a whig and having to appear in the bar-room every day or two to answer to the *Free Soilers* for all the sins of omission as well as commission, of the whole whig party –

Just think of these and a thousand nameless little things which conspire to fill up the out-of-school hours. . . . But three weeks more and I am returned to my father's house – Three weeks to night and another of those gladdest, those saddest of all the days of the year to me – Another Thanksgiving is over –

From his teaching post in Boston, a few months later, the news was not much better, to judge from Emily's letters of commiseration and encouragement—with some concern for the Irish children (then flooding the Boston schools) who had incurred Austin's wrath. "Father remarks quite briefly," she wrote, "that he 'thinks they have found their master,' mother bites her lips, and fears you 'will be *rash* with them' and Vinnie and I say masses for poor Irish boys souls." Austin was happy neither in his work nor in his new surroundings. Both sisters urged him to be more sociable, to see more people, and warned him against loneliness. "I wish you'd go into society a little more Austin," wrote Lavinia, "t'would be better & happier for you I know. Just try it & see." Emily urged him to see more of his friend Edmund Converse, whom he had recently brought home for a visit:

Now Austin – you have no friend there – why not see Converse often, and laugh and talk with *him?* I think him a noble fellow – it seems to me so pleasant for you to talk with somebody, and he is much like you in many thoughts and feelings. I know he would love to have you for a comrade and friend, and I would be with him a good deal if I were you.

She also urged him not to deny himself new girl friends in Boston out of loyalty to those at home (clearly, by this time, the Gilbert sisters, Susan and Martha):

I am glad you like Miss Nichols, it must be so pleasant for you to have somebody to care for, in such a cheerless place – dont shut yourself away from anyone whom you like, in order to keep the faith to those you leave behind! . . . On the contrary, Austin, I am very sure that seclusion from everyone there would make an ascetic of you, rather than restore you brighter and truer to *them.*

This was fine advice (and a bit ironical, coming from the "Queen Recluse" herself), but it was unavailing. He seems never to have been happy in Boston. In July 1852 he came home, his teaching days over. In early March 1853, after another stretch of reading law in his father's office, he entered Harvard Law School. Graduating in July 1854, he accepted his father's offer of a partnership and practiced law in Amherst the rest of his life.

Exactly when Austin's buoyant youth clouded over, it is hard to say. His unhappiness in Boston was partly homesickness, surely; partly the loneliness that Emily and Lavinia warned him against; partly his tendency, sharpened by loneliness, to brood and worry. For one thing, he was in the wrong profession. His gestures at schoolteaching were obviously a mistake—and perhaps a bit below the current level of Dickinson dignity. There is no sign that any of his family encouraged him, and Emily herself took a skeptical view. Once, urging him to come home from Sunderland for the annual Cattle Show, she wrote: "School masters and Monkeys half price." She never could see why he wanted to waste his time on "those useless boys." But admitting his mistake could not have been easy for one of his pride. When he finally fixed on the law as a career, the question of moving away from Amherst was a real and perplexing one. Like many other young people of the time, he felt the impulse to go west, and a few months after graduating from law school he went to Chicago to explore possibilities. By this time he was engaged to Susan Gilbert, who apparently would have relished the move. That he decided against it has been attributed most often to the influence of his father, who added to the partnership an offer of a fine new house next the Homestead for him and Susan.[9]

9. In his decision to stay in Amherst (according to Millicent Todd Bingham), Austin followed "the course his father had charted" (*Home*, p. 255). Throughout, Mrs. Bingham makes much of Edward's authoritarian nature, especially in the home, where "no one openly opposed his decisions" (p. 3). She finds "traces of command" (p. 410) even in Edward's last letters to his son; in short, Austin stayed in Amherst because his father wanted him to. More recently, in Cody, *After Great Pain*, p. 19, Austin is said to have "capitulated" to his father after "teetering on the verge of emancipation." Perhaps. But there were many other reasons, and it is clear that Austin was perfectly free to move had he so desired. In the spring of 1854, he wrote his fiancée, Susan Gilbert, "I shall keep it in mind – & wait the result of my trip West, and a plain frank talk with father – & then perhaps, *perhaps* a little variation from the present plan –" (*YH* I, 305). That fall he spent a full month in Chicago. Susan, ambitious, eager, and certainly not rooted in Amherst, would have offered no objection to moving west. But Austin was a New Englander, an Amherst boy, a Dickinson. He had been homesick even in Sunderland. Later, on another trip west, he was repelled by what he saw and couldn't wait to get back to Amherst. There was much more than the strong will of his father operating in his decision to make his career in Amherst. On November 27, 1851, Austin wrote Susan: "I love this Thanksgiving day – Sue – it is so truly New England in its spirit – I love New England & New England customs & New England institutions for I remember our fathers loved them and that it was they who founded & gave them to us –" (*YH* I, 226). So, if in the "plain frank talk" Austin had with his father, Edward's wishes prevailed, it must be remembered that many of Austin's basic wishes went the same way. Sue, perhaps a little disappointedly, described the decision to her brothers (*YH* I, 332; mid-May ? 1855):

Austin's plans are now definite, as he is writing you – tho' they have resulted very differently from our previously formed expectations, we are both happy in them, and hope they may strike you as pleasantly – Austin's Father has overruled all objections to our remaining here and tho' it has been something of a sacrifice for Austin's spirit and rather of a struggle with his pre-conceived ideas, I feel

While his father's offers undoubtedly influenced Austin's decision, there were other factors, and Emily may have been one of them. It may be too much to say that he depended on her in these early years as he certainly did later, but there are hints that it came close to that. On the most superficial level, a young man of his tastes and talents might have hesitated to leave behind so fascinating a sister for what seemed to him the cultural wastes of the Midwest. But there were deeper levels. Emily's long, newsy letters to him during his teaching and law-school years show a constant concern for his morale: "Take care of yourself, Austin, and dont get melancholy." " 'Let not your heart be troubled' – . . . believe also in me!" "And Austin, dont you care about anything else that troubles you – It isn't anything – It is too slight, too small, to make you worry so." Austin was perfectly frank about his own tendency to brood and worry. Once, ill and home from Sunderland (which in retrospect looked better to him), he described his dark mood to Susan Gilbert, whom he had by then (December 1850) begun actively to court:

> My last week's indisposition, and consequent seclusion brought back to me my old companion Reflection – whose presence had not obscured the brightness of my course for ten weeks – He yet tarries with me – and his children, The Blues – who ever accompany their Father, frisk about me – to my exceeding discomfort and gloom. . . . While in Sunderland, my mind was engrossed in matters of business, exciting and agreeable [by] nature, and to be at once transferred from scenes of activity and health and enjoyment, to the lonely, cold, dark, dismal, north room, whose four blank, meaningless walls have shut me from the world for the most of the last eight days, with memory, officious to remind of all done amiss in the Past – with Imagination, ready to predict the Future – and severe Physical Pain to render tedious the Present. . . .

But there is little to indicate that Susan, at least in these early years and perhaps never, was much of a help to him in his moods. She had many fine qualities, but her nature was hardly *sympathique*. Even in this letter, Austin complained, "I never *did*, and don't *now think*, we understand one another." And Austin's need for understanding was great. Emily sensed this and gave him what she could. If he stayed in Amherst partly for her, it has been suggested (such was the bond between them) that the reverse might have been true:

> To know Emily's brother as well as her father is to understand much of her own behavior. For it was her life work "to make everything

---

satisfied that in the end it will be best and he will be fully rewarded for his filial regard – He goes into partnership on even terms with his Father, the first of June – Earlier (*YH* I, 312, August 13, 1854), when her hopes were up, she had written her brother Dwight: "You may like to know that Austin is going to Chicago early in the Fall with a view to settling there – How would you like to dine with me there some fine day in about a year –"

pleasant for father and Austin," as she said, and when Austin's life turned to tragedy, his suffering forged yet another link in the chain which held her fast at home.

It was not until some years later that Austin's life could be said to have "turned to tragedy," and there were many other reasons why Emily stayed at home. But Austin was right (in this letter to Susan) in his gloomy imaginings about the future. The course of his courtship of Susan was anything but smooth and the degree of understanding between them at best erratic. It is clear that his parents could help him only in practical matters, like a job and a house. During these early years, he was a confused young man, emotionally, intellectually, spiritually. His courtship letters to Susan, and a notable one of the same period to her sister Martha, show him in torment and ecstasy—but mostly in confusion.

For all the "Miss Nicholses" he met in Boston or might have met in Sunderland or Cambridge, no one seems to have attracted him outside the Amherst circle; and the two to whom he was most attached from college days on were the "Gilbert Twins," as they were called, although Martha was a year (or more) older.[10] Both girls were born in Greenfield, Massachusetts, where their father kept a hostelry. In 1832 the family moved to Amherst, where for the next five years Mr. Gilbert ran the Mansion House, a tavern and livery stable not far from the Dickinson Homestead. Mr. Gilbert's reputation was not high—"his convivial habits were well known"—but there is no clear indication that the girls suffered any embarrassment in the town from their origins. At any rate, they were cut off from any parental influence, good or bad, when they were orphaned in their early teens. Their mother died in 1837, and their father in 1841. Following their mother's death, they lived for several years with an aunt in Geneva, New York, dividing their time, after 1832, between Geneva and Amherst, where they lived with their married sister, Harriet Gilbert Cutler. Both attended Utica Female Seminary, and in Amherst Susan went to Amherst Academy for a term (at least) in the fall of 1847, which was Emily's first at Mount Holyoke.[11] Susan joined the First Church in 1850, went to Baltimore to teach school in the fall of 1851, and returned to Amherst permanently the following summer, much to the delight of Emily, who by that time thought of her as her dearest friend. Emily seemed delighted, too, with the growing intimacy between Susan and Austin, who became engaged the next spring (1853). They were married in Geneva on July 1, 1856. Next year, in Amherst, Martha

10. Records differ about the date of Martha's birth. The dates on her tombstone in Geneva, New York, have her born on April 13, 1827, whereas the Greenfield church records say 1829 (*Home*, p. 496). Mrs. Bingham and Jay Leyda (*YH* I, xlviii) accept the former, Thomas Johnson and Theodora Ward the latter (*L* III, 954).

11. Records conflict (again) about the goings and comings of the Gilbert sisters during the decade of the 1840s. I have pieced together what seems most likely from *YH* I, xlviii–xlix; *L* III, 939; and *Home*, p. 110.

Commencement daguerreotype, 1850         About 1854, as law student ( ? )

Daguerreotype, about 1856

AUSTIN AS A YOUNG MAN

Susan Gilbert

Martha Gilbert

"THE GILBERT TWINS"
ABOUT 1851

married John Williams Smith and went to Geneva to live, where Smith was in the dry-goods business.

The Gilbert sisters, though close enough to be called twins, were very different. Whether, in Austin's mind, it ever came down to a choice between the two cannot be said; probably not; but even at the height of his courtship of Susan, his letters to Martha were warm and loving and remarkably frank. That, of the two, he married Susan, and *why* (provided, at this distance, motives on such delicate matters can be ascertained), is of the utmost importance. In the light of what happened, it seems to have been a tragic mistake for all concerned, including Emily. It would be nice to say that, after her first flush of enthusiasm for Sue, she tried to dissuade him, but there is no evidence that she did. The best that can be said for both Austin and Emily is that the rest of the family (with the possible exception of Lavinia) warmly approved of the match. Edward, he who had been so prudent and careful in his own choice of a wife, was especially delighted. Susan made herself one of his favorites. Her background may not have been up to Dickinson level, but she was handsome, bright, and ambitious, one of the acknowledged leaders of the younger set. When she got the catch of the town, there was general applause.

Apparently none of their intimates foresaw difficulties.[12] But in what survives of Austin's turbulent courtship letters (or rather drafts), signs of trouble ahead are unmistakable. The letters are so different in every way from the reasoned discourse and restrained affection of Edward's to Emily Norcross as to stand almost as a paradigm of a new era and a new sensibility. No wonder there was so little communication between the generations in the Dickinson home—they lived in different worlds. It is as if, in thirty-odd years, New England youth had swung from the Age of Reason, with its outward thrust and its concern for the Amelioration of Man, to the most intense kind of romantic introspection. We see Austin embarked upon his own "Campaign inscrutable," groping (especially in the letter to Martha) in the darkness of self-doubt and cosmic questioning and, in the drafts of his letters to Susan, baffled by the extremes of his own emotional nature and trying to fathom and to find rest—it seems in vain—in hers.

It is best to start with Austin's letter to Martha, to whom he entrusted a more sustained, and more composed, bit of self-analysis than anything that survives in the drafts to Susan. With Martha he was less tense, less on edge; her nature was more serene and sympathetic than her sister's. "Mat is very shy," Emily wrote Austin in May 1852, during his schoolteaching in Boston. "She was going to send you some flowers in a box, the other

12. I have found record of only one misgiving: Mrs. Harriet Cutler's. In the drafts of Austin's letters to Sue there are several references to sister Harriet's watchful eye. At one point, he writes: "Does Mrs. Cutler ever [suggest?] her fears now Sue, that 'you & Austin will have a falling out by & by – & then if you ever do it will be an awful one' – Does she ever hint any suspicions – or look knowing?"

day, but you had'nt answered her letter, so you see why you did'nt get them." A few months earlier, when Austin had sent her a bracelet, her "sweet face grew radiant [Emily wrote] and joyful that blue eye." Always Martha seems the gentle and submissive one, with Susan more forthright and self-possessed. Their brother-in-law, Samuel Learned, contrasted them about this time: Martha, he said, "may not be quite as handsome or as brilliant but is just as good a girl." Martha had flowers for Austin when he left for Boston, and one of his first letters home was to her. Though Emily surely encouraged Austin's relationship with Susan, even to the point of what she called "clandestiny," she repeatedly wrote him how much Martha inquired about him, missed him, and looked forward to his return. She wrote him once about a long soulful talk with Martha, when they both wept together. Apparently, at least in these early years, she would have welcomed either girl as a sister-in-law.

Austin's first letters to Martha from Boston are warm and affectionate, full of thanks for her attentions and for the memories of happy times they'd had together. Then, in the spring of 1852 (May 11), after a miserable winter, came a long, introspective letter, perhaps the most revealing we have from his formative years. He is entirely clear about his purpose—to give Martha "a tolerably fair idea of me . . . a glance, *only* a glance, at my inner life," a selection, at least, "of my varied thoughts & feelings & experiences, and hopes & fears. . . ." It is in no way a love letter, simply the outpouring of a troubled mind to a receptive listener. It is worth pausing over in some detail for the light it throws on the problems that beset these young people, especially on Emily's problems (at age twenty-one)—the kind of thing, perhaps, she and Austin discussed in those long talks when "the just" were asleep. On such matters, mostly religious and philosophical, she *could* be of help to him. She had done a good deal of pondering herself.

There is a lot of Emily in the letter, her problems and her tone, the sense of bafflement, the search for identity. There are the same extremes of mood, the light and dark, the ecstasy and despair, the heaven and the hell in the heart, that run through many of her poems and letters. After a brief preliminary, Austin begins:

My moods are so changing from day to day (& sometimes even from hour to hour) and with them my views of all about me. . . . For the shadows of life, with me, are so constantly changing from light to dark, from dark to light, sometimes as bright as bright can be, & at others, dark as a starless night, sometimes full of only lights of beauty & sounds of joy, & fragrant perfume, and every delightful sensation, and I feel the warmest, kindliest sympathy with all mankind, and can imagine then how no one can be *less* than happy in this world of such beauty & grandeur, nor how a heaven can be more perfect than the one that fills my own heart. And, at *others,* as entirely cheerless—no scenes meet my eye, but those of sorrow & misery, no tales, but of woe, my ears, and not the faintest glimmer from the faintest star of Hope, to encourage, or bec[k]on to a Future of promise.

It was only a few days later that Emily wrote Austin of the "long, sad talk" she'd had with Martha (obviously occasioned by this letter) "about Sue and Michigan, and Life, and our own future, and Mattie cried and I cried," among other things, surely, about Austin's unhappiness.

In the next paragraph Austin goes deeper, and again there is a good deal of Emily in what he says, the sense of bewilderment, jostle, even the "frightened child" pose:

> Sometimes its [Life's] end [is] clear as light, & its manifold duties & relations, and, at others, all an awful, bewildering mystery. I startle in broad day, like a frightened child from sleep, as if I had just woke for the first time, to consciousness of my existence & the world around me, and wonder where I am, & *what,* and what my destiny, and the meaning of all this bustle & parade I see, and this jostling and crowding of all these ten thousand men, in every respect like myself, this way & that, and all these signs of *power* impressed on all around.

Then Austin becomes philosophical, setting his broodings in the context of the mysteries of Time and Space and the Infinite. He is appalled at the paradox of the human mind (here the impact of his scientific studies is clear) that understands so much and yet so little. He stares into "the profound darkness" and contemplates the possibility of "blank nothingness" as the reality of human destiny. Emily knew these same moments,

> With Midnight to the North of Her –
> And Midnight to the South of Her –
> And Maelstrom – in the Sky –        ( #*721, about 1863* )

and brought these same themes to great intensity in her tragic poems years later. Two years before Austin wrote this letter to Martha, Emily, apparently in the midst of some such thoughts, had set her course for the open sea, crying buoyantly to a pious friend, "I love the danger!" Austin here describes himself as "still drifting."

> I feel the presence of that within me, unseen, yet indescribably mighty, that can comprehend worlds & systems of worlds & yet cannot comprehend itself. That with the aid of history, history, not as written in books, but imprinted on the everlasting hills, & deeply imbedded rocks, may last through long ages of a remote past, before Time began, and learn of the lives & changes & ends of races of beings before man was, and yet cannot assure me of a single event of the Future. That can estimate the distances and weights of burning suns, far off in the trackless wastes of space, & yet can find nothing to satisfy its own eager, restless longings for knowledge of itself, & its Infinite author – and I tremble & my brain reels as I think, with all this amazing power, *passing* wonder, and all the susceptibility to pleasure or pain, I am still drifting on I know not whither – I look around me, to see what others are doing, whether *they* too are suffering in the same anxious suspense, or whether it is to me alone Life is a sealed book. Here & there I behold a solitary *one,* groping on in the profound darkness unknowing

whether this course or that will lead him if indeed *any*where, if he may not, with the next step plunge into blank nothingness –

Perhaps all this was frightening to Martha, with her modest capacities and (at least there is no evidence to the contrary) orthodox piety. The specifically religious doubts that he went on to disclose may have been too much for her. Just as Emily in her distaste for creeds and doctrines parted spiritual company with her pious friends, so Austin charted a course that Martha could not follow. Except for the few "solitary gropers" like himself (and Emily?), he wrote:

I see them [mankind] marshalled in mighty hosts, yet under different banners, and marching on to the word of their several leaders, whom they believe, each his own, have received from the Omnipotent himself the true, and *only* true chart of the route to knowledge, to happiness everlasting & to him. And now *new* doubts encompass me, for if *either*, and only *one, which* is *right?* I am besought on the one hand to join one standard & on the other, another – the advocates for the standard of the "Cross" appeal to me in the most solemn manner, as I value quiet from the gloomy doubts & fears within me – as I value perfect peace & perfect happiness through a life eternal, in *God's* name to join them, for so surely as God is God, all the rest are marching on to death & perdition – but when I survey their ranks, and observe their comparative thinness, I hesitate. I ask myself, Is it possible that God, all powerful, all wise, all benevolent, as I must believe him, *could* have created all these millions upon millions of human souls, only to destroy them? That he *could* have revealed himself & his ways to a chosen few, and left the rest to grovel on in utter darkness? I *cannot* believe it. I can only bow & pray, Teach me, O God, what thou wilt have me do, & obedience shall be my highest pleasure.

At this point Austin catches himself, realizing how painful his confession must have been to Martha: "But Mat, what am I writing you? Something I am afraid you will be sorry to read from me." But it would have been worse, he goes on, had he not written thus frankly about himself. He asks her pardon for hurting her but (showing a candor quite like his sister's) not for telling the truth:

And now that you have a glance, *only* a glance, at my inner life, you can appreciate a little the reason for my not liking to write as I should were *I* more settled in my feelings. I despise untruthfulness to friends, and yet I hesitate to do anything that may tend, in the least, to dim their sun-light. –

Austin's next two (and last) letters to Martha are full of questions as to why she never wrote him any more. Perhaps she hesitated to navigate further on these troubled waters. Perhaps, knowing what was going on between Austin and her sister, she decided to bow out.

What seems the real source of the moodiness he described to Martha, and perhaps the occasion of the soul-probing and the cosmic questionings, was not so much his career problems or religious uncertainties as the vicissitudes of his relations with Susan Gilbert. Begun as a pleasant flirtation during the spring of his senior year in college, the romance by this time (spring 1852) was growing in intensity—at least on his side. His moods went up or down according to Susan's attitudes, which sent him into raptures or plunged him into the deepest gloom. Out of the strange jumble of the courtship documents,[13] at least one thing stands out clearly: Austin's extraordinary capacity for feeling. He loved Martha, but with Susan he was in love, passionately, even wildly (a word he used himself). With Sue, there are no long contemplative religious discussions; indeed, a recurrent theme is Sue's distaste for his heterodoxy, and he approached the subject gingerly. Once the early battle-of-the-sexes sparring was over, all is feeling, sentiment, passion, sometimes elevated and calm, sometimes anguished and desperate; and always there is the sense that Austin is reaching out for more than Susan was prepared to give. There are some periods of calm joy when he seems to be sure of her:

> Oh the virtues of love! the vastness of life – How few know anything of it & how solemn a responsibility upon those to whom it has been disclosed –
> Oh Sue, *Sue* – not the pumping of air in and out of the lungs – eating lest the body fall away – sleeping at night from weariness of the flesh – Life Soul Life – I have read of it – I have *felt* it with you – you are the light & you the genial warmth that have made the closed germ within me to expand & send up its tender shoot – & you the sweet influence that is to cherish it to its perfect flower.

In such moods he looks forward to the home they will one day share. "What a dear home ours will be. . . . What a world of things we shall have to say to each other while we are growing old together – Growing old! It hardly seems possible *we can* grow old – at any rate we shall never *feel* old –" Like Ik Marvel's Bachelor, whose *Reveries* was then making the rounds of the younger set, he dreams his enchanted dream of the perfect home, with husband and wife attentive to each other's every need, happy together through thick and thin: "What precious evenings we will have around our fireside Sue, & let the wind blow, & the rain pour – What

13. The letters are in the Dickinson Family Papers (Folder 8) in the Houghton Library, Harvard University. Leyda (*YH*, passim) printed some significant excerpts; Cody was the first to make extended biographical use of them. So far, they are the only source of even an approximately coherent account of this troubled romance from its beginnings about 1850 (Austin apparently destroyed Sue's letters to him). They present problems. Few are dated (although some can be dated fairly precisely from internal evidence), and it seems unlikely that they can ever be arranged in chronological order that will meet general acceptance. They are full of revisions and cancellations and are, in spots, almost illegible. It is impossible to tell how many of the drafts were put in final form and sent. Although they spell, all in all, confusion and turbulence, the course of the affair can be traced with some confidence, if not step by step, and certain major themes recur that illuminate both Austin's problems and probably Emily's. Although Dr. Cody's psychosexual analysis, especially of Austin's moods, often rings true, I do not follow his theory of the Austin-Sue-Emily triangle (brother and sister in love with the same girl) nor of Emily's being crushed when she lost Sue (by then her surrogate mother) to Austin.

care we?"—a thought not far, except in expression, from Emily's own (and famous)

> Wild Nights – Wild Nights!
> Were I with thee
> Wild Nights should be
> Our luxury! . . .                    (#249, about 1861)

He could sentimentalize on the idea of home along with Ik Marvel and Emily at their best:

> A home, Sue! It's too beautiful a word for this world. It means too much – It's an ideal realized by not one in a thousand – for it's not a house & barn & orchard. . . . It is the type & symbol of a heaven promised the followers of him who went about doing good. It is the center & spring of all living. It is the choice blossom of love – the beautiful answering of the dearest dream.

(If Austin is here apostrophizing the home of his boyhood, this is a fine tribute. But in view of what actually happened in the home he and Sue established next door, it is sadly ironic.)

Another effusion shows him again dreaming his dream of perfect love. There is little evidence that Sue shared his feelings with anything like his fervor, and there is a good deal of evidence that she did not. In such moments he seems blissfully unaware of the *other,* so rapt he was in his own inward vision. (In one of his first letters to Sue—one of the few that can be dated fairly accurately and itself a very effusive one—he had woven a poetic fantasy about himself as Narcissus, he who fell in love with his own image.) Like his sister Emily, he was inclined to see in others what he wanted to see.

> I don't know what to say to you, Sue. Maybe I'm brimming full of what I have to have you know. Perhaps your own heart can tell it all. I feel so dreamy, Sue. So strangely, wonderingly dreamy, for I dreamed a dream – a dream of the sweetest, sweetest love – and though I seemed waken the dream went dreaming dreaming on. And the joy of it never ceases – and whether I waken or whether I sleep – and whether the days are real and the sun is really up – or whether only the calm moon is shining in upon my eyelids – and lighting up a fancy of more than earthly beauty I sometimes hardly know. I want you to be glad and happy darling, and hopeful darling. I love you so and want you so to be – and God's and each other's – we'll [trust?] with his love our hopes – and pray if we sleep we may never waken – we sleep so sweetly – and if we waken we may never sleep. . . .

He was like Emily, too, in asking more of others than they wanted to, or could, give. For all his moments of rapture, the prevailing tone of the courtship letters is uncertainty, doubt of Susan's love, and tension that at times seems intolerable. Twice he speaks of his nerves as ready to snap under the strain, even when he most exults in what he thinks to be the certainty of Sue's love. (He has Emily's sense of being able to "wade

Grief – / Whole pools of it," but tipping "drunken" at "the least push of Joy.")

> I am overwhelmed with my emotions.
> I can't write. I haven't slept.
> All the night has a crowd of strange, tumultuous feelings made wild riot in my heart.
> O my God I am worthy of nothing – thou hast granted me everything. I tremble in my very joy. But I thank thee. I thank thee and pray that thou wilt continue thy care over me, support me, calm me for my shattered nerves are ready to snap.
> The excess of my joy is very pain.

"I love you Sue up to the very highest strain my nature can bear," he wrote, " – the least tension would snap my life threads – as brittle glass – more – you could not ask – more man could not give – Love *me*, Sue – *Love* me – for its my life."

His pleading is perhaps sufficient measure of Sue's response. He was troubled by her moods, which ranged from "stately indifference . . . unapproachable dignity . . . rigid formality" (as he described her once, whimsically, in what appears to be an early letter) to the stormy and unpredictable. Here he discusses them composedly:

> You seem to live in a rather tempestuous latitude, where tis a common thing for a bright day to be suddenly overcast with dark clouds – where the conflicts of the various elements are severe, yet unheralded – But do you not, sometimes, endeavor to account for these sudden & fierce storms? You designated the one of Wednesday last an "Equinoctial" – What corresponds in your "inner world" to the sun's crossing the line in [the] material?

(Or, as Emily said years later, "Susan fronts on the Gulf Stream.") But when Sue chides him—often, it would seem, for his religious views and perhaps for his overly aggressive courtship—or when he has doubts about his ability to make her happy or whether she really loves him, he is frantic. Only a week or so after a most rewarding meeting with her at the Revere House Hotel in Boston (the date was March 23, 1853; Austin had just settled in at the Harvard Law School), where amid kisses and confidences they had, it would seem, plighted their troth, he is thrown into despair by an unexpected reversal in one of Sue's letters:

> I read under the sting of these lines that told me that almost within one short week – and while you sat by my side – & pillowed your head upon my bosom & felt my arm around your neck & my lips on your cheek & my heart beating in its great love for you – Even there & then – you were doubting – *doubting* – questioning if after all you had any love for me – while I all unconscious of where your thoughts strayed – was ascribing every not perfect moment to your fatigue from your journey.

He has an impulse to give the whole thing up (the thought struck him several times during the courtship, even toward its end):

[T]hen Sue, the sooner I know it the better – then let us think no more of ever marrying – let our past be only as a dream that is soon forgotten. . . .

The very next evening, he retreats a bit: "I can hardly see to night how I happened to fix so closely upon those few lines"; but another letter from Sue a few days later, this time (it seems) questioning his religious belief, plunged him down again. Why the theological issue should have been so important to Sue raises a question. Though she was never famous for her piety, it may have meant much to her at this stage, only three years after she had joined the church, a step Austin had not taken. (Not to have publicly accepted Christ as one's Savior was to be marked out, even among the younger set.) Or she may simply have been impatient with Austin's spiritual gropings. (Martha met them with silence.) Or she may have used her objections—and her moods—as ways of keeping Austin at bay. It may be unfair to say that she was still playing the Amherst field, but as late as January 1853 she was still writing to Edward Hitchcock, Jr., and Austin mentions a certain "Jim" several times as a rival. And once, in a draft written apparently well after their engagement, he asks, "Does it ever seem to you you could live happier – better – unmarried – or married to some of the many others whose hearts you have unwittingly won?" At any rate, Sue's criticism on this occasion tore him apart:

Your last letter Sue has almost killed me – *Did* you mean all you said? & may I never write you again one word upon that one subject that I hope & feel is only for a time to separate us? till I can write just *your* words will it cast me from you Sue, *now!* Oh why is this. Has God permitted me to set you in my heart & watch you & cherish you there, till you have grown into its very fibre – become a part of it, only then to tear you thence – & leave me mangled, bleeding – dying — Oh Sue – I love you with a love that has almost driven me wild – I have centered everything in you – every hope – every aspiration – I've given you everything I have – all I am – & all I can make myself – & will you forsake me now – will you forsake me for only loving you too much?[14]

14. Sometimes the shoe was on the other foot. In two letters, apparently written fairly late in the courtship (in both there are references to his being in the "office"), Austin apologized profusely for wounding Susan's feelings. Both show signs of strain, not only in the frequent cancellations, illegibilities, and garbled sentences but in the abjectness of Austin's humility as he throws himself at her feet again and again, swears that his intentions were good, begs forgiveness, and vows eternal love. One letter (or draft) concerns a remark of Austin's that Sue had interpreted as "trifling" with her love. She had written him "a beautiful, dear note" forgiving him—to which he replied (in some thousand words) that he never meant it in the first place. He wonders how "for a single instant" it could have crossed her mind "that I could have meant or could have looked the slightest, faintest shadow of ridicule toward you . . . towards you (——?) to you as my life . . . nay, my life itself . . . toward you – so great a gift I tremble while I call you mine . . . No my own Sue, no thought of trifling with anything connected with you ever ventured its shade upon my mind. . . ." He wonders how she could have suspected an attitude toward her who had brought him tenderness for the first time in his life: "Ten-

Apparently, Sue had accused him of willfully refusing conversion (he did not join the church until 1856, six months before they were married).

Will you tell me it is only my *will* keeps me back – & if it is not – will you reproach me for not doing what you tell me of myself I cannot? Do I not believe in God – Do I not bow before the author of my being & do I not acknowledge His power – & worship Him for His goodness! Do I not know my own weakness – my own unworthiness of the many daily blessings of which He is the constant giver – Am I not ready to serve him in whatever He may command & yet am I so wicked Sue – you can't love me? *Am* I as wicked as you say, Sue – Oh I'm sick – I want to go home – I want to see Vinnie & Emily & father & mother & see if they'll notice me – if they will speak to me – if I shall not find the doors of my home closed on me –

Emily (it may be noted), showing a willfulness that worried her friends, *never* joined the church. Had she been aware of this impasse between Austin and Sue, there is no doubt whose side she would have been on. Austin concluded the letter with a burst of self-drama quite like some of Emily's early letters, the kind of thing that, at her best, she not only objectified but brought to new life in her poems. Here, quite explicitly, the clouds are gathering:

---

derness has not been so common a thing to me in the years that I have so far numbered as to have become valueless in my estimation. I have never before received any – from anybody – I never would. [He forgets, or ignores, Martha here, and his sisters.] I wanted to feel it all, in all its deliciousness, all its purity, all its vastly increased exquisiteness – from long fainting for it – I feel it for the first time from her from whom I am to receive all that I ever receive . . . from the only woman of all the world whom I 'could not chose but love'. . . ." No, he concludes, no such "trifling" from that "surpassingly great love that for two long years has so worn & worried me – . . ."

The other letter, shorter but even more frenzied, begins: "And I have made you cry Sue – you whom I have (told I?) (taken to?) love – and who have breathed out your love upon me. . . . Have made you cry – you whose every moment I ought to brighten . . . whose every sorrow to lighten – whose every joy to heighten [he shared this epistolary trick with Emily]. I have made you cry – and I have made you feel alone again in the world. . . ." All of which, of course, was farthest from his thoughts: "Can I have been unkind to you! The subject of all my love [written boldly over canceled "affection"] – and as fond a love as ever filled a man's heart!" The gist of the matter seems to have been the thought he came to next: her failure to understand him. She won't feel these hurts, he seems to be saying, "when you have learnt me as well as I know myself (then / when?) (dear Sue?) you have only fully (finally?) known me –"

For a young man supposedly engaged for some time, these letters show at the very least a precarious uncertainty. They protest too much. What Sue's attitude was can only be conjectured. She must have known how deeply Austin was in love. How could she have suspected him of being willfully unkind or of "trifling" with her affection? How long would it take for her to "know" him? It almost seems as if she had provoked the episodes behind these letters, perhaps to keep him off balance. While Austin seems almost lost in love, Sue could write the Bartletts in Hanover (July 7, 1853), "I have *not* forgotten you my dear friends, neither am I blind or sick or married but hale, single, eyes strong . . ." (*YH* I, 279).

Tell me again you love me Sue, tell me you *will* love me – tell me what love you have for Earth shall be mine – tell me God will bring us together in our religion – Tell me to be calm again – to study, to trust, to pray – tell me you will never leave me – but for God – or my star of hope has set – a blight has overspread my youth and a darkness has overshadowed my morning's Sun – the chill touch of Autumn has come upon me in the "April hour" of my life & the flower of my Spring has faded in its earliest blossoming –

I'm faint when I ought to be strongest & old while I'm yet young. Are you surprised, Sue, to read such a letter from me? Then you have not known how deeply an occasional reproach – an occasional doubting expression has sunk into my heart – then you have not known all the passion that has lain there.

On March 27, 1853, only a few days after the Revere House meeting, when Austin had felt so secure in Sue's love, he drafted a curious letter to Mattie, who had heard from Sue (apparently) about the engagement and had written her congratulations: "Heaven bless you – Mattie [Austin replied] for those kind . . . words that told me you were glad I loved Sue – & she loves me – " And then, strangely, he proceeds to explain their love. One gets the impression that he is explaining it to himself.

It seems strange to me too – does'nt it to you, Mattie – that just such characters should have chosen each other to love, that two so tall, proud, stiff people, so easily miffed, – so apt to be pert, two that could . . . stand under the "oak tree" just at the setting of a glorious Sunday's sun – & speak words – & look, look, so cold, – so bitter, as hardly the deepest hatred could have prompted a pair as would the guiltiest wretch – & his most wronged victim – that two who could love so well, or hate so well – that two just such *could* not choose but love each other! – but we *could not* Mattie –

We have loved each other a *long time* – longer than either has guessed, but we were too proud to confess it – How we at *last* broke down – I hardly know . . . Forgive me now Mattie will you for not writing you before – It is not because I have not thought of you – nor because I do not love you – I *do* love you Mattie – just as well as Emily and Vinnie . . . & you all enter into all Sue's & my plans for the future –

This hardly sounds like the agonizing, pleading, passionate young man of the courtship letters. The love-hate he confesses so frankly to Mattie tells more, perhaps, than he intended. He hardly seems to know his own mind. He may have been posing a bit—presenting himself as he would like Mattie to see him, "tall," "proud," giving in to love only because he had to. (Emily enjoyed this self-drama in her correspondence, often bafflingly.)

The question is, did he talk or write to Emily this way? and how much did she know about the ebb and flow of his feelings during this turbulent period? Her letters to him stay mostly on the surface of things, with only occasional warnings against melancholy and loneliness. But when he told Sue he wanted to come home to "Vinnie & Emily & father & mother," it is fairly safe to say, from what we know about the other three, that Emily was the one he wanted to talk to.

If we can trust the evidence of several letters to her brothers, Susan approached the marriage coolly and unromantically. Her attitude was eminently practical. After her unsettled youth she wanted a home of her own, and she was confident that Austin could provide one. She asked her brother Francis, "Why don't you write to me Frank and congratulate me, that I have found some one who is going, by and by, to encumber himself with me?" She thought he would like Austin: "I see no reason, viewing the subject as I try to, without prejudice why you won't like Austin and find in him all you could desire in the companion of your sister –" He is "poor and young," she wrote, "and in the *world's* eyes these are great weaknesses – but he is strong, manly, resolute – understands human nature and will take care of me –" Although she admitted that he had not yet decided where he would settle in business, she was sure that they would "have a cozy place some-where, where the long-cherished wish of my heart to have a home where my brothers and sisters can come, will be realized." Either she still failed to understand Austin or she was putting up a bold and somewhat false face to her brothers. At age twenty-five, son of one of Amherst's leading citizens, with a fine education, including a law degree, he could hardly be called "poor and young." On the other hand, how could Sue, knowing his painful indecision about a career, his spiritual bewilderments and emotional insecurity, have called him "strong, manly, resolute"? Perhaps she, too, was posing a bit.

In September 1854 Susan wrote to her brother Dwight that "Austin *now* expects our marriage to take place the following Fall" but, she added, "all earthly plans are so *mutable*." Though one of the reasons for putting off the marriage was a practical one—the completion of the new house—the fact is that by the time they were married (July 1, 1856) they had been engaged for three years. As dates were shifted and plans changed, the whole affair began to seem unreal to Sue. She wrote Dwight in this same letter: "I have always felt so like a *child* the idea of really being married seems absurd enough and if the event ever occurs I think I shall experience a feeling of odd surprise." With no proper home of her own, she hesitated about where to have the wedding, Amherst or Geneva. Only a few weeks before the wedding, she finally decided on Geneva and her Aunt Sophia (Mrs. William Van Vranken), but only "after mature deliberation on my part – a balancing of the gains & losses &c &c"—so she wrote to the Reverend Samuel Bartlett and his wife (Samuel Learned's sister) of Manchester, New Hampshire, formerly of Amherst, who had shown special interest in the Gilbert girls. Mr. Bartlett (later president of Dartmouth College) had been her choice to perform the ceremony—and to perform it in Amherst. She told the Bartletts that her aunt "through the Winter has been besieging me to come to her house to be married. . . . The decision made great shaking among the old plans, and thawing of fancy's frost-works, but for reasons I cannot explain, both for prudence and prolixity, it was advisable." What the word "prudence" concealed, we may never know precisely. But tensions were developing on several fronts. If Sue was thought by her contemporaries to be a little cool and calculating, it was because—given her ambition—her background and precarious home situation demanded these qualities. The rest of her letter to the Bartletts shows her at her ingenious best, patching things up with them and taking a pleasantly nonchalant attitude toward the whole affair.

No Mr Bartlett to marry me – or Mrs Bartlett for guest – strange hands to tie the silken knot, and some strange eyes to look on the tying – so I have said good-bye to some of the sweet old plans and pretend to believe the new ones are best – Yes my dear friends I am to be married the fourth week in June if God so wills and after a little jaunting, by way of matrimonial preface to return to Amherst to the new house Austin is building as fast as possible – I shall have a quiet wedding – a very few friends and my brothers & sisters a little cake – a little ice-cream and it is all over – the millionth wedding since the world began –

The wedding took place on July 1, the ceremony being performed by Professor Haven of Amherst. Apparently none of Austin's family made the trip to Geneva. On July 6 Austin made a curiously uncharacteristic request of a friend in New York, Gordon Ford: "May I ask if you will do me the kindness to see to the notice of my marriage in the New York 'Tribune' & 'Times.'" Both papers carried notices of the wedding in their issues of July 9. In both, Austin's bride is listed as "Miss Susan H. Gilbert, of Geneva." Why Sue's lifelong association with Amherst, much of it in residence, was thus slighted is not known. She was an "Amherst girl," like Emily.

By the middle of the month the two were settled in the new house— the Evergreens—next the Homestead. This was a fateful proximity, as it turned out. But all Amherst seemed pleased. Jane Hitchcock, the president's daughter, wrote a friend in September of the "beautiful new house" Austin and Sue moved into. Indeed, the Dickinson houses (she wrote) were "now quite as attractive" as any in Amherst.

With Austin and Sue established next door and little need for letters between the Homestead and the Evergreens, contemporary evidence is scant for a coherent, step-by-step account of the marriage. It was not until a full twenty-five years later, with the advent of Mabel Loomis Todd, that Austin unburdened himself; or, if he had confided in anybody before then (how he could have kept his troubles a secret from Emily is hard to see), no one recorded his confidences. Like his father, he grew more taciturn as he grew older. Until Mrs. Todd entered his life, there were no such outpourings as in the letter to Martha or the impassioned drafts to Sue. That strange late romance in his life, and what we can piece together of Susan's part in the marriage and its bearing on her long relationship with Emily, are reserved for later chapters.

Susan Gilbert Dickinson

The Evergreens

"THE OTHER HOUSE" AND ITS MISTRESS

Amherst, about 1875. The Dickinson Homestead in center, just above the word "Main"; the Evergreens to the left, across Main Street; hat factories in foreground

But, first, a look at the externals of Austin's career, since it is important, with these introverted Dickinsons, to be reminded that they lived busy, active lives—including Emily, in her own way. We may begin with one general comment: as with both his grandfather and his father, Austin's public success—his steadily growing stature in the affairs of town, church, and college—was in ironic contrast to his personal frustrations and private tragedy. Such a situation, repeated in the three generations, seems almost to have been a Dickinson pattern. Emily shared in it, and escaped it—again, in her own way.

Austin's story is one of increasing burdens and responsibilities, both domestic and professional. Domestically, his and Sue's life was complicated by the arrival in 1858 of the orphaned Newman sisters, Clara and Anna, who were to spend the next ten years with them in the Evergreens. The arrangement was not entirely harmonious. But the girls were useful, especially when Sue's first child, Ned, was born in 1861 and her second, Martha, five years later—sufficiently so that when Clara married in 1869 and Anna went to live with her, a family friend wrote acidly: "So Marm D—— will have to wait on her own children – "

Socially, Sue set up a lively establishment. The Evergreens, rather than the Homestead, became the center of attraction. When Emerson spoke in Amherst in 1857, he was entertained by the Austin Dickinsons, an event of which Sue has left a rapturous record.[15] Emily was a frequent visitor during the first few years after Austin and Sue were married and in 1859 felt that they were all she wanted of society: she called them "my crowd." This happy state did not last long, however. Sue's temperament, tastes, and social ambition created an atmosphere in which the Dickinson qualities, at least Austin's and Emily's—given more to the creative and speculative, and requiring solitude—found less and less sustenance.

There is no doubt about Sue's success in what she set out to do. She became the chief hostess of Commencement Week; Samuel Bowles, who regularly reported the festivities in the *Springfield Republican,* wrote her after the Commencement of 1877: "You & Judge Spofford & Dr. [Edward] Hitchcock [Jr.] won the honors of the week – You ought to have a de-

15. Emerson's first lecture was on December 16, 1857. His topic was "The Beautiful in Rural Life." The *Hampshire and Franklin Express* (in an article that helps explain Aunt Elisabeth's satiric stanzas to Austin about Transcendentalism) said in its issue of December 18: "Ralph Waldo Emerson's lecture greatly disappointed all who listened. It was in the English language instead of the Emersonese in which he usually clothes his thoughts, and the thoughts themselves were such as any plain common-sense person could understand and appreciate" (*YH* I, 351). Sue wrote in "Annals of the Evergreens" (see Appendix I): "I remember very little of the lecture except a fine glow of enthusiasm on my own part. . . . I felt strangely elated to take his transcendental arm afterward and walk leisurely home. . . . he was our guest at the time." It is not clear where he stayed on his next visit to Amherst, when he gave a course of six lectures (October 1865) on "Social Aims" (*YH* I, 351; II, 102), perhaps with the Lucius Boltwoods. (Mrs. Boltwood, his cousin, was frequently his hostess on his Hampshire County lecture trips.)

gree." There are many tributes to her social leadership, perhaps the most famous being from Professor John Burgess, who graduated from Amherst in 1867 and taught there from 1873 to 1876:

The society of Amherst . . . was, though limited, really charming in its simplicity, geniality, and intellectuality. In my day there were six chief social rendezvous in Amherst: the Austin Dickinsons', the Mathers', the Clark Seelyes', the Tuckermans', the Joneses', and the Stearns'. The social leader of the town was Mrs. Austin Dickinson, a really brilliant and highly cultivated woman of great taste and refinement, perhaps a little too aggressive, a little too sharp in wit and repartee, and a little too ambitious for social prestige, but, withal, a woman of the world in the best sense, having a very keen and correct appreciation of what was fine and admirable. Her imagination was exceedingly vivid, sometimes so vivid that it got away with her and she confounded its pictures with objective things. If she had had sufficient application, she would have rivaled Cervantes as a writer of romance and adventure. . . . Here at commencement time were to be met the élite of alumni: Henry Ward Beecher, Richard Salter Storrs, Frederic D. Huntington, Alexander H. Bullock, Edward B. Gillett, John E. Sanford, and the like. . . .

Mrs. Dickinson was, I suppose, by descent a Puritan, but she was not much of a Puritan in her mentality. She was decidedly aristocratic in her tastes, and her friends among the alumni were generally scions of the best American families or men who had distinguished themselves highly.

This confirms what Mabel Todd found to be true of her in the early 1880s: "the most of a real society person here," as she described her in a letter home. But for Austin, not only was Sue's "salon"—the teas, the musicales, the dancing parties (oyster stew at ten)—expensive, and for this reason alone a burden, but the whole affair rang increasingly hollow. In his diary for these later years, he spoke often of "Sue and her crowd" and absented himself frequently from their functions. He spent more and more time in the Homestead. "We almost forget," Emily wrote in 1883, "that he ever passed to a wedded Home."

What sustained Austin, besides Emily and the retreat the Homestead offered, was his absorption in his work, his hobbies (his paintings, his fine horses), and especially his love of nature as displayed in the Amherst countryside. This last deserves a special word. The beauties and mysteries of nature had been opened up for him in his boyhood by Professor Hitchcock [Sr.], whose lectures and writings influenced several generations of young people in Amherst, Emily most surely among them. The inciting event that led Austin for nearly a half century to incorporate some of this natural beauty into his beloved town was a series of lectures Hitchcock gave in 1850 after a five-month tour of Europe, during which he was particularly impressed with shade trees and shrubs in the continental cities and towns. One of the major steps in Austin's campaign to beautify Amherst came in 1874 with the draining and planting of the village common, still the handsomest feature of the town. During his tenure as treasurer of the college from 1873 until his death, it was his peculiar pleasure to see to the landscaping of the college grounds and especially the several buildings whose construction he supervised. His delight in nature was an enthusiasm that Emily, of course, understood and shared, and it became one of the strongest bonds between him and Mabel Todd. Sue's interests, apparently, went in quite different directions.

The list of Austin's civic projects and responsibilities reads much like his father's. He moderated the town meetings from 1881 to the time of his death. He was president of the Village Improvement Association. In 1874 he drafted the articles of incorporation for the Amherst Library Association and served on its board. He was on the board of Amherst Academy, the Amherst Savings Bank, the First National Bank of Amherst, the Amherst Water Company, and the Amherst Gas Light Company. He helped found Wildwood Cemetery and directed the laying out of its grounds. One of his most notable contributions to the community was his part in promoting and supervising the construction of a new building for the First Church in 1867–68. He was at his best in the task of uniting the congregation behind the project and then in the practical problems of the construction itself. There is a legend that Emily "crept out one evening with her brother as far as a certain tree in the hedge in order to see the new church," perhaps a measure of how reclusive she had become by that time—even toward an affair in which her family was deeply involved. Her father gave the dedicatory speech (on September 23, 1868) to an audience "filled to overflowing with the worthy people of Amherst."

All this, plus his law practice, his duties as treasurer, and the management of a difficult family which, after Edward Dickinson died in 1874, included the three next door—Emily, Vinnie, and (until 1882) their invalid mother—stretched Austin's endurance to the breaking point. Mabel Todd teased him about being the indispensable man in Amherst. "I suppose nobody in the town could be born or married or buried, or make an investment, or buy a house-lot, or a cemetary-lot or sell a newspaper, or build a house, or choose a profession, without you close at hand." But it was no joke; Austin had earlier written her: "I am crowded with work and can with difficulty keep abreast of the demands upon me. I seem to be too convenient for too many people, in too many ways." He once remarked to Mrs. Todd: "I have a very expensive family." Austin seriously overtaxed his strength, and it was generally agreed that his final illness was brought on by exhaustion.

In this crowded life, the early literary inclinations Austin shared at least to some extent with Emily never flourished. He was interested enough in the epistolary style of both his sisters to comment in an older-brotherly way. He knew, certainly, that Emily wrote poetry; but there is no sure evidence that he was aware of its quality. His sense of what he was to call her "genius" came late, probably stimulated by Mabel Todd's influence. At one point, apparently during the very week of his engagement to Sue, he sent Emily some of his verse. Emily's reply, dated March 27, 1853, hailed him as "Brother Pegasus" and teased him properly in a letter that shows their relationship at its sprightliest. He must have sent a considerable sample of his work to have evoked such a response, though Emily gives no hint of its substance. (Her last sentence, it is to be noted, shows that she had begun thinking of herself as a poet well before this episode.) After some preliminary fooling, she writes:

> And Austin is a Poet, Austin writes a psalm. Out of the way, Pegasus, Olympus enough "to him," and just say to those "nine muses" that we have done with them!
> Raised a living muse ourselves, worth the whole nine of them. Up, off, tramp!
> Now Brother Pegasus, I'll tell you what it is – I've been in the habit *myself* of writing some few things, and it rather appears to me that you're getting away my patent, so you'd better be somewhat careful, or I'll call the police!

Only one scrap of what has been called, perhaps too charitably, "a tentatively light poem" of Austin's has survived. It was sent to Sue (visiting in Grand Rapids) on October 19, 1882:

> Oil is no name for it,
> Peace is not
> Quiet is not – nor
> Rest.
> Serene doesnt ma[t]ch(?) to it,
> Tranquil doesnt.

(A postscript adds: "All and more but feebly convey the ineffable – The utterly utter dumbness and smoothness of life on the magical Terrace since Tuesday.")

Although Austin's one publication—his address at the one hundred and fiftieth anniversary of the First Church in 1889—was strictly local, written in the line of duty, it is worth notice, like anything from a Dickinson pen so near Emily's. The topic was a large one, certainly for the twenty minutes he was given on the program and for the short time he was given (he complained) to prepare. But when "Representative Men of the Parish, Church Buildings and Finances" was published next year by the press of the *Amherst Record* in a volume containing the proceedings of the occasion, it came to a full 7,500 words and obviously had involved research and careful composition. It contains indispensable background material for all Amherst—and for all Dickinsons.

There is little of the "Pegasus" in the essay and not much to suggest that he was the brother of a poet. The writing is hardheaded, forthright and firm, sure in its command of fact. The most striking family resemblance is a kind of wry humor toward the past and its dignitaries, reminiscent of Emily's (and Vinnie's) occasional reverent irreverence toward holy things. There is an occasional turn, also, to metaphor. The passage on the third meeting house (1829)—"The First Church in Amherst was built in the years 1867-8. . . . Before that we had meeting-houses and went to meeting"—has the tone and design of some of Emily's satiric letters:

> It was a substantial structure, is still, and may have fulfilled the hope and purpose of the building committee; though architecturally it could hardly have been thought an inspiration even then, and the discussions were many among the students as to the age and order which it represented. It was more commonly classed as Tuscan, that being the most elementary described in the books; but by some to be back of books – ancient Egyptian. This was the claim of Tutor March of the class of 1845, while one of the French professors in the early days pronounced it the Eighth Astonishment.

Austin made pleasant fun of the various stages by which the "meeting house" developed into the "church": the introduction of pews ("every man was buttoned tight in"); stoves ("As I remember them they stood within this circular wall, the pipes running the whole length of the side aisles directly over the centre, entering the chimneys at the west end, with tin troughs underneath to catch the creosote which dropped from the joints"); horse sheds, which came in 1838; a bell in 1839 ("Down to 1862 this bell rang at noon and at 9 in the evening as notice for dining and retiring"); and, also in 1839 (an event which made a lasting impression on Austin and, if on him, surely on Emily), the purchase of the double bass viol, "the first musical instrument ever owned by the parish."

> With my first recollection Josiah Ayres managed it, and the tones he drew from its lower chords in his accompaniment to the singing of some of Watts' Favorite Hymns, haunt me even now. Such lines as

> > "That awful day will surely come,
> > That last great day of woe and doom,"

> and

> > "Broad is the road that leads to death," etc.,

> seemed to me sufficiently depressing in plain print; sung with the accompaniment, they were appalling – to a boy.

In 1854 a movement was started among the young people to replace the bass viol with an organ ("a small second-hand" one). Austin reports:

> There was a great deal of doubt about this: there was a suggestion of Rome and Episcopacy in this instrument not brought up by the double bass viol,

but some of the young people were very urgent, and it was decided to let it be tried.

"Things were running now on rather a high key," Austin resumes; and in 1857, when there was a proposal to raise seventy-five dollars for four kerosene chandeliers, the liberals had a rough time of it. The "hunkers," as he calls them, asserted themselves.

> This [the chandeliers] was too much, a step too far for those who held religion rather as a matter for the practice of fine economy. They said it portended the theatre: they thought – as some of us believed – it would add to the burden of maintaining public worship; and threats of signing off were loud if the unsanctity were persisted in: the air was thick; there was concern on the part of the movers in the project and hesitation, but somehow the breakers were cleared and the chandeliers hung.

Once the parish recovered from the "shock of this innovation," things proceeded quietly until 1864, when the matter of the new building, often brought up in meeting but successfully quashed, would not down. Finally, after "numberless meetings" about plans and sites, the new church became an accomplished fact—"not without effort, not without opposition, not without sacrifice."

And here Austin embarks on a series of sketches of the leading men of the parish, past and present, to whom the First Church stood as a monument. He pays tribute to all those "strong and earnest men" who had been prominent in Amherst from the beginning, "when town and parish were the same": "The Bakers, Boltwoods, Clarks, Churches, Cowles, Dickinsons, Eastmans, Hawleys, Kelloggs, Montagues, Smiths, Strongs"; and others, "unrepresented among us now," the "Chaunceys, Colemans, Fields, Ingrams, Nashes, Porters, Warners"—an Amherst honor roll. The style in which he describes them is strong and earnest, like the men. We have already seen his tribute to his grandfather, Squire Fowler. Coming down the generations to his father, Austin shows the same bold Dickinson front to the world, excluding for public purposes all that was warm and personal, or amusing. Here again is the "River God," standing perpendicular in the community:

> Edward Dickinson, proud of being of Amherst soil, of the sixth generation born within sound of the old meeting-house bell, all earnest, God-fearing men, doing their part in their day toward the evolution of the Amherst we live in; in the front from earliest manhood, prompt with tongue, pen, time, money for anything promising its advancement, leading every forward movement, moral or material, in parish and town; holding many positions of trust and responsibility, never doubted, the soul of integrity and honor, fearless for the right, shirking no duty, and dying at his post as representative of his district in the Massachusetts Legislature where, in his seventy-second year, he had gone to help in shaping legislation proposed affecting the interests of the Central railroad.

First Congregational Church, erected 1867–8. Construction and landscaping supervised by Austin Dickinson

Rev. Aaron Merrick Colton, pastor
of the First Church, 1840–53

Rev. Jonathan Leavitt Jenkins, pasto
of the First Church, 1867–77

Dr. Timothy Gridley, physician
Austin: "strange, queer, eccentric, fascinating"

Deacon David Mack
Austin: "I thought I had seen God

Austin's sketches of other Amherst notables gain in humor and immediacy the farther he moves from his family. One of the town worthies, William Cutler, was "naturally slow and cautious, more apt to see objections than advantages – the course of events never quite to his mind – finding much to condemn, little to approve outside Daniel Webster and the old Whig party." Sidney Adams was "amiable, seeing only the sunny side, useless in a tempest, but using a good oar in smooth water." Dr. Timothy J. Gridley, the Amherst physician of Austin's and Emily's youth (he died in 1852), was one of the town's leading eccentrics:

> . . . that strange, queer, eccentric, fascinating man; doctor, politician; hated, admired, distrusted, believed to carry life in his hand; apparently not knowing day from night, that Sunday came the same day every time, his own house from another's; who wouldn't go straight if he could go across; regular only in being irregular; a most picturesque character.

And finally (his masterpiece) a tribute to Deacon David Mack, who with his family had lived in the west side of the Homestead during Austin's and Emily's childhood:

> . . . a man to command attention anywhere, tall, erect, of powerful build, with a fine head finely set, clear, exact, just, a believer in law and penalty for its breach; strong as a lion, pure as a saint, simple as a child, a Puritan of the Puritans: I remember my first sight of him – I was four years old – I thought I had seen God.

His review of the heroes of the parish leads Austin to some melancholy thoughts: "Has manhood gained?" he asks. "We cannot fail to perceive that we are counting fewer and fewer in numbers of the kind of men that save cities." The small country towns are being drained of those "independent, strong characters – men of mark – who used to be scattered over our hills." They have heard the call and have gone to the cities to join in "the struggle for wealth and power and fame – a struggle as fierce and desperate as the struggle of battle." Amherst and towns like it, he warned, must look to themselves.

Austin concludes on a curious, apologetic note, explainable in part by the chivalry demanded of the occasion but also perhaps by a fact of his biography. For all his qualities as leader and as spokesman for the parish, the color and texture of his later life was determined by women. After his father's death in 1874 the Dickinson enclave was dominated by females, and he felt himself more and more enmeshed. "Women," he wrote a friend, "you may or may not know, are very unreasonable, and very unmanageable, at times, and a man had better stand from under, if he can, and as far as he can." In the light of such a remark, his tribute to the women of the parish becomes all the more ironic:

> But the women count in our modern census. They have appeared above the surface in the last generation, and become a power, nowhere more than

in parish affairs, where they have found a congenial field for their activities and displayed them to good advantage. We no longer go home and tell them what we have done at parish meeting; they tell us what they have done at the sewing society. They are hardly longer the power behind the throne; they are a good part of the throne itself.

It is not quite easy for a masculine man to admit all this; but if he will live in the country, he might as well – and thank God for salvation even so.

As we shall see shortly, the situation in Austin's private life in 1889 (the year of the address) was such that there could hardly have been a person in the audience who would not have perceived the irony. But there is still another, and final, irony to be perceived in his address, also of unhappy implications.

Although Austin touches upon his grandfather's and father's service in the Massachusetts Legislature—that is, their part in affairs *outside* Amherst—it is curious that he omits his father's term in the House of Representatives in Washington, the high-water mark of Dickinson public achievement. The purely local aspect of his own career would have become, by contrast, all the more obvious, and he may have wanted to play it down. A document recently come to light shows him quite conscious of his provincialism and, for so dedicated an Amherst man, curiously frustrated by the limitations of small-town life. This, in spite of the fact that since young manhood he seems to have been ill at ease away from home—in Sunderland, Boston, and Cambridge. He could have settled in Chicago as a young lawyer, but he did not. He traveled infrequently, and seldom for the sake of traveling—his scorn of people going hither and yon was like Emily's (and Thoreau's). Although, when he became treasurer, he went often to Boston and New York in the service of the college, there is record of only one extended trip made for its own sake, a six-week journey to the West and South with his friend, John Sanford, in 1887. He got to New Orleans and as far west as St. Louis. His letters home (the only ones we have are to Mabel Todd) complain of almost everything: the noise, confusion, discomfort, people. One of his remarks sounds like a shaft from Emily herself: "I wouldn't give a volume of Emerson for all the hogs west of the Mississippi." In short, to this complete New Englander, one might think that success in his beloved Amherst would have been enough. But a draft of a letter to a friend in Omaha, dated August 8, 1893, shows him thinking quite different thoughts. While his domestic troubles may have eroded by then whatever joy he took in his work for the town and the college, his discontent apparently went deeper. However much, in his church address, he may have lamented the departure of so many good men to the cities to join in "the struggle for wealth and power and fame," he apparently wished he had gone, too. The letter shows the frustration in which he lived, the sense of unused talents and energies that might have carried him far in a larger community. One interesting fact also emerges: he attributed these same longings to his father.

*William Austin Dickinson*

Amherst, Mass.
August 8th, 1893.
[Hon James Clark]
DEAR SIR

I have received yours of 3rd inst – and again carefully considered your several propositions for my joining you in Omaha.

I have thought more than ever in the last six months of trying to get away from Amherst, where so many unpleasant animosities surround me, and I am strongly inclined to feel that, with the opening you offer to make for me, now is the time and Omaha the place.

It would ordinarily be thought a little late to pull up old and put down new stakes – at sixty, but according to Depew, Vanderbilt made the larger part of his fortune after he was seventy, and I have always held that it is never to[o] late to attempt the right thing. Besides[,] the lines you lay out for me – while in accordance with my general training and experience are even more congenial to me than what I have been accustomed to, and on those I should see more men – men of the world and affairs, which I greatly miss here, as my father did before me. The same lack which drove our mutual friend Gibbs from Norwich [?] to New York.

Unless then something which I do not now foresee occurs to prevent, I think I will plan to come out about the 21st, look the matter all over on the ground, and decide then. I will have my business here in such shape that I can leave by that time.

[P.S.]
Of course you will say nothing about this anywhere at present.

The "unpleasant animosities" mentioned in the second paragraph and the secrecy enjoined in the postscript are part of the story of his involvement, then nearing a crisis, with Mabel Loomis Todd. It is possible that these animosities may have soured his attitude toward Amherst only temporarily; but the letter throws a sad light over his whole career. Emily could have understood this, too. Like her father and brother, she too at one time had her eye on a larger world than Amherst. All three knew frustration of this sort.

Externally, save for what in the Mabel Todd affair became public knowledge, Austin's life during its final few years was more of the same, the endless duties of any pillar of a small-town community. Looking back over his life—from the famous "hurra" of his boyhood, through the passion of his romance, to the intense dedication to his work—one is struck, perhaps chiefly, by his enormous vitality. The years of his relations with Mabel Todd reveal but a late manifestation of it, remarkable in a man half his age. Though not explaining, it enables us to approach with less surprise the miracle of his sister's extraordinary creative power.

Another fact of Austin's character and experience makes a similar trait in Emily more understandable—his response to the phenomenon of death when it struck close to him. Emily's poems and letters are full of the shock of death and its mystery, sometimes to the point of obsession. Each

[ *123*

death seemed to her, as it apparently did to him, unprecedented, over-whelming, unfathomable. It was as if, each time, the old, grueling questions were opened all over again; each time she had to "regulate" her faith. And Austin had, at least once, to cling to his very life.

Although Austin has left little in writing, we have record of at least four occasions when his reactions were noted by others: the death of his friend Frazar Stearns, son of the president of Amherst College, in the Battle of Newbern (N.C.) in 1862; the death of his father in 1874; his beloved son Gilbert's death, at the age of eight, in 1883; and Emily's in 1886. These experiences appear to have been almost equally shattering. After Frazar's death, even Emily was distressed by Austin's behavior. (Perhaps there was a sense of guilt involved; he had paid for a substitute, while Frazar had joined up.) She described him as "stunned completely," and wrote to their friend Samuel Bowles:

> Austin is chilled – by Frazer's murder – He says – his Brain keeps saying over "Frazer is killed" – "Frazer is killed," just as Father told it – to Him. Two or three words of lead – that dropped so deep, they keep weighing – Tell Austin – how to get over them!

After his father's death he was similarly undone, about as little use to the family and their close friends as was Emily, who hid away upstairs. (It was Vinnie who bore the brunt.) Austin, wrote a friend, "is apparently the most shocked, stunned by the loss of his father." When Gilbert died, two close witnesses feared for Austin's life. Vinnie wrote some friends in Newport, "Of course you knew little Gilbert has disappeared & Emily & I have had hard work to keep Austin from following him –" Mabel Todd wrote in her diary the day after Gilbert died that Vinnie "says her brother looks like death" and later she wrote of the event in her journal: "Mr. D. nearly died too. Gilbert was his idol, and the only thing in his house which truly loved him, or in which he took any pleasure." It was weeks before he was himself again.[16] In a sense, Austin never got over Gilbert's

16. Gilbert was not only Austin's idol, and much cherished by Emily; he was already, at age eight, something of an idol of the town's, beloved by all. A striking obituary appeared in the *Amherst Record* for October 17, 1883, some two weeks after his death.

DEATH OF A PROMISING BOY.

Gilbert Dickinson youngest son of Wm. A. Dickinson died on the afternoon of Friday, October 5th, after a very short but severe attack of fever. He was at school on Thursday of the week before. He was only eight years old, and yet we are astonished to find how many Gilbert interested. His frankness and simple-heartedness were charming, but these are the common charms of childhood. There was in him also, a self-reliance, rare in a boy so gentle and sensitive, which seemed, somehow, to lift him into the sphere of men. He became not only interesting but companionable. People not only played with him to see the child-life show itself, but they talked with him for their own pleasure. When the village heard of his death we felt as if one had gone who had established a place for himself among us. We loved him as one in whom the qualities that men "Tie to" were freshened by the dew of childhood. Nor did this lessen his hearty

loss, nor did Emily. It was about this time (autumn 1884) that she wrote, "The Dyings have been too deep for me, and before I could raise my Heart from one, another has come – ." When Emily herself died a year and a half later, the loss was another fearful shock for Austin, even though there had been many premonitions. Mrs. Todd wrote in her diary on May 14 (Emily died the next day) : "He is terribly oppressed." And the entry in his own diary for May 15 speaks for itself:

> It was settled before morning broke that Emily would not wake again this side.
> The day was awful. She ceased to breathe that terrible breathing just before the whistles sounded for six.
> Mrs. Montagu and Mrs. Jameson were sitting with Vin.
> I was nearby.

There is no entry at all for May 16, an unusual blank in the eight volumes of his diary that survive. When he picked it up again on the seventeenth, he was his usual laconic self, "I attending to some necessary things, seeing a number of people, and was at my office an hour in forenoon and a little more than that P.M." What sustained him this time was Mabel Todd, who wrote in her journal for September 1, 1886:

---

enjoyment of all that children delight in. He was a real child only his interests were very broad for such a little fellow. As if by intuition, he found the real stuff of humanity beneath all sorts of garbs and in persons old as well as young. The best in people he brought to the surface, and it met his friendship. His circle of friends therefore was wide and varied. That he liked a person was enough. Whatever others might think of his friends he was loyal always. He liked so many that he took it for granted that people liked him and when he stopped an older person in the street to see him ride his velocipede, it was not because he thought he rode better than other boys but because of a common interest he supposed people had in each other. The richest kind of democracy had taken possession of that little heart. But his affection was not less intense because it was broad. At times he could not bear to see even the picture of one of his little friends who had left town. It must be turned to the wall. And this wide and intense affection found abundant, even delicious expression in his words to those he loved. How this giving of his love evoked a rich return those who received it well understand. He taught how blessed it is to give as well as to receive. Hopes are always buried with children but not often do we lose in the death of so young a boy so much of actual fruition. He not only promised much but he already had provided much.

Or as Emily put it, a year later, in a letter to Sue (*L* III, 842; October 1884):

> Twice, when I had Red Flowers out, Gilbert knocked, raised his sweet Hat, and asked if he might touch them –
> Yes, and take them too, I said, but Chivalry forbade him – Besides, he gathered Hearts, not Flowers –

> > Some Arrows slay but whom they strike –
> > But this slew all *but* him –
> > Who so appareled his Escape –
> > Too trackless for a Tomb –               [#*1565*]
> >                 EMILY –

[ *125*

It [Emily's death] was a very great sorrow to Austin, but I have lived through a greater with him – when poor little Gilbert died. He and I are so *one* that we comfort each other for everything perfectly.

This final remark is a measure of Austin's need in the presence of death. He was well into his maturity when Frazar was killed, a leading figure in Amherst and seemingly all-in-all sufficient by the time his father died, and fifty-four when Gilbert died. And yet, each time he was "stunned." Emily was not the only one in the family for whom the "Dyings were too deep."

One can only speculate about causes. A fearful mother or a father who had made both children overly dependent on him are hardly sufficient explanations. Vinnie apparently escaped such parental influences. One recalls Austin's gropings into "the profound darkness" in his letter to Mattie and the "maelstrom" poems by Emily. "Eternity," she said after her mother died, "sweeps around me like a sea." Or one has recourse simply to the heightened sensitivities of the poet, or the man of poetic nature, and to the imagination which is at once the poet's glory and his curse.

When Austin himself died (August 16, 1895), the Amherst shops were closed during his funeral as they had been during his father's. "The woods and fields and mountains," said the report in the *Springfield Republican* (August 20), "which were so dear to Mr. Dickinson . . . seemed to his mourning friends never more beautiful." The obituary in the *Republican* the day after his death presented the main outlines of his career accurately enough and caught some of the nuances of his character, probably because of the long association of the Bowles family with the Dickinsons (young Samuel had become editor of the paper when his father died). "Amherst Loses a Strong Man," ran the headline, "A Useful and Worthy Life Devoted to Amherst College and Town," and the first sentence called him "the most influential citizen of Amherst."

Much was said in the obituary that might have been expected—tributes to "his tremendous will power" in his final fight for life, to the sacrificial nature of the work that brought on his last illness ("There is no doubt that his death was hastened by overwork, and that by a long rest at the right time he might have been spared for years of usefulness"), to his "universal" service in town affairs, especially his leadership in beautifying Amherst. He "exerted a potent influence with the faculty and the trustees in the administration of the internal affairs of the college" and showed "excellent judgment and fine taste" in his care of its buildings and grounds. It was noted that as a lawyer he "never attained prominence as a practitioner before the courts"; as a speaker "he had not much gift" and tended to avoid court cases. But he was an "excellent" Town Moderator and "he could condense into a sentence what would take others minutes to express"—a point of style shared by another member of his family. Politically, he had "usually acted with the republicans" but latterly had become independent of party politics. Mention was made of his charming home in Amherst, "embowered in trees and surrounded with lovely shrubs and flowers," and of the many prominent men he had entertained there. "He was exceedingly fond of fine pictures and had many of his own. He was also a most appreciative reader of the best literature."

What is most striking about the obituary is its sensitivity to certain shadings in Austin's character amounting, almost, to the same paradox that the *Republican* had found in Edward Dickinson years before: the public vs. the private figure. Such perception could have come only from firsthand observation; one suspects the hand of a Bowles in both documents. Again, it is the strong, austere exterior in contrast to the "real" man within.

> Mr. Dickinson was a strong and forceful personality. He had an open, frank and vigorous way of speaking to and looking out at the world that commanded respect and confidence from the moment that he appeared on any scene. But his nature was all gentleness and refinement, and there were a shyness and reserve in his composition, coupled with an intensity of feeling, that were almost pathetic at times. . . . [He was] best liked by those who knew him best. Many thought him austere in his nature, but with closer intimacy that idea would vanish.

The obituary spoke, too, of his superior abilities that fitted him "to fill a larger sphere," but it missed the sad truth as Austin had put it in the letter of 1893 to his friend in Omaha. The obituary merely said, piously, that he was

> content to devote his life to the local institutions and interests, amid which he had been born and which he loved with a deep and abiding affection. . . . His love for Amherst was so strong he did not care to spend a vacation elsewhere, and he always expressed the satisfaction he had on returning to the town from a trip of even a few days' duration. . . .

So far into the Dickinson interior the eulogist went—but no further—and we are in the presence of those same qualities we have seen developing since Samuel Fowler: the love of Amherst; the sacrificial dedication; the angular exterior ("the face of flint") belying the passion within. A later section, "War between the Houses," will reveal more not only about Austin and Dickinsons in general but about that figure to whom the obituary paid this passing tribute:

> One of his sisters was the late Emily Dickinson, the literary recluse whose singular life and wonderful writings in prose and verse have only recently become known to the world.

# 7

# Lavinia Norcross Dickinson

LAVINIA DICKINSON (1833–1899) outlived all her family, and her comments during later years on the Dickinson scene have done much to clarify, color, and in some important ways distort our view of it. Summing up the inmates of her houshold, she said of Emily that "she had to think – she was the only one of us who had that to do," and added of the others: "Father believed; and mother loved; and Austin had Amherst; and I had the family to keep track of." Of the five, she came closest to the truth about Emily, her mother, and herself. From what we have seen of the family so far, she had Austin and her father the wrong way around. It was Edward Dickinson who "had Amherst"—and the railroad, and the college, and politics. His "belief" seems to have been more of an inherited discipline than a living spiritual experience. It guided him in his duty and set the tone of his public utterances, whether in leading family prayers (a phenomenon which must have impressed Lavinia as it did Emily) or in speaking at the dedication of the new church building. He left no record of any such spiritual anguish as Austin went through. Austin was more of a believer by temperament; at least, he was more expressive about spiritual matters, which is all we have to rely on. He "had Amherst," to be sure, and gave himself to it. But his loyalty to it was more like Emily's than his father's was; he was *in* it but not quite *of* it; his values and style of life were not identical with it, as (so far as we can see) Edward's—and Lavinia's—nearly were.

As an observer, Lavinia was never noted for her profundity; there were things about all her family she missed. If she was right that Emily "had to think," she seems to have been unaware of how much she had to write. At least, the surprise she expressed at finding, when Emily died, such a vast amount of writings tucked away in her room seems to have been genuine. As to her mother, it was to Vinnie's credit that she saw (for all the dark stories she told later about early days in the family) that her mother "loved," even though Vinnie's tenderness toward her came late. And it is to her credit, too, that she saw her own role in the family about right, though in this summary she did not do herself justice. She "kept track" of them, surely, but she was more than the family watchdog or drudge. As Emily's closest associate for more than fifty years, she became indispensable to her in many ways, if not in the same way Austin was. As a personality, she was indispensable to the family's solidarity. And in one final way she was indispensable to posterity. Her complete belief in Emily during her life was transferred to the poems after Emily died. Without that belief, which approached fanaticism, we might never have had them.

The questions will be asked: Who was Lavinia? What did she mean to Emily more than the guardian's role she is usually given? It cannot be insisted too much that, in Emily's limited circle, everyone counted. "Area – ," she once remarked, "no test of depth." To adopt an image from one of her poems, she "measured" people with "narrow, probing, Eyes," and she focused as closely on those nearest her as she did on the new visitor. She measured her father and mother with tender precision. She could make mistakes, and at times she could be impatient with people, especially bores. Sue, for instance, never bored her; but her misjudgment of Sue's future in the family circle shows how far wrong she could be, especially in this instance, about the character and needs of her own brother. It was an early mistake about "depth."

Lavinia, though in many ways the least of these, came under the same scrutiny. Fortunately, she involved Emily in no such problems as the others did. She was not by nature a griever. Though Austin was closer to Emily in temperament and mentality, she turned to Vinnie, the "uncomplicated" Dickinson, for daily living and the long pull. Vinnie functioned most notably in what might be called the comic side of the family drama. She early developed enough spunk and wit to make her a formidable figure even in a family of wits. Emily, older by two years and two months, kept a sisterly eye on her during their youth and, when Vinnie was fifteen, boasted to a friend that she had been "instilling many a lesson of wisdom into the budding intellect of my only sister." But neither the solicitude nor the humor was all one way. A few years later the roles were reversed. Vinnie wrote to Austin:

I think Emilie is very much improved. She has really grown *fat,* if youll believe it.
    I am very strict with her & I shouldnt wonder if she should come out bright some time after all.

There was the usual family bickering. "Emilie tells storys about me," Vinnie complained to Austin. "Dont believe her." She preceded this charge with a few comments on Austin's complaint about her handwriting. She is in fighting trim:

If you cant read my writing, Austin, perhaps twill do no good to say any thing to you. I really dont understand your inability to read what has always been called *plain*. I think you must be growing blind. I would advise you to consult Dr. Reynolds speedily, else secure a pair of Fathers glasses which have proved themselves *"uncommon"*.

(Austin's complaint, incidentally, could justly be leveled by generations of editors and biographers against the whole family, his own handwriting especially. It is sometimes almost indecipherable.)

As the sisters grew older, Emily became dependent on Lavinia in many practical ways, and there is no sign of discord. Emily loved her, respected her abilities, even felt a little humble, perhaps, in the presence of one so well adjusted to the world and confident in it. That she outgrew her was inevitable and no disparagement to Vinnie. But it did mean that above a certain level there was little communication between them. Vinnie was simply unequipped to function on her level.

As one who knew both girls during their formative years, Joseph Lyman sensed this difference, implicit in his remark about Vinnie's not being "inside the ring" as Emily was. She was "very pious and very pretty," and Joseph enjoyed his evenings with her. But it was Emily whom he took seriously. A letter of January 23, 1851, from his classmate, Daniel Bonbright, shows that even then the difference between the girls was common gossip among the young people. Bonbright, speculating on Lyman's activities during a short vacation, writes, "Or it may be, and I think this the more probable supposition, you are in Amherst, playing – what? 'spooney,' I suppose with Vinnie, or sitting up late of nights to talk with Emily, when less spiritual beings, such as watchful parents, are fast asleep."

Austin saw this difference, too, and Lavinia was occasionally miffed by his clear preference for Emily, who once scolded him for his favoritism: "Vinnie says she thinks you dont pay much attention to her." They all put much of the practical matters of the household on Vinnie's shoulders, and even Emily could be a little patronizing. She wrote to Austin that she would leave "all the matter o'fact to our practical sister Vinnie" and reserve for herself the interesting things to write about. Once she complained: "I dont see much of Vinnie – she's mostly dusting stairs!"—and sometimes to her annoyance:

We cleaned house all last week – that is to say – Mother and Vinnie did, and I scolded, because they moved my things – I cant find much left anywhere, that I used to wear, or know of. You will easily conclude that I am surrounded by trial.

In this situation, as the only other daughter, Vinnie understood and accepted her role. But she sometimes wrote about it plaintively, as in her apology, when she was nineteen, to Austin for filling her letters with matters of business: "the folks make me do all the errands, else I should sometimes say some thing different." That she was capable of something different soon became clear. A little later, Austin spoke of a letter from her that surprised him: it was "more beautiful," he wrote to Sue, "than I supposed she *could* write." Emily never gave her full credit; even in later years, she summed her up too quickly as "happy with her duties, her pussies, and her posies."

But Vinnie had talents and a style of her own, and Emily was aware of them. Beyond some minor flaws, the relationship between the sisters was warm and vital. Once Emily did the personal side of it full justice in a late letter to a friend who had just lost his brother. In these later years she recognized not only her indebtedness to Vinnie as a protectress—by then Vinnie had become her "Soldier and Angel" carrying "a 'drawn Sword' in behalf of Eden"—but she paid tribute to a quality not often remarked in Vinnie: "Your bond to your brother reminds me of mine to my sister – early, earnest, indissoluble. Without her life were fear, and Paradise a cowardice, except for her inciting voice."

It would be interesting to know precisely what Emily meant by "her inciting voice." She may have had in mind what I have called Vinnie's style, a quality of bearing and attitude as well as her manner of expressing herself. It is clear from Vinnie's letters, from her witty sayings that have come down to us, and from descriptions of her by her contemporaries, that she *had* a style and that it was pungent, racy, very much her own. These qualities were noted in a eulogy of her that appeared, shortly after her death, in the *Springfield Republican,* by a friend of her later years, Professor Joseph Chickering of Amherst:

> I suppose people called her peculiar, a favorite term in the vocabulary of mediocrity. To me she was unique, rather than peculiar. She never said things as other people said them. I think she abhorred the commonplace in speech almost more than the vulgar. . . . Her views of life were those of an onlooker, not a participator in the affairs of men, and they were at once shrewd and amusing to a remarkable degree. Her conversational and literary gifts would have been more highly appreciated and more widely known, but for the extraordinary powers of her famous sister.

It is clear from Emily's many comments that her pleasure in Vinnie's style was important in her life. What the Dickinson family needed for its day-to-day health and good spirits was a leaven, someone to offset its tendency toward introspection and brooding. Father never played, and Mother, so the tradition runs, was more solicitous about the dust on the piano than about the music it could make. Emily complained that when Austin was away, there was no fun any more; and when he "went East," as she described his marrying, all she had left for daily fare was Vinnie and that inciting voice.

What is impressive about Vinnie, certainly in her youth and until the 1880s and 1890s, when her involvement in the trouble emanating from the Evergreens made her devious and bitter, is her forthrightness. It is the basis of her style as a conversationalist and correspondent. She was the most outgoing and the least inhibited in the household. As a girl, she was not only pretty, she was "pert." Emily, writing to Austin, saw her at eighteen as growing *"perter* and *more* pert day by day," a word that in her lexicon meant not only "lively, brisk, smart," but "forward, saucy, bold, indecorously free." She had wit and a talent for mimicry. According to Jane Hitchcock, her roommate at Ipswich Female Seminary, it was she who made life bearable at school. In a letter to Austin, Jane all but despaired over the stuffiness of the Seminary:

> Now such things would crush me, and take away every bit of spirit and life I ever had, and I should become a blue-stocking, or book-worm, were it not for your dear sister Vinnie. . . . Vinnie writes all the funny letters that go from this room. . . . Fortunately she still retains her ability to "take off" people. You have seen her, enough to know how well she does it. I assure you it is a real comfort. And now and then we have a good laugh together.

Several years later, during her visit with her father at the Willard Hotel in Washington in 1854, Vinnie was just as successful before a larger audience, sufficiently so to be commented on many years later, again by Professor Chickering:

> [Lavinia] was a clever raconteur, and when in Washington during her father's term in Congress, was quite the center of a little circle at Willard's, who were refreshed by her unique wit and impersonations.

Vinnie often used her talent to refresh the members of her family, conversationally and in her letters, and this may be part of what Emily meant by her inciting voice.[1] For her brother Austin, drudging away in Boston at his schoolteaching, she embellished her report of some pleasant Amherst news with a description of the complaints of a certain Mrs. James. She had Emily's excellent ear for the idiom and rhythm of local speech.

> There was a pleasant little gathering at Tempe [Linnell]'s, Friday eve, Martha [Gilbert] is better, Mrs "James' lungs are all tied up in a knout & she haint got nothin to hitch her breath on to & her vitals are struck." This is a true statement Austin, the poor lady really thinks she does suffer & "if it had'nt a been for [Dr.] Gridley she'd a went," that time.

Her letters have color and pace. Her forthrightness, whether naïve or calculated, is the most refreshing thing about them. She never wasted words, or minced them. In a family that went in for the slant, or oblique, approach, Vinnie's attack was direct and frontal. About a picture she had just had taken, she wrote to Austin:

> I will send you my picture, but I dont like it at all & should be sorry to have you or any one else think I look just like it. I dont think my real face is quite so stupid as the picture, perhaps I'm mistaken however.

1. For Vinnie's style, conversational and epistolary, for her reading and her (limited) prowess as a poet, see Appendix I.

A little later, sending Austin some mail, she enclosed a scatter-shot note that covers in fourteen abrupt sentences subjects that would have kept her brother and sister, at that time in their discursive period, busy for many pages. She marches swiftly through such important matters as Austin's neglect of his friend and her sweetheart, Joseph Lyman; the state of her health and her sanity; news of Father, Sue, and Emily, and of "that pretty cousin Lizzie" and her approaching wedding:

> These documents came last night & I opened Joseph's thinking there might be some thing for me in it. I guess you won't care. You *must* write to Joseph. I think he feels badly that you dont. I've recovered from my head-ache. Father is coming this noon. It's dreadful lonely with out you Austin. Sue spent yesterday afternoon here. I've been thinking lately how easily I could become *insane*. Sometimes I feel as though I should be. Emilie & I had cards from Mr White, too. I am tired of receiving wedding cards, they come from some where, every day, that pretty cousin Lizzie sent me hers Monday. Now Austin, write to Joseph right off.
>      Write to us when you can.
>
> > > > > > Good bye.
> > > > > > V<small>INNIE</small>

Vinnie cultivated the staccato pace. An earlier note exceeds even the one above and ends with a flourish.

> Martha is sick. Emilene is sick too. Mrs Nash goes there often. Mr. Godfrey is visiting New York now. Thompson was here last week. I. F. Conkey has a new span of the blacks, rides out &c. Jane is at home. Kate will be married soon. Weather cold, corn high. Metaphysics clear, other things to match, Sir.

In 1852, when she wrote these letters, Vinnie was nineteen and at something of a crisis in her life. Joseph Lyman was in the deep South and (it seemed to Vinnie) losing interest in his Northern friends, including her. Only a few months before, she recorded in her diary,[2] "Received offer of *marriage*," presumably from "Tutor [William] Howland," mentioned twice in the same brief entry. But that, too, came to nothing. And, although Lyman wrote his mother as late as 1855 that he still had serious intentions toward Lavinia, he was a long way off, and Austin was doing nothing to help her, by way either of brotherly advice or of intercession. No wonder she felt frustrated by the steady flow of wedding cards. If her thoughts of insanity have more to do with Dickinson rhetoric than with Dickinson neurosis—Emily's similar thoughts were sheltered in her poems—they show that she too knew what pressure was and sensed a breaking point, even at this buoyant age.

Vinnie's way of coping with it, however mildly it burdened her, was through activity, seemingly ceaseless and mostly non-intellectual. She was the permanent "head of the committee on arrangements," the planner and doer about the house. Domestically, Emily was kept busy with her plants

2. Vinnie's tiny line-a-day diary, now in the Dickinson Papers, Houghton Library, covers only the year 1851 and a few days of 1852.

and flowers, her cooking and sewing and tending her mother's frequent illnesses. The prickly part of housekeeping was left to Lavinia, to whom the family and the house and the garden (Emily called it "Vinnie's sainted Garden") became a vocation. At twenty she was already beginning to take over: "I feel unusually hurried just now," she wrote to Austin, "so many plans suggest themselves to my mind for improving the house & grounds." Emily later warned their less robust cousin, Frances Norcross, against trying to keep up to such a pace: "I fear you are getting as driven as Vinnie. We consider her standard for superhuman effort erroneously applied." And still later she described Vinnie's harried life to Mrs. Holland: "Vinnie is under terrific headway, but finds time to remember you with vivid affection"; and to young Ned, vacationing in the Adirondacks: "Vinnie is still subsoiling, but lays down her Spade to caress you."

If Emily's rhetoric is a little patronizing, she never underestimated Vinnie's usefulness to the family and to herself, no little of which lay in Vinnie's being what she was, a phenomenon, remarkable in her own way in a remarkable family. The whimsey does not preclude real admiration:

> Vinnie is far more hurried than Presidential Candidates [she wrote Mrs. Holland during the election year of 1880] – I trust in more distinguished ways, for *they* have only the care of the Union, but Vinnie the Universe –

Next year, complaining about some little contretemps in the house, Emily concluded her letter by urging the Norcross cousins not to worry, either about herself or about Vinnie, who "was only sighing in fun":

> Vinnie [is] spectacular as Disraeli and sincere as Gladstone. . . . When she sighs in earnest, Emily's throne will tremble . . . [but, as of now] Vinnie "still prevails."

Before Vinnie began "prevailing," she led a gay social life, probably the most active of the three children. She had many affairs of the heart. At what point she ceased being the pert, popular figure in Amherst circles and gave herself up to her "duties, her pussies, and her posies" cannot be determined any more precisely than Emily's withdrawal. Both girls drifted into their eventual ways of life gradually, although Emily sensed her vocation earlier and made a much more complete withdrawal. Vinnie was an inveterate caller to the end, went on trips, and made long out-of-town visits until she was well into middle age. A letter to Joseph Lyman congratulating him on his engagement to Laura Baker in 1856 showed that at that time she was still entertaining thoughts of getting married, and when she wondered in 1853 what their father would do "when *we* are *all* gone," she apparently thought that Emily would get married, too. She eventually said of Emily's withdrawal that it "was only a happen," springing from family circumstances. It was more than this, of course, but there was a good deal of happen in it; and there may have been even more in Vinnie's own ultimate way of life, into which she settled only after several doors were closed to her, perhaps by Howland, certainly by Lyman, and presumably by several others. Whether in some instances she herself closed the doors, it is hard to tell. Her letter to Lyman on his engagement gives the impression that she still held the initiative, but she may simply have been maintaining a bold front. She was nearly twenty-four, and she had her pride:

> You asked me who I will marry, Joseph. I wish I knew. I have some dear friends. I have promised to decide *the* question before winter is all gone. Perhaps I may give them all up. I shall always love to hear from you, Joseph, & trust you will be *good* & prosperous. God bless you! Joseph,
>
> Good bye
> VINNIE

The affair with Joseph Lyman, by far the best documented of all the youthful Dickinson romances, tells us most about Vinnie; and since Joseph was an intimate friend of both girls, and often compared them, it reveals much about Emily as well. The story begins with the friendship of Joseph and Austin at nearby Williston Seminary, where Joseph had gone to school from his home in Chester, Massachusetts, some forty miles west of Amherst. The two boys roomed together, and Joseph paid an extended visit at the Dickinson home in the mid-1840s. (Edward Dickinson, in a gesture of thoughtfulness not usually considered characteristic of him, suggested the visit so that Austin could have a friend to keep him company during a term he had to be at home.) We know from Joseph's accounts that he enjoyed himself hugely, especially the family conversation. It was then that he found the Dickinson household "that charming second home of mine in Amherst," and later prized his friendship with the Dickinsons above all others. During his long visit Joseph became fond of Vinnie and began the "spooney" in which, according to his descriptions, she distinguished herself by quite un-Dickinsonian behavior. He never forgot her kisses, which he was fond of describing in the language of his favorite poem, *Maud,* as " 'sweeter, sweeter than anything on Earth.' " On both the first and later visits during his college years at Yale, he had long talks with Emily, helped her with her German, and joined the family and their Amherst friends in festivities like the annual sugaring-off parties.

One of these, during his last spring in New England, he later described in nostalgic detail to his fiancée, Laura Baker. Here, too, Vinnie distinguished herself as anything but shy. She was in love with him and wanted to display her love for all to see. But he was on the point of leaving Amherst and New England, and his own mind was far from made up about Vinnie. He recorded, for Laura's benefit, a snatch of their conversation on that last afternoon. When it came time to go home in the carriages, Vinnie begged him to ride with her. He held back. Vinnie came to him, took his hand, and said:

'O Joseph I havn't seen much of you today. Howell has been with me all the afternoon but I would so much rather have been with you.' I say 'My dear Vinnie, I thought it best under the circumstances not to pay you very marked attention before all these people. I would avoid every thing like gossip.' Vinnie loq. 'I know Joseph, but I love you, and I'm proud of you and of your love – I want people to know that you love me – come, Joseph, they are all going to the carriages. Let me take your arm and we will sit together in the carriage. – O Joseph *must* you go tomorrow!'

To Vinnie's sorrow, New England (and Yale, from which he had graduated in 1850) had made him restless. His farewell to Vinnie that day turned out to be for good. He left a few weeks later for the West and South. Vinnie wrote in her diary on March 26, 1851:

Letter from E.[liza] Coleman [Joseph's cousin]. Walked with Joseph. Now he is gone! Attended meeting, made calls, visited John Sanford, met Storrs there. Had maple Sugar. Joseph has gone, two years is a long time!

As Joseph later wrote to Laura, "Poor little soft-lipped Vinnie Dickinson."
The next stage in the story began in 1856. Lyman was in New Orleans, a rising young lawyer and engaged to Laura Baker, of Nashville, the two having met during Lyman's sojourn there on his way south. In the many and voluminous letters he wrote Laura between then and their marriage in 1858, he told her all about himself, his past, his present, his aims. He harked back frequently to his wonderful New England youth, not so much to his boyhood in Chester, or his years at Yale, but mostly to his memories of Amherst, particularly the Dickinson girls. Of all the girls he ever knew (and by that time his list was formidable), they understood him best. Of all his friends and many relatives in New England (in Chester, Amherst, Pittsfield, New Haven), it was they he wanted most to see again. As the story of his affair with Vinnie unfolds, with frequent references to the household in general and to Emily, some of our stock notions about the town, the family, and the girls are reversed, or at least heavily qualified. From hot and steaming New Orleans, Amherst seemed like a lost paradise to Joseph. He remembered the Dickinson house (it was the one on Pleasant Street that he had visited) as set in a "garden of roses." Far from being a prison dominated by an ogre father, he remembered the Dickinson home as one of freedom, love, gaiety, and good talk. We hear nothing about the depressing presence of parents; indeed, they seem tactfully to have retired, evenings, to leave the field open for the young. We see Emily as the good housekeeper—and Vinnie scarcely deigning to soil "her little fat hands." Indeed, Vinnie, not Emily, seems the delicate and protected one, unequipped for the "central strenuous life" that Lyman had chosen for himself.
The differences between the girls develop sharply in the course of Joseph's comments to Laura—Emily "inside the ring," Vinnie not; Emily platonic and intellectual, Vinnie warm and pliant. Perhaps by way of rationalizing his none-too-gentle rejection of Vinnie, he played her down

Lavinia Norcross Dickinson, about 1852

Joseph Bardwell Lyman, about 1850

The North Pleasant Street house occupied by the Dickinsons 1840–55
Lyman: ". . . my charming second home in Amherst"

a little heartlessly in the letters to Laura. She was "gentle" and affectionate (in this respect he several times held her up to Laura as a model), but she was otherwise not only unimpressive but had "radical defects":

I was very happy once in Vinnies arms – very happy. She sat in my lap and pulled the pins from her long soft chestnut hair and tied the long silken mass around my neck and kissed me again & again. She was always at my side clinging to my arm and used to have a little red ottoman that she brought & placed close by my chair and laid her book across my lap when she read. Her skin was very soft. Her arms were fat & white and I was very, very happy with her. But that was all. Vinnie hasn't brains at all superior. She is a proud, wilful, selfish girl. The only thing she wanted was to have me with her that she might be happy. She never forgot herself. She viewed everybody and every plan only as it might affect her happiness. All this in a quiet lady like way – "for Nelly was a Lady" but none of her blandishments could keep my calm impartial intellect from seeing all those radical defects of character. I never thought she would make me a good wife.

His "calm impartial intellect" may have told him at this point that she would not make him a good wife, but for a period of several years he had serious thoughts of marrying her. If not, he told his mother a downright lie, for he had twice within a year been very explicit. On May 23, 1854, he wrote his mother:

You ask me about my Amherst attachment. It is all right. Vinnie loves me and I love Vinnie and mean to marry her God willing – God and her old folks – and I have reason to think they do not object very much.

And again on February 12, 1855:

Vinnie Dickinson continues to love me very truly and writes me beautiful letters from Washington where she now is staying with her Father. She is a Christian girl and begs me to be very good. I think her parents object to her coming South but Vinnie declares that she can never love anybody else and I think I shall go on and marry her some of these summers if we live.

Joseph's meeting Laura and another remarkable girl, Araminta Wharton, in Nashville during 1856 apparently altered his perspective on Vinnie, whose stock steadily declined from then on. "Vinnie was not very noble or accomplished," he wrote Laura. "She could hardly be called 'a woman of superior merit.'" But no sooner had he written this than he was lost in memories of the little red ottoman and of Vinnie's "beauty . . . grace & gentleness," of "the simple unalloyed happiness of those sunny hours," the "beauty & purity & grace & gentleness that we may dream of but rarely see under the sun."

As Vinnie loses favor, Emily gains. Although Vinnie provided the romantic idyl in his life, it was Emily he admired. She saw the ambition in him and was aware, as Vinnie was not, that he was destined for a greater world than Amherst and that he even then was eager to be on his way. Emily had conveyed her impression to Lyman in a figure he later passed on to Laura:

Emily Dickinson, who by the bye was the most appreciative lady friend I ever had till you, in those years of late boyhood when she knew me used to say of me that I seemed ever to carry an arrow in my hand so distinctly and persistently did my whole nature point to what was before me.

Several times he associated Emily with Araminta Wharton, "one of those [as he described her to Laura] to whom God gave a white soul, and she, beside that natural endowment is in the number of those who have been made perfect through suffering." He asked Laura's permission to continue to write, after their engagement, to "such friends as our sweet Mintie and to Emily Dickinson"—not, be it noted, Vinnie. He enclosed a blue slip on which he had written the famous verses from Revelation (III: 4-5) which may have some bearing on Emily's later habit of wearing white:

. . . and they shall walk with me in white: for they are worthy.

*He that overcometh* the same shall be clothed in white raiment; and I will not blot out his name out of the book of Life. . . .

It is possible that even then Lyman thought of both Emily and Araminta as in the "white company" of those born pure and made perfect through suffering, although Emily's suffering was surely not from physical causes like Mintie's, who died of tuberculosis when she was twenty-seven. This spiritual quality—however achieved, and something he never found in Vinnie—is the theme of his most significant comparison of Emily and Mintie:

My friendships for Emily Dickinson & Mintie Wharton are much alike. They are both noble women – neither one of them will probably ever marry tho' both would make most true & devoted wives while they lived and both are deeply imbued with the essential spirit of the New Testament and of our Lord & Savior Jesus Christ.

His last glimpse of Emily had been during the morning of the sugaring-off party in March 1851, when he had said goodbye to Vinnie. He "had been with Emily a good deal." It is worth noting that even this early—Emily was only three months past her twentieth birthday—her character was sufficiently formed for Joseph to carry away this lofty view of her. (And, in fairness to Vinnie, it must be remembered that she was barely seventeen.) Although he sensed the essence of Emily's spirituality, he apparently did not know that she had refused to join the girls at Mount Holyoke who recognized Christ as their Savior and that she had not joined her family's church in Amherst (and never did). He would have been surprised, perhaps, to hear her call herself a pagan. But his impression of her as "noble," his notion that she would make a "true & devoted wife" even though she would probably never marry—all this helps to offset the traditional notion of her as fragile and timid, a moth-like creature who lived apart.

Lyman made another point of contrast between the girls—their verbal expression, a matter of interest to him as one who had literary ambitions. There is no indication anywhere that he knew that Emily wrote poetry, although in the "long and beautiful letters [as he wrote his mother]" which came to him from "Miss Emily Dickinson in Amherst" he had ample evidence of her power with language. As she did with many of her intimate friends, she may have sent him some of her poems. But, if only from her letters and from her talk, he had a strong sense of her style, and he admired it tremendously. He found in it another example of her superiority to Vinnie. On the eve of his marriage to Laura, he received congratulatory letters from both girls and, in an upsurge of the old feeling for the Dickinsons, sent Laura some excerpts. Writing to her from New Orleans, he expressed the hope that both girls would accept her "into the fold of their esteem & love. . . . Emily I know will. Vinnie somewhat reluctantly unless she marries soon & happily." He knew Laura would be interested in how differently the girls expressed themselves:

Emilys letter is very fine & has some rare delicate touches – let me copy some of them. She commences – "May. We parted in the spring, Joseph. It is natural that we should meet in months of the same name. I dare not count the crocuses that have sprung since then. It would bring us all nearer than we are fit to the Eternal Gardens. The "Kingdom by the Sea" never alters, Joseph but the "children" do – meeker and wistfuller on our part and more athletic-minded I believe on yours. . . . I suppose the grass is growing over much that is dear to us both but we'll leave that till we meet. . . . Are you well, dear Joseph? I am afraid of those Great Suns. I give his Tropics charge! Shall you not be carefull. When you know that the fires never burned low on the hearth stone of remembrance you will forgive us. Write to us again, dear Joseph, keep us in your prayer and in strong vesper we will bear you up – Good night – 'Good night' grows weary. I long to cry "Good Morning" so! Affecty Emilie" –

Vinnie talks more human like and passionately in this wise. Amherst May 1858 "Dear Joseph. Vinnie has not forgotten you in all these months of silence. Old times and old friends are still fresh in my memory and dear to my heart. Come back to us Joseph and you will then be assured that we love you still! Our new house [on Main Street, to which they had moved in the spring of 1855] is beautiful, Joseph, not so modest as the old one but *so pleasant*. I walk about in my garden in the bright mornings and then I think about the dear absent ones "– What is gone & what is left." My flowers dont know how far my thoughts wander away sometimes. Amherst is improved since you were here. Come & see for yourself. I wonder if we would know each other if we chanced to meet! Perhaps you are in your own home now. How queer it will seem to know that you are married! I would like to see you before that event takes place. I expect you have become very dignified & experienced but I guess we – we would be children again for a little while if we were together! Austin & Sue are close by us. Sue is a dear Sister, etc.

[ *139*

etc. . . . do come & see us before we are old people & wear caps and spectacles. Believe me always your true friend – Vinnie.

The two styles are distinguished accurately: Emily's "rare" and "delicate," Vinnie's "more human like" and passionate. Joseph's estimate of their letters corresponds roughly with his estimate of them as people, Emily noble and spiritual, Vinnie worldly and pleasure-loving.

Directly following the excerpts, Joseph embarked again upon the theme of Vinnie's inadequacies, which would seem in actuality to have been not so much radical defects of character as symptoms of a girl's first love encouraged a little irresponsibly by an older and more worldly young man. (He was Austin's age.) And now, to Laura, he put the blame for the failure of the affair on Vinnie. He rationalized his own conduct outrageously and attributed to Vinnie much of his own frank hedonism:

How much like "Maud in her Garden of Roses!" If Vinnie had been fit to be the wife of a self-made man I would have married her some time ago. But she is only a 'milk white fawn' – But her kisses – those kisses! – It is 7 years ago now since I kissed her among the crocus flowers. *They* and the daffodils and the little arbutus had left their sweetness on her lips! No wonder when she walks among her flowers that Maud 'remembers'. "I remember – I remember". I wish 'Maud' would forget that spiritual faced student boy that loosened the earth with his spade around the roots of her roses in the springtime so long ago! She has been up and down in the world – spent a winter in Boston – in Philadelphia – at Washington while her father was in Congress but no body talks as he talked – whispers as he whispered – kisses as he kissed! Poor Maud. If she had not thought so much of that fine house & carriage & roses her student lover would have 'come back' long ago. I was afraid she would miss them. So I left her with them. . . .

However unfair, it is remarkable that this portrait could have been written at all about a Dickinson. Vinnie hardly sounds like the scion of Puritan stock; nor do we recognize "our practical sister Vinnie," the planner and doer of the household, the "Soldier and Angel" with her " 'drawn Sword' in behalf of Eden." There is little trace of Vinnie the wit and mimic, the pert and peppery one. Although the letter shows that Joseph kept in touch with the family—he notes the visits in Boston, Philadelphia, and Washington—the Vinnie he depicts is still the Vinnie in her sentimental girlhood, well before she started "prevailing."

Five years later Joseph would have found a very different person, ready to take on, as Emily said, the "Universe." Far from developing as a Maud in her garden of roses, Lavinia became the family's front line of defense against the world. She ordered, shopped, bargained. Vinnie "cruises about some to transact the commerce," as Emily put it. She developed a combative streak that, with her wit, made her one of the most respected and feared tongues in town, to be surpassed (and this may have been a source of the later ill feeling between them) only by her sister-in-law, Sue.

*140* ]

When Vinnie was only twenty, she contemplated a passage-at-arms with the important Mrs. Luke Sweetser and her accomplice, Mrs. Fay, in a matter touching the family honor. The ladies in their gossip had accused the Dickinsons of slighting their four orphaned cousins, the Newmans, who had been living with their aunt, Mrs. Fay, for the past year. Her letter to Austin about the matter shows her fighting style at its best. (The letter begins "Dear *Rooster*" and is signed "Vinnie Alias, Chick.")

Sue was here this afternoon & told us a long story that Mrs Sweetser had told Harriet [Cutler] about us this morning. I have not been able to go out since Friday, but hope to get out again tomorrow & then Mrs Luke will get such a lecture from me as she never heard, I guess. She says we dont treat the Newmans with any attention & that Mrs Fay has talked with her about it & all such stuff. I shall first go to Mrs Luke & give her a piece of my mind, then Mrs Fay another piece & see what effect will come of it. Mrs Sweetser has interfered with my business long enough & now she'll get it, I tell you. I'll bring up all past grievances & set them in order before her & see what she'll say for herself. I hope to start by 11 oclock in the morning to deliver my feelings. I *certainly shall.* She has watched me long enough in meeting & her bonnet has bobbed long enough & now I'll have a stop put to such proceedings, I will indeed.

Austin, replying two days later from Cambridge, congratulated her on "rather the *smartest* note I have in your hand," and tried to soothe her spirit. He started with a bit of whimsey characteristic of the family's way of taking each other down:

*Will* those desiring have an opportunity to view the *remains* of the mischievous lady of the woods [the Sweetsers lived in the grove back of the Homestead on Main Street] when you get through with her, what few there may be left!

His counsel from then on was sober and judicious. The matter was a serious one. Besides the good advice he gave her, it is worth noting that he cleared with *her* (not Father, or Mother, or Emily) all the practical details of his expected trip home the following Saturday: the trunks, meeting him at the depot, his laundry. But it is his advice to Vinnie that tells most about himself, and Vinnie, and their relationship—and about certain realities of Amherst life:

My own notion would be, Vinnie, not to say a single word to Mrs Sweetser on the subject. She is not our master, nor are we in any way responsible to her for anything we are, or have. Let the woman talk if it makes her any happier. She cant hurt us, we dont care for her, and seems to me it would be making her of rather too much importance to take all the trouble to go up there & give her such a pommeling as you propose. I dont doubt your *ability* to raise an *awful* breeze around her ears, but is it on the whole best? Wont it be very apt to please her very much to know she has put you into such a fever?
I dont believe, Vinnie, that you could possibly tickle her so much as by

just the course you promise yourself. If you want to punish her the severest, just let her alone severely. Let her passion for slandering & insinuating against you, or any of us, fall upon herself alone. Do nothing which shall divert it from her for a single moment. Keep quiet & let it burn away there as long as it will, and it will burn nobody but her own dear self. And that miserable, fretful, old maidish widow [Mrs. Fay], let her alone too. Dont say a single word to her, only if she barks too loud, & troubles your sleep, tell father & have him inform her her services are no longer needed, and hire some more serviceable girl to take charge of those children. We can turn her out of the house any day and she cant say one word.

Vinnie probably took the advice; at least we hear no more of the affair. But Joseph Lyman would have been surprised to see his "milk white fawn" eager to enter the lists as the sole representative of the family against two ladies twice her age, and entirely confident of her ability to put them down. She might have been more useful to him in the "central strenuous life" than he thought. Professor Chickering, in his eulogy of Lavinia in the *Republican,* spoke of her "heart of adamant" and of her courage: "Did ever so valorous a spirit lodge in so frail a tenement?"

As she grew older, Vinnie's loyalty to her family became her vocation. Much has been made of her uncritical devotion to Emily, but it extended farther. She would tolerate no criticism whatever of any member of the family. Even Professor Chickering, her admirer, saw it as an obsession:

> It seemed impossible for her to realize that any other estimate than hers could be held of their gifts and graces, their abilities and achievements. Her fiercest denunciations were reserved for those who ventured to oppose or even call in question the opinions of her father and brother on matters of public concern. No other opinions were either conceivable or allowable.

Emily was amused by this quality in Vinnie, but she was grateful for the protection. She may have been grateful in still another respect. Although she herself shunned open battles and "fierce denunciations" as she did august assemblies, she was impressed by qualities in others that made them fit for such confrontations. The rhetoric she used in describing Vinnie—Gladstone, Disraeli, the Guardian Angel—was not necessarily facetious. There was something sharp and clear and tonic about Vinnie's belligerent loyalty, her dividing the world into Friends and Foes of Dickinsons. "Vinnie demurred," Emily once said, "and Vinnie decides." Once she described her in action:

> Vinnie is full of Wrath, and vicious as Saul – toward the Holy Ghost, in whatever form. I heard her declaiming the other night, to a Foe that called – and sent Maggie to part them –

Emily was a little like Keats in this—the Keats who relished the display of human passion even in such sordid affairs as street fights. What she heard that night in Vinnie's tussle with the Foe may have been another aspect of what she had in mind when she spoke of her "inciting voice."

Lavinia in the 1860s

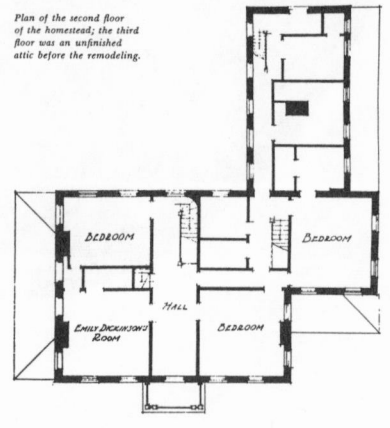

A later picture of the Homestead on Main Street

Floor plans of the Homestead

*Plan of the ground floor of the Dickinson homestead (before remodeling in 1916 by Howe & Manning, Boston).*

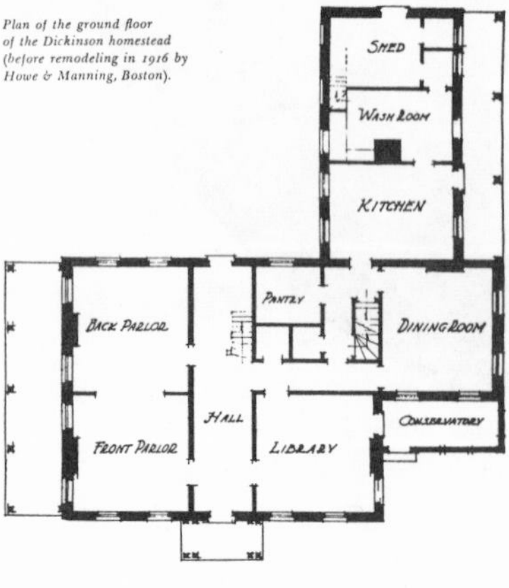

*Plan of the second floor of the homestead; the third floor was an unfinished attic before the remodeling.*

SHED

WASH ROOM

KITCHEN

PANTRY

BACK PARLOR

DINING ROOM

HALL

FRONT PARLOR    LIBRARY    CONSERVATORY

BEDROOM    BEDROOM

HALL

EMILY DICKINSON'S ROOM    BEDROOM

The degree of Emily's so-called dependence on her sister deserves some scrutiny. Rhetoric here as elsewhere has too often been taken at its face value. When Vinnie was off for the winter taking care of her aunt, Mrs. Loring Norcross in Boston, Emily wrote a friend in what would seem to be a state of minor panic:

> I would like more sisters, that the taking out of one, might not leave such stillness. Vinnie has been all, so long, I feel the oddest fright at parting with her for an hour, lest a storm arise, and I go unsheltered.

She once referred to Vinnie as her father confessor: "if she says I sin, I say, 'Father, I have sinned' – If she sanctions me, I am not afraid." We have already heard her speak of Vinnie as her "parents," although here she suggested that the dependence was mutual: "[Vinnie] has no Father and Mother but me and I have no Parents but her." Yet Emily probably was never so dependent on anyone as these remarks would suggest. Vinnie came nearer to what seems the truth when she said that the family lived together like "friendly and absolute monarchs, each in his own domain."

One action, however, speaks louder than any of Emily's rhetoric and suggests the true nature of her need of Vinnie. When Emily was about to come home from Cambridge after a long stretch of treatment for her eyes in 1864, she wrote Vinnie a brief note which concluded with a significant request: "I shall go Home in two weeks. You will get me at Palmer, yourself. Let no one beside come." A few days later she repeated it: "Vinnie will go to Palmer for me certainly?" Months before, she had written Vinnie from Cambridge, "I miss you most," and perhaps she had. But her singling Vinnie out for the lone meeting at Palmer should be viewed in the light of the possibilities she was excluding. While it is understandable, knowing what we know of her, that she would not want a delegation, Austin was available, and Sue, and her father and mother; and presumably all would have been eager to go. Her choice suggests, perhaps, not that she was so dependent on Vinnie, or loved her most, but that she felt most at ease with her. Vinnie's nature was the least likely to key her up. What she needed at this juncture, and to a certain extent all her life, was a stabilizing influence and someone to look after the details. Of all members of the household, Vinnie was best suited to fulfill this function. This was what she had in mind, perhaps, when she said that Vinnie had been "all" to her for so long.

What Vinnie's calming influence meant to her, and what it meant to the whole family in the Homestead after Edward Dickinson died, is nowhere better illustrated than in Emily's account, in a letter to the Norcrosses, of the fire that destroyed the business center of Amherst early in the morning of July 4, 1879. The letter—and I give it in full as the work of art that it is—is the most intimate glimpse we have of the family constellation during the later years. Vinnie is the heroine. Emily's narrative powers were never better, or her descriptive eye, or her humor, or her sense of character in action, or her command of sound and rhythm—all qualities, it should be said, that argue against the notion that her powers sadly declined after the miraculous production of the early 1860s.

Did you know there had been a fire here, and that but for a whim of the wind Austin and Vinnie and Emily would have all been homeless? But perhaps you saw *The Republican.*
We were waked by the ticking of the bells, – the bells tick in Amherst for a fire, to tell the firemen.
I sprang to the window, and each side of the curtain saw that awful sun. The moon was shining high at the time, and the birds singing like trumpets.
Vinnie came soft as a moccasin, "Don't be afraid, Emily, it is only the fourth of July."
I did not tell that I saw it, for I thought if she felt it best to deceive, it must be that it was.
She took hold of my hand and led me into mother's room. Mother had not waked, and Maggie was sitting by her. Vinnie left us a moment, and I whispered to Maggie, and asked her what it was.
"Only Stebbins's barn, Emily;" but I knew that the right and left of the village was on the arm of Stebbins's barn. I could hear buildings falling, and oil exploding, and people walking and talking gayly, and cannon soft as velvet from parishes that did not know that we were burning up.
And so much lighter than day was it, that I saw a caterpillar measure a leaf far down in the orchard; and Vinnie kept saying bravely, "It's only the fourth of July."
It seemed like a theatre, or a night in London, or perhaps like chaos. The innocent dew falling "as if it thought no evil," . . . and sweet frogs prattling in the pools as if there were no earth.
At seven people came to tell us that the fire was stopped, stopped by throwing sound houses in as one fills a well.
Mother never waked, and we were all grateful; we knew she would never buy needle and thread at Mr. Cutler's store, and if it were Pompeii nobody could tell her.
The post-office is in the old meeting-house where Loo and I went early to avoid the crowd, and – fell asleep with the bumble-bees and the Lord God of Elijah.
Vinnie's "only the fourth of July" I shall always remember. I think she will tell us so when we die, to keep us from being afraid.
Footlights cannot improve the grave, only immortality.
Forgive me the personality; but I knew, I thought, our peril was yours.

Curiously, "our peril" did not involve, at least by name, that of Sue and the children next door. Or perhaps "Austin" was a sufficient summary. Curiously, too, there is no mention of any help from the Evergreens. Vinnie prevailed.
Emily's most extended and most poignant comment on Vinnie is in the letter to Joseph Lyman in which she had so much to say about her father and where she documents, in family terms, her famous complaint, "All men say 'What' to me." The theme of the letter, or that part of it

which Joseph preserved, is the failure even of her intimates to understand her. Here Vinnie joins her father (and, we can assume, her mother) among the bewildered ones. She acknowledges her dependence on Vinnie in one vital matter and at the same time indicates the level on which she functioned in complete independence of her:

> And Vinnie, Joseph[,] it is so weird and so vastly mysterious, she sleeps by my side, her care is in some sort motherly, for you may not remember that our amiable mother never taught us tayloring and I am amused to remember those clothes, or rather those apologies made up from dry goods with which she covered us in nursery times; so Vinnie is in the matter of raiment greatly necessary to me; and the tie is quite vital, yet if we had come up for the first time from two wells where we had hitherto been bred her astonishment would not be greater at some things I say.

Concluding the letter, she declares her independence of Space and Time and in a phrase hits off what might be properly called the motto for her life: "My Country is Truth." But she adds a wry note: "Vinnie lives much of the time in the State of Regret."

The remark is not only a measure of the extent to which Emily outgrew her sister; it explains much about Vinnie's later development, the fanatic family loyalty, the sharp tongue, the bitterness. What did Vinnie "regret" besides her idyllic childhood and lost youth? Howland? Lyman? At any rate, there seems to have been a vacuum in her life, not to be adequately filled with domesticities, not at least for a person of her emotional capacity, her energy and abilities. This, along with her father's lonely and austere life and Austin's domestic misery, Emily had to witness, too. That she was extraordinarily sensitive to the vicissitudes, physical and spiritual, of every member of her family needs no more proving. Once, writing to the Hollands about Vinnie's difficulties with a headache, she made a classic statement:

> Vinnie is sick to-night, which gives the world a russet tinge, usually so red. It is only a headache, but when the head aches next to you, it becomes important. When she is well, time leaps. When she is ill, he lags, or stops entirely.
>
> Sisters are brittle things. God was penurious with me, which makes me shrewd with Him.

Vinnie's life had its tragic side, too, and its deep frustration. And happening "next" to Emily—no one closer—it became important.

On the whole, Vinnie did well, considering the disappointments in her life. At least she never became melancholic or hangdog. If, according to Joseph Lyman's impression, she was made for marriage (though not with him), at least she adapted herself to her spinster's life with good grace, until the pressures became too much for her. She identified herself with her family, both in Amherst and in distant places like Boston, when for a winter she helped with her ailing Aunt Lavinia. She was at her best in time of crisis. When Edward Dickinson died and Austin was too stunned to be of much use and Emily was hidden away upstairs, it was Vinnie who took charge. "The world seemed coming to an end," Martha Bianchi wrote later. "And where was Aunt Emily? Why did she not sit in the library with the family if he [Austin] could? She stayed upstairs in her own room with the door open just a crack, where she could hear without being seen." Vinnie's conduct on the occasion so impressed Professor Chickering that he mentioned it twenty-five years later in his eulogy:

> She who because she was sure her father would have wished it, denied herself to no one in the hours that succeeded his death, could weep with those who wept, and tried in gentlest ways to ease the burden.

And the Dickinsons' Amherst friend and neighbor, J. L. Skinner, wrote to his wife three days after the funeral:

> Spent half an hour with Austin at his office this morning, and half an hour with Vinnie. . . . I thought Vinnie's character as it shone out in her face today was beautiful.

Nine years later when Gilbert died, it was Vinnie again who provided the main support. Vinnie's letter to some friends in Newport is one of the fullest accounts we have of the effect of the death on the family. Her own essential function was never more clearly illustrated. The letter is dated November 16 (1883), just six weeks after Gilbert's death.

> MY DEAR FRIENDS:
> A Newport paper was a gentle reminder of you, some weeks ago, but now Susan has come & I have been so absorbed trying to comfort Austin that all else has been neglected though not forgotten – Of course you knew little Gilbert has disappeared & Emily & I have had hard work to keep Austin from following him – His fever was short & fierce & little more than one week ended his happy, brilliant life – His home is greatly changed for Gilbert was "the Child of the Regiment" as you well know – Emily received a nervous shock the night Gilbert died & was alarmingly ill for weeks – She is much improved at present but still very delicate – You can imagine my anxiety for all that's left of this home – Emily was devoted to Gilbert & was there the night of his death – I have longed for you both in these last weeks – why did you go away – Please write to me & I wish you would write to Austin.

There is much to be noted in this letter. Austin's grief was nearly mortal, we know, and it is clear from the letter that, among the members of the family, the burden of keeping him from complete despair fell mainly on Vinnie. How much Emily helped is hard to tell. Vinnie's account of her nervous shock on the night of Gilbert's death, and of her delicate condition for weeks following, is borne out in more detail by the report of a friend and neighbor, Mrs. John Jameson, who wrote to her son John:

> Miss Emily Dickinson . . . went over to Austin's with Maggie the night Gilbert died, the first time she had been in the house for 15 years – and the

odor from the disinfectants used, sickened her so that she was obliged to go home about 3 A M – and vomited – went to bed and has been feeble ever since, with a terrible pain in the back of her head –

So it was Vinnie as usual who was the most active in keeping together "all that's left of this home." Her energy was tried to the limit. A week after Gilbert died, she was treated by Dr. Cooper for exhaustion, a detail which she does not mention to her friends in Newport.

After Gilbert's death, Lavinia was more preoccupied than ever with looking after her home. Her mother had died the year before after years of incapacity, and Emily never fully recovered her vitality. Vinnie's life was not a happy one as Emily's health declined. Although there is record · of a pleasant visit with Mrs. Holland in Northampton the spring of 1884, of sleighing with Austin that winter—" 'Tom' whirls us over the white country at a flying pace"—about the only solid pleasure in her life during these years seems to have come from her friendship with Mrs. Mabel Todd, who had arrived in Amherst in the fall of 1881. This, in light of events shortly to be discussed, turned out to be a mixed blessing. The trouble came from next door. The impact of the arrival of this young lady, beautiful, sociable, talented, and half the age of the Dickinsons, will concern us next. It is a complicated story, climaxing and documenting the tensions between the two houses long sensed by biographers. It led directly to Vinnie's later woe.

For Vinnie the story begins with a perplexing conversation Mabel had with Sue in early September 1882. Sue, for reasons to be discussed later, warned her about the loose morals of the sisters in the Homestead and urged her not to call on them. Mabel, however, called immediately, and Vinnie apparently was grateful for her act of defiance. Within a few months after that first call (surely by the following spring) the relationship had become more than merely social. "I'm surprised at my missing you so much, for I have seen you only a little," Vinnie wrote Mabel in Washington. Eight months later she wrote again (Mabel was once more in Washington), this time more fervently and even a little desperately:

> I miss you every day & your companion also, whom I consider *gold* in character.
> Winter is here & Sunday was a dreadful day for gloom & cold. How I did wish you were in reach of my summons. Austin is so oppressed by these "glad days" [the Christmas season] & I hardly know how I shall cheer him so many weeks without you to help him. Write to him often. I have almost forgotten how joy feels, anxiety for others beside my own sorrow has for the time hidden all light. "Without hope" is a doomed thought. . . . I know what Washington life is & sometimes I wonder if *I* could be whirled into forgetfulness by social excitement. Pardon my way of talking & make no allusion to it when you reply as your letters are read by more than me. . . .
> Emilies love

The phrasing might have been her sister's—"I have almost forgotten how joy feels" and " 'Without hope' is a doomed thought"—but the problem was hers: how to keep up Austin's morale without Mabel Todd and with Emily in delicate health, and how to keep up her own spirits in so gloomy a situation. Her thought of being "whirled into forgetfulness by social excitement" is a touching throwback to the days when Lyman knew her and the Amherst boys were courting her. Mabel, who was having her usual busy and exciting time in Washington, was a reminder of all that she had missed.

It is easy to see how Mabel cheered Vinnie's gloom, but there was more to their friendship than that. As Mabel's relationship with Austin grew more intense, Vinnie was at the center of it, offering her house as a meeting place and acting as go-between in many ways. She was confidante, messenger, and scribe, often addressing envelopes to avoid telltale handwriting. Mabel was grateful for her loyalty; and Vinnie, on her part, welcomed a new ally against Sue. In the innumerable diary entries recording her calls on Vinnie from about 1883 on, not once does Mabel speak of meeting Sue at the Homestead, or of seeing Sue and Vinnie together.[3] Sue could hardly have helped knowing about their friendship—and hating them both for it—a fact which must have drawn them closer together. When, after Emily's death, and despairing of Sue, Vinnie finally took Emily's poems to Mabel Todd for editing, the reason for her secrecy, for the nocturnal visits and clandestine arrangements we will hear about, was fear of Sue's anger. And when Sue found out, she was furious; but the conspirators, then as in the early years of this drama (according to Mabel), kept their heads high.

Although Vinnie was often impatient with Mabel's progress during the long and difficult task of editing, their association seems to have been amicable. From the late 1880s until Austin's death in 1895, the calls and

---

3. Vinnie's relations with Sue seem to have been at best erratic, even during Austin's courtship, when at one point Vinnie apologized to Austin: "I love *Sue* most dearly & will try & never do her injustice again" (May 6, 1853; *Home*, p. 282). Firm evidence is scanty for the long years between Austin's marriage and Mabel Todd's arrival in Amherst. Vinnie gave Sue a copy of "H.H." 's *Verses* for her birthday in 1870 (*YH* II, 160). But by 1878 things were bad enough to start gossip in town. A "faculty wife" wrote to her son, abroad, on June 11: "I dont think [the Mathers] are quite as thick with the Dickinsons as they used to be – They are very sorry for Miss Vinny – Mrs Austin rides it rough shod over her – Prof M. says Ned D———— grows lordly and cynical –" (*YH* II, 294). So, five years later, it is not surprising to find Vinnie taking Austin's and Mabel's part against Sue. In a letter to Mabel of September 25, 1883, Vinnie wrote: "I *know* there is no change of feeling toward you, save one house & there I never hear your name & am never there!" (*YH* II, 405). In *AB* (p. 59), Mrs. Bingham described the situation seven years later (1890): "Without at this time going further into the matter of her relationship to her brother's wife—whom she called 'the Old Scratch,'—it is at present enough to say that they were at swords' points"—mainly (in 1890) over the publication of the poems. The distressing (and perplexing) events of Vinnie's last years are considered in Chapter 13.

visits continued at an average, according to Mabel's diary, of two or three a week. If Vinnie (as Millicent Todd Bingham has suggested) all this while was growing jealous of Mabel's success with the poems,[4] both as editor and as lecturer, there is nothing in the letters or journals of either to show it. There are signs, however, of a rift between the women in the spring of 1895. It may have arisen from Vinnie's resistance to Austin's suggestion that Mabel be compensated for her editorial work by the gift of a strip of land which they owned in common from their father's estate. Vinnie apparently resented this public acknowledgment of indebtedness to Mabel, who, she felt, was sufficiently recompensed by the literary fame the work brought her. Evidently Vinnie gossiped, for Mabel (in her diary for June 2, 1895) accuses her of "treachery." After Austin's death on August 16 there is an unmistakable change. Mabel mentions not so much as a chat with Vinnie until October 1. Her entries for weeks after Austin's death are short, often only a sentence, and given over almost entirely to her own grief. There is no sign that she turned to Vinnie for comfort, or Vinnie to her. Then, on October 6, there is a disturbing entry, followed by silence until the very end of the year. The entry reads:

> I went to see Vinnie in the morning, and I find she is going to ignore Austin's request to her – that she shall give to me his share of his father's estate. She is, as he always told me, utterly slippery and treacherous, but he did not think she would fail to do as he stipulated in this. Oh, it is pitiful! He had an entire contempt for her; but we talked it over, and it seemed the safest way to leave it. If he knows, how sorry he must be!

It is hard to tell how much Mabel's statement is colored by what seems to be her justified indignation. Austin had indeed made this request (although why, as a lawyer and with such an opinion of Vinnie's trustworthiness, he failed to put it in legal form is also hard to see); but whether he had always thought of Vinnie as "utterly slippery and treacherous" is open to question. He was often critical of her, but there is no evidence, except this statement of Mabel's, that he ever thought of her so harshly. He had welcomed her assistance, and trusted her, in his secret communications and meetings with Mabel, and so had Mabel. There is one redeeming note in Mabel's entry for December 29, 1895: "I went to see Vinnie just before tea – and had a talk with her. She is going to do one lovely thing." She concluded the entries for what she called her "tragic year" without specifying what the "lovely thing" was.

Vinnie thoroughly deserved Austin's harshness when she sued the Todds three years later for the land. To put it briefly, in bringing suit she was disloyal to Austin's wishes and to her friendship with both the

---

4. But Mrs. Bingham concludes her analysis of Vinnie's complicated attitude (and by this time Vinnie was a most "complicated" Dickinson) with a despairing "'Jealousy' is too simple a word to apply to her feelings" (*AB,* p. 213). "For Emily belonged to her" (*AB,* p. 211).

Todds; she lied to her lawyer; and in the course of the trial she perjured herself in court. She may have been induced to do all this by Sue, who wanted nothing more than Mabel's public humiliation. She was in her mid-sixties, living alone, and full of fears. Even then, it is hard to understand her almost complete collapse of character. For years she was so devoted to her family that her loyalty became a byword, and she had stood up bravely against Sue in the matter of the poems. What seems like the failure of all her fine qualities gives some notion of how powerful the forces were in this tense family situation.

One further thought suggests itself: there may have been some truth in Austin's distrust of Vinnie, even though Mabel's report of it may be extreme. If there was, then his isolation in the family circle was more complete than other evidence suggests. And did Emily share his distrust of Vinnie? Emily seems to have been the only one in the family whom he trusted completely. This final revelation about Vinnie, however ambiguous, brings Austin and Emily closer together. It is obvious where the spiritual refreshment of his daily calls on his sisters really came from.

But Vinnie must have her due both as a person and as a source of insight into the baffling problem of her sister.

If the image she gives us of Emily is far from complete—and colored by her idolatry, her possessiveness, and her desire to protect—certain truths about Emily, or facets of her life, become clearer because of her. We see how independently life could be pursued by the inmates of the household, containing as it did, in a fair degree of harmony, people of such different natures. Edward Dickinson, traditionally thought of as the tyrant, does not seem to have cowed Vinnie's spirit any more than Emily's. Vinnie's busyness was often Emily's, too. They had to work hard. Against this background, Emily's literary production, her determination and energy in the pursuit of it are all the more striking. Vinnie's gradual retirement after the sociable life of her girlhood makes Emily's more understandable, even if Vinnie never secluded herself so completely. Vinnie's feud with Sue uncovers a trouble in which Emily shared. Her belligerent defense of the members of her immediate family had its counterpart in Emily's anxious love. Her style may have been unliterary, but, written or oral, it was tough-minded, direct, down to earth. She made herself heard in her own way. Bereavements did not desolate her as they did Emily and Austin; she was more resilient, but she knew their meaning. After her mother's death, Vinnie wrote to Mabel Todd: "I still envy your possession of Father & Mother. Realize the joy to the full for memory is a poor substitute for reality. I *know* what *each* means."

Vinnie even wrote a few verses, a handful of which survive.[5] They show almost no talent; but it is reassuring to know that she felt the urge

5. See Appendix I.

for such expression and could thus bring some understanding to Emily's lifelong vocation. The verses are on subjects that Emily made poems of, the things of nature (trees, stars, fireflies), pain, the indifference of friends, bits of gnomic wisdom. There are four epigrams, or attempts at the form: "New pleasures bring new anxieties" is perhaps the best. The slim collection shows a kind of rugged angularity—and no sense at all of how to round out a quatrain neatly. Perhaps its greatest virtue is its independence (though not quite complete) of the mawkish popular verse of the day,[6] a virtue she shared with Emily. And, although she was no "Sister Pegasus," her furious determination to get Emily's poems published, every one of them and immediately, may have come in part from her having shared, however humbly, in the practice of the art. The fact is that Vinnie threw herself into the project as Austin did not. His busy life with the college, the town, his legal practice, the demands of an expensive family, and his absorbing relationship with Mabel Todd—none of this explains why he left this important matter almost entirely to Vinnie. The question arises: Mabel Todd is rightly regarded as the savior of the poems, but what would have happened to them without Vinnie? There is no evidence that Mrs. Todd, fired by the poems Emily had sent her, rushed to the Homestead after Emily's death to inquire about her literary remains. And Austin made no move. It is possible that Vinnie knew more about Emily's literary work all along than she has been given credit for, so much has been made of her as the uncomprehending, Philistine sister.

So, when Emily says of her, as she did to Joseph Lyman, that "if we had come up for the first time from two wells . . . her astonishment would not be greater at some things I say," some discount must be made for Dickinson rhetoric. Emily never would have tolerated obtuseness, nor did she have to, in any member of her family. The more one looks into Vinnie, the quality of her character during the years of her prime, the texture of her mind as seen in her letters, in her recorded sayings, and even in these few fragments of verse, the more her stature grows. She had her admirers, a long line, from Tutor William Howland and Joseph Lyman in the early days to Professor Chickering and Mr. Melvin Copeland, bank president of Middletown, Connecticut, who sent flowers to her funeral. Lyman's negative estimate of her character (after his ardor had cooled) and the eccentric old-maid image that still clings to her must be qualified by the tribute of John Franklin Jameson (his family lived across Main Street from the Dickinsons), who was then on his way to academic fame as a historian. He writes in his diary:

> Went to call on Miss Vinnie. . . . I know her very little, but I do like her. She is a noble, good and kind woman in spite of her occasional sharpness of sarcasm, of which in talking with me there was little.

6. See Appendix IV.

That she became bitter and deceitful toward the end of a life that had in some ways been parallel in its frustrations to her sister's is a comment on the superior resources Emily brought to her problems. There was something of the loser in this generation of Dickinsons, a quality that in all of them except Emily evokes pity. They all, including Emily, suffered heartbreaking disappointments, and in this sense, perhaps, Emily like the others could be pitied. But none had a fulfillment like Emily's, and pity is hardly the dominant response to one who wrote what she wrote.

With Vinnie the pity is dominant, especially after Austin died and left her defenseless. Her life is what Emily's might have been, nurtured similarly as they were, had it not been for Emily's extraordinary gifts. This is not to say that Vinnie was a poet *manqué* who needed only some talent to transcend her troubles; it is simply to acknowledge that she had enough of Emily in her to understand her sister, if not deeply, at least better than has been thought. For one thing, she had sense enough to see how important it was for Emily to live her life in her own way, and in this, like Austin, she was way ahead of the Amherst gossipers who turned Emily into a hopeless eccentric, or those who, following Thomas Wentworth Higginson, could regard her as a "partially cracked poetess." As early as Emily's twenty-fourth year, her friend Eliza Coleman wrote to John Graves, Emily's handsome cousin, in concern even then for Emily's fate at the hands of those who failed to understand her:

> *Emilie* . . . sends me beautiful letters & each one makes me love her more. I know you appreciate her & I think few of her Amherst friends do. They wholly misinterpret her, I believe—

It is notable, and to their credit, that both Austin and Vinnie took Emily exactly as she wanted to be taken. Mabel Todd said that Austin was merely amused at the gossip. Vinnie defended Emily from it and from all other intrusions. Not only this, but somehow or other, by affinities or perceptions she has been thought incapable of, she saw that Emily's poetry must be published.

A final example of her insight and devotion has come to light recently. A letter of January 29, 1895, is her answer to what she considered the growing misrepresentation of Emily's character and career. The myth-makers had been at work, and Vinnie was shocked to read the account of Emily in the *Boston Transcript* for December 22, 1894, by Mrs. Caroline Healey Dall. The article dealt in part with Emily's *Letters*, published that fall. Here is the passage that offended Vinnie:

> Some years ago a relative of Emily's came to see me. . . . "It was in Washington," said her friend to me, "that Emily met her fate. Her father absolutely refused his consent to her marriage for no reason that was ever given." It was probably, as he once said, when she wanted to go away and make a visit, because "he was used to her and did not wish to part with her!" When such a motive was urged, Emily could not resist. She would wait,

hoping, once, as we see in the pathetic little poem, "Almost". The lover came to see her and just missed her. His "soft, sauntering step" did not overtake hers. "Hope," she once wrote, had never "asked a crumb of her." It needed no sustenance, so immortal was her love, so elastic her spirit. And this answered until death came. In a few years her friend passed out of sight. I think from various indications that she never knew where his body lay, only he had gone after she had given her heart to him, and before her father would consent to ratify the contract.[7]

This has all the elements of the familiar story—indeed, several of the stories—said to explain Emily's "fate." Mrs. Dall's informant seems to have confused at least two, those involving her friendships with George Gould and (later) with Charles Wadsworth (whom, presumably, she met in Philadelphia, not Washington, but it was on the same trip). Here are the stock notions of the stroke of fate that cut her life in two, the possessive father, the life sustained on sad, sweet memories. Vinnie's reply to Mrs. Dall, as we have it from a typescript, signed by Vinnie, is a polite but earnest "You are wrong on every count":

Will Mrs. Dall pardon intrusion if I correct false statements that have been made *to her* concerning my sister and our noble father?

Emily never had any love disaster; she had the choisest friendships among the rarest men and women all her life, and was cut to the heart when death robbed her again and again. We were very fond sisters and, though I was the younger, I always took care of her, and we were never separated more than three months at any one time.

I was in Washington with her where we found the most delight-[ful] friends. Emily's so called "withdrawal from general society", for which she never cared, was only a happen. Our mother had a period of invalidism, and one of her daughters must be constantly at home; Emily chose this part and, finding the life with her books and nature so congenial, continued to live it, always seeing her chosen friends and doing her part for the happiness of the home.

Our father was the grandest of men, and never hindered our friendships after we were children. Emily had a joyous nature, yet full of pathos, and her power of language was unlike any one who ever lived. She fascinated every one she saw. Her intense verses were no more personal experiences than Shakespeare's tragedies, or Mrs. Browning's minor-key pictures. There has been an endeavor to invent and enforce a reason for Emily's peculiar and wonderful genius. This is not the first occasion that has forced me to right this cruel wrong (and, I think, always from the same source), the motive of invention being, I suppose, personal notoriety.

I am sure you will endorse my determination to extinguish all untruth relating to my beloved sister who is not here to speak for herself; if her life

7. *AB*, p. 319. Mrs. Dall (1822–1912) was a prolific author, lecturer, and advocate of women's rights. The "relative of Emily's" who visited her has not been identified. The poem she calls "Almost" is #90 ("Within my reach!"). The title was given by Higginson (for *Poems*, 1890).

*had* been a tragedy I should never speak, but I should appreciate the brutality of lighting a subterranean passage for curious eyes.

Will Mrs. Dall be so kind as to *tell* me if these words find her,
And believe me earnestly,

Emily's sister, –
Amherst, Mass.,
January 29, 1895.

Underneath. beginning at the left and in Vinnie's sprawling hand, is written: "Very Earnestly / Lavinia Dickinson / Amherst Mass – / January 29th '95."[8]

Most notable about the letter is that it squares perfectly with Austin's sense of the naturalness of Emily's way of life; and Sue, at least in the obituary of Emily she wrote for the *Republican,* seems to have held the same view. Vinnie's "only a happen" is too simple. Many of Emily's eccentricities—the long, intense seclusion; the refusal to call even next door; the interviews from behind doors or around corners or from the head of the stairs; her refusal to let doctors or dressmakers come near her or to let Mabel Todd see her when she called to sing—all this could hardly be called natural by any standard, nineteenth or twentieth century. Apparently what led those closest to Emily to call her retirement natural was its gradualness. Either that, or a family protectiveness that became all but conspiratorial. They seem, at least, not to have been disturbed by the eccentricities, so long and slow was the process of their development. But the rest of the world, waking up late to what had happened, saw them as very unnatural indeed and, as with all such phenomena, wanted an explanation. So the mythmaking began.

At the very least, I think we can agree with Austin and Vinnie that Emily's life is not to be explained by any one "love disaster." In the obituary, Sue attributed the withdrawal to Emily's "sensitive nature," insisting that she was "not disappointed with the world" but simply found in her own home "the fit atmosphere for her worth and work." Vinnie's reference to the series of losses from among Emily's "choisest friendships" seems more likely, if (which is hardly necessary) one looks to Emily's personal losses for an explanation of her withdrawn life. It is notable, also, that Vinnie considered the myth of the love disaster a "cruel wrong," the result of "false statements . . . always from the same source . . . the motive being, I suppose, personal notoriety." The source sounds like the Sue of the later years, who (Vinnie seems to be saying) was trying to get her share of the glory of being related to Emily, once the poems and letters had caused such a stir. The wrong was "cruel," one

8. The MS of the letter is in the Emily Dickinson Collection, Clifton Waller Barrett Library, University of Virginia Library, and is reproduced by permission. The typing was probably done by Mary Lee Hall, who later helped Vinnie with the transcripts of the poems, to be published long after Vinnie's death in *Further Poems of Emily Dickinson* (1929). See *AB,* pp. 371 ff. It is not known whether Vinnie ever got the reply she asked for.

gathers, both to Edward Dickinson and to Emily by making a tyrant of the one and a victim of the other.

Vinnie's comments about Emily's power with words need qualifying— save for the unexceptionable statement, "her power of language was unlike any one who ever lived." This remark sounds like a reference to Emily's spoken language and hence must long antedate Vinnie's full access to the poems. It alone would call in question the idea that her adoration was blind and uncomprehending. If, as Vinnie says, "she fascinated every one she saw," she fascinated Vinnie, too, and with the power of her language. Vinnie's remark about the poems—"Her intense verses were no more personal experiences than Shakespeare's tragedies, or Mrs. Browning's minor-key pictures"—is the same disclaimer that Emily herself had made years before to Higginson when she wrote him in July 1862, "When I state myself, as the Representative of the Verse – it does not mean – me – but a supposed person." Neither remark does justice to the whole truth, the truth of metaphor, Emily's characteristic vehicle, by which she could say a great deal about herself without seeming to. (She never lost a guinea in the sand, nor asked a merchant for Brazil, nor drowned at sea. But it is just as clear that at one time or another she felt *as if* she had done all three; and her life, even the simple, quiet life in the Homestead, was full of occasions that might have produced those feelings.) Both remarks are typical of Dickinson reticence, the fear of embarrassment, of "auctioning the mind," of exposing the soul *"at the White Heat."* The Dickinsons were not only reticent themselves; they respected each other's reticence, and protected it. Once in later years when Vinnie was asked if she could not get Emily to go out sometimes, she replied: "But why should I? She is quite happy and contented as she is. I would only disturb her."[9] An even more striking example of her respect for Emily's privacy is in one of her remarks recorded by a friend after Emily's death. She was asked whether she had studied her sister's poems extensively. She replied, "Certainly not. I never looked at Emily's poems except those she herself showed me. Had she wished me to do so, she would have made her wishes known."[10] Apparently she felt that even to

9. *YH* II, 273. This remark is quoted from Clara Bellinger Green's article on ED in *The Bookman*, November 1924, and dated as having been made in the spring of 1877. Mrs. Green's memories of Vinnie are as vivid as of Emily herself:

As young girls we used often to drop in after school to have a chat with "Miss Lavinia" as we called her, sure to be entertained by her droll, vivacious, and individual views on men and things. . . .

"I, you must know," she remarked one day, "am the family inflater. One by one the members of my household go down, and I must inflate them." . . .

10. *AB*, p. 146 n. The remark is from a conversation between Millicent Todd Bingham and Mrs. Edward Robinson. (The entire memorandum is in the Todd-Bingham Archive.) A subsequent letter from Mrs. Robinson contained this further comment on Vinnie: "Your letter has set me remembering Miss Lavinia who, I feel, was the important character of the family. A *dire* person! Perhaps she partly explains her sister." The reference is obviously to Lavinia in her declining years. See Appendix II, section 6, for a vivid glimpse of Vinnie in her later years, as Mrs. Bingham remembered her.

look at them after Emily's death would be disloyal. From all these remarks by Vinnie about the poems, it can be gathered how much Vinnie knew—Emily *did* show her some of the poems—and how much she did not know, not only about Emily's poetry but about the nature of poetry in general.

Finally, in the letter to Mrs. Dall, comes Vinnie's insistence that Emily "had a joyous nature, yet full of pathos," and that her life was not a tragedy. The joyousness is, of course, a major theme in Emily's letters and poems; it is nowhere more explicit, perhaps, than in her rejection of Higginson's solicitude about her starved and narrow life in Amherst: "I find ecstasy in living – the mere sense of living is joy enough." Then, as to want of employment and visitors, she told him, "I never thought of conceiving that I could ever have the slightest approach to such a want in all future time." Sue, in the obituary, and Mabel Todd, echoing Austin, both spoke of the "blossoming" of her nature, surely not a term denoting tragedy. Whether her life, for all its joy and richness, was, in a sense, a tragedy depends upon the reading of the whole. If, in spite of Vinnie and Austin, the love-disaster theory is insisted upon, her life could be called a tragedy; but even then the stress should be on her achievement as a poet, in spite of her tragic loss as a person. The same would be true if we accept the theory that her life was irretrievably warped by the inadequacies of her mother or the cruelties of a domineering father. If we accept the notion that her failure to publish her poetry blighted her life, then Bowles and Higginson become the antagonists in her tragedy, and her life after the age of thirty-one or thirty-two becomes a fifth-act denouement, a tapering off of unresolved tension. (If her rejection by Bowles was twofold, personal and professional, the tragedy deepens.) All these possibilities must be left open. So must Vinnie's formula that her withdrawn life was "just a happen," the result of nursing her mother through a spell of illness and liking the quiet life with nature and books. But Vinnie's explanation sounds too simple—as do all the single-cause theories, although each may contain a portion of the truth. All her intimates spoke at one time or another of her disenchantment with "the world" or "society." Such a large category could conceivably include a love disaster, a rejection by some representative of the world, or society; but it sounds more like a general rejection on her own part of a way of life in which she could not be happy and productive. There is something of Thoreau in the rejection, as has often been suggested. One surmises that he would have understood her better than Higginson did, and perhaps better than we can. We will come back to this problem many times.

One facet of it, and a major one, we shall now confront directly. I have already sketched some aspects of the distressing situation that developed in the family next door during the last five years of Emily's life. Although Vinnie certainly played a part in the situation, its origins go far back into the history of her generation of Dickinsons, and she was just as certainly its victim in many ways. Its virulence had a great deal to do with

Austin's premature death and even, in its long beginning (so Vinnie suggested darkly), with Emily's own. Its bitterness eventually spread into the town most divisively. Years later it was given a name, dramatic but descriptive, by Mary Lee Hall, Lavinia's friend and neighbor—"War between the Houses"—and it warrants a section to itself.

## "*War between the Houses*"

# 8

---

# Early Hostilities

THE ILL FEELING between the Homestead and the Evergreens had its origins in personal incompatibilities that go back to the time of Austin's troubled courtship and end only with Lavinia's death. It involved all three of the younger Dickinsons, plus two outsiders, Susan Gilbert Dickinson and (beginning in 1882) Mabel Loomis Todd. By Mabel Todd's time it had sufficiently advanced so that, at her first encounter with the Dickinsons, she realized that she was entering "a family quarrel of endless involutions." By the mid-1880s what had heretofore been kept under cover was all but open warfare, with Susan Dickinson and Mabel the chief antagonists. The quarrel by then, of course, was over Austin, whose affair with Mabel was being talked about in town; but this new development served merely to exacerbate old animosities and widen existing gaps.

We look in vain for explicit comment from Emily. But there are many reasons to believe that, in this situation as always, her sympathies were with Austin. In the 1890s it was Vinnie who got the worst of it, as the domestic tensions heightened and the personal problems involved in the editing of Emily's poems made matters worse. After Austin died in 1895, Vinnie and Sue were still at swords' points, until, by a curious switch whose rationale we can only guess at, Vinnie shifted to Sue's side and instituted the suit in 1898 against the Todds for the strip of land Austin had deeded Mabel Todd for her work on the poems. Vinnie died the next year, the last survivor in the Homestead; the Todds moved to the other side of town; and Sue and Martha (her loyal daughter) were left in possession.

But the real possessors were the bitterness and vindictiveness from which all have suffered, participants and posterity. To follow this story and sense its meaning is to gain new perspective on much that perplexes us about the Dickinsons, especially Emily: her withdrawal; the tragic, often violent tone of many of her poems; even, perhaps, her failure to publish. Seeing her against a background of anguish, frustration, and cruelty, we no longer have to ask how, in her quiet life, she came to know these things. Here is the real "Vesuvius at Home." All the characters in her limited circle take on new dimensions. Austin's story alone, now at last documented, shows him again passionately in love but this time a mature man, in firm control, glorying in a love that was fully reciprocated, and doing so in bland defiance of convention—and Amherst convention at that. Susan Dickinson emerges as one of the most impressive and formidable people in Emily's life, perhaps a decisive one. We see why the poems and letters were so long delayed and given to the world piecemeal and (for long) inaccurately. We see also why (by another curious switch) Emily's life and character were so sentimentalized by her niece Martha as to obscure for decades their stern and powerful reality.

As with any story of intensely private lives, of passions to which none of the participants ever publicly gave a name, the problem of the narrator is (again) delicate. The story must be pieced together from many sources, none of them free from bias. Sides are still taken, passionately. Often one must proceed by inference and intuition; and, as in all judgments of character and motive, conclusions must be tentative. But the story must be told, at whatever risk. Emily Dickinson did not write in a vacuum. The tangled relationships that developed into this final tragedy were a reality in her life, and an agonizing one, from her girlhood to the day she died.

One of the major themes in our treatment so far of the Dickinsons has been the closeness of the family, the interdependence of its members, and ultimately a pride that amounted to arrogance. Tradition may have exaggerated Edward Dickinson's petty tyrannies in the family, but there is no doubt that he kept a careful eye on the young men who came to call on his daughters. He was protecting the Dickinson name. He might have kept an equally careful eye on the young ladies who attracted his son. But, like Emily and all of Amherst, he was charmed by the dynamic young Susan Gilbert, who was clearly one of his favorites. He escorted her home on various occasions and called on her in Baltimore[1] (where she was teaching) when he went to the Whig Convention in June 1852. They joined the First Church on the same day, August 11, 1850. What Edward failed to see was that in encouraging the match between Susan and Austin, he was inviting into the family an alien and disruptive element. This is not a moral judgment; it is simply a fact.

To understand the disharmonies that soon arose, the nature of the conflict they developed into, and its effect on Emily as well as Austin, we

---

1. "Susie and I went to meeting last evening and Father went home first with Susie and then with me. I thought the folks would stare. I think Father feels that she appreciates him, better than most anybody else" (*L* I, 250; ED to Austin, May 16, 1853). "Father writes [from Baltimore] that he's called on Sue, twice, and found her very glad to see him" (*L* I, 213; ED to Austin, June 20, 1852).

must return to the early records for hints of trouble over and above the obvious frictions of Austin's courtship. Emily's early letters to Sue (there are none extant from Sue to Emily in this period and only one later) disclose a relationship which, on the face of it, seems rapturous. From the first letter (December 1850), Emily poured out her heart to her friend, showered her with affection, pined for her when she was absent, scolded her when she was offish. Her letters to many of her girl friends, like Abiah Root and Jane Humphrey, are insistent and effusive enough; the letters to Sue, even discounting the romantic style then in fashion and her own flair for rhetoric, are nothing less than love letters.

Even in its early stages, however, this relationship explains much that happened later. It has usually been taken at its face value—a girlish infatuation that developed, according to Martha Dickinson Bianchi's account, into lifelong devotion, with no rifts or seams. But there were difficulties from the start and rifts that opened wide in later years.

The question is: What is the truth behind the romantic rhetoric of the early letters? What did Sue really mean to Emily? It is clear, for all the gushiness, that she meant a great deal. By her twentieth year, Emily was consciously narrowing her circle, as one by one her friends, male and female, died or departed. More and more she saw Sue and Austin—and Vinnie in her own way—as supplying all the society she needed. As she looked forward to Austin's marriage, she saw Sue as her second sister, living only a hedge away. Discussions of life and love and literature would go on endlessly as they had begun in the letters. We "please ourselves with the fancy that we are the only poets, and everyone else is *prose,*" she proclaimed to Sue when they were twenty. She knew Martha as the sweeter of the two sisters and apparently would have been happy had Austin married her. But Sue was the fascinating one—more "brilliant," as their brother-in-law had said—and for Emily the future lay with her.

Perhaps the closest we can come to explaining, if not explaining away, the fervor of the letters is by way of a literary parallel known to both girls. Several times Emily referred to Longfellow's *Kavanagh,* a novel published in 1849 and smuggled into the house despite Mr. Dickinson's watchfulness.[2] It was one of those books that he feared would "joggle the Mind." In the novel, the relationship between Alice Archer and Cecilia Vaughan might well have been taken by Emily as an idealized statement of what she hoped, at least, was true of her and Sue. She could have seen herself as Alice Archer:

> She had a pale, transparent complexion, and large gray eyes, that seemed to see visions. Her figure was slight, almost fragile; her hands white, slender, diaphanous. . . . She was thoughtful, silent, susceptible; often sad, often in tears, often lost in reveries. She led a lonely life.

2. So Higginson wrote his wife (*L* II, 475, August 17, 1870): "Her father . . . did not wish them to read anything but the Bible. One day her brother brought home Kavanagh hid it under the piano cover & made signs to her & they read it: her father at last found it & was displeased."

Cecilia was in as sharp a contrast as, in real life, Sue was to Emily: beautiful, confident, outgoing, much sought after by young gentlemen. Longfellow pointed up the contrast in a passage that predicts precisely the theme and imagery of a poem Emily later sent to Sue (early in 1862), "Your Riches taught me Poverty":[3]

> ... what a contrast was there between the two young friends! The wealth of one and the poverty of the other were not so strikingly at variance, as this affluence and refluence of love. To the one, so much was given that she became regardless of the gift; from the other, so much withheld, that, if possible, she exaggerated its importance.

If Emily's letters to Sue sound like the sentimentalizing of a second-rate romantic heroine, *Kavanagh* was just one model: the sighing and the kisses, the heart-to-heart talks and the "long and impassioned letters" are

---

3. The poem (#299) illustrates the difficulty of assigning ED's apparently occasional poems to any one set of circumstances. It exists in several versions. One was sent with three other poems to Higginson in July 1862, identical with the "packet" copy (see *P* I, 219 n.). A third copy was sent to Sue early in 1862, with this concluding note:

DEAR SUE –
You see I remember –
EMILY.

In his note in *P* I, 220, Johnson tentatively accepts George Frisbie Whicher's suggestion (*This Was a Poet*, p. 92) that the poem was written in memory of Benjamin Franklin Newton, a law student in Edward Dickinson's office and an early friend and admirer of Emily's. Johnson goes further and suggests, in the light of ED's "unfailing" memory of anniversaries, that the poem was written on the ninth anniversary of Newton's death (March 24, 1853). However, the editors of the *Letters* (Johnson and Theodora Ward) three years later opened up another possibility (*L* II, 401–2): "On the other hand the poem may not be an elegy, but written about a person living whom ED feels that she has lost, perhaps Sue herself." The lines that echo (whether it was ED's intention or not) the situation and imagery of *Kavanagh* are:

> Your – Riches – taught me – poverty!
> Myself, a "Millionaire"
> In little – wealths – as Girls can boast –
> Till broad as "Buenos Ayre"
> You drifted your Dominions –
> A Different – Peru –
> And I esteemed – all – poverty –
> For Life's Estate – with you! . . .
>
> At least – it solaces – to know –
> That there *exists* – a *Gold* –
> Altho' I prove it, just in time –
> It's distance – to behold!
> It's far – far – Treasure – to surmise –
> And estimate – the Pearl –
> That slipped – my simple fingers – thro'
> While yet a Girl – at School!

all there. To this extent, Emily and Sue, like Alice and Cecilia, were (as Longfellow describes them) "in love with each other":

> They were nearly of the same age, and had been drawn together by that mysterious power which discovers and selects friends for us in our childhood. They sat together in school; they walked together after school; they told each other their manifold secrets; they wrote long and impassioned letters to each other in the evening; in a word, they were in love with each other.

Or (and this is the point) at least Emily was in love with Sue. By her early twenties, Sue was something of a woman of the world. As an orphan, she had known uncertainty and a good deal of knocking about. She took the teaching job in Baltimore as a gesture of independence and to make things easier for her sister, Mrs. Cutler. Her practical and matter-of-fact letters to her brothers before her marriage show that she knew where she was going. Austin's letter to Martha announcing the engagement described Sue as anything but sentimental: "tall," "stiff," "proud" were the words he applied to her as well as to himself. It is hard to believe that Sue responded to Emily's fervor in kind; the likelihood is that she was repelled by it or, at the very least, found it too demanding.

After she and Austin became engaged in 1853, it goes without saying that Sue could not have sustained anything like the relationship Emily wanted. Early in September 1854, ten months before Sue and Austin hoped to be married (the original wedding plans were for the summer of 1855), a letter of Emily's to Sue indicates a break that was by then inevitable. The letter starts bluntly, goes straight to the point, and ends with finality:

> Sue – you can go or stay – There is but one alternative – We differ often lately, and this must be the last.
> You need not fear to leave me lest I should be alone, for I often part with things I fancy I have loved, – sometimes to the grave, and sometimes to an oblivion rather bitterer than death – thus my heart bleeds so frequently that I shant mind the hemorrhage, and I only add an agony to several previous ones, and at the end of day remark – a bubble burst! . . .
> Sue – I have lived by this. It is the lingering emblem of the Heaven I once dreamed, and though if this is taken, I shall remain alone, and though in that last day, the Jesus Christ you love, remark he does not know me – there is a darker spirit will not disown it's child.
> Few have been given me, and if I love them so, that for *idolatry,* they are removed from me – I simply murmur *gone,* and the billow dies away into the boundless blue, and no one knows but me, that one went down to-day. We have walked very pleasantly – Perhaps this is the point at which our paths diverge – then pass on singing Sue, and up the distant hill I journey on.

The letter is an extraordinary one for Emily, the nearest approach to surliness and dismissal of any that survive. She is, quite simply, telling Susan off—her brother's fiancée and supposedly the darling of her heart.

Her own offense: "idolatry." The mysterious metaphor of the "darker spirit [that] will not disown it's child" is of a piece with similarly veiled prophecies she had been making for some time in letters to Jane Humphrey and Abiah Root but never with such an implied threat. What the substance of this immediate quarrel was we can only surmise. Religious differences between the two girls may have had something to do with it.[4] In a letter written a few weeks earlier, in August, Emily had said, "I was foolish eno' to be vexed at a little thing," and she asked God to forgive her—"as he'll have to many times, if he lives long enough." But the main point seems to have been Sue's neglect ("I have not heard from you"). With the September letter she sent a poem—"I have a Bird in spring"— that may have taken some of the sting off, since the poem says that the Bird (Sue?), though flown, will return some day with "Melody new for me." Then will come a time when "Each little doubt and fear, / Each little discord here" will be "Removed." But the doubts and discords were at that time real—and ominous.[5]

Whatever the cause of the quarrel, this apparently was not the first. Sometime in the early 1850s Austin drafted a strange letter to Sue. It is dated "Boston Sept. 23." In *The Years and Hours,* Leyda, associating it with the September "go or stay" letter, ascribes it to the year 1854, while the editors of the 1958 *Letters* place it in 1851. It is a chaotic scribble of nine pages, with many false starts, cancellations, and repetitions. Austin himself was apparently in trouble with Sue. First, he apologized profusely "for any reflections" he may have unconsciously made on her "honesty and honor," spoke acidly about not liking to hear "my plans ridiculed," and in conclusion put himself solidly on Emily's side in the impasse to which their relations had apparently come:

> As to your deprivation of "Spiritual converse" with my sister – I Know Nothing – I was aware that you had been in correspondence for some time, but had never had an intimation that the correspondence was at an end –
> I have full confidence in her good sense – as guide in this respect – So you

4. This is Thomas Johnson's explanation: "The letter . . . bears every evidence of telling Sue that she cannot honestly declare her faith, and therefore will not do so; and that if Sue's friendship is contingent upon such a declaration, the tie must be broken" (*Emily Dickinson: An Interpretive Biography,* p. 17). The falling out may have had some such origin, but it seems to have gone far beyond the religious issue, at least with Emily. Was the "darker spirit" the devil—or her own "pagan" Muse and its temptations?

5. Here (P #5), too, one hesitates to assert an absolute, one-to-one relationship between the poem and any specific person or experience. There almost always are other possibilities. For instance, Inder Nath Kher, *The Landscape of Absence: Emily Dickinson's Poetry* (1974), identifies the bird in the poem with Emily's Muse, her poetic inspiration. Certainly such bird symbolism can be seen in many later poems. Though the reference to Sue in "I have a Bird in spring" seems all but unmistakable, it is entirely possible that ED was writing on both levels at once: the Bird was Sue; Sue was her inspiration—her Muse—of the moment; with Sue out of her life, her poetry, for the time, dried up. The poem can be about both Sue *and* ED's poetry.

will not suspect me of having interfered with your epistolary intercourse with her –

Her choice of friends and correspondents is a matter over which I have never exerted any control –

Knowing therefore that you will not suspect me of having interfered with your epistolary relations & assuring you of my sentiments of regard for yourself – my respect and admiration for the President of the United States and the Gov Gen of Canada – I remain yours truly – Wm A Dickinson[6]

Sue herself had a reputation for being cool and self-possessed, but this (if we can take it even half seriously) goes beyond anything we have of hers from the early days. The line-up is significant: brother and sister versus the outsider.

Among the early hostilities that were later to develop so disastrously must be counted Lavinia's. Like all the family, she seems at first to have been charmed by Susan, half in love with her herself. Emily made a special point of it in a letter to Sue of April 1852:

> Mother sends her best love to you. It makes her look so happy when I give your's to her. Send it always, Susie, and send your respects to father! And much from Vinnie. She was so happy at her note. After she finished reading it, she said, "I dont know but it's wrong, but I love Sue better – than Jane, and I love her and Mattie better than all the friends I ever had in my life."

Vinnie was then nineteen. A year later, March 1853, she was "vexed" with Sue for neglecting Emily—a sign, among other things, of how the Dickinsons rallied to each other's support and, in particular, of Vinnie's growing sense of guardianship of Emily. Susan had been away and had failed to keep up her share of the correspondence. Vinnie complained to Austin:

> I think shes staid a long time & during it all she has written but a short note to Emilie. It has made E. very unhappy & me vexed. I dont understand what it means.

Two months later she wrote Austin the apologetic note about her quarrel with Sue, a premonition (as we can see now) of the later years of wrangling that came in the end to open warfare.

6. *YH* I, 316. The printed text of this draft gives a most inadequate idea of the MS. It is a curious mess. What it indicates about Austin's state of mind—or whether it was just another example of how seriously these young people took the discipline of epistolary composition—is problematic. It may have been a joke, pure and simple—but it has a sharp edge. At one point, Austin writes: "If you have occasion to address me on any subject again – please direct to the care of J. W. Norcross or if you are this way your card will find me at 19 Hancock St." The earlier date for this strange epistle (it was apparently never sent) seems more likely. During his first weeks as a teacher in Boston, Austin lived with the Norcrosses, then moved to a boardinghouse. In September 1854 he was in Amherst, preparing to go west in October. If the letter is serious, it is as little reassuring about the early relationship of Austin and Sue as about that of Sue and Emily. (The dating in the 1958 *Letters* [I, 307 n.] reverses Thomas Johnson's 1855 ascription in *Emily Dickinson: An Interpretive Biography*, p. 18.)

I saw *Sue* this afternoon, & everything is right between us now. We shall
never have any more troubles. I confess I did wrong to suspect her, but
sometimes I feel rather depressed & then I see every thing through cloudy
spectacles. I love *Sue* most dearly & will try & never do her injustice again.

Actually, Vinnie saw more clearly through her "cloudy spectacles"
than she did with them off. Her complaints against her sister-in-law in the
later years were venomous, although for a while "so delicate," according
to Mrs. Adelaide Hills, a close neighbor who often spoke critically of both
Dickinson families. Mrs. Hills wrote to her husband (December 9, 1866):

Vinnie called here the other day – she said she had not seen Mrs. [Austin]
Dickinson yet or the baby [Martha.] It had been nearly a week since the
baby was born. I think if it had been me I should have felt quite badly –
they try to be so delicate –

Mabel Todd was probably right when she said later that Vinnie and Sue
came to "hate each other black and blue."

Between the "go or stay" letter and Austin's wedding there are only
two letters from Emily to Sue, one at Thanksgiving that same year (1854)
and the other the following January. There are the usual protests of
loneliness and love, and only one mention of the previous quarrel.

I miss you, mourn for you, and walk the Streets alone – often at night,
beside, I fall asleep in tears, for your dear face, yet not one word comes back
to me from that silent West. If it is finished, tell me, and I will raise the lid
to my box of Phantoms, and lay one more love in; but if it *lives* and *beats*
still, still lives and beats for *me*, then say me *so*, and I will strike the strings
to one more strain of happiness before I die.

Mostly, the two letters are concerned with sensible, gossipy matters, a
welcome change from the saccharine (the September letter excepted) of
the earlier ones. Perhaps Emily was consciously taking off the high sentimental style. Walking the streets alone at night and falling asleep in tears
seems pure *Kavanagh*. But the words "If it is finished" and the "box of
Phantoms" (a metaphor she used to conclude another friendship about
that time) ring true. Later developments in Sue's character, in her
marriage with Austin, and in Emily's own way of life bear out the
prophetic hints here.

A poem Emily sent to Sue two years after the wedding, usually taken
as a sign of Emily's total devotion to her sister-in-law, should be reexam-
ined in the light of these early frictions. In the poem, Sue is again a Bird,
and this time she has come to stay.

> One Sister have I in our house,
> And one, a hedge away.
> There's only one recorded,
> But both belong to me.

One came the road that I came –
And wore my last year's gown –
The other, as a bird her nest,
Builded our hearts among.

She did not sing as we did –
It was a different tune –
Herself to her a music
As Bumble bee of June.

Today is far from Childhood –
But up and down the hills
I held her hand the tighter –
Which shortened all the miles –

And still her hum
The years among,
Deceives the Butterfly;
Still in her Eye
The Violets lie
Mouldered this many May.

I spilt the dew –
But took the morn –
I chose this single star
From out the wide night's numbers –
Sue – forevermore!                    (#*14, late 1858*)

Is the poem a pledge of eternal loyalty—or an elegy on a youthful friendship and a bitter reminder? From what we know about the "Dickinson
difference" and about the relationships that were developing in this tightly
knit group and even then worsening dramatically in the Evergreens, the
lines that need stressing are the first two of the third stanza. The ironic
implications of the images that follow the nostalgic stanza 4 are clear
enough, a far cry from the kisses and comforting embraces of the early
letters.

In view of the animosities that developed in the ensuing years, and in
view of the possibility that Austin (or Mabel) exaggerated his early experience, a comment in Mabel's journal for December 16, 1885, may be too
melodramatic a conclusion to this first stage of the "War between the
Houses." But it is part of the record: Susan, wrote Mabel, "made him
marry her, in spite of his terrible repugnance to doing it (he said he felt
as if he were going to his own execution the day he was married) . . ."

# 9

## Mabel Loomis Todd and Austin

THERE SEEM TO HAVE BEEN only two people in the world to whom Austin Dickinson, in his maturity, at one time or another poured out his heart. One was Emily, who, if she recorded the results at all, did so in her poetry, obliquely. The other was Mabel Loomis Todd (1856–1932), who for thirteen years was Austin's confidante in a relationship of complete intimacy. She has left us three major records: her daily diary from 1881 on; her journal, in which she wrote from time to time more fully than the size of the diary would permit; and her letters to and from Austin, from 1881 to the time of his death.[1]

Mabel Todd has appeared peripherally in our pages so far, but it is time now to bring her to the center. She not only precipitated the climactic conflict between the households, in both of which she was at one time intimate, but her records provide the materials for a striking new view of Austin and his private sorrow, of Sue and Lavinia, and ultimately of Emily as seen against the thirty-year background of family tensions. Furthermore, to follow the course of the complicated relationship she developed with both families is to see how she achieved the peculiar intimacy with things Dickinson that led her, finally, to edit the poems. True, she was technically the best-equipped person in town to do the work. But other qualities and insights and knowledge were needed. Jay Leyda's brief reminder gets at the heart of the matter.

> If David Peck Todd had not been appointed director of the Amherst College Observatory in 1881 we might not today know that a poet named Emily Dickinson ever wrote a poem. It is possible that Lavinia Dickinson's persistence in keeping her beloved sister's memory alive might have found someone, somehow, to watch over the publication of the poems, but it is

1. These materials, as noted above, are in the Todd-Bingham Archive, Yale.

extremely unlikely that she would have found an editor with the faith, sensitivity, and industry of Mabel Loomis Todd.

As we proceed with the story, unfolding as it does mainly from Mabel Todd's records, certain caveats are necessary. No one can claim that Mabel was an unbiased observer. She was every inch a participant, deeply in love with Austin, taking his side on every issue, and (in her journals and letters) defending her love against the world; and even if her reports of what Austin told her were truthful, it must be remembered that he, too, was in love, openly defying convention; and to justify himself to Mabel he may have exaggerated, knowingly or unknowingly, his previous difficulties with Sue—as in his remark about his wedding as his "execution." Nevertheless, the remark is not without some meaning, and, like everything she records, must be given its due. If nothing else, her account is by far the most complete we have, and impressively detailed. She was a veteran diarist, hardly missing a day from early girlhood on, and to read her daily entries is to gain confidence in her respect for fact and accuracy. She was twenty-seven years younger than Austin, she revered him, and she gives the impression, at least, of trying to put down on paper what he told her, even if in her youth and passion she made no discount for what may have been his colorations. And Austin's letters to her and to others over the thirteen years confirm, in general, her reliability, though with a lawyer's discretion he was seldom explicit on paper about details. Other observers corroborate her views of character and situation, although (again) no one of them is unprejudiced.[2] Mabel often rationalized her own behavior naïvely, and in the self-consciously literary manner of the day tended to overdramatize situations. But it seems to have been her sincere purpose to record the truth as she saw it, youthful, passionate, self-centered as she may have been.

Mabel Todd came to Amherst on August 31, 1881, with her husband, David Peck Todd, who had graduated from the college six years before. They had been married on March 5, 1879, in Washington, D.C. Their daughter, Millicent, was born on February 5, 1880. Mr. Todd had just been appointed, at the age of twenty-six, instructor in astronomy and director of the Amherst College Observatory. His wife was twenty-four, full of spirit and ambition, and fresh from a vibrant, social girlhood in Washington, where she had been brought up, we are told, "among distinguished scientists and men of letters."

Mrs. Todd made an immediate impression on Amherst, as did Amherst on her. Her journal and her letters to her family record exuberant enthusiasm over her first impressions of her new life. Her early tributes to the town, its blend of natural beauty with cultural and social amenities, should be put side by side with the dour comments of other observers, like Higginson, who found the atmosphere stifling. Her enthusiasm recalls the

2. The pertinent documents are assembled in Appendix II.

vivacious comments Emily made about the stir and bustle of Amherst in her youth ("Amherst is alive with fun this winter"), although the tone is quite different. In her journal for October 26, 1881, Mabel wrote:

> Do you know, I think Amherst is in many respects quite ideal. I always did like a college town, with its air of quiet cultivation, & by living in such an one it is possible to combine two things which are otherwise generally not found together. I mean the possibility of living in the country, amid the luxuriance of nature, and yet of having refined & educated society at the same time. . . . I have been entertained with a great deal of quiet elegance here, and I have had a really very brilliant experience. I was "taken in" at once, and have been constantly invited, for weeks.

Mabel Todd brought zest and color to this quiet elegance, and soon became a leading figure in many branches of the town's activity. She was the central attraction at parties and outings and the star of amateur theatricals, like the performance in 1883 of Frances Hodgson Burnett's *A Fair Barbarian,* a piece which Emily had read with amusement in *Scribner's,* and which, she said, amused "even the Cynic Austin." She became the leading soloist in the First Church and sang the lead in a performance of Handel's *Esther* in 1887. She held musical evenings, gave music lessons (she had studied piano for two winters in the New England Conservatory of Music in Boston), and according to the custom of the day was constantly calling and being called upon.

From girlhood on, she had literary ambitions; in later years, writing and lecturing became her major pursuits. She tried her hand at short stories and novels, she wrote and lectured about her travels with her husband on his scientific expeditions and, following her work on the *Poems,* about Emily Dickinson.[3] Her charm as a lecturer put her in wide demand. At the height of her career, her speaking schedule, which took her all over the East and once to San Francisco, was little short of professional. She became a steady reviewer for Wendell Phillips Garrison's *Nation,* carried on a book column for *Home Magazine,* and was a frequent contributor to other journals. A major frustration of a life sprinkled with minor successes was her failure to achieve the first-rate literary success—as a novelist—she had always dreamed of.

One of her compensations, besides music, was her love of nature and her flair for painting it. Since childhood she had lived in its influence. Her

3. For Mrs. Todd's speaking schedule on Emily Dickinson for the years 1891–98, see *Ancestors' Brocades,* pp. 211–12. Her publications include a short story ("Footprints," *The Independent,* September 27, 1883; reprinted separately, Amherst, 1883); two volumes of poetry (*A Cycle of Sonnets,* 1896; *A Cycle of Sunsets,* 1910); three serialized novels, *Home Magazine,* Washington, D.C., and Minneapolis, Minnesota ("Stars and Gardens," 1899–1900; "A Better Part," 1902–03; "Polly in Japan," 1904); three books on travel (*Corona and Coronet,* 1898; *Coronet Memories,* 1899; *Tripoli the Mysterious,* 1912); two popular works on science (*Total Eclipses of the Sun,* 1894; *Steele's Popular Astronomy,* revised by David Peck Todd and Mabel Loomis Todd, 1899); and two essays, one posthumously published ("Witchcraft in New England," 1906; "The Thoreau Family Two Generations Ago," 1958).

MABEL LOOMIS TODD

Senior year, Amherst College, 1875
Professor of Astronomy, 1884

DAVID PECK TODD

father, Eben Jenks Loomis, of Concord, was a friend of Thoreau—indeed, was invited by him at one point to go on a camping expedition in Maine, an invitation that had, sadly, to be refused. On her visits to Concord as a girl, she was constantly in and out of the Thoreau household, and called Maria and Sophia Thoreau her "aunts." As she grew older, she began to paint and sketch with an eye trained to the closest observation. The panel of Indian pipes she sent Emily (in September 1882) is an example of her art—but crudely represented, it should be said, in the cover design she later used for the first edition of the *Poems.* (Emily thanked her for "the preferred flower of life" and sent her the famous *quid pro quo,* the poem "A Route of Evanescence," with the remark, "I cannot make an Indian Pipe but please accept a Humming Bird."[4]) The most impressive public recognition of Mabel's art came when Samuel Scudder, the great ento-mologist, used her full-color study of the monarch butterfly as the frontis-piece of the prospectus for his *Butterflies of the Eastern United States and Canada* (1889). Her talent was (again) of professional quality and her production voluminous.

With all these gifts and her abounding energy, it is no wonder that her impact on Amherst was felt immediately, and especially in the Ever-greens, where Susan by that time had established Amherst's closest approach to a salon. Very soon after their arrival in Amherst, the Todds were entertained by the Austin Dickinsons and taken up by them. Or rather, since the ladies were the socially aggressive ones, Mrs. Todd was taken up by Mrs. Dickinson. In the early weeks, Mabel wrote several times to her family about her first impressions of the Dickinsons. This was when she found Mrs. Dickinson "the most of a real society person here." "Her presence," she added, "filled the room with an ineffable grace and elegance." She was impressed by the Dickinson affluence—"they are quite wealthy"—and by their style (letter of October 2, 1881):

> We met her [Mrs. Dickinson] the other morning driving with a handsome double carriage & pair, & coloured driver. . . . She is said to give extremely elegant little entertainments and musicales.

In her next letter to her parents (October 4, 1881), her enthusiasm soared:

> Last evening . . . we went to return the Dickinsons' call. I told you I ad-mired Mrs. Dickinson at first, but I am thoroughly captivated with her now. She does, as I supposed, live very handsomely, & she is so easy and charming, & sincere – and she understands me completely. She has a beautiful new up-right piano, & her young daughter and I played some duetts, & then I sang. . . . Her husband was not at home last night – but I was very much im-pressed with him in various ways. He is fine (& very remarkable) looking – & very dignified & strong and a little odd.

4. ED had already sent copies of the poem (#1463, about 1879) to Helen Hunt Jackson, Mrs. Edward Tuckerman, and Higginson. Evidently one of her favorites, it went this time as a tribute to a fellow artist. Some sixty of Mabel Todd's nature paint-ings (oils and watercolors) are now in the Hunt Institute for Botanical Documenta-tion, Carnegie Mellon University, Pittsburgh, Pennsylvania.

By October 12 she was spending "the morning with Mrs. Dickinson," playing and singing "three hours to her." Five months later she wrote in her journal (March 2, 1882): "I have been at Mrs. Dickinson's a great deal since my return. . . . She appreciates me completely, and I love and admire her equally. She is a rare woman, & her home is my haven of pleasure in Amherst." Five months later (diary, July 18, 1882), the Dickinson home had become her "ideal place" and the Dickinsons her "ideal people."

Thus the Todds were well launched, to the delight of all. The relations between the two families ran smoothly for at least the first year and a half. But this pleasant state of affairs did not last. Mabel soon learned that Susan Dickinson was known in town for her violent but short-lived enthusiasms. She took people up—and dropped them capriciously, a fate (Mabel was warned) that might befall even Sue's "darling Toddy."[5] Sue, however, was not the immediate cause of trouble. What led to an open break was that Ned, Austin and Sue's twenty-year-old son, in his enthusiasm over this brilliant newcomer fell in love with her, all within the first few months of the Todds' arrival. Mabel's diary, during her first year in Amherst, records frequent visits from Ned, whom she found charming and chivalrous and whose attentions she welcomed, especially the long rides in the fall, the sleighing in the winter, the waltzing lessons (Ned taught her the new steps) at the Dickinsons'. By mid-winter 1882 Ned was calling on her almost every day, and by spring Mabel was disturbed. She admitted later that she should have seen what was coming; but she was only twenty-five herself, used to many suitors, and devoted to her husband ("I love him better every day," she concluded the entry in her journal for March 23, 1882, "I have made *the perfect marriage*"). So she planned a two-month visit with her parents in Washington, among other things to give Ned a chance to cool off. But as she wrote in her journal (April 10, 1882), she was not at all sure, knowing his character as she did, that his feelings would have changed much when she returned in June. She was troubled:

> We left Amherst on Wednesday, the twenty-ninth of March. Ned went with us as far as Palmer, on his way to Boston. The dear boy felt more badly about my leaving with every mile. He to all appearance was talking in a lively mood to me, on the train, but I could see that he felt dreadfully. I never had a more intense lover, and I don't know what to do about it. . . . he is in character a very determined and steadfast person, and I mistake him very much if his feelings will have changed at all toward me by June. Of course, I am a woman, and I am older than he, and I know more of life than he, and I can help him somewhat against himself, and I will try. But that is all I can do. . . .
>
> Well, time alone can extricate him – if he is to be extricated.

5. Mabel wrote in her journal, September 16, 1883: "It was a matter of wonder with my friends that there had been no break before. It was Mrs. D's way to have some 'fuss' on hand most of the time." When things were going right, Sue called Mabel her "darling Toddy," according to Mrs. Bingham (in conversation).

When she returned, Ned had not changed. All seemed serene on the surface. The gay outings and cheerful parties continued; but when he persisted to the point of openly declaring his love, saying that "if he should let go his fierce hold of himself, he could not answer for anything" (journal, September 15, 1882), she realized that she had to call a halt. So she added, "Ned and I have tacitly abandoned our little affair."

But it was not all that easy. Obviously, the affair was anything but little to Ned. He felt jilted and aggrieved; and (sometime in the late fall of 1882 or the early winter of 1883) in his bitterness he went to his mother with some startling accusations. In the journal for February 3, 1883—the first entry since a most happy one of December 11—Mabel is distressed:

> The root of all my trouble is that I allowed that affair with Ned to pro-gress too much. I got over all especial feeling for him in the summer, and supposed he did for me. But . . . he cared more for me than ever when I came back in November, & said he had given up the struggle to get over it. I talked very wisely & sensibly to him – & out of it might have sprung a pleasant & lasting friendship. But he is of a very jealous disposition, & began to think I must care more for his father than himself. So he got angry, and went to his mother with some very mean things – among other things telling her that I was an awful flirt – & having allowed him to fall in love with me, I was now tired of him & was trying the same thing with his father. Of course this troubled her very much, & she began to look about.

The root of the trouble was not simply Ned, of course, for by then her affair with Austin was well advanced; but she was right that he was the immediate cause. When she returned from another visit to Washington on January 6, the atmosphere had changed. Her February 3 entry continues:

> She [Sue] had always known that her husband was fond of me, & was very glad; but at Ned's soreness, and anger, she – being utterly devoted to him – began to think perhaps I *was* a flirt, & so she got jealous, too. When I came back from Washington in January her manner was so different that I had to ask an explanation, and we had a long conversation, which was conducted with fairness (in general) on both sides.

"Since then," she went on, "things have been better," and, indeed, the diary records pleasant doings—rides, calls, teas—between the families for the next year or so. But she was right when she concluded the entry by admitting, "The old cordial, frank relations I am afraid can never be resumed."

These mild words do not begin to convey the seriousness of the situa-tion then developing, with herself at the center. Though she blamed herself for the affair with Ned, and rightly, there is in the journals and letters scarcely a word of self-reproach for her part in her affair with Austin, by this time five months under way, and potentially much more explosive.

In fact, Mabel was inexcusably naïve not to see this danger. By the winter of 1883 she and Austin were deeply committed, and tensions were rising. The course of their relationship and its effect on the families can be traced almost step by step in their letters and in her journal and diary. Austin's own laconic diary yields only one reference, but it is momentous.

Mabel's presence in the Evergreens had at first been a joy to all, including Sue. Perhaps Sue saw that Austin, fifty-two when the Todds arrived, was at a kind of dead center in his life and needed sprucing up. At any rate, he did respond to this vivid new personality, and there are numerous references in Mabel's diary, during the first year, to happy family gatherings and to walks and rides with "dear Mr. Dickinson." The Amherst countryside provided a special bond. She wrote in her journal for May 12, 1885, "His love for nature is as intense & necessary to him as mine is, & we see things just alike."

It was during one of their excursions to the country—on September 11, 1882, just a year after the Todds came to Amherst—that they recognized the full truth. Austin's diary for that day contains, along with some neutral items, one otherwise inexplicable word: "Rubicon." On that day seven years later, he wrote Mabel:

A full 7, rich – and richer with every one –
      Recall – remember – supply
         Nor rose –
         Nor earth –
         Not Heaven –
September 11 1889
September 11 1882      It was so ordained

Mabel reciprocated in a letter of November 7, 1889:

—how I live without you I do not see. Of course it is not living, but every moment of my life has been waiting ever since September eleventh, 1882. I had my vision then, and it has never wavered or faltered or grown dim since.

Following the day of days, their intimacy grew steadily, encouraged by circumstances. For three weeks beginning on October 19, 1882, Sue and daughter Martha were out of town attending a wedding in Grand Rapids. On November 10 David Todd left for the Lick Observatory in California to be the official photographer of the transit of Venus on December 6. He was gone two months. Mabel Todd became practically a member of the Dickinson family after he left, constantly in and out of the Evergreens and spending many nights there. One plaintive comment about that late autumn in Amherst has come down to us from David: "I never should have left her."[6]

The first few months of the romance, before suspicions were aroused,

6. Again, this was told me by Mrs. Bingham as her memory of what her father said. See also Appendix II, 5. Section 6 of this appendix assembles some striking sketches (from Mrs. Bingham's memoirs) of Austin, Vinnie, Mabel, and David.

seem to have been blissful. Twenty-two letters from Mabel to Austin, written between November (1882) and the following February, tell the idyllic story. One of them, written in mid-December, described the famous September 11 and set the tone—with one exception—for all the others:

. . . You thought you were all alone in the "by paths" – You loved the grass and the blue sky and the birds and the crickets – And you said you wanted the crickets to chirp about you when you were finally sleeping – You did not know then to whom you were saying that exquisite thing. But she loved those lonely walks too, only now they were not lonely – and she is thrilled with every bit of lichen on an old stone wall, and the scent of dead leaves, and the passive little buds that know so wondrously when to awake and breathe the rapture of spring.

And we walked toward the sunset – and leaning on an old fence, began to reach [each] other a very, very little – It was very peaceful, and very bright – but it was the beginning, unmistakably. . . . You reached out your hand without knowing it, almost – in the darkness – and you met another – warm and tender. You clasped it – knowing it was your fate – and it staid with you. It will never be withdrawn. . . .

Good night, beloved . . . Love me. Love me every minute, and think of me. The stars are shining brilliantly. I see many bright things for us in the future. Good night.

As the other letters pour out their protestations of love, the one exception to the idyllic tone emerges. Though their love "grows and grows . . . wondrously and beautifully," certain anxieties appear: "I hope everything was in a lovely and serene state upon your return," she wrote on December 5. "How is the Home atmosphere? I am anxious to know that." She hesitated to send some of her more passionate letters in the mail. In Washington, where she had gone for the Christmas holidays, she worried about not hearing from Austin:

. . . I am wondering too how the "Powers" are talking and acting and feeling – I hope it is not they – in any way – who keep you from writing. . . . It may be some idea of danger to us that keeps you from writing to me – and so it may not be safe for me to write to you even in the manner you suggested. . . .

Back in Amherst to greet her husband's return from California on January 6, she wrote in alarm over an evening at Sue's (Austin was in Boston):

The evening was too horribly chilling – The whole atmosphere was cruel – I felt as if all the surroundings were pitiless – What new thing has occurred to make everything so dreadful? I must see you – It is necessary for me to see you soon. . . .

Things were better a few weeks later (January 29), "but still the constant air of watchfulness is very uncomfortable."

It was in this letter that she urged Austin to burn all her letters. "But above everything, *do* be careful of this note. It frightens me when I think of your having it with you when you come home." It apparently frightened Austin, too. He burned them, all twenty-two of them—but not (curiously) before making copies. These, in his own hand, he placed in an envelope and entrusted it to Vinnie. On the envelope he wrote a surprising directive:

VIN –

If anything happens
    to me
        Burn this package
at once –
    without opening.
Do this as you love me.

    W A DICKINSON

The "War between the Houses" was on in earnest.

Lavinia directed operations from the Homestead, addressing envelopes, delivering messages, arranging meetings. Austin's real center was there, too. In 1861 Emily had written a friend that Austin "married—and went East"; it was about this time (March 1883) that she wrote: "My Brother is with us so often each Day, we almost forget that he ever passed to a wedded Home." Whatever Emily's part was in all these doings, she had ample opportunity to hear about them. On July 12, 1885, Austin wrote Mrs. Todd about a custom of his that had obviously been going on for some time. It is a crucial one.

> I have two or three little visits with my sisters every day, and we talk you over, always. . . . I see Vin and Em more than I did and you are the constant theme.

By then Austin's alienation from his own home seems to have been complete. The loss of his son Gilbert in the fall of 1883 had been all the more grievous because Austin, according to Mabel, looked upon him as the only member of his household who understood and loved him.

The remaining years of this ill-fated love affair present a harrowing story of frustration and despair that in the end were almost too much for both Austin and Mabel. At first, when Sue's hostility became apparent, they were defiant. Two notes from Austin sounded the trumpet. The first (April 6, 1883) called for courage and belief in themselves (the envelope is addressed by Vinnie):

> . . . Hope you are holding up. It is the part of a man or a woman, to meet what they must in a noble way, even if it kills. Honor and nobleness are far beyond life.
>     Besides what is there from which either should shrink!

The next, written on July 12, when Mabel was vacationing at Hampton, N.H., is more militant. The spring in Amherst had been difficult:

Cast of *A Fair Barbarian,* November 23, 1883
David and Mabel Todd, sitting, center


DIVERSIONS IN AMHERST, 1882–3


"The Shutesbury School of Philosophy" (after a picnic, July 1882)
Mabel Todd, center, standing; David Todd, far right; Susan Dickinson, with
Gilbert on her lap, seated, center; Mattie Dickinson, seated, right; Ned
Dickinson, front right, with tennis racket

Indian Pipes, on black gilt-edge panel, by Mabel Todd. Sent by her to ED, September 24, 1882

A final version of this poem, here in worksheet draft, went to Mrs. Todd in return. This is the only known version without the word "revolving" in line 2. The variants show the care with which ED arrived at her final choices

. . . I hope the summer may be most pleasant to you, that the brightness of the passing days at Hampton may crowd down all memory of the unpleasantness of the days here, and that circumstances may so change as to make your return here in September easy and agreeable. I cannot but believe they will.

I suffer for every wound you have received from my family, but for the time have seemed powerless to prevent them.

What strength I have however will be pitted against any more of them.

I will straighten the matter out before the summer is over or smash the machine –

I had rather be under the wreck than under what I am. There would be several other broken heads, certainly, and I would take the chance of coming out on top.

Nothing in Austin's actions bears out these brave words. Perhaps Gilbert's sickness and death in October took the heart out of him. What eventuated, in spite of repeated protests of defiance in their correspondence, were twelve years of double living—with this notable exception: they made no attempt to conceal their love for each other from their spouses. In his July 1883 letter, Austin described the following scene in the Evergreens:

. . . At breakfast . . . the question came square, after leading up properly, "Did you see Mrs. Todd?" I had anticipated it and said at once, "Certainly, that was what I went to Boston for." This unhesitating frankness was somewhat stunning, and the rally wasn't prompt. When it came, it was, "She told me she was to spend a few days in Boston before going to Hampton, and I concluded you would see her." I replied, "Yes, I *said* I did." This ended it. There has been no allusion to it or you, since. I don't know whether on the whole I am supposed to have lied about it or not, but *you* know I spoke the Truth.

David Todd was equally aware of the relationship but tolerated it in his gentle way. A man deeply engrossed in science, he wanted nothing more than to have his brilliant Mabel happy. His role in this extraordinary affair was, of course, crucial. It could be said that, by his very virtues of restraint and tolerance, he contributed to the prolonged frustration and agony of all concerned, including himself. But he was a man of mild temper and of such devotion to his wife that her will was his will, even if it was her will to love another man. Of his feelings toward Austin, twenty-six years his senior, two things must be said. First, he revered him and loved him. In later years, he told his daughter, "I loved him more than any man I ever knew."[7] Second, in the early 1880s, Austin Dickinson was

7. This, too, was communicated to me by Mrs. Bingham. Since she died, its accuracy has been verified by three entries in David Todd's diary at the time of Austin's death: "My best friend died tonight, and I seem stranded." Next day, he wrote: "Impossible to do anything today. The loss of our dear friend is unspeakable – he touched and pervaded everything." On August 19: "The saddest day of my life – the funeral of our best friend." These entries were called to my attention by Polly Longsworth, currently engaged in a study of Mabel Loomis Todd.

[ *179*

one of the most powerful men in Amherst College. President Merrill
Gates was neither a very forceful nor an entirely well man and depended
on him a great deal. Young Professor Todd's tenure was far from secure.
Part of his hesitancy to interfere with his wife's relationship with Austin
might have been due to his regard for Austin's influence.

But the larger truth seems to have been that David Todd was deeply
impressed by Austin from the start, delighted and flattered by his frequent
visits to his house, and came to be very fond of him, as Austin came to be
of him. In 1885, when Mabel was in Europe for the summer, while the
two men consoled each other's loneliness, Austin actually speculated on a
*ménage à trois*[8] to solve their problems. The three spent much time together—on outings and drives, at theater parties in Boston, with occasional meetings in New York, and a trip to the Chicago World's Fair in
1893. David Todd might at one point or another have taken a firm
stand—or bowed out. But he did neither, nor did Austin ever seek a
divorce. When he came at last to realize how deeply his wife was involved, he made up his mind to live with it, which he did with grace and
magnanimity. But it was a design for living that ultimately satisfied no
one. His daughter Millicent, during her girlhood, remembers hearing her
father whistling a tune from *Martha* when he came home from the
Observatory late at night. Only later did she realize that this was a signal
to forewarn Austin and Mabel of his coming. Only later did she realize,
too, why so many Amherst citizens refused to speak to her on the street.
And she later saw that it was the strain of this trying and irregular
relationship that contributed to her father's ultimate mental breakdown
and hospitalization.

Often in her journal Mabel faced the anomaly of her situation but
declared herself capable of loving two men at once, though each in a
different way. A few sentences from a passage to be quoted in full later
provide an example of how she thought it out to herself:

> I thank God again and again for him [Austin]. I do not love David less –
> he is sweet & gentle & tender – but I have found my very own. That is all.
> . . . And yet I will never make David unhappy. He has been wondrously
> generous & noble, and I appreciate, & will make his life just as happy as
> every possible sweetness & attention can make it. But I cannot be untrue to
> myself & shut the door on my real self for conventionality. I know that
> Austin belongs to me, & I to him.

Five years later (journal, May 13, 1890) came an even bolder defiance of
convention. She had just visited her friend Mrs. Chant's "Refuge" for

8. On July 12, 1885, Austin wrote Mabel, traveling with her friend, Mrs. Caro
Andrews:

. . . I look after David – as a part of my charge. He seems to like me – to rely upon
me – and to confide in me to a remarkable degree. I think we three would have
no trouble – in a house together – in living as you and I should wish. He admires
you more than Caro – but with you away and Caro present he would be filled –
while I should die – and wouldn$^{nt}$ you without me!

fallen women in Chicago and found herself unable to condemn any of the inmates who had acted out of true love: "If it is something they have done for the love of a man, then it is a sweet and pure thing. . . . Mrs. Chant thinks so too, & she is the only person I ever saw – no, not quite, but nearly – who looks on such things as I do." So much for the "Dimity Convictions" of the gentle folk who surrounded her at Amherst. Apparently, what kept Austin and Mabel sustained during the long years of frustration was the idea (as far as one can see from hints and suggestions in the letters and journal) that they would somehow miraculously outlive their spouses, or (a thought shared between them many times) that they would be joined together forever in Eternity.

David Todd might acquiesce, and Mabel might justify, but neither Sue nor the community were prepared to understand. Despite their protestations of divinely sanctioned love and their contempt for town gossip, Austin and Mabel decided at an early stage to keep visible signs and public encounters to a minimum. They habitually met in the dining room in the Homestead and had private places of rendezvous for drives and walks. They concocted code names and code messages for communication by telegram. Austin had self-addressed, stamped envelopes printed for Mabel's use, to divert attention from her handwriting. David Todd addressed most of the letters that went from Austin to Mabel in Europe during her summer abroad. They adopted, in short, what Mabel called a "policy"—"that wretched, hateful, loathsome word!" she blurted out in a letter of January 17, 1888.[9] The strain was great; but such were the times, or such were their natures, that they could never bring themselves (as Austin put it) to "smash the machine."

The dominant note in their letters throughout the thirteen years is one of utter, absolute devotion. Their passion transcended all obstacles. They wrote each other almost daily, and voluminously. With both of them living full professional lives, the wonder is that they had time for it all—Austin with his law work and the college, Mabel with her music and painting lessons, her writing and lecturing. Starting with the simple discovery (to quote from widely separated parts of the journal) that "we had a great many ideas in common" and the announcement of a "friendship which is the most true and satisfying I ever had," the rhetoric soars to crescendo after crescendo. Toward the end it had a religious cast. Their love lifts them "solemnly to God." "You are my Christ," Austin writes in August 1887. "Oh! my love, my king! My star and guide and heaven-sent

9. The "policy" involved many levels of deception, one of which Polly Longsworth discovered in her work on the Austin-Mabel correspondence. For many months during the early stages of the affair, they wrote each other two sorts of letters: one, staid and respectable, harmless if read by Sue or David; the other, love letters, intense and passionate. These were transmitted by various means of subterfuge—in self-addressed envelopes; tucked into books; or exchanged during casual encounters on the street. These they agreed to burn (although Mabel couldn't bring herself to destroy all of Austin's), and it was these that Austin copied in his own hand before burning the originals.

light," declares Mabel a year later (June 28, 1888). "Do you not know that my soul is knit to yours by an Almighty hand? Through you I see God."

Their mutual love of nature is a recurrent theme. There is seldom a letter without some reference to the weather, or flowers, or the hills. In an early letter (September 25, 1883), to bolster Austin's low spirits, Mabel reminded him of this great resource:

> How the crickets are chirping today, and how the asters shine from the roadside! There is surely no place for unhappiness of any kind in so beautiful a world. I think it is a mistake when there is any – the elements of joy are so simple: Could you not make a perfectly uncomplicated combination which would bring joy to you? I have been so busy all day, and now I am resting – under a rare sky, breathing an air full of quiet peace. . . .

Since meetings in town were risky, they took to the country for long walks and rides, as far from "the Powers" as they could get. Mabel wrote in her journal on May 12, 1885:

> Through all the crises & chaoses how tender & restful has been my dear Mr. Dickinson! He takes me off for long quieting drives under the trees & by brooks & through the sweet home of wild flowers. And I see such blue, blue skies & such thrilling clouds with him, and we hear the half-melancholy notes of wee frogs in the boggy fields, & ecstatic bird-songs in the woods.

Another major theme in the letters and especially in the journals is Austin's life before he met Mabel, its sadness and frustration. Several times she asked him to put in writing the story of his life, partly, perhaps, for her own protection. He came close to answering her request in 1883, probably in March; but what resulted was a love letter, one of the most ardent in the long correspondence. It deserves quotation in full for many reasons, but here it speaks simply for "Austin in love," fifty-four-year-old husband and father, a pillar of the community, orator at church celebrations, first in honoring his Puritan forebears—and the brother of the "Queen Recluse." When the Dickinson dam burst, the flood was a mighty one.

> Yes, my darling, I did promise you that sometime I would put into your hands the story of my life, to use as a shield, if ever, when I am not here to answer for myself, any attack should be made upon my love for you, or yours for me, or our relations to each other.
>
> And yet is it not better and nobler that I say nothing which involves any other, reflects upon any other! may offend or wound. Is it not better to begin with my meeting you, and for the first time feeling clear sunshine! What is the past in the face of the present and the future, as we now see it! Is it not better, and enough, for me to say simply, what I have said so many times before, that I love you, love you, love you with all my mind and heart and strength! and that I know what I mean when I say this, that with you my real life began! that with you I have found what life may mean! that in you I have found the sweetest, richest dreams of my boyhood, youth, and early manhood more than realized! That I have found in you what a woman may

I bless Austin every moment, not only for
all he was to me through the noble years
when he loved me so, and that he could
make so high and transcendent a love in
me for him – but I bless him for the
mere memory of it, now, which hallows
me, and makes the thought of every
place I have ever seen with him a
sacred thing. And I bless him for the
hope I have of finding him again – oh!
I long for that unspeakably.

My Darling and my King!

A page from Mabel Todd's journal, on board yacht *Coronet*, 1,600 miles from
Honolulu, June 4, 1896

David and Mabel Todd, at the Observatory House, their last home in Amherst, May 1907

be to a man, hope, courage, joy, inspiration, companionship, rest, peace, religion! That in you I have found my perfect soul-mate, for time and eternity! That in you I have found my longing satisfied – that through you my ideals have been excelled! That you are to me a constant wellspring of delight! more than any throne – than any fame! That I have come to live in you – and by you – and for you – that I admire you as well as love you. That I trust you implicitly, and feel with you my most complete freedom. That I have given myself to you, or rather that I have found myself yours! outside of all will or intent. That with you I breathe a new air, move in new realms, that by you I am enlarged, enriched, uplifted. That I thank God for you every hour. That I find in you everything most beautiful, most dear, most rare, and in you the promptest response to every subtilest feeling and movement of my nature – or do we not rather move toward each other by a common impulse! and in perfect unison! No words can express, dearie, the depth and strength of my love for you, its sacredness, its holiness. You can know it only by looking into your own heart and seeing there the love you have for me, for we have learned that there is no difference in the quality or quantity of the love which fills us both, and that is the Glory of it. I am yours, yours wholly, and only, living or dying. I didn't will it. I simply recognized it, and recognizing it, I could not, and would not deny it. The highest truth is above and beyond common forms and formulas. The spirit is greater than the letter. Conventionalism is for those not strong enough to be laws for themselves, or to conform themselves to the great higher law where all the harmonies meet. I love you, love you, now and forever, and it is my great joy that my love is as much to you as yours to me. The fulness and stoutness and brightness – and excellent happiness – and hope, and thrill, and ecstasy of the days since in that sudden flash of light when we stood revealed to each other, through and through, and saw that each was, in the divine order, the other's world – one part of one existence forevermore.

How much we have to be grateful for, even though we have been obliged to defer some of our hopes – everything will come in good time.

> Once more I love you,
> and again, I love you
> my dearest, dearest Mabel,
> and without my will, and
> with my will am your
>                     own Austin.

The sustained elevation, the almost awesome fervor of Austin and Mabel's love appear in letters throughout its thirteen-year course. The rhetoric becomes repetitious, but it is never exhausted. Mabel, of course, thought Austin's letters, if published,[10] would be "immortal," and wrote in her journal (September 14, 1886): "I have read a great many stories, & I

---

10. Many of them, it is to be hoped, will be published soon in a volume of selections from the Austin-Mabel correspondence now being assembled by Polly Longsworth and myself. A much more detailed account of the relationship will be possible there.

have had a good many love-letters, and I have heard a good many lovers talk, but I never heard or read or imagined such a wonderful putting-into-words. . . ." But Austin had little of his sister Emily's gift. What makes the letters remarkable is the completeness of the commitment they reveal, the outpourings of a heart too long frustrated and denied. One can only conclude that his hopes for happiness with Sue, stated with such fervor in the courtship letters, had long since come to nothing. Nor can one help thinking of Emily next door, at that very time pouring out her heart—also vainly, as it turned out—to Judge Otis Lord of Salem, pillar of the Massachusetts bar and eighteen years her senior.

As, month after month and year after year, the bright future that Austin and Mabel envisioned failed to materialize, signs of strain accumulated. The "Powers" became ever more formidable. The moods of the two lovers fluctuated more severely from hope to despair. "I have a strange sort of life," Mabel wrote in her journal on December 15, 1885, "it is not a bit like anybody else's . . . often far unhappier, it is sometimes infinitely happier." A hint of the martyr creeps into her complaints to Austin (and to her journal) about not being able to stand the strain much longer. By the late 1880s she was near the breaking point.

> I am so tired of *bearing* [she wrote to Austin on November 7, 1889]. If I could be once more happy – I have not quite forgotten how it feels – I could take breath for more pain. . . . I hope – I anticipate all. Some day it is coming.

The hope, or whatever it was, sustained her for another three years; but by then she was utterly exhausted. In a letter of July 28, 1892, she told Austin that she had reached her limit. She implied strongly that he had better *do* something:

> Your letter written on Tuesday, after getting my Sunday note, came this morning. I have just reread it, and I appreciate all you say. Whether I can live up to it or not I cannot say. There are qualities in me worth saving, I am sure. But I was not fitted to stand the kind of strain I have had, and it seems to have taken out from me the joyous, enthusiastic happiness in everything with which I was endowed by nature. I know it is nothing now but a question of will, as you say – but I have lived on will for ten years – even you do not know to what extent – and it has nearly used me up. Things must be happier soon, or my power of mental recuperation will give out. I could get back – *now*. . . .

It was soon after this, and probably in response to it, that Austin wrote to his friend in Omaha about the possibility of establishing himself there. One can hardly doubt that he had in mind a complete break with Sue and his family—and perhaps taking Mabel with him. But, like so many other frustrations in his life, nothing came of it. The letter to Omaha is only a draft; there is no proof that it was ever sent. The tensions continued. Austin showed more and more signs of fatigue. Two years later he was dead.

Mabel's grief demands a postscript. Whatever the verdict of history on her part in this whole troubled affair, there can be little doubt of the depth and sincerity of her love for Austin. Young, inexperienced, and incorrigibly romantic she may have been when she first came to Amherst, but once in love, she was in deep. She never wavered, and she never regretted it.

The entries in the journal for the months after Austin's death are short and stark. She did not indulge herself, as she sometimes had previously, in romantic rhetoric and posing. Three days after Austin died, she wrote (August 19, 1895): "I am utterly crushed. . . . I kissed his blessed cold cheek." Two months later (October 31): "It does not grow in the least easier." A month later (November 15): "I miss him so that I cannot adjust my life at all. . . . Well, my beloved Austin, there is no need to say good-night – you do not go away at all." And as late as the following January (the sixth): "I am so tired with grief that I am worn out." Early that spring, when the Todds were about to start on a scientific expedition to Japan in Arthur Curtiss James's yacht, *Coronet,* she was more composed, more literary, but still deeply involved. Writing of a prospect that would once have utterly delighted her, she had only one thought (March 30, 1896):

> Yet nothing on earth has power to really thrill me any more – one old brown coat and a big hat used to be enough to set every drop of blood in my body tingling and racing through the veins in tumultuous rush. The sound of his well-beloved knock almost stopped my heart with joy – and the singular part of it is that it was always so – after fourteen years I thrilled to his coming or his voice or his distant figure just as in the first wonderful months when we were finding out that each was for the other *forever.*

# 10

# Austin's Marriage

Although most of Mabel Todd's correspondence with Austin is taken up with their mutual love and though most of her journal, when she is writing about personal things, concerns that same all-absorbing topic, she touched frequently on a matter about which much has been implicit, and not a little explicit, in earlier chapters: Austin's marriage. It has long been known that the marriage was unhappy, if only on the evidence of the affair with Mabel. The gossip began in earnest in the mid-1880s, but there were murmurings before then. What Mabel says about it, along with other comments that have recently come to light, allows the fullest view so far, and it is a bitter one.

Mabel's account, of course, tends to justify her own part in a highly unconventional relationship by sharpening the outlines of the story, with Sue the villain, Austin the victim, and herself the one who rescued his life from disaster. What Austin told her, even if she reported it truthfully, must (again) be taken with caution, since he, too, must have been under some compulsion to justify his relationship with Mabel. What cannot be denied is Mabel's privileged position. At one point in her journal (September 14, 1886) she described Austin as having been "self-contained and reticent all his life" (a good description of the Dickinson front to the world). But as their intimacy increased from that crucial September day onward, his reticence diminished. On April 5, 1890, he wrote her, "You are my only confidante – the only one I ever had"—an exaggeration, surely, in view of his outpourings to Sue during the courtship, the long confessional letter to Martha Gilbert, the "kitchen talks" with Emily, and his almost daily visits to the Homestead in the early 1880s. But by 1890 Emily had been gone four years, the courtship days were a bitter memory, and this late but perfect intimacy with Mabel may have made her seem the first. Certainly Austin had ample opportunity to tell her everything there was to tell. Mabel's diary records his innumerable calls, their day-long walks and rides when, apparently, he spoke more freely about Sue and his home life than he ever did in his letters. Only a fraction of his confidences, it seems clear, ever reached the pages of Mabel's journal or diary. What *did,* for all its obvious bias, is always revealing (in one way or another) and sometimes startling.

Austin's description of his feelings on his wedding day—as if he were going to his execution—is a sample. Mabel's account makes it sound as if Sue pressured him into marriage to satisfy her social ambitions and her longing for security. The thrust of the courtship letters, in which Austin is the passionate, pleading suitor, is reversed. While Mabel wrote in her journal for December 16, 1885, that Susan "made him marry her," and while it is conceivable, of course, that if an accurate dating of the courtship letters were possible, Austin's passion might be shown to have ebbed· gradually as the wedding approached, Mabel's phrase about Austin's "terrible repugnance" cannot be otherwise documented and tells, perhaps, more about Austin's accumulated bitterness over the years than about his feelings on his wedding day. Mabel's account of his motives in choosing Sue also seems overcolored, although she purports to be quoting him. Austin thought (she wrote in this same entry) that by marrying Sue, a tavern keeper's daughter, he would be introducing "bodily vigor" into the Dickinson line, more so than if he married a "gentle lady"—a revelation that moves Mabel to comment: "It does not do for persons of entirely different social grade to marry." She continued with a panegyric on "the most intimate and tender friendship . . . the most delicate chivalry and courtesy" she has always enjoyed with Austin—all those blessings, she implies, that Sue failed to give him.

On one important point she is positive. In the same passage that described Austin's repugnance toward his marriage, she continued: ". . . he found himself wofully mistaken in it all – at once." If this is true, or even approximately so, it shows how soon the shadow fell over Austin's life, and it throws a somber light over those gay evenings in the Evergreens we hear about during the late 1850s. What it meant for Emily we can only speculate.

In the journal, shortly after the first rift in the relations between the families in the winter of 1883, Mabel touches on the specifics of Austin's wretched domestic life. Other details, some of them harrowing, appear off and on throughout the next seven or eight years. Her account begins in a long journal entry for April 10, 1883:

> Mr. Dickinson has told me a great many things since I last wrote. . . .
> It seems he & his wife have not been in the least happy together, although for the sake of appearances & the children, they have continued to live together. Notwithstanding the utter lack of love between them, the fact that he is so interested in me has stirred her beyond the power of words to express. And she makes it pretty dreadful for him at home. I have seen some

developments in her character which are very startling. . . . Mr. Dickinson's life has been very barren.

What these startling developments were can be inferred from subsequent entries. On September 16, 1883, Mabel described Sue's behavior on a drive in the country, in which both families joined, as "still very chaotic and not sweet," and added that she has given Austin "a wretched life at home, in spite of the perfect house & grounds, the carriages & horses, pictures & luxuries generally." Relations between the families were now threatened with a permanent break, with the two ladies as antagonists. The journal commented:

> Mrs. D. is so well understood in Amherst that the fact of her breaking with us cannot redound to her credit. . . . Mr. D. says she fears me – the first woman who ever really crossed her path.

What Mabel meant by the "chaotic" in Sue's behavior soon becomes apparent. As the entries accumulate, Sue's character gradually takes on darker and darker colors. In this same entry, Sue's present anger and frustration appear (to Mabel) as the inevitable result of her failure as a wife from the beginning.

> I cannot blame her for her frantic efforts to regain the respect & love of her husband – which she has not had for more than twenty years. . . . Though she has gone her own way all these years, & never tried to keep him, doing all the time things morally certain to do worse than alienate him from her – yet now when she sees he has turned to me . . . she chafes & raves & cannot endure it. The greatest joy in life lay beside her for years, & she never moved to retain it, even pushed it from her. Now it has left her irrevocably, & she sees the awful loss & void. She has the husk, from which the soul has departed. And I cannot blame her, nor do other than deeply pity her.

Sue, added Mabel, has tried "coldness, hauteur, affectionateness, commanding, indignation" but "nothing succeeds."

All this made for unhappiness at home and social unpleasantness abroad, but it was superficial compared with the much deeper incompatibilities from which it apparently sprung. Not only had Austin's romantic dreams (as he had poured them out to Sue in the courtship letters) come to nothing; but, according to Mabel's account, Sue was an unwilling partner in his more realistic hope of strengthening the Dickinson line, or even perpetuating it. What he discovered—and "at once"—wrote Mabel in her journal (December 16, 1885) was Sue's "morbid dread of having any children." In her final summing up, in 1932, of her relations with the Dickinsons,[1] Mabel returned to this theme of Sue's distaste for marital relations. Sue, she wrote, called them "low practices" and kept Austin from her for many months after the wedding. Sue's attitude "hurt and distressed his life to the quick. . . . His life has been in all home things a terrible failure." Ned, the first child, was born a full five years after the

---

1. See the document "Scurrilous but True," reproduced fully in Appendix II, 4.

wedding and only after Sue (according to the journal entry) had "caused three or four to be artificially removed" and had failed in repeated attempts to prevent his birth. Years later (journal, October 18, 1891), Mabel reiterated that statement. Speaking of Austin's life of "bitter pain and disappointment," she wrote, "Sue's unnatural, cowardly horror of having any children turned all life dark to him for years – she had four killed before birth." To add to Austin's miseries, Ned became an epileptic (the result, thought Mabel, of Sue's efforts to "get rid of him"). Here, too, Sue turned out to be no tough and capable daughter of the soil. According to Mabel, she cowered in terror while Austin dealt with Ned's nocturnal fits, whose thrashings fairly shook the house. This "night horror" (as Mabel called it) was a severe strain on Austin, whose "nervous system [is] so exquisitely delicate and high strung."

These revelations may all be factual; they may not be; they may be partly so. In "Scurrilous but True," Mabel set them in the broad perspective of Sue and the town and brought in another witness to Austin's confidences, her husband David.

> While never saying anything unjust of his family, Austin told us, gradually, the entire tale of his life's utter disappointment, not only in the affected and pretentious Sue, but of her having caused his son Ned and his daughter Mattie to assume the attitude of utter superiority to the town and all his neighbors which they preserved through life and which caused profound anger in many persons quite as good in family and attainments as the two young people. Their mother had so instructed them that neither could act naturally or honestly toward the world. He also told us the real cause of Ned's delicacy – which cannot be repeated here.

A penciled scrap in the Todd-Bingham Archive, in Millicent Todd Bingham's handwriting and apparently a memorandum of a conversation with her mother, adds some specifics to the charge of the abortions and Ned's poor health:

> Sue had several abortions. Dr. Breck of Springfield, as she thought it disgusting to have children. She tried to get rid of Ned but he was born in spite of her but was an invalid, epileptic fits in his sleep. . . . His mother afraid of him so father had to go to him & he thought it gave him (Austin) heart disease. Ned woke on such mornings with a sore mouth from having bitten his tongue.

The darkest revelation of all is recorded in the long entry of December 16, 1885. It gives disturbing substance to Mabel's rhetoric—the "wretchedness" and the "horrors" of Austin's home life, Sue's "chafing" and "raving" and her "chaotic" behavior. As to its credibility, it at least is in line with a cluster of facts, near-facts, and allegations about Sue that all point to something ruthless and ungovernable in her nature: her bursts of temper, people leaving town because of her cruelty, her alleged alcoholism (supposedly inherited from her father), Vinnie's mortal fear of her after Austin died, and Vinnie's charge that Sue by her "cruel treatment" shortened Emily's life ten years. The crucial passage from Mabel's December 16 entry, furthermore, contains the very wording of Austin's cryptic directive to Vinnie on the packet of letters: "If anything should happen to me. . . ." The difference is that it specified the reason for his alarm:

> Her [Sue's] fits of horrible & entirely unrestrained temper have put Austin several times in danger of his life, & he says if anything should happen to him suddenly we may be tolerably sure she has killed him in a sudden wrath.

Then, as if to sum it up, there is a scrap in Mabel's hand that has survived in the family papers. Enclosed in an envelope labeled "Austin's statements to me," it is Austin's life as he described it to Mabel Todd. The items are numbered.

1. Fly in spider's web
2. Entire disappointment in all so-called married life
3. Destruction of various children (not intimated but expressed)
4. Carving knife thrown at you & other fits of diabolical temper
5. The spoiling of your life until you found me – that is, only coming to your own, after years of mistake & endurance.

There is little to corroborate these charges in Austin's letters and diary, though there are the directive to Vinnie, the repeated insistence that he knew no happiness until he met Mabel, the references to his family's behavior that made him want to "smash the machine," and the "animosities [that] surround me" of the letter to his friend in Omaha. We have seen how, in the impassioned letter to Mabel of March 1883, he did *not* write the story of his life, as he set out to do, thinking it would be "better and nobler that I say nothing which involves any other, reflects upon any other! may offend or wound." Once Mabel Todd praised him for his restraint. "He knows his life has been all but spoiled," she wrote in her journal on September 14, 1886, but he is "gentle and generous in his feeling toward the Spoiler." He often admitted to her that the original mistake had been his. "He says she was not made to understand him – so far she could not help." He blamed her only to this extent: "If she had done even as well as lay in her, he could never have blamed her, but not doing even that, & going through life wholly selfishly, & worse. . . ."

It is this last theme—Sue's selfish, pleasure-seeking life—that is reiterated in the surviving volumes of Austin's diary. Even here, whether through reticence or a lawyer's shrewdness, he is terse and detached. His infrequent comments seldom go beyond irritation with Sue's ways, or weariness with the social gatherings in his house. From 1880 on, the references are frequent to "Sue and her crowd," their outings, dances, "sprees," "riots": "A riot in the house till 10½" (June 17, 1880). On June 19, 1882, the party for Ned's twenty-first birthday lasted until one in the morning "in a wild tear and revel, everything being turned inside out and upside down, and one dancer jamming right through a register." At another time he declared himself "tired to death" with his family's pursuit of pleasure and called his house (June 20, 1882) "my wife's tavern." On May 11, 1883, two friends of Ned's arrive "to commence a series of orgies here." But there is no indication anywhere in the diaries of the kind of pressure or fear that Mabel Todd reported; compared with her rhetoric, Austin's is neutral indeed. The many entries about Ned's epileptic seizures make no complaint about Sue's lack of cooperativeness—nor, for that matter, do they mention her help. All that can be gathered from the diary is the impression of a busy man whose tastes, interests, and friends differed diametrically from those of his wife. He loved nature—his daily entries never failed to mention the weather and the look of things—while Sue loved society. He worked, while Sue (as he saw her) played. Emily hit off at least this superficial difference between them in an epigram in 1877: "[Austin] is overcharged with care, and Sue with scintillation."

Mabel Todd's youth, involvement, egocentrism, her turn for the dramatic—all these must be considered in evaluating her account. Her own behavior was not above reproach, and there were those in town who reproached her severely. During its thirteen-year history, in spite of all precautions, her affair with Austin became public knowledge, and gossip flew. On one side, she was branded as flirt and troublemaker (as Ned had accused her to his mother); on the other, there were those who blamed Sue for making Austin's life miserable and wished him joy of Mrs. Todd. (The second Mrs. Mather, wife of Professor Richard Mather and close neighbor of the Dickinsons, is reported to have said, "If after all his years of misery, Austin can get any joy from Mrs. Todd, he deserves it.") Still others thought that Austin was shockingly irresponsible and self-indulgent. In the eyes of the town, none of the three principals was blameless, and one would gladly dismiss the affair as another village quarrel were its implications not so important.

At the very least, the gossip that has come down in bits and snatches has tended to erode the notion of "Sweet Sue" as surely as the notion of "Our Emily" must now be relegated to myth. Life in the Evergreens can no longer be regarded in the idyllic light of the early biographies of Emily Dickinson. Though Austin had enemies, he was generally respected and loved and hence was less the target of gossip than the others. Young Mrs. Todd was much criticized at first for her "modern" ways but only later came in for vindictive gossip. Socially, Sue was a ruling power for sixty years in the town. (She was so good at it that Samuel Bowles would have given her a degree.) But she made many enemies. "Never have I lived where one family ruled as the D[ickinson]'s did in Amherst," wrote Lavinia's friend Mary Lee Hall, who came to the town shortly before Emily died and lived there twenty years. By "Dickinsons," she meant Sue. It will be clear later how far from benign she thought that rule was.

The recurrent themes in the gossip about Sue are snobbery and love of dominance. When the orphaned Newman sisters came to live in the Evergreens in 1858, Sue seemed to enjoy "treating them like poor relatives."[2] Clara reported that, for punishment, Sue made her study entire evenings "in a lighted bay window with the shades up," an indignity she remembered the rest of her life. A faculty wife wrote to her son in 1876 that Mrs. Jenkins, wife of the minister, at first a great favorite of Sue's, had become "disgusted – with the patronizing and the flattery and the hollowness." It was this same faculty wife who described the Mathers two years later as being "very sorry for Miss Vinny – Mrs Austin rides it rough shod over her – "

There are many other scratchy comments in the annals. Two more will suffice. They point, in different language, to the same thing. Professor John Burgess, whose praise of Sue's social talents we have already heard, admitted that she was "a little too aggressive, a little too sharp in wit and repartee, and a little too ambitious for social prestige." Alfred E. Stearns, recalling in 1946 his boyhood in Amherst, put it less politely:

> In my boyhood days and in common with my friends I had heard stories of a mysterious woman who with her less gifted but equally peculiar sister lived in the house next to that occupied by Austin Dickinson, the treasurer of the college. I knew that these spinsters were sisters of the treasurer and, for this was common gossip, that his wife and daughter Mattie, commonly regarded as the town's outstanding snobs, were a bit ashamed to acknowledge the relationship and treated them as strangers or worse.

As he continued with his reminiscences, Stearns's treatment of what he called the "Todd-Dickinson episode" is decidedly comic, as it must have seemed to a young man who knew very little about it. Austin, thought Stearns, liked Mabel because she was the only one in town who shared his interest in landscape gardening, and the love affair had been blown up by the gossips because someone had seen them out driving together. All smoke and no flame, he concluded.

Whether or not Sue brought her troubles on herself, there is no doubt that she had plenty to bear, much of it far from comic. Life in the Evergreens became unbearably tense, for Sue and the children as well as for Austin. On December 7, 1884, Sue wrote to her daughter: "I carry very many burdens, so heavy that I sometimes feel that you and Ned will be left ere very long without any one but each other"—the assumption being that they had already lost a father. Austin regarded Ned and Mattie as on their mother's side and said as much in his will. That short document left the Homestead and Austin's share in his father's estate to Lavinia, two pictures to Mabel Todd, and all the rest "real and personal" to Sue;

2. From Millicent Todd Bingham's penciled notes on an interview with Mrs. Clara Newman Pearl (Mrs. George E.), Clara Newman Turner's niece, in Haverhill, Mass., September 13, 1932. The whole passage reads:

[After the death of their parents] the two younger girls [Clara and Anna] were put into Austin's family after his marriage and had a hard time of it. Though they had money, Sue took pleasure in treating them like poor relatives, and made Clara look out for Ned and Anna for Mattie. She was ingenious in cruelties. They went to the Amherst public schools. Sue had a very difficult disposition.

Edward Dickinson (Ned)
Martha Dickinson (Mattie)

Gilbert Dickinson (Gib)

then: "I make no special mention of Ned and Mattie because they are practically one in interest and feeling with their Mother, and would I presume prefer it in this way to any division." He was completely right about Martha, who was very much her mother's child (as Gilbert was Austin's) and carried on her mother's battle to the end. Ned's loyalties seem to have been mixed. One of his letters shows compassion for his mother; on March 5, 1885, he wrote Martha:

> If there is any beautiful, peaceful, restful place hereafter and [Mother] dont have a seat among the Saints & martyrs – I dont care to go there – Such superhuman efforts to keep up & cheerful, for those around her – mortal eye never witnessed. . . . My only ambition in life . . . is to have a quiet, pleasant little house somewhere – with you and Mother in it, where things can be *pleasant* – No fame, no brains, no family, no scholarship, *No Anything* amounts to anything beside that. . . .

But if this seems to place him completely on his mother's side, later testimony puts it in question. Mary Lee Hall's letters to Mrs. Bingham in the early 1930s several times touch on Ned's attitude toward the family situation. Ned, apparently, became a frequent caller at the Halls' and gave them a sad picture of life in the Evergreens:

> Ned told us that his life had been a "hell on earth," & that the early hour that he daily spent in reading really worth while things, was what kept him sane, and half decent.

In another letter (three years later) Miss Hall returned to the "hell on earth" theme, with a pathetic Austin-Sue scene and more than a hint of Ned's attitude:

> I have wondered if Sue and Mattie knew that he [Ned] came to the house, and talked freely about the home life. He told of the friendship of Austin and your Mother, said he could not blame his father, altho' he called the attention indiscreet because of the terrible scenes it caused in the family. There were weeks when Sue would not speak to Austin, and when Austin would not speak to her. Ned had seen his Mother kneel at his father's feet, and beg him to speak to her. I truly believe that in his heart, Ned put most of the blame upon his Mother. He said that he and Mattie had grown up in an atmosphere of Hell.

In another of Ned's comments his feelings are put more precisely. He told Miss Hall that he "had always admired [Mrs. Todd], and had never changed in his feelings for [her], but he felt obliged to hide his feelings, and to stand by his Mother even though he considered her to be entirely responsible for what had happened."

Such comments seem sufficient, at least, to rule out the possibility that Mabel Todd willfully falsified her account of Austin's marriage. And it should be said that she, like Ned, had sympathy for Sue and (to her credit) recognized Sue's abilities from the beginning and never ceased admiring them. Even during the painful months of 1883, when the affair

[ *193* ]

with Ned opened the first rift between the families, Mabel wrote to Austin in February, just after the distressing evening:

Can you see how I can still love her very much? But I do – she stimulates me intellectually more than any other woman I ever knew. She is fascinating to me. I would do *anything* to make her like me again. . . . I do care a great deal for her – and I am inexpressibly sorry for her –

Seven months later, when things were even worse, she noted in her journal (September 16, 1883): "Notwithstanding all that I hear about her, I do admire her mind."

By the time of Susan's death in 1913, much had happened to fix forever the hostility between the two women. Sue had been furious when she heard that Lavinia had engaged Mabel to edit the poems. No one in the Evergreens was allowed to speak to Vinnie for months; Sue forbade the mention of her name—and Emily's—in the household. Mabel wrote (journal, November 30, 1890):

[Vinnie] is constantly exasperated and outraged at Susan – as well as hurt and wounded to death by her cruelties. She seems at times to be curiously in fear of her, and she used to wish not to offend her. Of course she knew that Susan would want to kill her as soon as she found out that I had brought out the poems.

Her "crowning atrocity," as Mabel called it, was to claim that Emily had bequeathed the poems to *her* and that Vinnie's actions were illegal, a charge, however, that Sue never pressed. When Vinnie took legal action in 1898 against the Todds for the strip of land Austin had deeded them, Mabel, of course, saw Sue's hand in the operation, and all chance of reconciliation was gone. So it is noteworthy that in her diary (May 13, 1913) for the day after Susan died, Mabel, though still critical of Sue, was capable of some admiration and compassion. At least she seems to have understood, as Emily did, the paradox and the power of Sue's nature:

Poor old Susan died last night. A very curious nature, full of (originally) fine powers most cruelly perverted. She has done incalculable evil, and wrought endless unhappiness. At times she seemed possessed of a devil – yet could be smoothly winning & interesting. Close to the surface was always the Tartar.

Mabel's final deposition, the document "Scurrilous but True," came nineteen years later, the year, as it happened, of her own death (1932). To one familiar with the journal and letters, it presents few surprises. The old charges are there: Susan's aggressiveness in getting Austin to marry her, her attitude toward having children, Austin's mistake in thinking that, by marrying out of his social class, he would strengthen his family line, Sue's cruelty to people in the town and the town's "thorough distrust" of her. There are some interesting additions, however, to certain aspects of the situation already familiar to us. She described her first impression of Austin and Susan:

. . . when these two called upon me, as they did shortly after my arrival in Amherst, I was much impressed with both. He was a truly regal man, tall and magnificent in bearing, and she well-dressed with an India shawl over her shoulders, which became her dark beauty.

She recorded her first intimations of trouble, intimations in the form of warnings from both Vinnie and Sue:

"I hope you will not go very much to the other house," said Vinnie one day shortly after my visits there had become regular and expected; "I have seen too many hearts broken there," she went on, "and always to those liked and loved at first."

It was on this occasion that she saw herself becoming involved in "a family quarrel of endless involutions," the "mazes of feeling between the two houses." Vinnie warned her about the Evergreens; Sue warned her away from the Homestead. The battle lines between the houses were well established by the early 1880s:

About this time Sue, as she was called in the village, began to tell me about a remarkable sister of Austin's who never went out, and saw no one who called. I heard of her also through others in town who seemed to resent, somewhat, her refusal to see themselves, who had known her in earlier years. Then came a note from this mysterious Emily's housemate, her sister Lavinia, demanding that I call 'at once, with my husband'. Sue said at that, 'You will not allow your husband to go there, I hope!' 'Why not?' I asked innocently. 'Because they have not, either of them, any idea of morality,' she replied, with a certain satisfaction in her tone. I knew that would interest my good husband, and pressing her a little farther, she added, 'I went in there one day, and in the drawing room I found Emily reclining in the arms of a man. What can you say to that?' I had no explanation, of course, so I let the subject drop, notwithstanding which I went to the ancestral mansion in which the two lived a few days later.

Sue's disparagement of Emily here brings up the entire problem of the Sue-Emily relationship later described so confidently by Martha as a "romantic friendship" that extended "from girlhood until death."[3] The

---

3. *The Single Hound* (1914), ed. Martha Dickinson Bianchi, "The Editor's Preface," p. v. Cf. Martha also in her *Life and Letters of Emily Dickinson:* "Her sister Sue recognized her genius from the first, and hoarded every scrap Emily sent her from the time they were both girls of sixteen. Their love never faltered or waned" (p. 64). In *Emily Dickinson Face to Face,* Martha becomes even more lyric; speaking of the notes Emily sent in a continuous stream across the lawn, she writes (p. 176):

Scores of such short notes were also given in the text of "Life and Letters," as they best flash a quick hint of the varied sympathies always existing between Aunt Emily and my mother – from their first girlish wonderings about life, on through the books they shared, the flowers they tilled, the friends they loved, their culinary wizardry, their domestic crises, their absorption in us children, their fun and fears, their gay whimsies and tragic realities; all their deepening experiences uniting to weld the confident and profound devotion enduring unto death.

following passage from "Scurrilous but True," however biased it may be, at least shows how questionable Martha's description is. During her first talks with Vinnie, Mabel continued:

> It quickly came out that Vinnie was herself nearly heart-broken over Sue's treatment of Emily, and herself too, only she never counted anything done to herself in comparison with anything involving her adored Emily. She often said she knew that Emily would die years before she ought owing to the cruelties practiced upon her almost ever since poor Austin was "taken in" and made to marry outside of his normal class, socially. Her account was really sad and terrible. At first Emily had tried to make her only brother like and marry her early friend, Sue Gilbert, and for some years she aided and abetted the match, which had made Austin at first melancholy to an unprecedented degree. . . . For years before I came to Amherst Emily had not had any affectionate relations with the Sue once so loved, and Vinnie had not been to her brother's house for years. . . . Every day he visited them, and it was really a genuine refreshment of spirit to him.

Here is Mabel's summing up of Sue, the marriage, the "War between the Houses" and Austin's role in it:

> "Sue" was a person full of certain kinds of ability, never used in any noble manner as help or affection for her fellow townsmen, but practically always in their detriment; for many years before my coming to Amherst there had been no real communication between the two Dickinson homes. The two sisters lived their own life entirely independent of the "other house" and Austin was the only link between. He went to see his sisters every day, and they loved and revered him all the more since his profound unhappiness in his marriage had left him few satisfactions in his home. The story of his disenchantment with Sue was told me, first by indifferent persons in town, and then more in detail by Lavinia with a few comments by Emily in her curiously interrogative voice from the next room.

The tone, compared with the letters and journal, is detached; but the position is the same. Sue, the alien element, had brought on the war and wrecked their lives. There is no word of self-reproach, no sense that she, Mabel Todd herself, had entered the situation as an alien element and had precipitated its worst phase. Her position was simple: Austin had been hers by divine right; Sue had forfeited him.

# *11*

---

# Susan and Emily

SUSAN," said Emily, "fronts on the Gulf Stream." "What depths of Domingo in that torrid Spirit!" Whatever these two remarks (both in notes to Sue during the last three years of Emily's life) may imply in a moral way about Emily's estimate of Susan's character or behavior, they are tributes, if nothing else, to her power. To have lived next door to such a person for thirty years was an experience, and what Sue saved of the notes that crossed the narrow strip between the Homestead and the Evergreens fairly tingle with it. What Emily made of the experience, what it did for her or to her are vital questions. At the very least, her relationship with Sue was one of the controlling influences in her life. The girlhood phase did not last long and ended sadly for Emily. What scars it left can only be guessed at. Emily in her maturity was seldom discursive on any aspect of her personal life and never on this.

The materials to go on are few and ambiguous. The most important, of course, are the dozens of notes that Sue kept. These are mostly very brief (Emily's early effusive style disappears soon after Sue's marriage); many of them are cryptic, or gnomic, or Delphic; and many can be dated only approximately. There are a few comments by observers, like Lavinia's as passed on by Mabel Todd and Mary Lee Hall, and then there is Martha Dickinson Bianchi's account, which gives only the happy side. There is a brief, troubled letter from Sue to Emily. There are a few poems that mention Sue by name and a cluster of others that by imagery, metaphor, and similar phrasing seem fairly surely to be about her or to have come out of their relationship.

Even a casual run through the notes makes the problem clear. In spite of all we know about the "War between the Houses" and what it tells about Emily's estrangement from Sue, terms of endearment persist to the end.

There is no clear evidence of a break—nothing as forthright as Emily's youthful pronouncement: "Sue – you can go or stay." There are some edgy notes and signs of strain. There is one bit of verse about a rejection that may be a cry from the heart. But, though not always loving, the tone of the thirty-year correspondence is mostly cordial. One wonders if Emily was being characteristically reticent, or hiding her true feelings behind irony and wit, or trying to keep the surface of things smooth for Austin's sake. Or Martha Bianchi, to give the impression of a love that never faltered, may have suppressed evidence or altered dates in her zeal to defend her mother.[1] The problem may never be solved, but it is important that its terms be understood.

A few general truths seem beyond question. We have seen that Emily had an all but obsessive concern for every member of her family. She kept an anxious eye not only on their private concerns (Father's loneliness or Vinnie's headache), but she was interested all her life in their public lives—whether her father's associates in Washington understood him, or how Austin was getting along with his students in Boston. Even when her withdrawal was most complete, her letters are peppered with gossip and personal matters. We know how close she and Austin were from the beginning; she had early spotted him as a worrier, and she worried about him. We know that she felt herself a part of his courtship, and it is inconceivable that she did not become involved in the much more intense drama of his marriage. When the Homestead became Austin's spiritual home, at the very least a refuge from the tensions of the Evergreens, Emily would hardly have tolerated his daily conversations about Mabel Todd (as he described them in the summer of 1885) if she had not long understood his situation and sympathized with him.[2] And there is the report by Mrs. Jameson that on the night of Gilbert's death Emily had come to Sue and Austin's house for the first time in "15 years." On an even more general level, the "Dickinson difference," an axiom of Emily's youth, reflects her hope that Sue would join the inner circle and be one of them, a true sister. But the fact is that the loving and fruitful relationship Emily hoped for did not materialize.

It may have been just as well for Emily's poetry, if not for her happiness, that Sue turned out to be a very un-Dickinsonian Dickinson. She

---

1. Cf. David Higgins, *Portrait of Emily Dickinson: The Poet and Her Prose* (1967), p. 37: "Sue's daughter, Martha Dickinson Bianchi, fostered the image of 'Sister Sue,' Emily's *alter ego* with a 'sixth sense for Emily's real meaning.' In doing so, she misdated poems and letters until it seemed that Emily had praised Sue in prose and verse from the mid-eighteen forties to the end of her life." Higgins appends a revealing note: "The misdating began with Sue. In March 1853, when both Sue and Emily were twenty-two, Emily sent Sue [the poem] 'On this wondrous sea.' Mrs. Bianchi wrote on the manuscript, 'The first verse Aunt Emily sent to Mamma – (She *thought* when both were sixteen or so.)' Sue's later transcript of the poem survives; on it she wrote '1848.' See *P* I, 6–7."

2. For "the little visits with my sisters" (letter of July 12, 1885), see Chapter 9, p. 178.

expanded Emily's horizon and was a vital part of her education. In 1882 (late enough to be a summing up), Emily put the matter to Sue in her usual ambiguous way: "With the exception of Shakespeare, you have told me of more knowledge than any one living – To say that sincerely is strange praise."[3] "Strange praise," surely, if she implies what seems obvious: a Shakespearian range of temperament and qualities, evil as well as good—as Mabel Todd (and, as we shall see later, Mary Lee Hall) summed them up, the "originally fine powers," the charm and wit, the touch of the devil and "the Tartar." Clearly, Emily reveled in the wit and the fine powers; it also seems clear that she felt at times the touch of the devil—the "Gimblets – among the nerve – " She learned from both.

For two years after the wedding (July 1, 1856) there were no letters— at least there are none extant. Whether Emily knew that Austin realized his mistake in marrying Sue—"at once," as Mabel Todd said—is impossible to say. At least his alleged unhappiness did not prevent Emily's frequent visits to the Evergreens. It was in 1859 that Emily called Austin and Sue "my crowd." When the correspondence resumed in the fall of 1858, there was some, but not much, of the old feeling and a good deal of verbal play. On September 26, a brisk, cheerful, gossipy letter went off to Sue, then visiting sister Martha in Geneva.

> I hav'nt any paper, dear, but faith continues firm – Presume if I met with my "deserts," I should receive nothing. Was informed to that effect today by a "dear pastor." What a privilege it is to be so insignificant! Thought of intimating that the "Atonement" was'nt needed for such atomies! . . .
>
> Ah – Dobbin – Dobbin – you little know the chink which your dear face makes. We would'nt mind the sun, dear, if it did'nt *set* – How much you cost – how much Mat costs – I will never sell you for a piece of silver. I'll buy you back with red drops, when you go away. I'll keep you in a casket – I'll bury you in the garden – and keep a bird to watch the spot – perhaps my pillow's safer – Try my bosom last – That's nearest of them all, and I should hear a foot the quickest, should I hear a foot – . . .
>
> God bless you, if he please! Bless Mr John and Mrs Mat – Bless two or three others! I wish to be there – Shall I come? If I jump, shall you catch me. . . .

And so on, with some tender farewells to the whole household. It is a cordial letter, surely, but the old passion and the yearning are gone. Emily, it seems, has learned that Sue the married woman was not to be the soul mate and confidante so longed for in the early years. Rather, Sue emerges as someone with whom, at a safe distance, she could at least play at wit and love. Such, at any rate, appears to be the meaning of the strained

3. The editors of the 1958 *Letters* (III, 733 n.) comment as follows on this remark, a complete letter in itself: "The strain between the two houses about this time had perhaps a temporary fission. . . . It is probable that Sue's resentment concerning the attachment of Emily to Judge Lord was made clear to Emily, and may account for this note of 'strange praise.'"

metaphors—the piece of silver, the red drops, the casket, her pillow, and her bosom. It can hardly be imagined that Sue took them seriously.

On the social level, Emily learned much from Sue, and much that was good. Her parties helped keep Emily in circulation, at least for a while. There were lively evenings at the Evergreens, during one of which Edward Dickinson himself arrived at the indecent hour of midnight to fetch his daughter home. Emily played and sang (we are told) her inimitable songs, and there was much laughter. Often there were interesting people at Sue's, and, much as she was inclined to run from them, Emily enjoyed their talk. She described a typical evening in a letter to Mrs. Holland (about February 20, 1859):

> . . . sitting next evening with S[ue],[4] as I often do, some one rang the bell and I ran, as is my custom.
> What was my surprise and shame, on hearing Mr. Chapman ask for "Mrs. D!" K[ate] S[cott], a guest of [Sue]'s, was my confederate, and clinging fast like culprit mice, we opened consultation. . . .

They were "detected" and Emily "gasped a brief apology":

> I do not mind [offending] Mr. Hyde of Ware [whom, with Mr. Chapman, the Edward Dickinsons had entertained the evening before], because he does not please me, but Mr. Chapman is my friend, talks of my books with me, and I would not wound him.

At least at Sue's she could talk books and get away from the austerity that, with Austin gone, was settling in at the Homestead. Whatever she said later about Sue's scintillation, at this point she delighted in it.

Intellectually, Sue was as lively as anyone in town. The two exchanged books, gave them to each other as presents, and (presumably) discussed them. Although, after the early years, Emily never unbosomed herself on important, personal matters in her extant letters to Sue (she *did* to other intimates, like the Hollands and the Norcross cousins), there is enough in her tiny notes to Sue to show rapport on many levels, if not the deepest. They enjoyed Biblical and literary allusions, usually with a whimsical turn and often so private as to be a kind of code language between them. (In the "Gulf Stream" note Emily comments on a coincidence that gave her pause: "Do you remember what whispered to 'Horatio'?") They

---

4. *L* II, 348–49. Sue's name was originally deleted by Austin. Millicent Todd Bingham (*Home*, p. 54) gives the following explanation:

> Mr. Dickinson stipulated that if Emily's letters to him were to be used [in the publication Mrs. Todd was then preparing in the early 1890s], the name of one of her girlhood friends must be left out – that of Susan Gilbert, his wife. But omitting her name was not enough. Before turning over the letters he went through them, eliminating Susan Gilbert's name and in some instances making alterations to disguise a reference to her. He asked my mother to make sure he had overlooked nothing. In the published volumes Sue's name does not appear. It has been said that her name was omitted at her own request. This is not the case. Mrs. Dickinson was not aware that publication of Emily's letters was in prospect.

indulged their private skepticisms and being quizzical together. Emily called it "the clandestine Mind" and practiced her gnomic style on Sue. "In a Life that stopped guessing," she wrote, "you and I should not feel at home – "

The extent of Sue's help with Emily's poetry is impossible to document, except for the one instance of the poem "Safe in their Alabaster Chambers." She praised the poem, with reservations:

I am not suited dear Emily with the second verse – It is remarkable as the chain lightening that blinds us hot nights in the Southern sky but it does not go with the ghostly shimmer of the first verse as well as the other one – It just occurs to me that the first verse is complete in itself it needs no other, and can't be coupled – Strange things always go alone – as there is only one Gabriel and one Sun – You never made a peer for that verse, and I *guess* you[r] kingdom does'nt hold one – I always go to the fire and get warm after thinking of it, but I never *can* again – . . .

The note, besides being remarkably perceptive criticism, shows Sue as a mentor of some standing. In reply, Emily composed two alternates for the second stanza, chose one, and sent it to Sue with the question, "Is *this* frostier?" She appended a note that is as close as she got to announcing her literary ambitions in these years (the time was about 1860 or 1861) and is a measure of her confidence in Sue's judgment:

DEAR SUE –
Your praise is good – to me – because I *know* it *knows* – and *suppose* it means –
Could I make you and Austin – proud – sometime – a great way off – 'twould give me taller feet –[5]

After the "Alabaster Chambers" episode there is no record of Emily's asking Sue's opinion again. Emily may have sensed a barb in Sue's "You never made a peer for that verse, and I *guess* you[r] kingdom does'nt hold one – " The emphasis in Emily's reply—*"suppose* it *means"*—might imply a doubt of Sue's kindly intentions. Only a few months later she turned to another mentor, Thomas Wentworth Higginson. At any rate, her respect for Sue's mind, and style, never wavered. In two separate notes of about 1881 she wrote: "Balm for Susan's Voice – Could sooner spare the Nightingale's – " and "Your impregnable syllables need no prop, to stand – "

Sue was not only capable of impregnable syllables, she brought out some of Emily's best. If Emily's audience had all been Sues—at least Sue of the "Alabaster Chambers" exchange—the history of her publication might have been different. Emily's virtuosity is seldom as brilliant as in these messages that sped from one house to the other. They are in a style she particularly (though not exclusively) reserved for Sue: tight, elliptical, almost always figurative.

5. The story of this exchange is told in full, and the episode dated summer 1861, in *P* I, 151–55, n.

The dominant tone is clear: it is one of admiration and gratitude for the privilege of living near such a person as Sue. The language is almost never neutral. Hyperbole is the rule, and images of uniqueness, size, power, totality abound. "Only Woman in the World, Accept a Julep – " "That Susan lives – is a Universe which neither going nor coming could displace – " "To thank one for Sweetness, is possible, but for Spaciousness, out of sight – " Sue is at one time her "vast" and at another her "great" sister. "I must wait a few Days before seeing you – You are too momentous. But remember it is idolatry, not indifference." Ten years earlier (about 1868) it had been: "Susan's Idolator keeps a Shrine for Susan." "To miss you, Sue, is power. The stimulus of Loss makes most Possession mean." The qualities in Sue that irritated many people in town—her social ambition and worldliness—Emily apparently cherished as welcome change from the usual Amherst fare. "To see you," she wrote Sue, "unfits for staler meetings. I dare not risk an intemperate moment before a Banquet of Bran." Whatever else she might have been, Sue was not pure Amherst. "Susan breaks many Commandments," Emily wrote her about 1879, "but *one* she obeys – 'Whatsoever ye do, do it unto the Glory' – " And once, thanking Sue for a visit: "Thank her dear power for having come, an Avalanche of Sun!"

If all this time Sue (as Vinnie charged) by her "cruel treatment" was shortening Emily's life, there is little in the notes to suggest it. There may be some ill feeling in a cluster ranging over a period of a dozen years (beginning in 1869) that play on the notion of Sue as Cleopatra. One complete note of about 1874 is typical: " 'Egypt – thou knew'st' – " "Tell the Susan who never forgets to be subtle, every Spark is numbered – " wrote Emily about 1884 and included a poem that may have implied a reproach to the "torrid Spirit":

> The farthest Thunder that I heard
> Was nearer than the Sky –
> And rumbles still –
> Though torrid Noons –
> Have lain their Missiles by – . . .                    (#1581)

And in 1878: "Susan knows she is a Siren – and that at a word from her, Emily would forfeit Righteousness – " Again (about 1869): "Dont do such things, dear Sue – The 'Arabian Nights' unfit the heart for it's Arithmetic – " She called Sue her "pseudo Sister" in a letter to Higginson about 1881—perhaps a rebuff, but possibly only a good-natured pun.[6] For Christmas 1876, Sue sent Emily a copy of *Of the Imitation of Christ,* inscribed "Emily with love," and in 1880 a copy of Disraeli's *Endymion*

6. Thomas H. Johnson, *Emily Dickinson: An Interpretive Biography,* p. 41, sees in it a hint "at some kind of alienation."

SUSAN GILBERT DICKINSON
From a medallion now hanging in ED's room, the Homestead.
Date and artist unknown. Perhaps taken from Sue's pose in
picture of "Shutesbury School of Philosophy"

Facsimile of "Safe in their Alabaster Chambers"
Emily to Sue, early summer 1861(?)

with the inscription: "Emily / Whom not seeing I still love,"—ironic in view of the proximity of the two houses. By this time, apparently, both women realized the distance between them. In late 1885, Emily concluded a brief note with the sentence: "The tie between us is very fine, but a Hair never dissolves." This may relate to a more explicit comment by Mary Lee Hall: "Emily turned against Sue, when Sue deceived her, and was not friendly toward her for more than a year before her death. . . ." What the deception was is not stated.

Two documents from the early 1860s, perhaps an exchange, indicate a much earlier breach than Miss Hall thought. The editors of the 1958 *Letters* suggest that the one from Emily to Sue was written shortly after Ned's birth (June 19, 1861) and is a complaint about Sue's neglecting her for the new baby. The note is a stanza of three lines:

SUE –

> Could *I* – then – shut the door –
> Lest *my* beseeching face – at last –
> Rejected – be – of *Her?*     (#*220, and L II, 381 n.*)

Perhaps Emily felt neglected while Sue was preoccupied with the new baby; but one wonders. Sue had plenty of domestic help (the Newman girls, both able and in their mid-teens, were in residence). Emily was fond of children, welcomed all of Sue's into the world and became devoted to them, as they to her. The note is characteristically ambiguous. It may be Emily's way of leveling an accusation: "Could *I* ever reject you as you have rejected me?" Or it may be part of a dialogue, an answer to an accusation that Emily herself has been aloof, or offish: "I could not possibly have rejected you, as you charge, if only for fear that you will some day ('at last') reject me." At the very least, it indicates trouble; there is no play here. But it is curiously isolated among the steady stream of friendly communications. One can only suspect that others of a similar nature have disappeared.

The other document is a note from Sue to Emily, written in late October of that year.

*Private* I have intended to write you Emily to day but the quiet has not been mine – I should send you this, lest I should seem to have turned away from a kiss –

If you have suffered this past Summer I am sorry [*cut*]. *I* Emily bear a sorrow that I never uncover – If a nightingale sings with her breast against a thorn, why not *we?* [*cut*] When I can, I shall write –

SUE –[7]

7. The MS (Dickinson Papers, Houghton Library, Harvard) is in three scissored pieces, as indicated by the bracketed "*cut.*" The scissorings seem to have been made for the purpose of deletion; but by whom, and why, is unknown.

There is no hint as to the cause of all this suffering—whether, for Sue, it had something to do with Austin and their marriage, or the birth of an unwanted child, or something in her relations with Emily. As for Emily's suffering "this past Summer," our only recourse is to other and not very clearly established facts of her life about this time. This was the year (1861, as far as can be determined from her handwriting) of the second and most anguished of her "Master" letters, drafted but never sent, recipient unknown, and whose theme is passionate and unrequited love. Many of the poems of this time are about loss and rejection. The search for specifics has led to many suggestions, ranging from personal and professional disappointment to anguish over the Civil War and back to premonitions of trouble with her eyes—whatever it was that in a letter of April 25, 1862, to Higginson she had in mind when she wrote, "I had a terror – since September – I could tell to none – "[8] And, according to this note of Sue's, *she* had a sorrow she could tell to none. Sue's nightingale with her "breast against a thorn" makes one suspect a romantic pose. But if Emily's verse note can be related to the withdrawn life that was shortly to intensify, there may be something more to it. As early as the quarrel in 1854, Emily had spoken of their "diverging paths," and now Sue, with her family and social life, was going a way which was clearly not Emily's. At the very least, the idea of rejection was in the air; and from what we know of Emily's sensitive relations with Sue, it would have taken only a hint. And it could have been either way: Sue might have rejected Emily, or Emily might have rejected Sue.

So, for fifteen years, according to the local estimate, Emily withdrew to the Homestead, not once venturing to the Evergreens until Gilbert's death, October 5, 1883. Had he lived, this remarkable child might have brought about some reconciliation between his parents and the two houses. Though there is no record of any loving, conciliatory meeting between Emily and Sue in their grief, the letters that Emily wrote Sue during the next months are among the tenderest since their girlhood. One is perhaps the finest she ever wrote anybody:

DEAR SUE –
The Vision of Immortal Life has been fulfilled –
How simply at the last the Fathom comes! The Passenger and not the Sea, we find surprises us –
Gilbert rejoiced in Secrets –
His Life was panting with them – With what menace of Light he cried "Dont tell, Aunt Emily"! Now my ascended Playmate must instruct *me*. Show us, prattling Preceptor, but the way to thee!
He knew no niggard moment – His Life was full of Boon – The Playthings of the Dervish were not so wild as his –
No crescent was this Creature – He traveled from the Full –

8. I have reserved full discussion of these matters for subsequent chapters.

Such soar, but never set –
I see him in the Star, and meet his sweet velocity in everything that flies –
His Life was like the Bugle, which winds itself away, his Elegy an echo –
his Requiem ecstasy –
Dawn and Meridian in one.
Wherefore would he wait, wronged only of Night, which he left for us –
Without a speculation, our little Ajax spans the whole –

> Pass to thy Rendezvous of Light,
> Pangless except for us –
> Who slowly ford the Mystery
> Which thou hast leaped across!       [#*1564*]
> Emily.

But beautiful as the letter is, Sue, the grieving mother, is hardly in it at all.[9]
In most of her letters of condolence—and no one surpassed her in that
delicate art—Emily offered comfort and help and love to her bereaved
friends. Here there is only the wonder and beauty of the lost child and the
mystery of death. Within a few days of Gilbert's death, Emily sent a
flower with a tiny note to "the dear, grieved Heart"; and another note of
about the same time spoke more to Sue's grief: "Hopelessness in it's first
Film has not leave to last. . . . Intimacy with Mystery, after great Space,
will usurp it's place – " But a poem that went with the note is all about
the dead boy.

> Expanse cannot be lost –
> Not Joy, but a Decree
> Is Deity –
> His Scene, Infinity –
> Whose rumor's Gate was shut so tight
> Before my Beam was sown,
> Not even a Prognostic's push
> Could make a Dent thereon –

9. Mrs. John Jameson, a neighbor "intimate with both Dickinson households"
(*YH* I, lvii), wrote her son Frank three weeks after Gilbert's death. Sue's grief,
though apparently not so devastating as Austin's, is sharply etched. (So is the village
gossip. Sue's period of formal mourning was indeed, at least in the eyes of Austin and
Mabel, unduly prolonged. In their letters she was often called "the great big black
mogul.")

I called on Mrs Dickinson this week and she *kissed* me when I went and when I
came away. She is a sad woman – and in fact the whole family are changed. . . .
Mrs. D. has seen no one except Madam Stearns and myself – says she cannot, she
will break down – and yet – someone said to Helen [Mrs. Jameson's daughter]
today that Mrs D. would probably "make a parade of her grief." What an
abominable place, a village is, for defamation of character and how easily the
worst will be believed of folks – (*YH* II, 411).

> The World that thou has opened
> Shuts for thee,
> But not alone,
> We all have followed thee –
> Escape more slowly
> To thy Tracts of Sheen –
> The Tent is listening,
> But the Troops are gone!                    (#1584)

Emily never fully recovered from Gilbert's death. It was a staggering loss. Indeed, in sharing their grief, Emily and Sue might have done much for each other; but there is no sign that they did. When Vinnie described the shock and grief in the two households and confessed her anxiety "for all that's left of this home," it was Austin, not Sue, whom she described as the stricken one. She spoke of her own and Emily's "hard work to keep Austin from following" Gilbert. Not once did she mention Sue as sharing in their efforts. There is no record that Emily's single visit that sad night led to any others.

Searching the poems for what they reveal about the relationship between Emily and Susan also has its problems. A few poems, like the two discussed in an earlier chapter—"I have a Bird in spring," sent in the "you can go or stay" letter in 1854, and "One Sister have I in our house," a letter poem of 1858—are clearly to the point. Both contain elements that qualify the adoring tone of the early letters and foreshadow later rifts. One other early poem that contains Sue's pet name, Dollie, and was probably sent to her, seems even more clearly to reflect early tensions. It is of a piece, surely, with the tone and idiom of that plaintive letter Emily wrote Sue in January 1855 shortly after the quarrel of the preceding September. The theme, we recall, was: "Tell me that you still love me." She missed Sue (then visiting in Michigan), mourned for her, walked the streets "alone – often at night":

> If it is finished, tell me, and I will raise the lid to my box of Phantoms, and lay one more love in; but if it *lives* and *beats* still, still lives and beats for *me,* then say me *so,* and I will strike the strings to one more strain of happiness before I die.

The poem seems to come so directly from this state of mind and heart (or from one very much like it) that it is tempting to suggest an earlier date for it than the 1860 assigned in the 1955 *Poems:*

You love me – you are sure –
I shall not fear mistake –
I shall not *cheated* wake –
Some grinning morn –
To find the Sunrise left –
And Orchards – unbereft –
And Dollie – gone!

I need not start – you're sure –
That night will never be –
When frightened – home to Thee I run –
To find the windows dark –
And no more Dollie – mark –
Quite none?

Be sure you're sure – you know –
I'll bear it better now –
If you'll just tell me so –
Than when – a little dull Balm grown –
Over this pain of mine –
You sting – again!                                    (#*156*)

The girlishness of such poems soon gives way to sterner stuff. The tense "Could *I* – then – shut the door – " is of a different order. While two hundred and seventy-six poems are indicated in the 1955 *Poems* as having been sent to Sue, two more that mention her by name are worth noting. The shorter, a letter poem, is a throwback to the theme of idolatry, puzzling (as usual) in view of the background. It is dated about 1877.

To own a Susan of my own
Is of itself a Bliss –
Whatever Realm I forfeit, Lord,
Continue me in this!                                    (#*1401*)

At least it is "Susan" now, and not "Susie" or "Dollie." The longer poem presents a peculiar problem centering in Emily's striking alteration of the two concluding stanzas. As the poem appears in the 1955 *Poems,* the concluding stanzas sum up the theme of the mystery of Nature, developed in the poem through the metaphor of the well. It has been a favorite of the anthologists, mostly, perhaps, for its last two stanzas—the final one a little too neat for Emily Dickinson at her best:

What mystery pervades a well!
The water lives so far –
A neighbor from another world
Residing in a jar

Whose limit none have ever seen,
But just his lid of glass –
Like looking every time you please
In an abyss's face!

The grass does not appear afraid,
I often wonder he
Can stand so close and look so bold
At what is awe to me.

Related somehow they may be,
The sedge stands next the sea –
Where he is floorless
And does no timidity betray

But nature is a stranger yet;
The ones that cite her most
Have never passed her haunted house,
Nor simplified her ghost.

To pity those that know her not
Is helped by the regret
That those who know her, know her less
The nearer her they get.                    (#1400)

The 1955 *Poems* assigns no date to the poem, not even an approximate one, since there is no autograph of the entire poem to provide a handwriting clue. It is grouped among the late poems on the evidence of the two variant concluding stanzas, written in the handwriting of 1877, sent to Sue, and signed "Emily – ." Here the name "Susan" replaces "Nature." The change suggests a good deal about the long tension between the two women:

But Susan is a Stranger yet –
The Ones who cite her most
Have never scaled her Haunted House
Nor compromised her Ghost –

To pity those who know her not
Is helped by the regret
That those who know her know her less
The nearer her they get –

The change from "nature" to "Susan" raises many questions and possibilities. Which, in Emily's thinking, came first, nature or Susan? There may be a clue in a worksheet draft of a seventh stanza written in the handwriting of about 1871.

> How adequate the Human Heart
> To it's emergency –
> Intrenchments stimulate a friend
> And stem an enemy

In the light of this stanza, the well and its mystery would seem to be figurative of the mystery of *human* nature and the poem as a whole originating in her thoughts about the complexities of a human relationship, though whether Sue was the friend stimulated by Emily's "intrenchments" or the "enemy" stemmed by them must remain a question. Much of the figurative language of the letters to Sue describe her as a force of nature ("Gulf Stream," "torrid Spirit," "Avalanche"), and for Emily it was an easy step from there to a poem about Nature and its mystery. This personal origin, if it is so, may explain the clipped and tart tone of the last stanza of the version as it is usually printed. It has the snap of a retort, and may tell much about the strained relations between the two. But the stanzas still pay their compliment: Sue may have enjoyed being known as a mystery.

In approaching the many other poems possibly about Sue, we must walk warily. It is clear that in her poems and letters, Emily tended to associate certain images, or clusters of images, with specific people, experiences, ideas. Bees, birds, the sea, the crescent, "circumference" or the circle, names of faraway places, images of battle, victory and defeat, even the hour of noon and certain colors—each of these in her writing has a discernible frame of reference. But she was neither systematic nor consistent. She never set up private symbolic structures as Blake or Yeats did. Thus one shrinks from uniformly equating the sea with death, the sky with immortality, noon with perfection and fulfillment—or images of rejection, the sting of loss, and birds of passage with Sue.

Nevertheless, certain connections seem unmistakable. Emily sent "I have a Bird in spring" to Sue in the "go or stay" letter of 1854 and then four years later wrote a poem on a "missing friend" (the date may well have been earlier than the assigned "about 1858") whose second stanza begins:

> I had a crimson Robin –
> Who sang full many a day
> But when the woods were painted,
> He, too, did fly away – . . .                    (#23)

We can be fairly sure that the later one is a variant of the first and prompted by the same experience. Nor is it improbable that a poem assigned to the next year (or near it) is still another variant:

My friend must be a Bird –
Because it flies!
Mortal, my friend must be,
Because it dies!
Barbs has it, like a Bee!
Ah, curious friend!
Thou puzzlest me! (#92, about 1859)

The "barbs" here recall not only the "sting" of the last line of "You love me – you are sure –" but "the barbed syllables" of another poem also sent to Sue and of the same period. Here too, one recalls Emily's respect for Sue's "impregnable syllables" and the sense of loss in "Could *I* – then – shut the door":

There is a word
Which bears a sword
Can pierce an armed man –
It hurls it's barbed syllables
And is mute again –
But where it fell
The saved will tell
On patriotic day,
Some epauletted Brother
Gave his breath away!

Wherever runs the breathless sun –
Wherever roams the day –
There is it's noiseless onset –
There is it's victory!
Behold the keenest marksman –
The most accomplished shot!
Time's sublimest target
Is a soul "forgot!" (#8, about 1858)

If Emily could think of Susan as she plumbed "the mystery that pervades a well," it is not too much to suggest that she could think of herself here as the one "forgot." Again, the "epauletted Brother," slain by the barbed syllables of the word "forgot," recalls the "defeated – dying –" of the famous poem Emily sent Sue about the same time, the purport of which Sue could hardly have missed:

Success is counted sweetest
By those who ne'er succeed.
To comprehend a nectar
Requires sorest need.

Not one of all the purple Host
Who took the Flag today
Can tell the definition
So clear of Victory

As he defeated – dying –
On whose forbidden ear
The distant strains of triumph
Burst agonized and clear!                    (*#67, about 1859*)

What looks like an intentional summing up of their early relationship
occurs in a poem dated "about 1862" but which may have been written
much earlier. A copy was sent to Sue and signed "Emily – ." The first four
lines recall the metaphor Emily used in the "go or stay" letter of 1854:
"We have walked very pleasantly – Perhaps this is the point at which our
paths diverge – then pass on singing Sue, and up the distant hill I journey
on." The last two lines echo the theme, rhythm, and language of "Could
*I* – then – shut the door." The identification seems almost unavoidable:

I showed her Hights she never saw –
"Would'st Climb," I said?
She said – "Not so" –
"With *me* – " I said – With *me*?
I showed her Secrets – Morning's Nest –
The Rope the Nights were put across –
And *now* – "Would'st have me for a Guest?"
She could not find her Yes –
And then, I brake my life – And Lo,
A Light, for her, did solemn glow,
The larger, as her face withdrew –
And *could* she, further, "No"?                    (*#446*)

One could move down a long list of further poems about loss, rejection, separation, defeat. Of course, Sue was not the only cause of such
sorrow for Emily; her early years were filled with numerous, if not such
grievous, separations and losses. But, living next door for much of Emily's
life, Sue was a continuous reminder of old wounds that never entirely
healed. If these resulted from the "Gimblets – among the nerve," that
image suggests another poem of about 1862 in which Sue's social methods
at least, as many others besides Mabel Todd experienced them, are nimbly
hit off:

She dealt her pretty words like Blades –
How glittering they shone –
And every One unbared a Nerve
Or wantoned with a Bone –

[ *211* ]

> She never deemed – she hurt –
> That – is not Steel's Affair –
> A vulgar grimace in the Flesh –
> How ill the Creatures bear –
>
> To Ache is human – not polite –
> The Film upon the eye
> Mortality's old Custom –
> Just locking up – to Die. (#479)

If reports are true, however, Sue's motives were not so pure: she *knew* she hurt. A grim little poem of about 1863 may commemorate, if not the nadir of Sue and Emily's friendship, at least a moment of utter disenchantment. And here, even if the connection must remain problematic, we must keep in mind not only the divergent paths the young women had already taken, but all that Emily, by this time, had probably learned about Sue from Austin's disastrous marriage and his increasing defection from "Sue and her crowd."

> It dropped so low – in my Regard –
> I heard it hit the Ground –
> And go to pieces on the Stones
> At bottom of my Mind –
>
> Yet blamed the Fate that fractured – *less*
> Than I reviled Myself,
> For entertaining Plated Wares
> Upon my Silver Shelf – (#747)

One final poem, a later one, will serve as coda to this sequence of possibilities. In a way, recapitulating as it does so many of the themes and motifs of the notes and poems that went to Sue or were almost certainly about her, it is the most tempting, as it is the most moving, of them all. Here are the idolatry, the rejection, the strangeness and remoteness, the "Foreigner" living just a hedge away:

> Now I knew I lost her –
> Not that she was gone –
> But Remoteness travelled
> On her Face and Tongue.
>
> Alien, though adjoining
> As a Foreign Race –
> Traversed she though pausing
> Latitudeless Place.

Elements Unaltered –
Universe the same
But Love's transmigration –
Somehow this had come –

Henceforth to remember
Nature took the Day
I had paid so much for –
His is Penury
Not who toils for Freedom
Or for Family
But the Restitution
Of Idolatry.                    (*#1219, about 1872*)

It may have been that, while Emily "told the Truth" about Sue sufficiently "slant" in the poems she sent her to obviate an open breach
between them (but with ruthless directness in the poems she wrote for
herself), she kept up a pleasant surface relationship in the letters and
notes in the later years. If this is so, she was true to a frequent theme in
poems since the early years: the theme of the barb, or sting, or inner hurt
not perceived by others, and the protective covering assumed by the one
who has been hurt:

A *Wounded* Deer – leaps highest –
I've heard the Hunter tell –
'Tis but the Extasy of *death* –
And then the Brake is still!

The *Smitten* Rock that gushes!
The *trampled* Steel that springs!
A Cheek is alway redder
Just where the Hectic stings!

Mirth is the Mail of Anguish –
In which it Cautious Arm,
Lest anybody spy the blood
And "you're hurt" exclaim!        (*#165, about 1860*)

If this poem is really about Sue, her cruelties, and Emily's response, it
would alone go a long way toward explaining the cheerful face that
Emily put on their relationship throughout her life. It might explain
Martha Dickinson Bianchi's picture of Emily as humorous, whimsical,
roguish and of the relationship between Emily and Sue as idyllic throughout. It is possible that young Mattie never saw any other side, or was so
dazzled by her aunt's play-acting that she concluded the other side was
unimportant. At any rate, Emily's pose, if such it was, is essential New
England, pure Dickinson from Samuel Fowler to Edward to Emily and

Austin (Vinnie escaped)—the Puritan discipline of restraint. She may have suffered an early and painful rejection by Sue; or she may have rejected Sue and all she stood for. Some such hypothesis, more than Emily's shyness and eccentricity, seems necessary to explain the extraordinary fact that for "15 years," beginning sometime in the 1860s, she did not enter Sue's house only three hundred feet away. And this after a girlhood affection so warm, at least on Emily's part, as to evoke some of the most adoring letters she ever wrote.

# 12

## Publication of the Poems:

## Mabel and Austin

THE SAD COMPLEXITIES of Austin's marriage and his involvement with Mabel Todd had effects that lasted long after Emily's death in 1886, his own in 1895, and Lavinia's in 1899. The first, and by far the happiest, came in the late 1880s, when Mabel undertook the editing of the poems and (later) the collecting and editing of as many of Emily's letters as she could locate. This, in turn, led to the final and most public skirmish in the "War between the Houses," the trial about the strip of land deeded to the Todds, in which Susan may have played an important if invisible role. In any case, her treatment of the bereaved Lavinia was the subject of considerable gossip.

Mabel Todd's experience of Emily Dickinson from the beginning of their relationship, both as poet and as person, is important in more than one respect. First, her developing awareness of this strange sister of Austin's is figurative of the experience of all those who succeed in making the journey from the legend to the poet. Even though she never saw her face to face, it could be said that Mabel Todd penetrated, ultimately, to the "real" Emily Dickinson more surely than did any of Emily's close associates. Although she came to Amherst, and to things Dickinson, as the complete ingénue, susceptible to every wisp of sentiment and legend, the more romantic the better, her involvement with the family in the Evergreens led her steadily from youthful enchantment to realities almost too much for her to bear, in the light of which Emily as poet figured ever more powerfully in her consciousness. Second, on a more practical level,

[ 215

her intimacy with the Dickinsons, especially Austin, was essential to her undertaking the editorial task in the first place, and then, in spite of all her interests and distractions, bringing at least a good portion of it to completion. Without her intense loyalty to Austin and the insight and information he provided, it is hard to imagine her persevering in the enormous responsibility of transcribing the poems, a task often of cryptographic proportions, and then of persuading reluctant men of letters and editors that they were worth publishing.

How much practical help Austin gave her is hard to tell. He was continually at hand, in and out of her house on almost daily calls. At one point he presented her with a handsome quartered-oak desk to work on. There is evidence, in manuscript notes and jottings in the Todd-Bingham Archive, that they discussed Emily often. One disappointment, however, in reading through their thirteen-year correspondence is to find so little about Emily and especially about the poems. Apparently, their relationship and the difficulties attending it were too absorbing. What little we have from Austin on Emily comes from fleeting references, with one extended comment in a manuscript note presumably from the period of the editing. But his influence appears in many of Mabel's remarks in various contexts—her letters to her parents, her diary and journal, her prefaces to the *Poems,* her many lectures on Emily following their publication, and in the summary statement "Scurrilous but True"—and these are essential to our understanding of both the poet's retreat from the world and its discovery of her.

Mabel's first reference to Emily came in a letter to her parents of November 6, 1881, only two months after she arrived in Amherst. It had not taken her long to pick up the gossip. Unfortunately, the passage has become a *locus classicus* for most of the elements that make up the still-current myth:

> I must tell you about the *character* of Amherst. It is a lady whom the people call the *Myth*. She is a sister of Mr. Dickinson, & seems to be the climax of all the family oddity. She has not been outside of her own house in fifteen years, except once to see a new church, when she crept out at night, & viewed it by moonlight. No one who calls upon her mother & sister ever see her, but she allows little children once in a great while, & one at a time, to come in, when she gives them cake or candy, or some nicety, for she is very fond of little ones. But more often she lets down the sweetmeat by a string, out of a window, to them. She dresses wholly in white, & her mind is said to be perfectly wonderful. She writes finely, but no one *ever* sees her. Her sister, who was at Mrs. Dickinson's party, invited me to come & sing to her mother some time and I promised to go & if the performance pleases her, a servant will enter with wine for me, or a flower, & perhaps her thanks; but just probably the token of approval will not come then, but a few days after, some dainty present will appear for me at twilight. People tell me that the *myth* will hear every note—she will be near, but unseen. . . . Isn't that like a book? So interesting.

No one knows the cause of her isolation, but of course there are dozens of reasons assigned.

In her diary three months later (February 8, 1882) Mabel recorded her first experience of the poetry: "Went in the afternoon to Mrs. Dickinson's. She read me some strange poems by Emily Dickinson. They are full of power"—a response, incidentally, that joins Mabel with Helen Hunt Jackson as among the very few during Emily's lifetime who left on record unqualified approval of her poetry. Next month (March 26, 1882) she recorded proudly: "Miss Emily Dickinson sent me some exquisite flowers, with a verse."

A few months later (September 15, 1882) Mabel spoke again (this time in her journal), enlarging upon what she had written her parents about Emily. She repeated many of the details—the white dress, the fifteen-year retirement, the idea of "the Myth." In the meantime, however, she had actually visited the Homestead, sung for Emily, and been rewarded with a glass of sherry and a present; so it is not surprising that the Myth had taken on flesh and blood and that, such being Mabel's ear for gossip, the "dozens of reasons" for Emily's retirement were reduced to a few specific ones:

His [Austin's] sister Emily is called in Amherst "the myth." She has not been out of her house for fifteen years. One inevitably thinks of Miss Haversham in speaking of her. She writes the strangest poems, & very remarkable ones. She is in many respects a genius. She wears always white, & has her hair arranged as was the fashion fifteen years ago when she went into retirement. She wanted me to come & sing to her, but she would not see me. She has frequently sent me flowers & poems, & we have a very pleasant friendship in that way. So last Sunday I went over there with Mr. Dickinson. Miss Vinnie, the other sister, who does occasionally go out, told me that if I had been otherwise than a very agreeable person she should have been dreadfully tired of my name even, for she says all the members of her brother's family have so raved about me that ordinarily she would hate the sound of Mrs. Todd. But when I left her on Sunday she took my hand in the shyest, quaintest way, and said she saw plainly that she should have to yield to the same fascination which had enthralled her family; & when I come back [from Washington] she wants me to have stated & regular days for coming there to sing & play. It was odd to think, as my voice rang out through the big silent house that Miss Emily in her weird white dress was outside in the shadow hearing every word, & the mother, bed-ridden for years was listening up stairs. When I stopped Emily sent me in a glass of rich sherry & a poem written as I sang. I know I shall yet see her. No one has seen her in all those years except her own family. She is very brilliant and strong, but became disgusted with society & declared she would leave it when she was quite young. It is hinted that Dr. Holland loved her very much & she him, but that her father who was a stern old New England lawyer & politician saw nothing particularly promising or remarkable in the shy, half-educated boy, & would not listen to her marrying him. Of that I am of course not sure, but it might be so, for I know Dr. Holland has always been an intimate friend of the family. I have heard a great deal about Mr. Samuel Bowles who was the most intimate friend of both Mr. and Mrs. Dickinson. How they did love him!

It is unfortunate that the poem Emily sent in to Mabel with the sherry got less comment than the sentimental picture of Vinnie ("shy," "quaint") and the gossip about Dr. Holland and Samuel Bowles, but it at least gave Mabel another example of the "strange" and "remarkable" poetry that she was later to devote much of her life to:

> Elysium is as far as to
> The very nearest Room
> If in that Room a Friend await
> Felicity or Doom –
>
> What fortitude the Soul contains,
> That it can so endure
> The accent of a coming Foot –
> The opening of a Door –      (#*1760, about 1882*)

It would be interesting to know how Mabel Todd knew that this poem was "written as I sang." Did Emily tell her, through Vinnie? If the statement is true, it could tell much about the nature of Emily Dickinson's poetry and her method of composition, especially its speed. (The 1955 *Poems,* for instance, assigns an almost unbelievable 366 poems to a single year, 1862.) It might substantiate the theory that more poems than is usually thought came out of specific situations. But it may well be nothing but the product of Mabel's romantic imagination. Years later, in a little black notebook auspiciously labeled "Emily" but containing only the following entry of significance, Mabel again insisted upon the impromptu nature of Emily's composition. But she inserted some qualifying adverbs:

I used to sing to Emily frequently, in the long, lonely drawing-room. But she never came in to listen – only sat outside in the darksome hall, on the stairs. But she heard every note. When I had finished she always sent me in a glass of wine on a silver salver, and with it either a piece of cake or a rose – and a poem, the latter usually impromptu, evidently written on the spot.

It was during the editing of the poems and the letters that Mabel came closest to Emily Dickinson. The story of that undertaking, told by Millicent Todd Bingham in *Ancestors' Brocades,* is a tribute to Mabel's conviction and resourcefulness, though Mrs. Bingham gave only a few hints of the long personal background that made Mabel's involvement so intimate. If her sensitivity to the Dickinson style was not strong enough to keep her (as she explained in her journal, November 30, 1890) from changing "words here and there . . . to make them smoother"—an editorial license for which she has been sufficiently criticized—it is nevertheless safe to say (with Jay Leyda) that without the spiritual kinship she felt with the poet and with the poems we might have had no poems (or letters) at all.

This spiritual kinship is more important than it might seem. What the poems needed was somebody besides Lavinia to believe in them. Except for Helen Hunt Jackson, the professionals had been cool and unreceptive, and no one in Emily's immediate circle, except Vinnie, was moved to do much about them. Vinnie knew that she herself was incompetent. She tried vainly, with "fierce insistence" (according to Mabel), to get Sue to edit them. Mabel described the situation further in her journal (November 30, 1890):

> Susan is afflicted with an unconquerable laziness, and she kept saying she would, & she would perhaps, until Vinnie was wild. At last she announced that she thought nothing had better be done about it, they would never sell – there was not money enough to get them out – the public would not care for them, & so on – in short, she gave it up. Then Vinnie came to me. She knew I always had faith in the poems, and she begged me to copy and edit them – put them all into shape. Then she was sure Col. Higginson would write a preface, and somebody would be willing to publish them, and the desire of her heart would be accomplished. So I took them.

Thus Vinnie turned to Mabel not only as a friend of the family and a literary lady who knew something about publishing but as one who "had faith in the poems." There were many reasons why Mabel might have turned her down. She was deeply involved in her own literary affairs, in Amherst activities, and with Austin. She was giving art and music lessons, teaching school, and painting pictures. When Vinnie came to her, she was on the point of going to Japan with her husband. If she said yes to Vinnie, she knew she could count on Sue's antagonism—and that was something to reckon with. Then, too, the mere size of the task, the difficulties of the handwriting, the endless problem of the variants and the scraps, presented, as she wrote in her journal, an "appalling" outlook. But the years of anguish and frustration, with Austin so near and yet so far, had made her psychologically vulnerable. She too had begun to think of herself as something of a Queen of Calvary. As early as 1885 she wrote in her journal (November 10) of her "very happy & very unhappy" life: "I and my soul are becoming very well-acquainted." For all her intense sociability, she began to feel isolated. "I have a strange sort of life," she wrote (journal, December 15, 1885), "it is not a bit like anybody else's. . . ." She enlarged more and more upon "the ills which press upon me through small, narrow-minded people" (journal, April 30, 1889). Amherst, once so thrilling with its quiet elegance, became almost intolerable, especially when Austin was not there to sustain her. She became disgusted with the "cant" and "hypocrisy" of the preachers at the college church, and told her journal in blunt terms what Emily implied in many an irreverent poem: "Narrow, uncharitable, self-righteous, are the chief characteristics of the shining lights in this faculty" (November 30, 1890). She turned increasingly to her writing. There is even a faint echo, in a confession to her journal (July 15, 1889), of Emily's notion of the therapeutic value of writing—as Emily put it, the "palsy here, – the Verses just relieve –": "I feel more and more," Mabel wrote, "that I must write or die. A literary career is my only relief."

In such a state of mind (it was in the late 1880s that the words "martyr" and "suffering" began to appear in the journal), Mabel was ready to believe in the poems as no one else was. She recognized in them a suffering yet resilient spirit, a tumultuous inner life in sharp contrast to a placid exterior, a defiance of convention and orthodoxy suggestive of the attitude her own relations with Austin had forced her to adopt. As she worked, the sense of spiritual kinship grew (entry of November 30, 1890):

> The poems were having a wonderful effect on me, mentally and spiritually. They seemed to open the door into a wider universe than the little sphere surrounding me which so often hurt and compressed me – and they helped me nobly through a trying time. Their sadness and hopelessness, sometimes, was so much bitterer than mine that
>
> > "I was helped
> > As if a Kingdom cared."     [ #260, about 1861 ]
>
> . . . I was strengthened and uplifted.

If the poems could help her so, she felt that others could be helped, too. The project became a mission. She became convinced that Sue was wrong in thinking that there would be no public for the poems. She contrasted her conviction to Vinnie's "blind sort of faith," which came, she thought, from uncomprehending adoration, "not in the least from any literary appreciation of their power."

Mabel's long journal entry for November 30, 1890, provides a full account of the many obstacles (at least they seemed so to her) to be overcome. The first was Thomas Wentworth Higginson, whom Vinnie, knowing that Emily had sent him dozens of poems, had already approached without success. Higginson had always admired Emily's dazzling thoughts but had consistently deplored the form of her poems and had never urged publication. Mabel described his conversion when, early in November 1889, she discussed the poems with him in Cambridge:

> He did not think a volume advisable – they were too crude in form, he said, and the public would not accept even fine ideas in such rough and mystical dress – so hard to elucidate.
>
> But I read him nearly a dozen of my favorites, and he was greatly astonished – said he had no idea there were so many in passably conventional form, and said if I would classify them all into A B and C he would look them over later in the winter.

When, some months later (he was ill that winter), he finally got around to studying the typescripts Mabel had prepared for him, he declared himself "much impressed"—though not to the extent of backing them all for publication and letting them speak for themselves. He accepted Mabel's "A" list, promoted a few from her "B" and "C" lists which she subsequently rejected, made still further editorial changes, and, against Mabel's judgment, insisted on giving the poems titles, some of which were so clearly mistaken that she later had to intercede with the publishers to make changes.

Nevertheless, Higginson's general approval, as Mabel acknowledged, was essential in persuading the publisher to go ahead at all, and this he finally gave. Even here the route was not easy. Mrs. Bingham tells of her father's report that Higginson first submitted the poems to Houghton Mifflin, for whom he was a reader, only to have them rejected as "queer – the rhymes were all wrong," and his own judgment ridiculed. Higginson, apparently, then endorsed Mabel's suggestion that she take them to Thomas Niles of Roberts Brothers, he himself (so David Todd surmised) being reluctant to take them to another Boston publisher so soon after Houghton Mifflin's rejection. Niles was a likely publisher, but at first he too was reluctant. For several years after Helen Hunt had persuaded Emily to include "Success is counted sweetest" in Niles's No Name anthology, *A Masque of Poets* (1878), Emily had corresponded with him and had sent him seven more poems. But he did nothing with them for reasons he later described to Higginson during the negotiations (June 10, 1890) : "It has always seemed to me that it would be unwise to perpetuate Miss Dickinson's poems. They are quite as remarkable for defects as for beauties & are generally devoid of true poetical qualities." But an appraisal from Arlo Bates, a poet himself, and frequent reader for Roberts Brothers, recommended publishing a highly selected group in a small edition (five hundred copies). Its faults, Bates said, would be "colossal," but it would have "the real stuff in no stinted quantities." Bates's list of exclusions (among them the poems "I died for Beauty" and "I shall know why") infuriated Mabel, and she again had to assert herself. Niles agreed to the publication, provided "Miss [Lavinia] Dickinson will pay for the plates." When the book proved successful beyond the expectation of anyone but Mabel—even Vinnie had urged her to hurry before all of Emily's friends died or else there would be "no one left to welcome" the poems—it should be said to his honor that Niles withdrew the final proviso.

All this took time, courage, and faith. Aside from Austin, Mabel had much to overcome even in Amherst, what with Vinnie's passionate but unhelpful devotion and Sue's personal hostility and indifference to the poems (her daughter Martha was even then showing signs of talent that Sue was beginning to take more seriously than Emily's). And even Austin's help was limited. Although he could give her insights into Emily's character and way of life, he seems to have been curiously blind— or deaf—to the poetry. Millicent Todd Bingham says flatly that "he died without suspecting that his sister had been a great poet." Even after the first edition was well launched, his attitude was grudging and tentative. He wrote Higginson (October 10, 1890) to thank him for his article in the *Christian Union* (September 25, 1890) in praise of the *Poems,* just published:

> It struck me, as I read, that you had hit and revealed her exactly, and with great skill, taste, and good judgement. I do not see how she could have been brought before the world, if she were to be brought at all, more aptly and more favorably, and if the little volume meets with any success, I shall attribute it in the main to the labor of love which you and Mrs Todd have given to it, and of which I shall have something more to say hereafter.
>
> Whether it was, on the whole, advisable to publish is yet with me, a question, but my Sister Vin, whose knowledge of what is, or has been, outside of her dooryard is bounded by the number of her callers, who had no comprehension of her sister, yet believed her a shining genius, was determined to have some of her writing where it could be read of all men, and she is expecting to become famous herself thereby, and now we shall see.

If the editing of Emily's poems was to him no more than "a labor of love," of questionable permanent value, Mabel's persistence seems little less than inspired devotion.

Although Austin apparently held aloof from the process of the editing and publishing and never seems to have discussed Emily's poetry with Mabel or anyone else, there are two penciled documents in his hand in the Todd-Bingham Archive (with some scribbled notes in Mabel's on one of them) which show some understanding of what he called her "genius" and her chosen way of life. The first, with Mabel's notes, compares Helen Hunt Jackson and Emily as personalities. The closest he comes to Emily's writing is her schoolgirl compositions.

> It is a little remarkable that two girls – of the Genius of Helen Hunt and Emily Dickinson should have been within three or four years of each other in the same quiet New England village the one the daughter of a minister and professor in the College – the other daughter of a lawyer and Treasurer of the College – both attracting general attention in their childhood the one more by her wild romping rebellious Spirit and ways – the other by her intellectual brilliancy – the one as she grew up meeting the world fearlessly – and triumphantly – adding increasing fame with every year – moving through the country like a Queen – the other, after 18 or 20, gradually withdrawing herself from society till she saw very few except members of her own family – and was known only through memory or tradition – and her letters to those who especially interested her. In her school days – at the primary – at [word illegible] Amherst Academy and at South Hadley – she was not of the best scholars – but the brightest of any social group. Her compositions were unlike anything ever heard – and always produced a sensation – both with the scholars and Teachers – her imagination sparkled – and she gave it free rein. She was full of courage – but always had a peculiar personal sensitiveness. She saw things directly and just as they were. She abhorred sham and cheapness. As she saw more and more of society – in Bos-

ton where she visited often – in Washington where she spent some time with her father when he was a member of Congress – and in other places [*The following is crossed out:*] she could not resist the feeling that it was [terribly] painfully hollow. It was to her so thin and unsatisfying in the face of the Great realities of Life although no one surpassed her in wit or brilliancy. [*The text resumes:*] notwithstanding the fact that she was everywhere sought for her brightness – originality & wit –

Far as Austin may be here from Emily as poet, this sketch deserves a word of comment. In the summer of 1878, there had been a lively discussion in the local press (Springfield and Amherst) about the possibility that Emily Dickinson had collaborated with Helen Hunt Jackson in the writing of the "Saxe Holm" stories. "Saxe Holm" was an obvious pseudonym, and the stories were immediately (and correctly) attributed to "H.H.," or Helen Hunt. But an anonymous contributor to the *Springfield Republican* (July 25) found the stories much too "morbid, and morbid to the last degree," too "weird and improbable," for the Helen Hunt everybody knew—practical, sociable, "a woman of every day life." The style was altogether (thought the contributor) that of a recluse, timid, quaint, "exquisitely sensitive to the feelings produced by birds and flowers . . . a person long shut out from the world and living in a world of her own. . . . We cannot refrain, also, from picturing her robed in white, like Draxy Miller, whether it be a mourning for a friend, a religious notion like that of Hawthorne's Hilda, or, perchance, the result of some decree of fate. . . ." Before a week was out, the papers of the region (the *Springfield Union,* the *Amherst Record,* and the *Amherst Transcript*) had narrowed the field to one who "answers in private life to the honored name of Dickinson." This suggestion was promptly quashed by an editorial note in the *Republican:* ". . . we happen to *know* that no person by the name of Dickinson is in any way responsible for the Saxe Holm stories."

Despite the *Republican*'s welcome denial, many of the elements of the Myth (and some of the unfortunate ones) were now out in the open. Austin's sketch, with its insistence on Emily's wit and brilliance, her courage, her realistic view of things "just as they were," sounds like a direct answer to the statements in the *Republican*. Perhaps his sketch was an attempt to block out some ideas for Mabel's preface to the *Poems,* second series (1891), since by that time the interest in the poems had stirred up gossip about the Myth all over again. At any rate, the preface contained the gist of Austin's views. "Emily Dickinson scrutinized everything with clear-eyed frankness. . . . She had tried society and the world, and found them lacking." She was "never morbid or melancholy. . . ." Mabel went beyond Austin's sketch to add two other assertions, undoubtedly picked up from Austin (or Vinnie) in conversation: "She was not an invalid, and she lived in seclusion from no love-disappointment." Mabel's penciled notes on the manuscript of Austin's sketch show how closely she followed his lead. They show also the degree of her own empathy with her great subject:

It all seemed to her so cheap and thin & hollow as she saw it, with the solemn realities of life staring her in the face, that she wanted none of it. Never made any difference what sort of day it was – every day was a red-letter day. The greatness mystery & depth of life was so great & overwhelming to her that she could not see how people could go into all this littleness. No suggestion in all her life that she had done anything they did not know about.

And a final, detached jotting on another page:

Breezy & clear, opposite of morbidness.
Good judgment and adviser.

The second document in the Todd-Bingham Archive that may throw some light on Austin's view of Emily is a series of jottings on the subject of genius. It seems inescapable that he had Emily in mind. Perhaps some of the items are snatches from his reading, but most seem to be his own, the kind of thing he and Emily discussed together, or later, he and Mabel, when the talk turned to Emily and her genius. They show him in a rare, detached, contemplative mood, more like his sister Emily than the harassed figure we have seen. From the very first, we can almost hear Emily's remark to Joseph Lyman, "So I conclude that space & time are things of the body. . . . My Country is Truth":

Genius is Veracity

With Genius there is always youth and never the obituary eloquence of memory

Talent is Vice president and presiding officer never the King –

Truth is sensibility to the laws of the world and Genius is always governed by truth

Genius deals with the Elemental
the roots of things and takes nothing
second hand

Then, after a space, there are some jottings about "Fancy" and "Imagination." It is hard to resist suggesting that, in what follows, Austin had in mind not only Emily and the imagination to which (as he had written) she gave "free rein" but the two worlds of his own divided life—the world of the Evergreens with "Sue and her crowd" (the delights of Fancy) and the world of the Homestead, where he encountered true Imagination:

Everybody can do his best work easiest

Fancy is full of accidental surprises and amuses the vacant or idle mind –

Imagination silences Fancy –

## Publication of the Poems: Mabel and Austin

Fancy becomes speechless in its presence –

Imagination deals with the identity of things

It is more central, Tragic –[1]

If this last is indeed a comment on Emily's imagination, it is one of the best of its generation. One would like to think that Austin is here putting more briefly, and better, what he had written in the sketch—that Emily preferred contemplating the "Great realities of Life" to mixing in society. Mabel expanded upon the idea in her preface; for Emily Dickinson, she wrote:

> Every subject was proper ground for legitimate study, even the sombre facts of death and burial, and the unknown life beyond.

She denied the charge that Emily had no humor and reverted to the impression of the "strange power" she had felt in Emily's poems when Sue had first read them to her years before:

> She touches these themes sometimes lightly, sometimes almost humorously, more often with weird and peculiar power; but she is never by any chance frivolous or trivial.

Or, as Austin had written, "Imagination silences Fancy."

These comments of Austin's, however, still leave us far from Emily as poet. And yet he must have seen many of her poems, both those that came into his house addressed to Sue and the profusion of manuscripts that Mabel was working on. Early in her journal (September 15, 1882), Mabel called him a "silent poet" whose outlet was nature, not art; and though she later thought his letters publishable, she liked them for very different qualities from those she found in Emily's poems. They were ardent and strong, but she never mentioned any "weird and peculiar power." Austin was pleased, of course, by the popular success of the poems, but there is no evidence that he ever understood it. It can only be concluded that, like many of his more literary contemporaries, he had no ear for Emily's poems, much as he marveled at her "genius." The cadences of Tennyson and Longfellow and their hosts of imitators all but deafened, it would seem, not only Austin but a number of others, like Higginson, who might have helped her.

It was here, perhaps, that Mabel made one of her most important contributions. Though nothing she wrote ever came close to Emily's

---

1. On the reverse of the torn doubled sheet (9" x 6½") on which Austin jotted these remarks, he wrote the following:

"Page 275. Scruples are for common souls – The mark of a lofty heart is to desire all and to dare all – "

The page reference suggests that all these jottings were from his reading. But the remark on "scruples" seems to have been written at a different time and in a different context, probably that of his and Mabel's defiance of convention.

[ 225

poetry, she heard Emily's subtle music as the others did not. In a day that sought message and uplift and the charm of lilting meters, she was ahead of her time in sensing and articulating the rhythmic and melodic qualities that, among other things, make Emily's poetry remarkable. It is notable that Higginson was not converted to the poems until he heard her read them aloud. If she was first drawn by Emily's strange power and then, as she immersed herself in the editing, found spiritual support "as if a Kingdom cared," she came eventually to see, quite precisely, why it was the poems moved her so. In the preface to *Poems,* second series, she wrote:

> Like impressionist pictures, or Wagner's rugged music, the very absence of conventional form challenges attention. In Emily Dickinson's exacting hands, the especial, intrinsic fitness of a particular order of words might not be sacrificed to anything virtually extrinsic; and her verses all show a strange cadence of inner rhythmical music. Lines are always daringly constructed, and the "thought-rhyme" appears frequently, – appealing, indeed, to an unrecognized sense more elusive than hearing.

If any important figure of Emily's early years had brought this kind of sensitivity to her poetry, her life and her literary career might have been quite different. It is notable, too, that by the time Higginson came to write the preface to the first group published (1890), he had moved far beyond the negative advice he had given Emily in the early 1860s. Although his first praise (always sufficiently guarded to preserve his critical reputation) was for her insights and thoughts that "take one's breath away" and for her "words and phrases exhibiting an extraordinary vividness of descriptive and imaginative power," he spoke admiringly of "an ear which had its own tenacious fastidiousness." His suggestion that the closest literary parallel to Emily Dickinson was the poetry of William Blake must have been based on more than his sense of their sometimes kindred spirit. This new insight, it can be said with some assurance, he owed to Mabel Todd. Whether she was ever as successful in sensitizing Austin's ear to the "inner rhythmical music" of his sister's poetry, we do not know.

Where Austin obviously helped Mabel was in his knowledge of Emily's secluded life and the reasons for it, as he saw them. He took for granted what the community built legends about, and he brought Mabel down from her early lofty, romantic notion of the Myth. She, too, in her preface to *Poems,* second series, had come a long way. The gossipy speculations of the early letters to her parents and of her journal were replaced by a normalized view of Emily's life. She rejected the notion of a "love-disappointment" and described Emily's career as "the normal blossoming of a nature introspective to a high degree, whose best thought could not exist in pretence." In her journal for October 18, 1891, just a few weeks before *Poems,* second series, was published, there is a hint of how much of these opinions she owed to Austin. That month, Higginson had published an article on Emily in the *Atlantic,* with some of her letters. There had been much criticism, including Amherst President Seelye's remark to

226 ]

Mabel that it was "horrible" to publish the letters and even the poems of "that 'innocent and confiding child.'" Mabel dissented in her journal, and cited Austin's opinion:

> Yet my own opinion is that she thought sometime her own verses might see the light of print, only by other hands than hers. As to the letters, that is different. Those to Mr. Higginson are not of a private nature, and as to the "innocent and confiding" nature of them, Austin smiles. He says Emily definitely posed in those letters, he knows her thoroughly, through and through, as no one else ever did. He tells me many things quite unsuspected by others.

Millicent Todd Bingham, in *Ancestors' Brocades,* questioned her mother's conclusion about Austin's judgment here: "With the fate of her poetry at stake, it hardly seems likely that Emily Dickinson would have attitudinized in front of Colonel Higginson."[2] But it hardly seems likely, either, that among the "many things quite unsuspected by others" Austin told Mabel about Emily, he would have withheld any fact of sufficient importance to invalidate his "normal blossoming" idea of Emily's youth and his theory of her withdrawal. In "Scurrilous but True," Mabel's final comment on the subject is entirely consistent with her remarks in the preface forty years before:

> Her [Emily's] curious leaving of outer life never seemed unnatural to him [Austin]. He told me about her girlhood and her normal blossoming and gradual retirement, and her few love affairs. Her life was perfectly natural. All the village gossip merely amused him.

It is possible, of course, that New England reticence prevailed even over Austin's complete rapport with Mabel; but it is worth noting that

2. *AB*, pp. 166–67. Some slight corroboration for the "normal blossoming" view, at least as it discounts the notion that Emily's life was blighted by a hopeless love affair, comes in an item in the Todd-Bingham Archive. Although Ned Dickinson said he never lost his devotion to Mrs. Todd, he became engaged (a few years before his premature death at the age of thirty-seven) to Alice Hill (later Mrs. Franklin Harris). In a letter to Mrs. Bingham (June 1, 1945) thanking her for the "faint but convincing outline of Ned" in *Ancestors' Brocades,* Mrs. Harris added, "I wish I might have given him something of youth and joy, before he left his unhappy life"; and ten years later she wrote again to agree with one of the main theses of *Emily Dickinson's Home,* which had just been published (letter of June 14, 1955 ?):

> I never believed in any thwarted love affair, except perhaps in the vaguest sense.
> Martha [Dickinson Bianchi] once asked me if Ned had ever mentioned any man to me in connection with Emily – of course he never had – quite naturally she was never a subject of conversation between us – I wish she had been – . . .

In view of the certainty with which Martha Bianchi in *Life and Letters* told the story of Emily's frustrated romance, her quizzing Ned's fiancée seems curious. A final comment by Mrs. Harris, in view of the infinite involutions of the Dickinson family feud, is not surprising at all:

> I was in Amherst that summer Lavinia died [1899] – but [was] only told what they wanted me to know – I was vaguely troubled all the time by what I suspected –

Emily's closest associates agree. Sue's obituary of Emily in the *Springfield Republican* (May 18, 1886), three days after Emily's death, made the same point:

> As she passed on in life, her sensitive nature shrank from much personal contact with the world, and more and more turned to her own large wealth of individual resources for companionship, sitting thenceforth, as some one said of her, "in the light of her own fire." Not disappointed with the world, not an invalid until within the past two years, not from any lack of sympathy, not because she was insufficient for any mental work or social career – her endowments being so exceptional – but the "mesh of her soul," as Browning calls the body, was too rare, and the sacred quiet of her own home proved the fit atmosphere for her worth and work.

But by then the blighted-romance theory was abroad—perhaps, as some think, concocted by Sue for her own purposes and certainly, though much later, given to the world as gospel by daughter Martha for hers (now with the name of Charles Wadsworth publicly attached). The fact that Sue gave no hint of it in the obituary may be a clue to the element of artifice in it. One may be warned, in passing, against taking at face value Sue's assertion that Emily was "not disappointed with the world." What Emily might have been disappointed with, and might have withdrawn from, was precisely the kind of thing Sue would not have been inclined to understand—or, if she understood, to say anything about in public.

Such complexities Mabel ignored as, with Austin's views uppermost in her mind, she prepared to present Emily to the world. Whatever effects her efforts may have had in toning down the Myth, perhaps her greatest distinction was being among the first to "hear" Emily Dickinson and, far from being put off by her irregular form, to sense its creative power. Then she convinced Higginson, in itself a major achievement.

# 13

# Last Phase of the Quarrel

# and a Late View of Susan

M ANY OF THE COMPLEXITIES that Mabel sidestepped came grimly to
light during Lavinia's legal battle about the strip of land deeded
to the Todds in return for Mabel's work on the poems. If Alfred E. Stearns,
as we have seen, recalled the earlier stages of the Todd-Dickinson episode
as comic, he took the trial in 1898 more seriously. It rocked the town, he
wrote, dividing it into two irreconcilable camps. But even this, to Stearns,
had its ridiculous side—the gossip it evoked and the dinner parties it
spoiled. He sobered up when he came to Vinnie's curious reversal toward
her old friend and ally, Mabel Todd:

> What means were employed to bring her change of heart to pass can only be
> guessed. Town gossips played with the topic, suggesting such devious devices
> as hypnotism, threats, blackmail, and deceit, but these notions were the
> products of minds too much accustomed to thinking in terms of unsupported
> evidence and hence were not generally taken seriously. But whatever they
> were they proved immensely effective, and Lavinia, turning against her
> former friend and helper, allied herself with her belligerent relatives.

The suggestion here of unscrupulous methods, even if Stearns dismissed it as gossip, recalls other comments closer to the scene of action:
Sue "riding rough shod" over Vinnie; Vinnie "curiously in fear" of Sue;
Vinnie's charge that Sue shortened Emily's life by her cruelties. And
Stearns's report that Sue and Mattie were "a bit ashamed to acknowledge
the relationship [with Emily and Vinnie] and treated them as strangers
or worse" has the ring of something more than gossip.

Yet it is almost impossible to determine the facts here. Among the "cruelties" which Vinnie reported to her friends were Sue's setting her dogs on Vinnie's cats, appropriating Vinnie's cherished store of manure, and letting her horse trample Vinnie's lawn. Such incidents may be quite on the comic side, but Mary Lee Hall confirms their more somber implications in a late (1935) comment:

> Sue was relentlessly cruel to Miss Vinnie in every possible way, and they hated each other with a deadly hate. . . . I was called to Miss Vinnie's many times to quiet her nerves, and help her recover from Sue's *verbal* blows.

In assessing the situation, especially as Sue's character is brought under the most critical scrutiny, one can only invoke personal opinions and hope that the biases will even up. Mary Lee Hall's letters of the early 1930s are the richest source.[1] Although her friendship with Vinnie indicates her bias, she makes it clear that she lived quite outside the limits of Sue's influence and hence to that extent could write without prejudice. She observed Amherst life for nearly twenty years and wrote about it from the distance of some thirty years, enough time for feelings, it would seem, to cool. Her estimate of Sue, much darker than Mabel Todd's, is recorded with a vehemence that appears to come from deep conviction. "Sue was a jealous woman," she began in one of her milder charges; "she hated Vinnie because Vinnie knew too much about her." Writing to Mrs. Bingham, then collecting materials for the new edition of Emily's letters, she took a clear stand on the problem of the trial and its motivating force:

> Sue did everything in her power to *down* your adorable mother. . . . It must have been Sue who held a sword over Vinnie's head. . . . It was not Vinnie who started the trouble, I am sure of that. . . . she *dared not* do what would madden the enemy. . . . Sue was bitter, and cruel, & revengeful.

A little later, Miss Hall amplified her theory about Vinnie's part in the quarrel:

> During your Mother's absence in Japan, Sue found the opportunity of getting her chance for revenge, by telling Miss Vinnie about the strip of land, and she influenced her to do as she did, in order to get *in* with Miss Vinnie, that she might use her to get back the land, and to get control of her for the remainder of her life. For one thing, she feared that Miss Vinnie might make a will favorable to others, giving Ned & Mattie only what the law obliged her to give.

There are many difficulties here, although it is worth noting that Clara Newman Pearl agreed with Miss Hall's view: "I can remember hearing my father say that that last suit 'never should have happened,' but Cousin

1. For selections, see Appendix II, 1.

Susan Dickinson in 1897

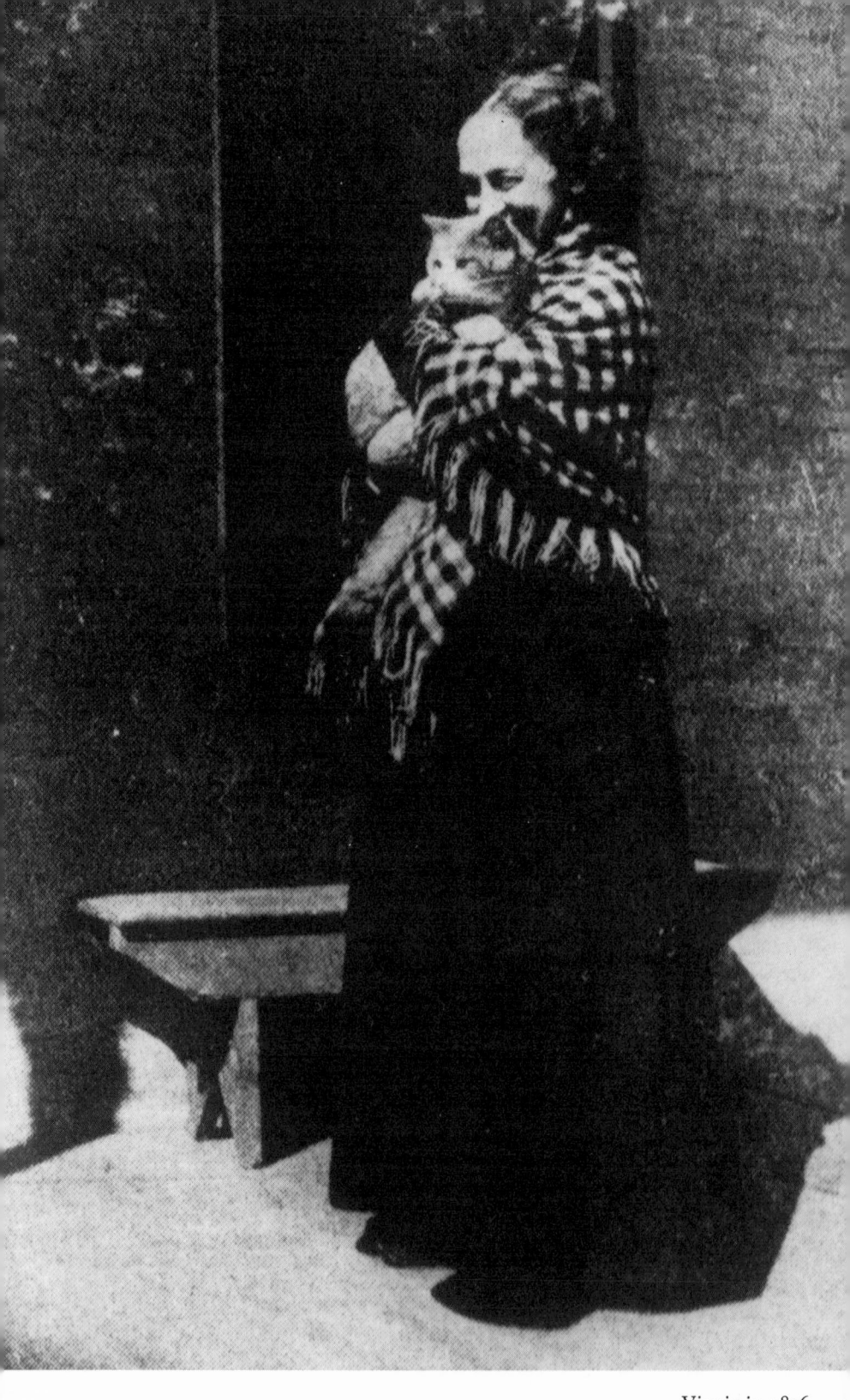

Vinnie in 1896

Vinnie was just a tool in others' hands." Vinnie did not need to be "told" about the land. In signing the deed of gift, she had broken her promise to her legal and financial adviser, Mr. Hills, not to sign anything without first consulting him, and she may have decided to sue for the land as a way of redeeming herself with him, for whom she seems to have had a special regard. At any rate, Sue's part in the proceedings is difficult to ascertain. She kept herself aloof from the trial itself, sending Ned and Martha to sit beside Vinnie in the courtroom. It was probably from Vinnie, whose habits of exaggeration were then fully developed, that Miss Hall heard about the matter of the bequests to the children. The passage is significant mainly as it shows how completely Miss Hall distrusted Sue. She subscribed to the local gossip about Sue's alcoholism (her comment recalls Austin's complaint about Sue's fits of temper): "I think Sue inherited her father's love of liquor, and that there were times when she actually did not know what she was doing, or saying."

Miss Hall's general estimate of Sue's character hardly allows even the ambivalence of Mrs. Todd's view—the fine abilities wrongly used. It is much less charitable. The contradiction in her nature, as Miss Hall saw it, would seem to make Sue—and not Emily—the object of psychiatric investigation. The charming exterior and the "black" interior could be reconciled only in terms of the demonic theme carried out in Vinnie's favorite term for Sue, "the Old Scratch"—at least so Miss Hall's rhetoric suggests:

. . . you never will know what an evil minded person Sue was. You cannot imagine such a fiend, for Sue could appear like "an angel of light," when it served her purpose to do so.

Such epithets persist in her invective—"black devil," "fiend," "Satan, or Sue"—and come to a head in her most extended characterization:

To me Sue was abnormally self-centered; an egotist; arrogant; haughty; pretentious; and, to give the Devil her due, she could be gracious, clever, entertaining on the surface, and black as the blackest ink inside, where truth is generated, and where it lives, if it lives at all.

In one important passage, Miss Hall brings all the scattered themes together: Sue's character, Austin and Mabel, the family conflict, and Emily's involvement:

Vinnie told me . . . that Emily was furious at Sue on account of her deceptions, and had little, if anything to do with her a year or two before her death. It may be that Emily became too much interested in your Mother [Mrs. Todd], that she defended your Mother. That probably enraged Sue.

"Furious" seems hardly the epithet for Emily, and what Sue's "deceptions" were is another of those charges hard to document. They may have had something to do with Emily's relationship with Judge Lord, which seems to have been very distasteful to Sue. When Sue warned Mabel

Todd away from the Homestead because of the "immorality" practiced there—she had found Emily "in the arms of a man"—the man (if any) must have been Lord. It has been suggested that at this time she started the rumors of Emily's early love for the Reverend Charles Wadsworth to deflect gossip, both from Emily's involvement with Lord and from the trouble in her own home. "So successful was the stratagem, if such it was," wrote Millicent Todd Bingham in 1954, "that until now the existence of an ardent attachment between Emily Dickinson and the venerable Judge has not been suspected." Much more could be said about this strange ramification of the family quarrel, even if all analysis must remain hypothetical. In her distaste for Emily's late romance, Sue may simply have been siding with Judge Lord's niece, Abbie Farley, who had kept house for him after his wife died in 1877. (Abbie was a special friend of Sue's and "Vinnie's special aversion." She thought her uncle's and Emily's friendship disgusting[2] and years later called Emily a "little hussy. . . . Loose morals. She was crazy about men. Even tried to get Judge Lord. Insane, too.") Also, Sue may have been jealous of the attention Judge Lord was paying to the other house. It is conceivable that she may for years have been storing up resentment at Emily's withdrawal from her sphere of influence: a brilliant, even if eccentric sister-in-law would have been an asset at her teas and receptions and musicales, and Emily's absence might have drawn comment not always favorable to Sue. An early, frustrated love affair and a broken heart could have served as an appealing explanation for Emily's withdrawal. The legend, given such currency in Martha Dickinson Bianchi's *Life and Letters of Emily Dickinson*, may have had just such an origin.

Of all these complications Miss Hall seems to have been ignorant. What made her "furious" was Martha's suppression, in her various writings on Emily, of the dark realities of the family situation, of Emily's uneven relations with Sue, of any hint that life in the Evergreens was anything but idyllic. She hoped that Martha's "deceptions" and "falsehoods" would be *"stabbed* with the true history of the lives of all the D. family" and in a notable passage made her meaning clear:

> I do hope that someone will write "The Life of Shadows," or the "House of Shadows," a book giving some of the *awful pressure* under which Austin, Emily, and Vinnie lived; the stern, austere, unaffectionate character of Edward D., and the soft, yielding, rather unstable one of his wife. I shudder as I recall the stories Vinnie told me of their little deceptions in order to get a drop of joy out of their gloomy home life. . . . Sue had a fearful influence over the three, as each one found her out to his and her sorrow.

2. "Abbie," writes Mrs. Bingham, "sensed power in the relationship . . . and, my mother thought, wanted to disguise it, to cover it up, feeling that it was somehow disloyal to her dead aunt. At any rate, she made sarcastic comments on the 'sweet' letters she thought 'Uncle Lord' was sending to the 'mansion' " (*Revelation,* p. 60). Jay Leyda adds: ". . . marriage was further discouraged by the Farleys, Mrs. Lord's family, who continued to live in Lord's Salem home" (*YH* I, lix).

There is no need to accept Miss Hall's Vinnie-inspired version of life in the Homestead, or her moral verdict on Sue, to agree with her about Sue's influence in the lives of all the Dickinsons, even if the word "fearful" does not cover all the cases, all the time. For Emily it had moments of exaltation and delight, certainly, as well as disappointment and bitterness. There was perhaps one thing about Sue that Emily and Mary Lee Hall would have agreed upon: her power.

So much (although the final word can never be said on such delicate and sensitive matters) for what Miss Hall herself called "war." For us, the problem is not one of moral judgment but of determining as precisely as we can the effect of it all on Emily Dickinson. To this end, every scrap of information or opinion, even gossip, emerging from the heat of the conflict or coming to light years later, becomes relevant. How does the accumulated evidence illuminate the setting, help re-create the atmosphere in which she wrote her poetry, and thus illuminate the substance of the poetry itself? Of few poets could the claim be made more confidently that her life was her work. To repeat: Emily, even "Our Emily," did not write in total isolation, shut off from the world, meditating among her flowers. Vesuvius was at *home,* Gethsemane "but a Province – in the Being's Centre –" And at the center of Emily Dickinson's being must have been the gnawing realization of an early mistake in judgment, hers as well as Austin's; a youthful affinity that came to nothing; the lifelong suffering to which that mistake had condemned her brother; and the tension and anxiety it had brought them all.

> Remorse – is Memory – awake –
> Her Parties all astir –
> A Presence of Departed Acts –
> At window – and at Door –
>
> It's Past – set down before the Soul
> And lighted with a Match –
> Perusal – to facilitate –
> And help Belief to stretch –
>
> Remorse is cureless – the Disease
> Not even God – can heal –
> For 'tis His institution – and
> The Adequate of Hell –            (#744, about 1863)

Whether it was her fault, or his, or Sue's, or, in its final stages, Mabel Todd's, is now beside the point. The tragedy only a hedge away had to be, and was, lived through. The paradox of its final stage must now be clear: without it, we might never have had the poems.

There may be comfort in the paradox, but it is chilly. The conflict took a long toll. It may be true that without Mabel Todd and her involvement

[ 233

with the Dickinsons, we might never have had the poems (she edited a third series, without Higginson's help, in 1896). And it was she alone who saw the importance of collecting the letters that made up her pioneer edition in 1894—an achievement ranking close to her work on the poems. Her lectures in the 1890s undoubtedly made many readers of Emily Dickinson, even if she was inclined to put a disproportionate emphasis on the mystery of Emily's life and personality. But when the trial over the strip of land ended disastrously for the Todds, she determined to have nothing more to do with things Dickinson, put all the manuscript materials, including some 665 of Emily's poems, in the famous camphorwood chest and shut the lid, as she thought, forever. Her withdrawal left Martha Dickinson Bianchi with a clear field, with what results we have seen. There was no possibility of cooperation between the two women. The poems came out piecemeal, unprofessionally edited, with Mabel's holdings, of course, still in the camphorwood chest, not to be opened until 1929, when Mabel, finally relenting, entrusted their editing to her daughter. But it was sixteen years before *Bolts of Melody* (1945) and another ten before all of Emily Dickinson's poems were brought together in a single edition, professionally edited, with variants, an approximation of Emily Dickinson's unique punctuation, and a tentative chronology. There is hardly a more erratic publishing record of a major poet in literary history. Finally, with the *Letters* of 1958, we were enabled to view Emily Dickinson in what seems close to entirety. This long, tortuous delay exposed her, of course, to many partial judgments and misconceptions; and much of it must be attributed to the tensions and ill feeling between the families—the "war," with its long beginnings and disastrous finale.

# 14

## The Dickinson Rhetoric and

## the Structure of a Life

Howled far from center the preceding chapters may at times have seemed, their purpose has been to present in reasonably full detail the givens of Emily Dickinson's life, what she was born into, what in a sense she could not avoid, the complex and powerful forces of her heredity and environment that she had to cope with as she shaped her life. Of course, we have seen much that she could have avoided. The story of Sue, in its early years, certainly shows her making choices; but Sue's thirty-year presence next door was an inescapable fixture of her maturity, as (for her) were her home, her family, and Amherst. We are by no means done with such matters, for her childhood, her schooling, her intellectual surroundings, and the hard facts of mid-century America (including the literary situation) are all part of her ecology. The aim has been, by first showing what she reached out from, to prepare the way for a better understanding of what she reached out toward and of her extraordinary achievement in evolving out of both a structured and creative life.

In the course of our chapters, a number of stock notions should have been laid to rest or so qualified as to lose the insistence they have often had in accounts of Emily Dickinson: that Amherst was no place for a poet to be born in; that she was the lone star in a colorless and insignificant family; that her home was either a prison to her spirit or, at the other extreme, a cozy retreat irradiated (after July 1, 1856) by the attentions of a loving confidante; that she lived apart from the passions and bitterness that plague the rest of humanity and, not knowing such things firsthand, made them up for the purposes of poetry; that a love tragedy is the only way of explaining her withdrawal from society (Austin and Lavinia denied its existence, and Sue in the obituary gave no hint of it); that she spent her day "meditating majestically among her flowers."

On the contrary, what should be emerging is a perceptive, critical, self-propelling person working hard in the midst of a busy town and a busy family and taking the measure of both. We have seen her through the eyes of her intimates, but mostly we have seen them through hers—which is as sure a way as any, perhaps, of getting to know her. We have had glimpses of her in action: outmaneuvering her father, coping with the housework during her mother's illness, advising her brother, depending and not depending on her sister, living out a curious love-hate relationship with her sister-in-law—and trying out her style on them all. There is much more of all this to come—the qualities and the actions, what she was born into and what she made of it. And most important, of course, the major action, her vocation, which gave the structure to her life.

In retrospect, one matter emerges that requires a further word: a phenomenon of temperament and need—and hence style and hence vocation—that subsumes certain themes touched upon so far and prepares for encounters and problems to come. This too was a family character-istic—hardly inherited but certainly shared by all three of the young Dickinsons, and thus, in a sense, part of the world Emily grew up in. So distinct is it from anything recorded in Dickinson annals before this generation, and so unparalleled in Emily's immediate cultural environ-ment, that it deserves a special term: the Dickinson Rhetoric.

The baffled Higginson once said, ruefully, "It is hard to steer safely among Dickinsons!" He found them a subtle and circuitous family, with Emily, of course, his first and central enigma. He complained that she surrounded herself with a fiery mist. What he meant, presumably, was her bewildering language, the slant and elliptical style of the poems and letters she sent him. Or perhaps what made the mist fiery was her ex-travagance, the hyperbole he found hard to believe, a tendency to exag-gerate of the sort we have seen in operation frequently in the preceding chapters, whether it was Vinnie telling Mary Lee Hall lurid tales of her youth, or Austin calling Mabel Todd his "Christ," or Emily saying that Vinnie was "all" to her. Heightened rhetoric seems in this generation to have been a family phenomenon, and it presents a particular problem: the problem of *pose*. When can we trust these Dickinsons? When are they posing, or dramatizing—or speaking simply, directly, as we would say "truthfully"?

To the biographer, these questions are crucial in regard to many of Emily's statements in her letters, the richest source we have of positive, concrete information about her life. What did she mean, for instance, when she told Higginson, twice, that he had "saved [her] Life"? that, by 1862, she had written "but one or two" poems? One does not look first for hard biographical data in the hyperbolic and figurative language of the poems, although their truth becomes more available the more we understand her medium, an understanding that must come gradually (and may never be complete). But Emily as she presents herself in the letters, where (we would like to think) we see her face to face, is a constant problem. She could adopt a persona or don a mask as readily here as in the more obvious art constructs of the poems. It is too easy to dismiss such tendencies as merely protective. Viewed more closely, and in their historical context, they may be related to the large creative effort of Emily Dickinson's life.

To go back: until Samuel Fowler Dickinson, there was nothing in Emily's lineage to account for the flair for language peculiar to her generation of Dickinsons; and he did little more than establish directions toward ideas, education, literary expression. Although he and his son Edward made reputations as orators, their public rhetoric was quite conventional. Edward's courtship letters were, for the most part, models of rational control, with only an occasional burst of feeling and then in a style that has nothing surprising about it, nothing misty or fiery. At home, in his soberer years, Edward was inclined to be taciturn. By Higginson's standard he probably *was* "speechless," though he could at times be moved to argumentative bouts with Austin, as Emily records, and her quotations from his conversation show a turn for terse, wry humor, mostly ironic and understated. All his children inherited some of this, especially his satiric bent and his gift for mimicry, but in general their tendency went in the other direction, toward a freer, more colorful rhetoric. Much of this could be attributed to the tendencies of the times, the loosening of the old formalism by writers like Emerson and Thoreau, to whom Emily and Austin responded immediately, or to the influence of contemporary popular literature, like Ik Marvel's *Reveries* or Longfellow's *Kavanagh,* in which the young Dickinsons indulged heavily in spite of their father's disapproval.

There must have been an inner need for verbal expression without which these influences would have had little effect. These Dickinsons, certainly Austin and Emily, faced a spiritual crisis unknown, or at least not articulated, by their elders. The old forms and formulations were losing their sustaining power. Austin's letters to Martha Gilbert are a case in point; he was bewildered and groping, and he was impelled to an expression unprecedented in the Dickinson line. Apparently, his heterodoxy was a real obstacle in his early relations with Sue; he, a Dickinson, had to plead with her not to dismiss him as an atheist. Emily spoke of at least one theological discussion she had with him, and it is likely that the nocturnal talks that both she and Joseph Lyman referred to when "the ancient people" were away, or asleep, covered many such problems. They discussed their difficulties in a way not recorded of their elders, who presumably found their answers in church—or, if not, kept up appearances in silence. None of the three children was especially pious or churchly. Although Vinnie dutifully joined the church during the Revival of 1850, there is nothing in anything she said or did, certainly not in the years when she needed it most, that shows she got much help from it. Austin worked hard for the church as an institution, but it hardly seems to have been a major source of spiritual comfort for him either. He turned to his intimates, at first Sue and Martha and then Emily (who became a constant); then to nature, to his passion for art, to his work for the college and the town; and finally to Mabel Todd, who as his "Christ" released in him the flood of rhetoric that had the fervor and many of the phrases of the old piety. That Emily stopped going to church regularly by the time she was thirty is a sign of more than mere reclusiveness; she refused to follow her pious friends to the ark of safety when she was a girl, and later she openly confessed a scorn of doctrines. She took it upon herself to fill the void left by these rejections with all the verbal resources she could muster. She would triumph by the word—her own Word.

Each one of these younger Dickinsons, at one time or another, took a stance that required new, fresh expression. It showed in such everyday but significant ways as their conversation. They were well known as talkers. If Higginson was struck by Edward Dickinson's speechlessness, he was all but overwhelmed by Emily's intense, electric talk. As girls, Emily and Vinnie were famous as wits, a little on the prickly side. Neither of them, or Austin, tolerated fools gladly, and they could sometimes be abrasive or abrupt. The Dickinson snobbishness had its rhetoric, too—cultivated, I think, by Emily for defensive purposes, as when she called her Aunt Elisabeth "the only male relative on the female side," or when she directed an elderly and tiresome lady, inquiring at the Homestead about lodgings in Amherst, to the cemetery, as Emily later said, "to spare expense of moving." Austin's brusqueness was notorious. Vinnie was peppery. Her safety valve became increasingly her sharp tongue. She could "raise an *awful* breeze," as Austin observed, and in later years she exercised her considerable talents defending her family against the world. It seems that all three set out at one time or another to surround themselves, if not all with fiery mists, at least with some degree of impenetrability, as if to fend off ordinary, boring human nature. There is more than a trace of it in Emily's poetry, as in her famous jibe at gentility:

What Soft – Cherubic Creatures –
These Gentlewomen are –
One would as soon assault a Plush –
Or violate a Star –

Such Dimity Convictions –
A Horror so refined
Of freckled Human Nature –
Of Deity – ashamed –

It's such a common – Glory –
A Fisherman's – Degree –
Redemption – Brittle Lady –
Be so – ashamed of Thee –        (*#401, about 1862*)

But Emily's fiery mist, her rhetorical virtuosity, was more than protective. Her problem was constructive, and ours is to penetrate the mist to the outlines of what it was she was constructing. Her poems employ the language of almost every conceivable action, from the most gentle to the most violent—passionate love, torture, shipwreck, battle, murder, and, as in the poem just quoted, rape. Not that a poet must fight in a battle or commit murder before he can legitimately use the language of such actions in his poems. But the perennial misgiving about Emily Dickinson, the Amherst recluse, comes from what appears to be the unexplained gap between rhetoric and reality.

What we have seen so far of the vital and often agonizing relationships by which Emily's life was crisscrossed should have bridged some of that gap. As her purpose and method as poet become clearer in what follows, the gap should close further. Once understood, the career she fashioned for herself can be seen in the light of a grand metaphoric design—a design that puts everything else, including her baffling private life and her rhetorical eccentricities, into believable perspective. As we follow her on her way, I propose one important criterion as a guide.

The task, as one confronts the recalcitrant and often paradoxical materials, is not unlike that of the novelist as he approaches his imagined situations. Indeed, this is why her life has been such a tempting subject for the writers of fiction and fictionalized biography. One is confronted with many questions that are unanswerable, and as clue after clue ends in an impasse, the temptation is to hypothesize and improvise. One is reminded of Joseph Conrad's struggle to bring into focus his romantic young hero Lord Jim. It is worth noting that both Marlow (Conrad's fictional narrator and control) and Higginson (who functions somewhat similarly in our early pages) used the image of mist to describe their difficulty: Higginson's fiery mist and the fog, or mist, that shrouded Marlow's enigmatic young protégé. Several times Marlow (like Higginson) confesses his bafflement: "I don't pretend I understood him. The views he let me have of himself were like those glimpses through the shifting rents in a thick fog—bits of vivid and vanishing detail, giving no connected idea of the general aspect of a country. . . . how incomprehensible, wavering, and misty are the beings that share with us the sight of the stars and the warmth of the sun. . . ." Sometimes Marlow's vision is dimmed by the dazzle of too much sun: "My eyes were too dazzled by the glitter of the sea below his feet to see him clearly; I am fated never to see him clearly." Some such thoughts must have plagued everyone, beginning with Higginson, who has assayed the life of Emily Dickinson. For Marlow, it was not until the action was complete, with Jim's final heroic stand at

Patusan, that his life assumed coherence and meaningful shape. What one concludes is that, with people who guard their inner natures so success-fully, either with reticence or rhetoric, we must look to their actions, or rather their life actions taken as wholes, for their overarching truth. This is the way Conrad solved his problem, as, under his treatment, the life action of his hero became metaphoric.

We would look, then, for Emily Dickinson's life action and its meta-phoric purport. The early letters, especially, show that she, too, had a problem of organization and coherence. They abound in energy and zest for living, but they show her groping for direction and meaning. She tried all the standard routes in vain and ran the gamut of the current senti-mentalities. She pummeled and browbeat her correspondents, or bathed them in the tender emotions. (No wonder they dropped off, unwilling or unable to keep up.) The wit, the whimsey, the turn for drama and exaggeration, the rhetorical tricks picked up at school or in reading or listening to sermons—all these entered into her brilliant young virtuosity, and all had, ultimately, to be brought under control. Her own word was "organized," as when she answered Higginson's charge that her poems lacked form: "When I try to organize – my little Force explodes." And often it did explode, especially though not exclusively in the early letters, into bathos, or rhapsody, or sheer indulgence. Later on, we detect her, in her rhetoric, stretching the truth, or posing, or just plain lying, as when she pictured herself as an ingénue to Higginson, with "one or two" verses to her credit, when we know that she had written hundreds, among them some of her finest. And many of the poems make denials or affirmations that seem startlingly at variance with the known facts of her life. We wonder what truth there is behind this seeming fantasia; we wonder where the ultimate meaning is.

Poets like Emily Dickinson may "lie" in their hyperbole and exagger-ated rhetoric. They may strike poses and don masks and speak through personae. But in their basic structures, where they begin, where they end, and how they got there, they do not lie. Certainly it was Emily Dickin-son's constant aim, her life action, to make her "truth" clear. Her poems, those "short sharp probings at the very axis of reality," show her in a continual effort to expand, deepen, clarify, and be ever more precise. That is why, perhaps, she tried her hand again and again at similar materials, sometimes forging new meaning, sometimes adding little or even slipping back (the curve is not always up), but in general continuing her course toward what she called "Circumference."

To watch her at work in one instance is a good way to get a sense of the configuration of her career. As poet, she worked from specific to general, concrete to universal. The phenomena of experience that surged more or less uncontrolled through the early letters came under increas-ingly sharp scrutiny. She became preoccupied with essence; the accidents (who? when? where?) did not concern her. The example at hand shows her moving from a specific early encounter and the rhetoric it evoked to what she ultimately made of much the same materials. Here, though hardly its finest achievement, is the type of her career as a whole.

The encounter, described in an early letter to Susan Gilbert, involved a bit of moon-gazing. She was twenty and at the height of her infatuation for Sue, at that time teaching school in Baltimore. She thinks of her friend as she gazes at the moon. In her fantasy, the moon becomes a fairy, sailing in a gondola, who coolly ignores her request for a ride to Baltimore and Sue, and sails serenely on. It is all very sad.

> I wept a tear here, Susie, on purpose for *you* – because this "sweet silver moon" smiles in on me and Vinnie, and then it goes so far before it gets to you – and then you never told me if there *was* any moon in Baltimore – and how do *I* know Susie – that you see her sweet face at all? She looks like a fairy tonight, sailing around the sky in a little silver gondola with stars for gondoliers. I asked her to let me ride a little while ago – and told her I would *get out* when she got as far as Baltimore, but she only smiled to herself and went sailing on.

Years later, after she had learned to disentangle essences from personal sentiment, the " 'sweet silver moon' " functions in two poems, "I watched the Moon around the House" and "The Moon upon her fluent Route," only in both poems far from sweetly. In the first poem, the moon, which in the letter played the stock role of uniting loving hearts only to prove fickle, becomes a symbol of much more than nature's coyness:

> I watched the Moon around the House
> Until upon a Pane –
> She stopped – a Traveller's privilege – for Rest –
> And there upon
>
> I gazed – as at a stranger –
> The Lady in the Town
> Doth think no incivility
> To lift her Glass – upon –
>
> But never Stranger justified
> The Curiosity
> Like Mine – for not a Foot – nor Hand –
> Nor Formula – had she –
>
> But like a Head – a Guillotine
> Slid carelessly away –
> Did independent, Amber –
> Sustain her in the sky –
>
> Or like a Stemless Flower –
> Upheld in rolling Air
> By finer Gravitations –
> Then bind Philosopher –

No Hunger – had she – nor an Inn –
Her Toilette – to suffice –
Nor Avocation – nor concern
For little Mysteries

As harass us – like Life – and Death –
And Afterward – or Nay –
But seemed engrossed to Absolute –
With Shining – and the Sky –

The privilege to scrutinize
Was scarce upon my Eyes
When, with a Silver practise –
She vaulted out of Gaze –

And next – I met her on a Cloud –
Myself too far below
To follow her superior Road –
Or it's advantage – Blue –                    (#629, about 1862)

For all the ladylike imagery and the detached, contemplative mood of the poem, the preoccupation is with a moon whose cold indifference implies an absolute break between man and nature—the guillotined head, the stemless flower: nothing less than the isolation and terror of man's place in the universe, where his "little Mysteries . . . like Life – and Death – " are of no concern whatever to anyone or anything but himself. In such moods, Emily Dickinson is as far as can be imagined from Emerson and the Transcendentalists. The snub she felt from Susie's moon and the sentimental cry it wrung from her young heart have been developed into a Pascalian contemplation of immensity and (poetically) into a coolheaded, beautifully controlled statement of alienated man. No poetic cliché is more weary than the moon, and yet every detail is new, every image precisely visualized. She has brought her ideas, her perceptions, and herself under firm control. One has the feeling that, having confronted the destructive element fearlessly and frankly, and having painted it where it stands, she can live with it.

The other, later moon poem (she wrote still others, and in varying moods) shows her in another stage of contemplation. This time she has, to some degree, distanced the sense of alienation and is on the verge of revelation. It is an austere little statement, gnomic and oracular.

The Moon upon her fluent Route
Defiant of a Road –
The Star's Etruscan Argument
Substantiate a God –

> If Aims impel these Astral Ones
> The ones allowed to know
> Know that which makes them as forgot
> As Dawn forgets them – now –      (*#1528, about 1881*)

The distance is not complete or the revelation fulfilled. The conditional "If . . ." and the sense that full knowledge is achieved only by those who have joined the Astral Ones—that is, died—show her still groping for a firm and abiding faith. But the orderly wheeling of the moon and stars provide an Etruscan argument (primal? sturdy? and hence encouraging?), and we are nearer knowledge than before, if only in the sense of its possible revelation after death. This is not new in her poetic or spiritual development. She experimented with the thought many times—for instance, the agonizing cry of the early poem:

> I shall know why – when Time is over –
> And I have ceased to wonder why –
> Christ will explain each separate anguish
> In the fair schoolroom of the sky –
>
> He will tell me what "Peter" promised –
> And I – for wonder at his woe –
> I shall forget the drop of Anguish
> That scalds me now – that scalds me now!      (*#193, about 1860*)

Here the lyric outburst of the young heart is everything, only more controlled and (one feels) much less staged than the moon letter to Susan. "I watched the Moon around the House" and "The Moon upon her fluent Route" do not seem staged at all. No one is likely to exclaim, "Mere rhetoric." Their truth stands clear and powerful. They are a measure of the growth of the poet in breadth of vision and in organizing power.

In miniature, such was the journey, the life action, of Emily Dickinson. It required extraordinary discipline and concentration. While Austin apparently submerged his early bewilderments in his profession and his good works, and Vinnie made a career of the Dickinson home and taking care of Dickinsons, Emily had other work to do. "She had to think," said Vinnie; "she was the only one of us who had that to do." Seeing her life and her work and what she accomplished this way makes the disparity between the quiet life and the tumultuous rhetoric understandable. The intense inner life she was born to lead, as the others were not, required no less a rhetoric for its full expression. For her there came to be no such thing as mere rhetoric. Every word was an experiment in meaning, a route toward the discovery of new meanings in the perceptions and thoughts that entered her teeming consciousness. This was her career, her journey toward Circumference.

Appendixes for

VOLUME ONE

# I
## Vinnie as Stylist, Mimic, Reader,
## and Poet

VINNIE'S PROSE STYLE, both written and oral, deserves attention. Like her mother, she did not enjoy writing. But she tried hard—if only to keep up with her brother and sister—as we know from a letter to Austin written when she was nearly seventeen (*Home,* pp. 87–89, January 11, 1850): "I thank you, for your good advice, concerning letter writing, & hope to profit by it. I have written one & generally two letters, evry Saturday, since I left home, &, though I've allways had a great aversion to writing, I hope, by consent practice, the dislike will wear away, in a degree, at least. . . . Write soon & dont ridicule this will you?" If in her letters she stuck to the "matters of fact" (which Emily relegated to her) and cultivated a staccato style, it was probably in reaction to the "metaphysics"—the "air"—she saw inflating the discursive paragraphs of her more literary siblings. "Emilie has fed you on air so long, that I think a little 'sound common sense' perhaps wouldnt come amiss[.] *Plain english you know* such as Father likes" (*Home,* p. 148; to Austin, June 30, 1851). She jammed her letters tight with gossip and crisp, sometimes enigmatic comments: "Emilie is pensive just now recollections of 'by gones' you know, 'Old un' &c." (*Home,* p. 206, December 29, 1851). She had a good ear and a keen eye. Her gift was for the satiric and combative, examples of which we have already seen. Mabel Todd described it as follows (*AB,* p. 6): "Lavinia was a brilliant exponent of ancient wit and comment not involving any superfluous love for one's fellow man. . . . I could not help a liking for the fierce denunciations which sprung forth from Vinnie's nimble tongue." Mabel once started a collection of Vinnie's sayings. To a woman who complained that Vinnie's cats were killing birds, Vinnie replied, "You must blame the Creator" (*Home,* p. 29). Hearing some working men cursing, she remarked, "At least they've heard of our Redeemer." After a tedious visit from Uncle Joel Norcross: "I have got tired of hearing about *Ego altogether.* He is never informed on any other subject" (*Home,* p. 297). She had other moods. "Vinnie says there is a tree in Mr. Sweetser's woods that shivers," wrote Emily to the Norcrosses (*L* II, 495, early May 1872). When a caller later, in 1895, urged her to look at the light on the Pelham Hills, she turned away and said, "There is no landscape since Austin died" (*AB,* p. 331).

The best account we have of Vinnie's gift for impersonation and imitation is in Susan Dickinson's monograph, "Annals of the Evergreens," a twenty-five-page, typewritten document (Dickinson Papers, Houghton Library, Harvard) written for her children as a memorial of the great days in the Evergreens when the Dickinsons entertained such notables as Bowles, Emerson, Wendell Phillips, Colonel Benton, Bishop Huntington, and Judge Lord. Susan exercises her own not inconsiderable style on each of these. One of her most entertaining passages is on Judge Lord, with Vinnie playing a strong supporting role—indeed, stealing the show. The episode—a Sunday dinner—might have taken place sometime in the late 1870s. Mrs. Lord is not present—she died on December 10, 1877; Vinnie and Sue seem on still cordial terms; Emily, of course, is not there; Austin is sick in bed, upstairs. Sue begins with an unflattering sketch of the Judge,

> . . . a perfect figure-head for the Supreme Court, from his stiff stock to his toes; never seem[ed] to coalesce with these men, although he was often here with them as the guest of your Grand Father – But his individuality was so bristling, his conviction that he alone was the embodiment of the law, as given on Sinai so entire, his suspicion of all but himself, so deeply founded in the bed rock of old conservative Whig tenacities, not to say obstinacies, that he was an anxious element to his hostess in a group of progressive and mellow although staunch men and women. At an informal dinner with him once we saw him at his best. Your Father was ill, and he kindly took the head of the table, your Aunt Vinnie, sat at his right, the other guests I do not seem to remember. Perhaps because it was Sunday, we naturally got upon the subject of hymnology in New England. The Judge remarking that he was brought up on "Watts and Select" unabridged, asked if any of us were familiar with the hymn beginning
>
> > "My thoughts on awful subjects roll
> > Damnation and the dead."
>
> In astonishment we answered, no! where upon he layed down his fork, made himself a little more stiff, and erect, behind his old-fashioned silk stock, than usual, if that were possible, and recited with an energy worthy himself and the subject, the whole hymn. There was really a horrible grandeur about it, although our nervous laughter might have misled one in the next room as to our real emotions. Your Aunt was inspired by this to give us one of her famous representations of the early choir, with bass viol accompaniment, as familiar to us in the Village church a generation ago when they worshipped in what is now called "College Hall." She sang stoutly and with real minor threat and pathos the first two lines of
>
> > "Broad is the road which leads to death."
>
> but in the third line, where "Wisdom shows a narrow path," the melody running too high for the superannuated Village soprano, she dropped off in a cracked subsidence from the key, leaving the bass-viol to moan in harrowing discord, rejoining it again, after an interval in the fourth line, where they each, somewhat spent, strove to deepen the gloom of "Here and there a traveler" – ! the viol quite outstripping its rival and prolonging the last few notes in such grating woe, that I remember in the old days, the little boys used to look round furtively after sitting down to the prayer, to see if anything was the matter, with the good old man who bullied this kingly, misplaced instrument. The imitation was a most remarkable artistic performance on your Aunt's part, arousing such applause that your Father's bell rang, requesting us to remember that it was Sunday. The suggestion of unmusical, quavering voices was remarkable in the imitation, without the astonishing reproduction of the sullen bass-viol.

As to Vinnie's reading, her diary (see Chapter 7, note 2) shows what she was up to at age eighteen.

Jan. 16   finished Adirondack. [Joel Tyler Headley, *The Adirondack, or Life in the Woods*, 1849]

Jan. 21   Received my usual magazine [*Harper's*. This was a monthly entry]

Feb. 4   Attended the Lyceum.

Feb. 7   Read this eve.

Feb. 14   Read some in "Woman in America" [*Her Work and Her Reward*, by Maria J. McIntosh, 1850]

Feb. 20   Commenced Reveries of Bachelor. [Ik Marvel, 1850]

Feb. 22   Finished *Bachelors Reveries*.

March 1   Tutor Holland . . . Lent me "French Revolution." [Carlyle, 1837]

March 19   Commenced *David Copperfield* [1849–50]

March 21   The reading circle commenced this evening

April 18   Finished *"David Copperfield."* Commenced German Story.

April 20   Read "Literary attractions of the Bible." [Not identified]

May 30   Attended *reading club* in evening.

May 31   Received *Music* and Magazine [June *Harper's*]

June 3   Attended Reading Society.

June 4   Arranged books in morning.

June 13   Emilie Fowler spent morning reading Shakespeare here.

July 5   Went to preparatory lecture.

July 8   Went to reading club.

Aug. 13   Heard Mr. Beechers *address* [on "Imagination"]

Aug. 17   Read "House with seven gables" [1851]

Sept. 9   Heard Othello at Museum [in Boston]

Oct. 9   Borrowed Upham's phylosophy. [Thomas C. Upham, *Elements of Mental Philosophy*, 1838]

Oct. 17   Begin reading "Second Love" [by Martha Martell]

Oct. 18   Finished Second Love.

Oct. 19   Commenced "Memoir of Lady Colquhoun." [James Hamilton, *A Memoir of Lady Colquhoun*, 1851]

Nov. 23   Finished Lady Colquhoun.

Dec. 7   Commenced reading Miss Lyons memoir. [Edward Hitchcock, *The Power of Christian Benevolence Illustrated in the Life and Labors of Mary Lyon*, 1851]

Dec. 16   *Read all evening.*

As Mrs. Bianchi remarks of Vinnie's diary (*Face to Face*, p. 108, n.): "It is significant that books and the names of books read, as well as allusions to the 'reading club', are to be found on almost every page"; and (p. 113): "For even then their home was a house of books and the talk of them." And (in *Life and Letters*, p. 13): "It was Lavinia who knew where everything was, from a lost quotation to last year's muffler." Emily writes to Austin (November 16, 1851, L I, 157): "Vinnie is eating an apple . . ., and accompanying it with her favorite [New York] Observer, which if you recollect, deprives us many a time of her sisterly society."

Although later evidence is scanty, we can assume that she shared the young people's interest in books like *Kavanagh*, that she kept up with the magazines (*Harper's*, the *Atlantic*, and *Scribner's*) that came to the house, and that, as with Emily, the Bible and Shakespeare were staples, even if as busy house-keeper she spent much of her time being "Atlas."

Although Vinnie as poet is hardly a topic of broad or deep dimensions, one document survives to show that, whatever posterity might think, she thought of herself as sometimes visited by the Muse. The document (Dickinson Papers, Houghton Library, Harvard) is a gathering of seventeen 5 x 8 sheets, each sheet containing a poem (or fragment), typewritten, with a title sheet as follows:

Poems

by

Miss Lavinia Dickinson

*Amherst, Massachusetts*

1898

The final sheet, signed "Lavinia Dickinson," is on different paper from the rest, and the writing is in what appears to be Vinnie's *youthful* hand. It is difficult to explain this—indeed, one wonders how these verses ever got type-written. Surely not by Vinnie. Perhaps by her friend Mary Lee Hall, who earlier had helped transcribe Emily's MSS.

Night

The stars kept winking and blinking,
   as if they had secrets to tell;
But as nobody asked any questions,
   Nobody heard any tales.

\*   \*   \*

The ingenuity of pain
   Groping for tenderest nooks
Then plants its fangs in quivering flesh.

\*   \*   \*

The pines let drop their needles
   As noiseless as the snow,
They carpet all the woods with plush
   And light the darkest paths.

\*   \*   \*

New pleasures bring new anxieties.

\*   \*   \*

Pain and I fought for the mastery
   But oh! the bleak, bleak battlefield
Before the victory.

\*   \*   \*

Indifference is as sure to kill
    As smokeless powder's mark,
So be cautious how you trifle
    With a heart of any size.

\*   \*   \*

Why should we hide our friendship
    From those who've earned the claim?
Is it disgrace to recognize
    A kindred heart and soul?

\*   \*   \*

### FIRE-FLIES

The fire-flies hold their lanterns high
    To guide the falling star,
But, if by chance the wicks grow short
    The stars might lose their way.

\*   \*   \*

The bells clang out the notice
    That the holy time has come, –
And man must cease from labor,
    And beasts may roam at will.

\*   \*   \*

Challenge makes contrast swift to hurt or heal.

\*   \*   \*

The wind hung high in the trees last night
    And threw the branches down,
And sang weird tunes the elfins made,
    And then the world was still.

               ["threw" is written in Vinnie's *late* hand]

\*   \*   \*

Appreciation is as rare as pearls in dusty streets.

\*   \*   \*

Forgetting to remember is such a little thing,
    But sometimes it snaps the heartstrings
And that's a little thing.

\*   \*   \*

Encouragement is like the dew
    That saves the breath of flowers,
Discouragement is drought
    That parches all their hopes.

\*   \*   \*

How easy 'tis to meet
　　The wrongs to others done,
But when we are hurt
　　The christian grace is not so manifest.

\* \* \*

Circumstances shatter vows, as autumn wind, the leaves.

\* \* \*

"And yet", is such a simple phrase, –
　　It hardly seems worth mending;
But many a bliss has tripped just here,
　　Because this fatal footing.

## II

### "War between the Houses": Documents

THE TODD-BINGHAM ARCHIVE is rich in gossipy memoranda. Much of it—interviews and correspondence—dates from the early 1930s, when Mabel Todd and her daughter were preparing the new edition of the letters, and later, after Mrs. Todd's death in 1932, when Mrs. Bingham was preparing *Bolts of Melody, Ancestors' Brocades,* and *Home.* Some of it is in Millicent Todd Bingham's hand; some of it typed, probably by her; some of it from other sources. The historical validity of such material, of course, is always open to question; but it is part of the written record.

　　To comment on the items in order: 1) Mary Lee Hall's bias is clear; she hated Sue and was fond of Vinnie. 2) Miss Jordan is also hostile to Sue, but, it should be noted, ambivalent toward Vinnie and Mabel Todd. (Mary Augusta Jordan was librarian at Vassar College following her graduation there in 1876. She taught English at Vassar from 1880 to 1884, when she went to Smith, where she remained a member of the English department until her retirement in 1921. She brought out editions of *The Vicar of Wakefield, Burke on Conciliation, Milton's Minor Poems,* and *Ten Essays of Ralph Waldo Emerson.* She received the honorary degree of L.H.D. from Smith in 1910. She died in New Haven in 1941.) 3) Mrs. Turner's memories of the Dickinsons in "My Personal Acquaintance with Emily Dickinson," edited by her niece Clara Newman Pearl, were drawn upon by Mrs. Bingham in *Emily Dickinson's Home,* by Jay Leyda in *The Years and Hours,* and are frequently mentioned in my own chapters; but the document, to my knowledge, has never been printed in full. It gains in color and, perhaps, in authenticity when one reads the whole of it. One can see, in action, the making of a myth. While not so acrimonious as Miss Hall or Miss Jordan, Mrs. Turner's bias for the Homestead over the Evergreens is clear. She can be inaccurate or sentimental, especially when she comes to the poems, to the earliest anecdotes about ED, to the last days, and to ED's funeral. But it is to be noted that she insists on the

gradual nature of Emily's withdrawal and rejects the notion of a single traumatic love experience. 4) I have also frequently referred to the document,
written or dictated by Mabel Loomis Todd the year before she died, "Scurrilous but True." It, too, has appeared elsewhere in part; but, again, it seems
well to present the document in its entirety. Mabel Todd's bias, her suppres-
sions, her vanity and snobbishness, are obvious enough. The document is important, however, for the kernel of truth in her side of the story. 5) Millicent
Todd Bingham's report of her interview with her father in his declining years
illuminates one of the saddest aspects of this drama of the Houses; and finally,
6) her sketches for her projected autobiography give revealing insights into
the drama's setting, and glimpses of some of its important personages.


I


THESE EXCERPTS from the voluminous correspondence between Mabel Loomis
Todd, Millicent Todd Bingham, and Mary Lee Hall during the years (1929–
39) of the work on the 1931 *Letters* and beyond give the context, and more of
the color, of Miss Hall's animadversions on the "War between the Houses."
In spite of Miss Hall's plea for confidentiality, and sensitive as the issue may
still be, it seems best now to put this material in the public domain. Its biases,
indeed its furies, have long existed underground, to surface occasionally and
tantalizingly, as in the brief selections in Mrs. Bingham's *Ancestors' Brocades*
and Jay Leyda's *Years and Hours*. The processes of history, new material and
new witnesses, will correct what is purely temperamental or untrue in them.
Several of Miss Hall's fixed ideas have long since been questioned, or are
questioned in my text: her notion of George Gould as the Lover and her melodramatic view of life in the "House of Shadows" in the early years. And when
she writes Mrs. Bingham that "the awful spirit rises in me whenever Sue and
Mattie are in my thoughts," she exposes frankly her own emotional bias, still
powerful after all those years.

Excerpts, first, from a letter from Miss Hall to Genevieve Taggard will
explain Miss Hall's involvement with Vinnie. It also establishes an important
priority: it was Miss Hall who got in touch with Mabel Todd, rather than
vice versa. The letter is dated November 4, 1929. Miss Taggard's biography of
ED appeared the following year.

MY DEAR MISS TAGGARD:

A friend sent me notice of the "Emily Dickinson Meeting" soon to be
held, and I am *very* anxious that Mrs Todd may add something quite interesting to her contribution on this special occasion.

How I wish I could follow my spirit, and be "present in the flesh", to
hear the truth about Emily Dickinson.

Please tell Mrs Todd – and she *knows* that I do not stand for falsehoods –
that Miss Vinnie brought the one hundred and fifty poems to my home, and
putting them in my hands asked me to copy them for her, and to let no one
know excepting my mother. I kept her secret until the "Further" poems
were published, when I broke my silence, and wrote to personal friends
about this incident.

Miss Vinnie asked me if it would "Hurt Emily" if the poems were published. I told her that *she* must decide that question, or ask some friend of Emily's who knew her in life.

I kept the poems six months, copied them as well as I could, and gave them back to Miss Vinnie who was not at all well at the time. (She did not live more than four months afterwards.) I asked her to put the poems in a *safe* place, or send them to a reliable firm to be published when she was able to attend to the matter. . . .

My heart and I rejoice that Mrs Todd is living, and will speak at this remarkable meeting – Give Mrs Todd my love, and ask her to let me know where the report of the meeting will be published, in what paper, that I may send for a copy. There are so many statements in the "Life of Emily Dickinson" written by her niece who wrote what she wished the world to believe, that I shall pray the good Lord to let me live to read your book. . . .

I am not sure of reaching Mrs. Todd in any other way, so I will be most grateful to you if you will share this with my dear friend of Amherst days, whom my mother and I admired tremendously, and trusted implicitly.

Most cordially yours

(*Miss*) Mary Lee Hall

*1313 South Roan Street.*
*Johnson City, Tenn.*

By late that month (November 1929), the correspondence between Miss Hall and Mabel Todd was in full swing. We begin with one of Miss Hall's typical blasts against Martha Dickinson Bianchi's alleged misrepresentations. (I have omitted from these excerpts the major passages appearing in the text.)

*Nov. 24, 1929*

MLH to MLT

No, never have I fallen so desperately low as to follow Mattie's black flag of spiritual illiteracy.

When Ned died Mother and I allowed his sister to come to the house and cry out her anguish in complete seclusion; that is all. Never did we accept any of the invitations from the two women behind the hedge of utter insincerity & deceit, which were showered upon us. A friend sent me the "Life of Emily Dickinson" to read and return – a book made with the undivine purpose of painting Sue's portrait for the world – that did not know her – to gaze on and admire.

Poor Vinnie received blow after blow, and Emily's love affair was mangled beyond all possible recognition.

Had Mattie taken her pen to paint her own character, as the object of her work, she could not more truthfully have portrayed her lack of righteous standards, her false judgement, and her intentional betrayal of trust. . . .

# "War between the Houses": Documents

*Feb. 26th, 1930*

MLH TO MLT

. . . The book [Josephine Pollitt, *Emily Dickinson: The Human Background of Her Poetry*, 1930] is interesting, and far superior in every respect to Mattie's "Life of *Sue*", as it ought to be called, yet it does not satisfy my hungry soul.

You know far more than any other person, probably, about the inner, personal history of the D. family. When you are at liberty to let your sparks fly, they will blaze a trail that will make other little by-paths look like spider tracks. Write it before I become immortal.

*June 25, 1930*

MLH TO MLT

. . . I knew Vinnie intimately, and I knew the dreadful warfare that kept her mind unsettled, but I did not know Emily excepting as I knew her through her poems that you edited, and I am sure the world owes you an everlasting debt. . . .

*July 29, 1930*

MLH TO MLT

A letter from you is an event and a most welcome one.

The "lover" of whom I wrote was not Emily's, but Vinnie's, a Mr Copeland – of the Copeland family of Northampton – and he was a banker at Middletown, Ct. at the time of Vinnie's death. . . .

The poems cannot be interpreted solely by Emily's love affairs, the *shadows* drove her into herself. She found much elation in the men who came into her horizon, and they seemed to be the matches that ignited her mental oil tanks. She was a poor, lonely soul, and so were the others. Each one had one or more romances, and they needed them. . . .

*Sept. 14, 1930*

MLH TO MLT

Vinnie gave me the "Further" poems to copy just after Christmas of 1898, and I had them until the last of May, or first of June 1899. When she became ill I felt that it was better that she should have the poems in the house, especially as she was having some serious battles with "the other house". She said she would hide them where prowlers could not discover them. Of course I did not ask about them after they left my hands. Mattie has claimed to have found them in an old box, where deeds & mortgages were kept, also between the leaves of a large book that was usually in Vinnie's sitting room – perhaps in various other places built for the purpose by her vivid imagination. Vinnie intended to publish the poems, but was never well enough to do so, & I did not want to have any part in such an undertaking.

Vinnie suggested that Mattie's poems were manufactured out of some of Emily's. I told her I thought *not*.

Vinnie made no pretence to me ever of having any affection for Sue or Mattie. She was bitter in her denunciations of them. She told me Sue had been cruel to Emily and herself, and they each had suffered keenly from her insincerities, her insane jealousies, as well as her intentional deceit. I know that Vinnie told Mrs Stockbridge that Sue never ceased to annoy her in every possible way, and that she felt she was trying to *kill* her, as she knew her heart was weak.

In one of Mr Copeland's letters to me, written during Vinnie's last illness, he asked if "the other house" was fighting Vinnie, or leaving her in peace to be cared for by Maggie: he wanted to assure Vinnie that if he could be of comfort or assistance to her, he was ready to go to Amherst at any time. Vinnie often said that Emily's life was shortened by at least ten years, by Sue's cruel treatment. I know Vinnie's life was a tragedy after Ned's death. Sue & Mattie claimed that his heart was weakened by his determination to "stand by Vinnie", during the trial at Northampton. She had a bad adviser, and there were times when she regretted the step she took, also the publicity. . . .

What a novel could be written about the D. family. . . . Only the absolute truth need be revealed, and that would be startling, & sensational enough for the most rabid devourer of novels. . . .

*Oct. 12, 1930*

MLH TO MLT

. . . Mrs. Davis came to see me one evening, and she was greatly agitated over a request from Mrs. Donald – that she "take a stand" against you, in favor of Sue D. Martha and Mrs. D. emphatically declared that Mrs Donald had been greatly mistaken if she expected any real friend of yours to be less a friend when you were under trial, and they decided that Sue was the one to be treated with disdain. Mrs. Davis said, "Why Sue drove Austin out of the house more than once when she was flirting with Mr. Sam Bowles, and *I* shall stand by Austin & Mrs Todd, and I am not afraid to show my colors either. I told Mrs Donald she was not setting a good example as a clergyman's wife, and I also told her that I could tell her a thousand things about Sue that would shock her." . . .

We refused to meet Sue for three years, and never accepted her invitations. One evening my brother and I went to the house to hear Mattie play, on Ned's invitation, & Mattie said she preferred to talk, and would not play. Sue & Mattie must have had a drink for they imitated Pres. Seelye, Dr. W$^m$ Tyler, John Tyler and many others, spoiling the evening for us. When we left we vowed never to enter the house again unless to attend the funerals of Ned & his father. We kept the vow.

After Austin's death Ned came to the house a number of times, and, to our surprise he told us that the day of his father's funeral he arranged that you should be in the house at least ten minutes while the family was at lunch, & he told the nurse never to let his mother or sister know you had been there. He said the nurse told him you had put something in the casket, and he remarked, "Whatever Mrs Todd placed in the casket remained there – and I am glad she had the comfort of that last few minutes with my father"—When Sue knew that some pictures had been left you, by Austin's will, she swore you never should have them. Ned said, "Father loved Mrs Todd, and desired her to have the pictures, so I shall see that she receives them, if I have to send Mother and Mattie to Europe in order to carry out father's wishes."

Ned said he had always admired you, and had never changed in his feelings for you, but he felt obliged to hide his feelings, and to stand by his Mother even though he considered her to be entirely responsible for what had happened. He said he and Mattie had lived in *hell,* and he believed no one could possibly suffer more than he had in trying to be loyal to family traditions. This is for you alone, & not to be used for publication.

*July 29, 1933*

MTB TO MLH

. . . I want to know anything, everything that is true regarding Emily and every member of her family. Speculation does not interest me. I have no theory to prove. . . . I want solely to prevent a tortured and grotesque picture of Emily Dickinson from being foisted upon posterity. . . .

You ask me to write you what I want to know. The trouble is, I want to know everything, every little nugget of truth. For instance; Between what dates did you know the Dickinsons? Did you ever see Emily? Did you know Sue? What did you think of her? What were her characteristics? Was she pretentious? On what sort of terms was she with Emily and Lavinia? What did Lavinia say about her? What was Emily's attitude toward her? Was there ever any harmony between the two households? What was the attitude of each to each? How can Mrs. Bianchi say that Emily adored Sue up to the moment she died, when Emily called her her "pseudo-sister"?

*Aug. 5, 1933*

MLH TO MTB

Soon I will answer your other questions. I only hope you will gather some pebbles from all the sand I have scattered on the beach. I feel as you do, that the falsehoods, and deceptions, and insincerities that fill the books Mattie has written ought to be *stabbed* with the true history of the lives of all the D. Family.

*Aug. 5, 1933*

MLH TO MTB

Your Mother's heart is strong in you, and I want to tell you all you wish to know because of my faith in her, and because of my faith in you. Then, too, I want the truth to be known in regard to the kind of life that was lived behind the hedges, – both hedges! . . .

Mrs. Hills invited us a number of times to meet Austin & Sue, but we had heard so much about the arrogance, and insincerity of Sue, that we were determined *not* to meet her, & we avoided her for several years, but

[ 257 ]

we consulted Austin about some business matters, and really liked & enjoyed him. . . .

Of course I kept meeting Mattie D. at parties, & receptions, and one morning half way between the First Church, and the Town Hall, I met Austin. He stopped me, and said, "I want to ask you a question. Mattie says you do not always recognize her – Why not?" To this I replied, "Having been introduced to your daughter twenty-six times, and having been snubbed by her quite as often, I have decided that I do not care to know her." Austin laughed, and so did I. He told me that I had a clear case against Mattie, one that he could endorse. Soon after, Mattie joined me after church service, and she said, "Ned and I are going to call on you some evening this week –" Hesitating a moment I said – "Oh, are you?" She tossed her head and replied, "You will soon find out." They called Wednesday evening, remained until half past ten, and we liked Ned. He was so outspoken and sincere, so courteous, and entertaining that we kept his friendship as long as he lived. Sue and Mattie did their best to dominate her [Vinnie], in every possible manner, especially after Ned's death. I have always thought that Vinnie never would have turned against your dear mother had not her mind been poisoned by "the two black devils," as Mrs. Tuckerman, the Esty boys' aunt, called Sue and Mattie. . . .

Vinnie did not dare say aught against your mother to me and she knew that I loved and admired the friend who really introduced Emily to the great literary world. I think *in her heart* Vinnie admired and loved your mother, but dared not admit it on account of some dire threat held over her head.

Vinnie told me of the lawsuit, and Ned talked it over with us, but it is not very distinct in my memory. I remember that Ned said, "If my aunt wins the suit, Mattie and I may join the church, as that would be the biggest thing we could do in this small college town."

The attitude between "the two houses" was one of war, and Sue was the cause of all the discord and strife as far as I could learn. . . .

. . . I copied many of them ["Further Poems"], and intended helping Vinnie to do as she wished me to, and there was "war between the houses", especially severe, and so much was done to cruelly hurt Vinnie, that she became seriously ill, and I returned the precious manuscript after keeping same for four or five months, giving them into Vinnie's hands, & telling her to hide them well. She hid them so well that they were not discovered for – was it twenty years, or thirty? If I am not mistaken Mattie has mentioned two, if not three places where she found them. In a box with old deeds, mortgages, etc. In a large book, and I can't tell where the third hiding place was. The Manuscript given me was *all* in Emily's handwriting. When Vinnie was so ill, Mattie came to see me one morning, and said, "By the Dr's orders, no one is to see Aunt Vinnie so please do not try to see her again." Vinnie had asked me to see her daily, and to write to her old lover, telling him of her condition. In the first letter that I received from Mr Copeland, he asked "Is there a battle going on between the two houses? Can I be of any help to Vinnie, if I visit Amherst?" As soon as Mattie was out of sight, I went to Miss Vinnie's, and met Dr Haskell, at the door. I asked if I might see Vinnie, or if he had given orders for me to keep away. He said, "Miss Vinnie wants you here as often as you can arrange to come – and, so do I." Before my visit ended that morning, Mattie came in with a handful of red roses, and she was furious when she found me there. She asked Vinnie if she was tired, and poor Vinnie who whispered all she had to say, managed to tell her that my little visits rested, and comforted her.

Never have I lived where one family ruled as the D's did in Amherst, and, as the Oliver Hunt family ruled in the First Church. And why? Was it because people were afraid of Sue's tongue, of what she might say? My brother and I went just once to the Austin D. house by invitation. That sufficed. . . .

You certainly will *feel* the awful spirit that rises in me whenever Sue or Mattie are in my thoughts, and I believe that generally speaking, Amherst people feel as I do, yet pretend otherwise for fear of the sulphur fumes of Mattie's condemnation. . . .

*March 13, 1934*

MLH to MTB

The *cause* of her [Vinnie's] last illness was Sue who terrified her, and treated her shamefully. It began in the fall of '98. Vinnie always had Emily's rose bushes, and other shrubs carefully attended to before cold weather. When the day came for having the work done, the man told Vinnie that all the "dressing" had been taken from under the barn, and Maggie found out that Sue had ordered it put on her flower beds and shrubs. That stunned Vinnie. She sent for me, and I found her hardly able to speak. When I learned the reason for her condition, I laughed, and said, "Miss Vinnie, just get Mr Lindsay to bring you a load of fertilizer, and say nothing to Sue. Let her find you equal to the battle, and *don't* let her hurt you". Her heart was so rapidly beating that I cautioned Maggie to watch her. Mr Lindsay came to the rescue, and then Sue began to send "Sport" over to Vinnie's, and he worried the pussies. Finally Vinnie could endure no more, and she went to bed. She asked me to write to Mr. Copeland, and he wrote beautiful letters of tender sympathy, offering to come to her if she so desired, and he wrote me, asking if "the other house" was causing any trouble. . . .

Vinnie was not well all winter, and was not up during the summer – it was "the Dickinson heart" as she called it, and Dr. Nelson Haskell was her physician. . . .

Vinnie did not see much of Sue for several years, and rarely after Austin's death. Ned was kind to his aunt, and did all he could to cheer her, and she was fond of him. . . .

I may have written your Mother, or told her, of my visit one Sunday, after service, when Austin was ill. I saw him alone on the piazza, and he greeted me most cordially, asked me if I thought it would do him any harm to take a trip by water. I felt that Sue was not far away, invisible though, and I said I thought, with a jolly good friend to go with him, the trip might do him good. "Getting away might give you a brace", I told him. Then Sue came out and asked if I intended to imply that leaving his family would help recovery. I said, "Sometimes it does. It might in this case." Sue left, and I did not remain long. That was the last time I saw Austin. How he *suffered*. . . .

*March 20, 1934*

MTB TO MLH

. . . Did Miss Vinnie ever talk to you about her suit against my mother? *Why* did she sue mamma for that piece of land – after all that mamma had done for her? Do you know why she did it? What was the real motive? I have wondered and wondered about it. Though it has warped my life, I never have fully understood it. Was Vinnie happy after she got the land back? If it does not tire you, please tell me sometime all you remember about it, and Sue's part in it.

The more you tell me about Vinnie the more profoundly sorry I am for her. Poor, lonely, loyal, terror-stricken last of her race in the grip of a relentless alien like Sue! What a tragedy! But my father still speaks of her with affection. Why did she turn away from her best friends – my mother and even more my father who was devoted to her? All you say is heartbreaking.

*April 10, 1934*

MLH TO MTB

. . . Yes Vinnie spoke several times to me of "the suit," and I thought that she greatly regretted having been forced into it. Really, if Sue had kept her finger out of Vinnie's pies, there would not have been trouble of any depth. Vinnie never was loved by Austin as Emily was, and had he lived, there would not have been a suit. Ned talked very freely about the matter but only in regard to Vinnie appearing in court. We have thought his death was hastened by the friction at home over the suit. He felt by "the traditions of the family," to stand by his aunt. . . . Sue did everything in her power to *down* your adorable mother, and it made her furious that she had absolutely no influence over "the Halls". Mrs. A.B.H. Davis told me that Mrs Neill, & Mrs Donald – whose husband was rector of the Church of the Ascension, in N.Y. City, at the time – urged her to take sides with Mrs D. against your Mother, and Mrs Davis told them that she admired your Mother very much, & always enjoyed meeting her, and saw no reason whatever for hurting her. She also said she had known Sue D. for many years, and she did *not* admire her, and she blamed *her* for having made so much trouble in town among people whom she pretended to like, and whom she had treated shamefully. It must have been Sue who held a sword over Vinnie's head, ready to let it drop if she did *not* get that land back. It was not Vinnie who started the trouble, I am sure of that.

Ned told us that his father left your Mother a picture, possibly two, that had hung in their parlor. Sue declared that the pictures never should be taken from the house, but Ned said he planned to take his mother & sister abroad for a few months, and would send them to N.Y. City for a few days while he closed the house. He planned to have the pictures boxed, and taken to your house, before leaving Amherst, and I suppose he did. He was loyal to Austin's memory, & especially after his father's death he was particularly fine.

Of course Vinnie missed your father – your mother also – but Satan, or Sue, was her deadly foe, and she *dared not* do what would ˙madden the enemy. She had no one to defend her, and Sue was bitter, and cruel & revengeful. . . .

*Feb. 20, 1935*

MLH to MTB

. . . If I remember correctly, Austin died in 1895, and of course Miss Vinnie was in the depths of loneliness; she had depended much upon her brother, and was ready to do whatever he wished her to regarding your Mother, and she did carry notes to him from your Mother during his illness, taking care never to be seen by any member of the family.

During your Mother's absence in Japan, Sue found the opportunity of getting in her chance for revenge, by telling Miss Vinnie about the strip of land, and she influenced her to do as she did, in order to get *in* with Miss Vinnie, that she might use her to get back the land, and to get control of her for the remainder of her life. For one thing she feared that Miss Vinnie might make a will favorable to others, giving Ned & Mattie only what the law obliged her to give.

Millicent, you never will know what an evil minded person Sue was. You cannot imagine such a fiend, for Sue could appear like "an angel of light", when it served her purpose to do so. . . . Miss Vinnie was devoted to Ned, and he was really a friend to her, but he was influenced by Sue, in the desire to get back the land, although he did his best to avoid the publicity of a law-suit, and it was one of the hardest things he ever did to go to Northampton with her, and remain by her side during the trial. Ned spoke freely to us about it, and he felt that his Mother was going too far in making such an exhibition of Miss Vinnie. . . .

My dear, your Mother never did anything to Miss Vinnie that caused her to act as she did. In her heart, she missed your Mother, but she *dared* not defy Sue. Sue was relentlessly cruel to Miss Vinnie in every possible way, and they hated one another with a deadly hate; even I was treated in the most offensive manner by Sue, but I simply ignored her, for I could do what Miss Vinnie felt she must not, on account of Ned. After Ned's death there were tragic battles between the two houses, and I was called to Miss Vinnie's many times to quiet her nerves, and help her recover from Sue's *verbal* blows.

*Dec. 29, 1939*

MLH to MTB

I do not think Emily was a victim of Amherst social life. Instead I think her home life, its atmosphere, and her father's austere and stern character had a large part in the kind of life she chose to live.

*May 3, 1940*

Mrs. S. S. Preston to MTB

. . . dear Miss Hall left us Feb 17 – . . .

# APPENDIX II

*May 13, 1940*

MRS. PRESTON TO MTB

Your letter inquiring about Miss Hall's letters, yes I can tell you about them she destroyed most of them before she passed away, and I destroyed what she left. The things (letters) she left was her late mail. But when she found her eye sight was failing so fast she went through her things and destroyed them. . . .

2

MRS. BINGHAM INCLUDED, IN *Ancestors' Brocades,* Miss Jordan's account of the trial much as it appears here, an obvious polishing up of what Miss Jordan recounted in conversation. The other gleanings from the interview with Miss Jordan seem to be from notes taken at the time, or hurriedly written up shortly after. In *Ancestors' Brocades* (p. 359), Mrs. Bingham describes Miss Jordan as an "eyewitness" at the trial. Her interest in the trial, her detailed memory of it over the years, and her seemingly intimate knowledge of Dickinson gossip indicate, if nothing else, the impact of the doings of this extraordinary family on that whole Connecticut Valley area. (It is to be recalled that Maria Whitney was a member of the Smith College faculty from 1875 to 1880.)

Mary A. Jordan to Millicent Todd Bingham, interview of November 3–4, 1934

Miss Jordan remembers the trial, the relations of the Dickinsons, the attitude of the public to my mother and father, all in the greatest detail. She says mamma had a rather superior way with people and they were rather pleased to see the verdict go against her. Moreover, they enjoyed the trial exceedingly, it was very amusing. In fact, it was *opera bouffe.* It was generally recognized that Lavinia was putting up a ludicrous testimony.

"Miss Dickinson, is not this your signature?"

"Yes – that is to say, that's my autograph. I understood that someone in Boston wished my autograph, and thought that was what I was doing when I wrote it."

"Did you know that this was a release?"

"Isn't that business? I know nothing of business."

"Did you not know that this was a contract?"

"Isn't that business, too? Father always attended to business."

"Miss Dickinson, did you never employ labor?"

"No."

"Do you mean that you never hired servants?"

With lifted, inquiring eye-brows, "Does he mean Maggie?"

The judge had the greatest difficulty to control himself.

Miss Jordan thinks that the decision went in her favor not at all because of facts, for everybody knew that she had known what she was doing, but because it was felt that she had changed her mind about wanting mamma to have the property, and she should be allowed to change her mind.

Miss Jordan thinks mamma was greatly to blame for having attempted

262 ]

to get her to carry through her promise and to sign the deed, even though it had long been her intention to do so.

Miss Jordan thinks that Sue did not intimidate her, because nobody could, not her man of business either, as Miss Buffum thinks. Besides that, she was a complicated and adroit liar. She lived entirely in fiction and in her own imagination.

According to Lavinia, via Miss Jordan, when Miss Lyon said to Emily, "Have you said your prayers?" Emily replied, "Yes, why shouldn't I? Though it can't make much difference to the Creator." Emily was not unsympathetic, indeed, she was very affectionate according to Lavinia. She gave this as an instance. Emily asked the milk-boy one morning, "How did the great grey cat strike you?" "She didn't strike me."

When it comes to Sue, she was a lady who was known to have doubtful relations with other men besides Samuel Bowles. Had county-family manner, which is exaggerated in her daughter. Miss Jordan understands Mattie perfectly, calls her vain and pompous, an accomplished liar and a seducer of youth. She described a dinner party when she took the actor, Mr. Harrison, an Englishman, to dinner at Mattie's and his horror when, trying to place the date when something happened, she said, "Oh, that must have been when I was lying in with my first book." She throws around names and facts with equal abandon, and always supplied a sensation in Amherst which relieved the monotony. I questioned whether there is any interest which is real in her life, one which keeps her going. Miss Jordan thought she must sometimes get tired of pose, of nothing else.

Once she came over to Northampton and tried to vamp George McCallum. She came with a maid, in lordly manner, to make sure that it was all right. She talked at length about the "Count" [Bianchi] and his ancestral jewels. Miss Jordan thinks she bought them herself. Though he posed as Russian, he was Austro-Italian. Professor Tyler tried to save her, for "After all, she is a Dickinson." Bianchi used up all her money, and only Professor Tyler saved her mother's money from going the same way.

At the time of the 1898 trial, Field brought the correspondence between Dr. Dickinson and mamma to Miss Jordan and asked her to read it, and she kept it from coming up in the trial. They intended to use it as evidence that this land was payment by Austin for services other than the editing of Emily's poetry. This of course I doubt, inasmuch as they had none of Austin's or mamma's letters in their possession.

Miss Jordan begs me to let the whole thing alone. If I attempted to deny anything she may say in print, I couldn't prove a thing. It would be her word against my word and she is enormously clever, and entirely unscrupulous. And as for Amherst, I couldn't count on anybody. People do not like to get mixed up in such things. She concluded with, "I wouldn't get between the upper and lower jaws of that tradition, if I were you."

Thinks mamma made Emily – calls it creative editing – says that a woman who couldn't choose among half a dozen words, was mostly juggling with the Dictionary. Thinks Emily artificial & living in imagination entirely.

[ 263 ]

# Appendix II

[The following is a transcript of Mrs. Bingham's penciled notes apparently from the same interview, followed by some jottings on separate, small scraps of paper.]

[Miss Jordan quoting Austin (?)]:
"People talk a lot about the play spirit. Never heard about the play spirit when I was a boy. When I was restless my mother put me in the wood-box and gave me an onion. Lavinia used to say, 'There ought to be an executive in every family. Father was always the executive in ours – After he died, [I] tried to be. I tried to be constructive. They said I should clean house. So I appointed the fourth of July – And had it done then. No calamity happened. So, if we got through it all right once, that ought to prove it can be done. And it did.' "

They were all remarkable. Was Sue? Oh yes, in her aplomb – She & her son & daughter put on all the airs of a county-family. They wanted to have a salon in Amherst with Samuel Bowles & his questionable relationship to Mrs. Austin as a background. They and their adjectives did not impress me. Mansion. Their statements of fact I sometimes questioned. (Miss Margaret Whitney in Farmington with Mattie. But Mattie didn't stay long) Mattie referred to her mother as "Dolly." In fact calling people by their first names was part of the technique of the salon – (Hitchcocks w[ith] all their integrities & all their angularities) Jealousies bet. Amherst & Smith – Bowles feminist & tried to get the Smith money to make Amherst coed and "a really 1st class institution" Resented the implication. Split the town – Over our dead bodies said the old timers. Seelye in particular – So Smith was founded, with L. Clark, who believed in the gentlewoman but not in feminism, at the helm – So close was he that Smith has more ready money than Amherst which added to the rift. Ned told Miss Jordan that she [Emily?] was a left-over of the Brontës. . . .

Miss Margaret, Emily & Maria Whitney, 186 Edwards St. – Miss Maria Whitney destroyed all her correspondence before she died as she wished to leave nothing to burden any relatives. Reserved, a great student & friend of prominent men. Loved teaching.

Further Poems in Atlantic not Emily
Sue a woman who despised her husband and was the soul mate of Sam Bowles.
Mrs. Bowles ill, [word illegible] for Republican & woman suffrage.
Miss Whitney an aristocrat who was conscious of it.
Lavinia said there ought to be someone in every family who would say Damn. Father did, but now up to her. "Damn, d.d." . . .

3

MY PERSONAL ACQUAINTANCE WITH EMILY DICKINSON*
by Clara Newman Turner

*Edited by Clara Newman Pearl*

SOON AFTER THE FIRST PUBLICATION of the Letters of Emily Dickinson in 1894, Mrs. Sidney Turner (Clara Newman) of Baltimore, a niece of Edward Dickinson, wrote for her friends a rather intimate account of Emily Dickinson's life. It was for them alone, for she felt that it would be sacrilege to give to the world the details of the private life of that shy, retiring personality. She remembered Emily's own words that she did not deem it "feminine" to publish. But after a lapse of more than thirty-five years I feel that I may be forgiven for publishing that account.

In March, 1852, Mary, a sister of Edward Dickinson, died. Mark Newman, her husband, followed her a few months later, and left his children and estate in the care of Edward Dickinson. He took the children to Amherst soon after the death of their parents, and after Austin Dickinson's marriage, placed the two younger children, Clara and Anna in Austin's family. Anna was my mother. She died when I was a child, but Clara, my aunt, the author of this account, born in 1844, married Sidney Turner, and lived to be seventy-eight years old. Mrs. Austin Dickinson was a woman of very peculiar disposition and the life of the two girls in the family of their cousin, Austin Dickinson, was far from happy. After my aunt was seventy years old I heard her say that she could not understand why Uncle Edward made them stay there when he knew how unhappy they were. For instance, my aunt to the end of her long life never willingly sat in a lighted room unless the shades were drawn for a favorite punishment of Cousin Sue's had been to make her study an entire evening seated in a lighted bay window with the shades up. It was my aunt's duty to take care of little Ned Dickinson, and my mother's to care for Mattie. My mother depended upon her sister always and my aunt in turn upon her Cousin Emily for counsel and support. As soon as an older sister, who had been placed in the family of William Dickinson of Worcester, married, both my mother and aunt went to live with her. My mother never went back to Amherst. My aunt went back each year to the old home and was married from Austin Dickinson's home. For many years the two orphan girls were in and out of their uncle's home almost every day. His two nieces never wavered in their love and loyalty to their Uncle Edward. . . .

Edward Dickinson has always been a very real person to me. His wife has not. As a child I remember standing beside my mother's sewing table and asking, "What was Aunt Emily like, Mother?" And her reply, "Aunt Emily was a Norcross." For years I wondered just what a Norcross could be.

I, personally, was brought up to believe that there never was what one would call a serious love affair. However, women of the old school, so

---

* Printed by permission of the Jones Library, Amherst. (Again, I have omitted the major passages appearing in the text or notes.)

called, like my aunt, did not discuss private family affairs with their "in-laws", nor a love affair before a young girl. I feel sure that the love and loyalty of the older generation were such that they never would have discussed the story of Emily's love affair with any outside person, even had there been such an experience in her life.

I never saw Emily Dickinson. In my childhood remembrance she is a dearly loved cousin who wore white in winter, as well as in summer, and who never would have her picture taken. This letter to my mother (the Madonna Anna) was rescued by my father when other personal letters from Emily were destroyed.

"It hardly seems credible that the brave little Boy and the celestial little Girl are Anna's, and yet would we not expect her to be the Mother of Poets and Prophets, were she the mother of anyone at all, as the Mail so sweetly assures us.

The bestowal of two such Fairies upon a sordid World, is of itself Prowess, and we give our hallowed congratulations to the Madonna Anna.

The picture of the pretty home is very warm and vivid and we half "touch" it too, unless softly forbidden-not with mortal Fingers, but those more Tidy, mental ones which never leave a blot. Thanks, dear, for the beatific Package, a murmur of the Saints, and never hide so long again from

your seeking Cousins,

EMILY."

I knew and loved Lavinia, her sister. I shall always remember Cousin Vinnie as she arrived at my aunt's home in Norwich, Connecticut. With her was Professor Todd of Amherst whose friendship and reliability never failed her. He used even to wind her clocks on Saturday night. Family and friends were gathered there at Norwich to pay their last respects to Sidney Turner, my aunt's husband. A slight figure wrapped in an old squirrel-lined circular flew up the steps and into the house. A rusty crepe veil fluttered in the wind as she hurried to my aunt's side. It was the first time that she had been out of Amherst for twenty years, and she was the center of attraction as long as she stayed. My fifteen year old curiosity made me ask why she did not leave Amherst more often. I remember well her reply. "Because, my dear, I do not like to travel. One sees so many people and things that one does not wish to see."

This letter to my aunt from Maggie speaks of the visit.

"MY DEAR MRS. TURNER

How kind of you to give me a thought in youre large Hart Where there is So Much Sorrow just Now. I wish I were big enough to have some of the outer Sorrow that Seround you. Bleve me that if my Sympaty could only Bring you back youre love again youre hart would never Know What Pain ment. I hope the dear one whome you grive for is Safe in that Heavenly home Where he is Master of Pain and dont remember the past you were So thoughtfull of dear dear Vinnia When she went to you that she Never Will for get, how beautifull every thing looked in youre lovely home and that nice vissit that you had with her in bed that morning She So ofton Spakes of it I hope you will come to Amherst some time this summer and have a nother Picknick with us in this dear old home We Will make you happy if we can Vinnia has not being Very Well this last few Weeks I hope she will sone be better The Doctor say she will to tell the truth of it She is not strong and cant get a long with things that She have no write to be troubled with it Will always be so as far as I see all are well around here / But a few are happy I hope the summer will give you a grate dale of Strenth and Some Plasure dont work for others have little thought for yourself

We have 5 cats 2 in the house and 3 in the Barren all well and good apetited so far again I think you for all youre kindness to me I hope youre hart will always remain here as there is not many more like it as I have reason to remember long, long, a go

> Some time I will Write to you on
> other Subjects
> youre servent
> Miss Emely.s and
> Vinnia.s
>
> MAGGIE"

My aunt went occasionally to Amherst for a visit with Cousin Vinnie. For years I think she was the only overnight guest in that household and I was always interested to hear about faithful and devoted Maggie and the humorous cats, each with its own saucer. During my aunt's visits she and her hostess always ate at two small tables, a not too sociable arrangement that alway excited my youthful interest. With a hesitancy bred by an association so intimate and yet so bound by decorum my Aunt Clara begins her article.

Since Death has loosened the clasps and opened the volume of Emily Dickinson's poetic life and the world is turning its pages back and forth— first with curiosity, then with curious interest—and closing the volume always with wondering admiration, perhaps it may interest you to take a little nearer look into that life, from the standpoint of one who was in and out of her home nearly every day for many years. You will pardon my own personal intrusion, as a necessary background to personal recollections.

I say *Poetic life* speaking as a whole, for from her mixing the bread her father preferred—in the kitchen—to her mingling of the sunbeams, the birds, and the flowers in the realm of her poetic thought, it was Fantasy all the way. Had not others preceded me, I should have hesitated long before bringing before any even private-public one so modest, so retired, so sensitive, who lived, as she said,

> "I'm Nobody! Who are you?
> Are you nobody, too?

[ 267 ]

> Then there's a pair of us – don't tell!
> They'd banish us, you know.
>
> How dreary to be somebody!
> How public, like a frog
> To tell your name the livelong day
> To an admiring bog!"

I am *not* the first, however, to draw aside the curtain, and enter the "Sanctum Sanctorum" of her lovely life, and can only hope her pardon will not have been quite exhausted before she reaches my offense, for I cannot but feel a little guilty, knowing her extreme retirement of nature, and remembering her own remark that she did not deem it "feminine to publish." The only warrant, as you know, which her publishers offer, is this little Prelude to the 1st Series.

> "This is my letter to the world,
> That never wrote to me –
> The simple news that Nature told,
> With tender majesty
>
> Her message is committed
> To hands I cannot see;
> For love of her, sweet countrymen,
> Judge tenderly of me!"

Perhaps this is sufficient, when you place with it the fact that there were found—after she went—over 700 of these little poems, tied in tiny booklets of six pages each. I feel impelled to say just here, however, as my own opinion, that I find no warrant, not even in the world's interested curiosity, or curious interest (as you will) for the first publication of her personally-private letters to a personal friend, on strictly personal, private, and home details. I cannot but feel the friend must ask very humble pardon at the door of her "Mansion", before he be quite acquitted. . . . [*Of Edward Dickinson, she writes:* In our National and State Congress, and holding high positions of public trust for over 40 years, the newspapers spoke of him, after his death, as leaving a name without a stain upon its memory. While making a speech in the Massachusetts Legislature upon the "Hoosac Tunnel bill" one hot day in June '74, he suddenly became faint and sat down. The House adjourned, and he went directly to "The Tremont House", where he died in three hours. It is one of the facts we call *strange,* that although in apparently perfect health, he had sat for his picture only a week or two before for the first time in many, many years, and the finished photographs surprised his home after he had been borne beyond its doors forever.

Mrs. Dickinson was a quiet, sweet, practical, unpretentiously-modest woman, with the sweetly-hushed voice of her daughter's inheritance, to whom I think Emily was a great mystery and constant surprise. The family would have died for each other, in their loyalty to, and pride in one another, but in my many years of daily intercourse with them, I never saw exchanged any marked *demonstration* of affection. I speak thus in detail, to give you a little glimpse of the characteristics of the atmosphere into which the daughter Emily was born in Amherst, December 10th, 1830. She was not born in the house in which she died, but was laid to rest—the light of her Day just set—only a few steps from where she opened her eyes upon her day just begun.

It is not what the world would call an *eventful life,* of which we ask. Her childhood and youth were as joyous as the birds she loved. Amherst was the home of her whole life and education, with the exception of one year, into which she crowded a two years' course of study in South Hadley under Miss Mary Lyon and a short stay in Washington while her father was in Congress. She was, while in South Hadley, the idol of the school and its Preceptress, and her appointment for a composition marked a "Red Letter Day." To illustrate the independence and honesty of her convictions, —Miss Lyon, during a time of religious interest in the school, asked all those who wanted to be Christian to rise. The wording of the request was not such as Emily could honestly accede to and she remained seated—the only one who did not rise. In relating the incident to me, she said, "They thought it queer I didn't rise"—adding with a twinkle in her eye, "I thought a lie would be queerer." This letter to my aunt, my *aunt* would never have published.

> "The cordiality of the Sacrament extremely interested me when a Child, and when the Clergyman invited 'all who loved the Lord Jesus Christ to remain', I could scarcely refrain from rising and thanking him for the to me unexpected courtesy, though I now think had it been to all who loved Santa Claus, my transports would have been even more untimely.
>
> Emily"

Her father's house was always the resort of the most cultured and refined, and such were her surroundings always. His home and grounds were thrown open annually for a Lawn Reception to the Alumni of the College and their friends, and at these gatherings Emily was accustomed, at first, to take a daughter's place. Later she was seen for shorter and shorter times, until in the latter years, her appearance was but a prelude to her disappearance, after just a word to one or two favored friends. She was full of fun and had a keen sense of the ludicrous, although I do not think you gather this from her poems.

To repeat, the world would not call her's an eventful life. *Her events* were the coming of the first bird;—the bursting of a chrysalis;—the detection of the fascinating spring fuzz of green in the air—the wondering opening on the new world of every little flower; an unusual sunset; the autumn changes—and the inexhaustible life. Her *Tragedies*—the wild storm:—the bruising of a plant;—the falling of a young bird from its nest;—a hurtful slight to an animal;—the falsity of a friend—a surprise upon her retreat;— an unfriendly act to *her* friend. The death of one she loved was to her the saving of them for her, I think, a little later on, and not so much a tragedy as would be a possible perfidy in life. . . .

Winter was the absence of Nature's Panorama, and was filled with excited anticipation of the renewal of her miracles. *Then*—her pictures, changed every morning, in the infinite resources of an Infinite Artist—were the "undressed hills";—the stalactites of Nature's enclosing circles;—and the

[ 269

Frost-King in his studio—Monarch only while the opposing sceptre of the Sun was withheld.

Her Opera was the trilling of the birds outside her window;—the buzzing of the bees;—the flitting in and out of the butterflies in their gauzy costumes. The crickets, and the frogs, and the breeze in its orchestra;—the many tinted trees, the sky and the clouds, the God-painted scenery—and though there were nothing to count to assure the fact, the auditorium was always full, because her great appreciative heart was all there.

Of her loves you can judge somewhat by this little tribute to her sister, in a letter to a friend whose brother had just gone. She says, "Your bond to your brother reminds me of mine to my sister—early—earnest—indissoluble. Without her, life were tears, and Paradise a cowardice, except for her inciting voice."

She was a great reader and a dainty reader. You remember her questioning the need of any other book after she had found Shakespeare. Her selections were the choicest—I should have as readily believed of her reading anything but the best, the purest, the most uplifting, as I should dream of the snow falling any other color than white. Her books? To quote her own words, "For poets—I have Keats and Mr. and Mrs. Browning. For prose—Mr. Ruskin, Sir Thomas Browne, and the Revelations. When a little girl I had a friend who taught me Immortality; but, venturing too near himself, he never returned. Soon after—my tutor died, and for several years my Lexicon was my only companion." Had her "Lexicon" been of her own making, we should not have called her poverty-stricken.

Listen to a few of her uncompiled definitions:—

> "*Presentiment* is that long shadow on the lawn
> Indicative that suns go down:
> The notice to the startled grass
> That darkness is about to pass.
>
> *Hope* is the thing with feathers
> That perches in the soul,
> And sings the tune without the words,
> And never stops at all.
>
> *Experiment* – to me – is every one I meet. If it contain a kernel?
>
> *Home* – is the definition of God.
>
> *Sunset*. Where ships of purple gently toss
> On seas of daffodil,
> Fantastic sailors mingle
> And then – the wharf is still.
>
> *Remorse* is memory awake
> Her companies astir;
> A presence of departed acts
> At window and at door.

*The Humming-bird.* A route of evanescence
With a revolving wheel:
A resonance of emerald
A rush of cochineal.

*The Sea* – An everywhere of silver
With ropes of sand
To keep it from effacing
The track called land.

*Prayer* is the little implement
Through which men reach
Whose presence is denied them."
(I think I'll finish this)
"They fling their speech
By means of it in God's ear,
If then He hear.
This sums the apparatus
Comprised in prayer."

(Webster, and Worcester, and Johnson, and the rest seem a little like prosaic Monday morning, do they Not?)

My own personal acquaintance with Emily Dickinson began when I was a young school girl, and many were the interests I took to her at our trysting-place, on the top stair of the flight leading down to a side hall. It was almost dark but opened into many retreats for my fawn-like friend. On a few never-to-be-forgotten occasions she read to me there a verse or two before enclosing in some friendly letter asking me to tell her what it meant to me and calling me her little *World*. I think I can never feel more proud than when she honored me by thinking I understood her. . . .

In one of her letters, you may remember, she says, "While my thought is undressed, I can make the distinction; but when I put them in a gown, they look alike and numb." And this was the reason for her asking at all, as she states in her first letter to Mr. Higginson. "My life," she says, "has been too simple and stern to embarrass any. 'Seen of Angels' scarcely my responsibility." In another place—"I do not cross my father's ground to any house or town." (To my knowledge she did not own a bonnet for 25 years or more.) Her own testimony elsewhere "I oftenest stay with myself", is, to me, a sad little knell of the absence of sympathy in her own peculiar introspective world. "Of shunning men and women," she says, "They talk of hallowed things aloud, and embarrass my dog. He and I don't object to them, if they'll exist their side."

In the first years of my knowing her, she would sometimes come across the grounds to her brother's home and spend an hour in chatting with us all. Gradually these "angel visits became few and far between" indeed, and more and more quaint like herself. For instance—I remember, as I confided my hopes and fears to her ever-sympathetic listening ear before the severe

APPENDIX II

examinations (taken alone) for entrance to the High School—then equal to
the College examination—she would only repeat "I am sure of success, I see
nothing else," until I met it brave in her courage. The morning of the
dreaded ordeal came a little note on this wise,—"A little flower is sitting beside me waiting to be a Crown."

Released from my hard day only just before supper, I had no time to
take her word that her kind prophecy was true, but I had no need, for,
being summoned from the table, I found Emily in the dark just outside the
door holding out the fair flower, and her sweet voice said, "Nobody came
to tell us, and the little flower was so impatient to be a crown, it insisted
upon bringing me over."

As this retirement grew upon her she rarely saw anyone outside her immediate home circle, although one and another of the Literati of the
country have come—at times far—to see her. A glass of wine and a flower,
accompanied with a note or line (as in one instance with a Cape Jessamine,
the quotation "I, Jesus, send mine angel") and the visitor must be sufficed,
if the Spirit within that strange little self did not move her to be seen.

I have been asked repeatedly what led to this withdrawing of herself
from the world—was it some disappointment? If, by this, disappointment
in love is meant, implying love unrequited, I answer almost an indignant
*No*. If disappointment in *Life* is meant, consider her intensely sensitive
nature, and exceeding individual mind and its longings, and you will readily
accept my reply that I am sure there were *many*—but Life is not all Love,
you know, although Love may be the sweetest part of all life. It began by
simply not joining in some things which were not congenial and a gradual
withdrawing from many things which we none of us hardly realized so
subtly did it come, until *others* spoke of her as a Recluse. You know how
imperceptibly such changes *can* approach.

One or two more little home incidents. Her little nephew, boy-like, had
a way of leaving anything superfluous to his immediate needs at Grandma's.
After one of these little "Sins of Omission", over came his high-top rubber
boots, standing erect and spotless on a silver tray, their tops running over
with Emily's flowers. At another time the little overcoat was returned with
each velvet pocket pinned down, and a card with "Come in" on one, and
"Knock" on the other. The "Come in" proved to be raisins;—the "Knock",
cracked nuts. Do you blame the little fellow for leaving his things round
over there? The boy was my care, but I never could be generous enough to
discourage the failing.

She was very fond of music, and at one time played not a little on the
piano. When I knew her, her Repertoire was quite limited—consisting of
but three tunes. One of these she called "The Devil", and it was weird and
quaint enough to warrant the title. She had learned it on an old-fashioned
piano, two octaves shorter than the modern "Chickering" which then
stood in her home parlor, and always before seating herself to play, she
covered these superfluous octaves, that the keyboard might accord with her
education. After she became more reclusive, and gave up the piano entirely
I had the pleasure of playing for her and quite often would come to me
just some little word as, "Emily is tired, and the sweet voice in the parlor
cannot speak to her alone," or "There's a voice in the down-stairs; I call,

272 ]

but it does not answer." I answered the summons when I could, and never without some acknowledgement. Sometimes a flower on the piano stool, again a little plate of fresh cookies, or, best of all, a word written out for me. How I regret we had not known the Angel-Genius we were entertaining, and so had preserved these little missives! Is it always "Unawares"? What hourly caution lies in the answer!

Returning each year after my marriage, for short stays to her own home, so long as my Uncle lived, my visits with Emily were always in her own room after the evening was done below stairs, and by appointment her door was left ajar. "I don't speak things like the rest" was her apology and her "speaking things" like herself would delight my very soul often far into the night, or even early morning. I was not present at Mr. Dickinson's funeral. The following Christmas when I enclosed a Christmas wreath for his grave with the little remembrances for the living, Emily wrote thus in acknowledgement, "I am sure you must have remembered that Father had become 'as little children' or you would never have dared send him a Christmas gift, for you know how he frowned upon Santa Claus, and all such prowling gentlemen."

The next time I saw her was at the burial of her Mother. Arriving only in time for the service, I saw nothing of Emily, save a line asking for a word as I went away. On our way to the train, we stopped at the door just a moment and Emily, calling me *behind* the door, looking pale and worn with her anxious watching and grief, said she just wanted to thank Mr. Turner and myself for coming so far "to speak to Mother. She cannot thank you herself today, you know, but some other day," and this was the last time I ever saw her sweet face.

She *died* (as we say) quite suddenly May 15th, '86, of a disease which owing to her extreme reticence and retirement of disposition, and reluctance to confer with a physician, was hastened, no doubt, when it might possibly have been retarded, though not cured. Two years before—breaking through all reserve, and at night—she had had a chill while ministering to death in her brother's house, and was taken home unconscious. Three times during those two years she had similar attacks, and from little casual remarks doubtless she knew within herself that her note of warning had been sounded and she had heard. On Thursday, May 13th, '86, the message came very tenderly, for she became unconscious almost at once and so remained until Saturday afternoon, when Death gave her Life "the other side." I think it must have been during these two years, (although there is no date) that she wrote these poems.

Greatly to my regret, I was unable to attend Emily's funeral, being called to sickness by a telegram received the same hour with that which called me to her. They folded her in a little white wrap* I had sewed for her myself the last Christmas, little dreaming I was weaving her shroud, and she lay in her white casket in the hall of her father's house, while the bees and the butterflies she had immortalized, buzzed a Requiem without the open door. A knot of field blue violets lay at her throat, and a wreath of the same modest flower was the only decoration on her casket. The ser-

* Compare "Emily Dickinson, Face to Face," p. 61, Mrs. Powell.

vice was very simple. The Pastor of the Congregational Church of Amherst read from the Scriptures. Rev. Mr. Jenkins of Portland led in prayer, and Col. Higginson followed with the reading of Emily Brontë's last Poem, prefacing the reading by this introduction, "I will read a poem, our friend who has just now put on Immortality, and who seemed scarce ever to have taken it off, used to read to her sister."

The brief service concluded, six stalwart men, with whose faces she had been familiar, and who had rendered glad service as she toiled among her out-door friends—the flowers—lifted her on their shoulders and bore her—into the street? Ah no! That would have been a way almost as strange and unknown for her, to pass, as is to us today that upon which she has entered, while we stand without, as yet unbidden to follow.

The Cemetery lay three fields away, and the bars being lowered between —the light little burden led the way through meadows *filled* with buttercups and daisies, and they stood sentinels of her path, or bowed their heads as the funeral train brushed them by. Place these facts by her poem.

> "Let down the bars O Death!
> The tired flocks come in
> Whose bleating ceases to repeat
> Whose wandering is done."

Following the benediction, they turned away to leave her numbered now with those of whom she had so beautifully said,

> "Deep in their alabaster chambers
> Untouched by moon, and untouched by noon;
> Sleep the mute members of the Resurrection,
> Roof of satin, and Rafter of stone."

And we spoke of her as *Dead!* How later facts have reproved our mistake! Like the butterfly she had shown to the children in her conservatory, she had burst the chrysalis only to find wings for a wonderful delight-giving life. The Recluse is entering stranger homes all over the land. The quiet sweet voice calls even across the great waters.

Although there is no "Mould of her"—pen pictures leave her no stranger. Her secluded home life is eagerly asked and entered by the wondering Many. The dainty Poems of the modest little woman who deemed it "unfeminine" to publish have reached edition after edition in publication. Can we say she *died?*

Beside her bequest of these Poems to her only sister, there was but one other, viz.:—

> "If I shouldn't be alive
> When the Robins come,
> Give the one in red cravat
> A Memorial crumb."

and to the executor of this bequest,

> "If I couldn't thank you,
> Being just asleep,
> You will know I'm trying
> With my granite lip."

I cannot but ask again and again, for what service beyond was this sweetly strange life a preparation? What has she found awaiting her in the fulfilled promise that we shall be *satisfied?* She, who so shrank from people —is she among the multitude who have gone before, and yet *satisfied?* Are there birds, and bees, and clover for her there? Does she go on "making verses", or was her gift only for *this side?* and on and on I question.

Surely since her going Heaven holds a new mystery, and I can only answer in her own words,

> "There are that resting – rise,
> Can I expound the skies?
> How still the riddle lies!
>
>     \*    \*    \*
>
> Faith faints to understand."

## 4

THE FOLLOWING IS A SYNTHESIS of three separate, brief MSS in the Todd-Bingham Archive. They are all in typescript, with a few penciled corrections in Mrs. Todd's shaky hand (the result of her stroke in 1913), and were enclosed in a manila envelope labeled, in Mrs. Bingham's writing, "Scurrilous but True," after a comment written by Mrs. Todd at the head of one of them. The three repeat one another often, sometimes at length, but each contains material not found in the others. The aim of this synthesis is to avoid repetition (although some still remains) while excluding no detail, not even the opening paragraphs about Mabel Todd's life in Washington, legends of Emily, animadversions on Vinnie, and the accounts of Mabel's work on the editing and of her stroke. All are relevant in some way, I think, to the "War between the Houses." The word "scurrilous" applies, of course, only to the paragraphs dealing with Susan Dickinson. (Words and phrases in brackets indicate, mostly, alternate readings in the MSS. In this instance, I have retained passages that appear in the text, since it is important that they be read in their original context.)

Our life in Washington was especially delightful. I had lived there ever since I was a small child, and my father's particular friends were chiefly the scientific men connected with the Observatory. He had gone from Cambridge where he had been associated with Professor Benjamin Pierce, Asa Gray the botanist, Louis Agassiz and other distinguished men connected with Harvard, James Russell Lowell, Professor Longfellow, and a unique combination of those in his own chosen subjects, and where he had helped to establish the American Ephemeris as distinguished from the British Nautical Almanac. His profession was really mathematics and astronomy, but that did not exclude him from the great interest he always felt in natural sciences as well as English literature, in both of which he was an authority. My grandmother was friendly already with some members of the Cabinet, Senator Hoar as well as Judge Rockwood Hoar, and from the beginning our life there was brilliant and satisfying. I was always on friendly terms with the young men who came to the Observatory from different colleges, to stay temporarily, or permanently as their gifts might develop, and among them was young David Todd, who had been invited to Washington as soon as he graduated from Amherst College (at the age of twenty) by Professor Simon Newcomb, a leading astronomer of America. He was engaged at once on the computations resulting from the last transit of Venus in 1874, and for some years he continued that congenial work. He meantime wrote numerous papers on allied subjects,—a continuation of De Damoiseau's tables of Jupiter's satellites to 1900, on an "Attachment for equatorial mountings to facilitate sweeping in right ascension", two upon his theoretical position of the possible trans-Neptunian planet, and many others which brought his name prominently before the astronomical world.

He soon became of all the young astronomers my best friend, and almost before I was aware of it I found myself engaged to marry him, and I was proceeding with wedding preparations, which culminated on March the fifth, 1879. For two years our brilliant Washington life continued, we made our home with my father and mother at their charming house on College Hill Terrace, where our constantly increasing number of friends augmenting every month gave me genuine happiness and satisfaction. My painting, piano-forte playing which I had pursued for years both in Boston and with Anton Gloetzner in Washington were of course continued, and our life was carried on with much satisfaction to us both. Then our daughter was born, and the days glowed with contentment and achievement.

Into the midst of this eminently happy experience came one day a letter from my husband's old professor at Amherst, Mr. Esty of the mathematics department, inviting him at the President's instigation, to return to Amherst and become Director of the Observatory there. He remarked that his especial student, David Todd, would remember that there was really no professor of astronomy, although his own chair was called "mathematics and astronomy", but what they now desired was an astronomer really, which they knew he was, and they both hoped that he would see the matter in the light they both regarded it, and come to his *alma mater* forthwith.

Of course we discussed this matter for several days. We really did not want to leave Washington even for distinguished consideration from Amherst. To be sure there was no great future in Washington, unless the appointment ultimately of "Professorship in the Navy" where the salary was settled and gradually increasing by slow degrees, but without great financial advantages. My husband had received invitations from one or two western colleges to become their professor of astronomy, which he had refused at once. But his own *alma mater* was slightly different.

At last, weighing advantages and drawbacks with perfectly honest study, we decided to go. Even now I can hardly say that our decision was a wise one. But the result caused our life to proceed on utterly different lines. A small village was henceforth to be our background. My husband's brilliant study of solar eclipses, throughout his life, founded as a basis on his constant expeditions to different parts of the world to observe the phenomena connected with those dramatic happenings in the heavens, made a specialty of the sun, which perhaps gave him wider reach than he could have had in Washington.

At all events, we were established in Amherst with our interest increasing in astronomy constantly, and with the hope that a friend of the college would soon give the funds for a new Observatory—as President Seelye had promised when we came to the little town.

The difference between life in the national capital and in a small New England village was very marked. At first we stayed at the Amherst House, a fairly good New England country hotel, and spent our time for a week or two in looking about the town for a permanent home. After many curious experiences we finally took rooms in a new and somewhat boxy large house "at the end of the village concrete sidewalk," as told us by the philanthropist who had presented the walks to the town. The door was opened upon our ringing by a very tall man in an unusually long linen coat, formerly a clergyman, with the air of a duke. He had been paralyzed to the extent that his left hand was peculiarly lifeless, only the right possessing initiative enough to put the left where it was required; after it was placed in position it could grasp anything wanted. His manner was unexpectedly courteous, and his language polished and elegant. For a time our meals were furnished by a dear old couple in the next house; also an ex-clergyman, as most of the dwellers in Amherst were, those not connected with the college. It was a quaint experience, and interesting to a degree, and almost at once we were invited to the homes of the college faculty so frequently that luncheons and dinners were nearly all taken in the homes of the professors.

Of course there were degrees of cultivation in the various homes, and I speedily made my choice of especial friends. One of the first places I particularly enjoyed was Professor Tuckerman's delightfully English mansion, and I continued to go there frequently all winter. The other was at the Dickinsons' charming home. Mr. and Mrs. Dickinson called on us very soon after we were established in the big new house. He was immensely impressive to me; and she was handsome, with a scarlet India shawl over her shoulders, which became her dark beauty.

That was the beginning. With her accustomed precipitancy she took an immediate fancy to me and to my experiences of life, and she followed me up with invitations until life began to take on a glamorous tint and to glow with colours beyond this existence. She talked to her son Ned and daughter "Mattie" of me until I should have thought they would despise the very sound of my name. But they too fell under the same spell, if so it could be called, which affected their mother, and I was the tutelary deity of their household. Unfortunately for me the son, Ned, fell violently in love with me, and just how to manage that romantic episode escaped my tact. I did not know how to take it. After a while Sue, Mrs. Dickinson, began to tell me about Austin's two sisters, who lived in the old family mansion, alone with a servant of ancestral manners and achievement and years a servant with them. Until that time I had not yet met them, Lavinia, the sister retaining her place in the world yet not frequenting its haunts; and Emily having been described to me as the "myth" and the "shadow lady." For nearly twenty years she had not left the house and grounds, for the last ten years the house was her only abode, and her curious habits formed the text for a hundred queer sermons and talks. There was a legend that she had crept out one evening with her brother as far as a certain tree in the hedge in order to see the new church which her brother had been the most instrumental in building. Old College Hall had been the church which she knew before the new stone Gothic building had arisen; so she went out actually from the house as far as would allow her a view of what she had heard about for months, but had not seen until the wonderful night which took her out into its view. And that was the only time, according to the eager gossips of the town, that Emily went out of the door of her dwelling in many years.

Poor Emily! To be the subject of so much speculation, so much "certain information" through all those years! She did not care—she was secluded from any pain of knowing what was said, and her curious, original life went peacefully onward as she came more and more into her own line of living.

The college, town and general life in Amherst were decidedly different in the early eighties from those in nineteen-thirty-one [nineteen-thirty]. People at that time were much more absorbed in the severities of living than in its gayeties. The faculty were elderly men, their wives estimable ladies of quiet tastes, dressing in dark colours, having their supper at six o'clock, dinner at one, or earlier, not playing cards nor dancing nor doing any of those things which I had been taught in Washington were a part of a lady's equipment; my first thoughts on entering this somewhat peculiar environment were rather amazed, even troubled.

Of course they were all courteous, called duly upon this young woman whose husband, notwithstanding his youth (then twenty-six) had acquired a great reputation for his scientific papers at the Observatory in Washington, had achieved a fine distinction by his observations of the sun's eclipse in Dallas, Texas, when he had been out of college only three years, and was bent upon making the little observatory at Amherst as noteworthy as possible.

My own opinion is that they did not wholly approve of me; the students were beginning their "promenades" and sóme fraternity dances, and they seemed delighted to have a member of the faculty for a chaperone, one who could also dance! They always supplied me with a dance programme completely filled out with names quite as if I had been a girl.

Every one began by telling me of town matters, explaining relationships, showing how this one and that one might be considered thus and so, and many other matters filled out my list of information quite completely within a short time of my arrival. I quickly learned that Austin Dickinson, the leading lawyer of the region and Treasurer of Amherst College, was deeply reverenced and loved, though slightly dignified in bearing; that his wife, Susan, was [quite generally disliked and] thoroughly distrusted. Notwithstanding, when these two called upon me, I was greatly [much] impressed with both. He was a truly regal man, tall and magnificent in bearing, and she well dressed.

Apparently they were not entirely congenial, a fact which appeared during the short call unmistakably. But I soon saw that life in the New England college town was not to be wholly circumscribed by the orthodox ideas of the majority of the faculty. We were soon invited to—not supper with scalloped oysters as in the majority of entertainments offered us (coming as we did from the native haunts of the oyster at home, oysters were not as foreign a delicacy to us as to the inland givers of suppers in Amherst)— but to dinner, and at half after six o'clock. This was like home, and I revelled in familiar surroundings.

The Dickinson home was very beautiful, planned after a generous Italian villa fashion, and fitted up delightfully inside. The pictures were especially lovely, and I learned soon after that Austin's chief extravagance, it could be so called, was in buying fine pictures. He had gradually accumulated through the past few years a splendid collection, greatly impressive to strangers or persons of susceptible taste [tastes].

About this time Sue, as she was [universally] called in the village, began to tell me about a remarkable sister of Austin's who never went out, and saw no one who called. I heard of her also quite constantly through others in town, who seemed to resent, somewhat, her refusal to see themselves, who had known her in earlier years. Then came a note from this mysterious Emily's housemate, her sister Lavinia. The writing resembled most perfectly the crawlings of a demented house fly, after having lain awhile in the family inkstand. As far as it was translatable I made out that Lavinia was demanding that I call "at once, with my husband."

Discussing this missive with Sue, she said quickly, "You will not allow your husband to go [there] to that house, I hope!"

"Why not?" I asked innocently.

"Because they have not, either of them, any [faintest] idea of morality," she replied, with a certain satisfaction in her tone. I knew that would interest my good husband, and pressing her a bit farther for information [a little farther] she continued, "I went in to the drawing room there one day a few years ago, and found Emily reclining in the arms of a man. What can you say to that?"

I had no explanation, of course, so I let the subject drop, notwithstanding which I went a few days later to the ancestral mansion in which the two [maiden ladies] lived. And then began the picturesque series of encounters which made life in Amherst far from commonplace to me.

Lavinia was a brilliant exponent of ancient wit and comment not involving any superfluous love for one's fellow men, and although I had as yet formed no active likes or dislikes in the town, I could not help enjoying [a liking for] the fierce denunciations which sprung forth from Vinnie's nimble tongue. Her two passions were cats and [her sister] Emily. Her wrath over any person, child or grown-up, who attempted to molest her cats was only equalled by anyone trying to impose upon Emily, for whom she was vigorously alert to protect.

"I hope you will not go very much to the other house," said Vinnie, once, soon after I had made her acquaintance; "I have seen too many hearts broken there," she went on—"And always of those loved and admired [liked and loved] at first." I speedily saw that I should become involved in a family quarrel of endless involutions if I inquired too much into the

[ 279

mazes of feeling between the two houses. The break between them was notorious in Amherst, and persons dropped by Sue used to fly at once to Vinnie, who comforted them after her own unique fashion, by her terrible diatribes against Sue, which grew more and more denunciatory as years went on.

It quickly came out that Vinnie was herself nearly heart-broken by [over] Sue's treatment of Emily, and of course [of] herself, also, only she never counted anything done to herself in comparison with those things [anything] involving her adored Emily. She often said that she knew that Emily would die years before she ought, owing to [the] cruelties practiced upon her almost ever since poor Austin was "taken in" and made to marry outside his normal class, socially.

Her account was really sad and terrible. At first, in earliest years, Emily had tried to make her only brother like and marry her old friend, especially while he was away, after graduation from Amherst, at the Harvard Law School, and for some years she aided and abetted the match [which had made Austin at first melancholy to an unprecedented degree]. When Austin returned, a graduate, he heard himself spoken of every where in town as "engaged" to Sue Gilbert. At first amazed, he denied vigorously any such idea, but finding that she also told "the lie" as he called it, he became so melancholy that life held very little to him with this incubus hanging over him. After a time he foolishly [finally] yielded, really a boy at heart, and consoling himself with the idea [hoping] that possibly his children [from such a match] might have stouter and stronger bodies from their mother being so much nearer the soil than his own inheritance could be [might inherit some strength of body from being so much nearer the soil in their mother's inheritance]. But that idea speedily vanished in her dread of having any children, and her determination to allow no indulgence [not to indulge] in those "low practices" of the average married couple. Finally she gave in, after a fashion, and then those without children [who did not have] were terribly denounced.

[One of the three MSS at this point gives a sufficiently differing version of Austin's courtship and early married life to warrant separate entry:]

At this time Austin was studying law at the Harvard Law School, and as will be remembered by his correspondence with Emily (her letters I published in the first volume of her *Letters*) he was on a really intimate footing with his dear sister. When he returned, flushed with his success at Harvard, he was spoken of in town as "engaged" to Sue. A complete surprise and not entirely a pleasant one, he denied it wherever he heard the assertion. Continual denials, however, seemed to do no especial good, and busy in establishing himself as a young lawyer he finally let the talk of him go, worrying no more about what he termed "silly gossip" about himself.

As it kept on with increasing volume, he was at last forced to pay some attention to the opinions of his neighbors. He comforted himself with the thought that if he really was obliged to marry in that unexpected way, at least he might anticipate that his children would come into the world with fine constitutions, that their health would be assured from the nearness to primitive conditions in their mother's heritage, and his own more delicate ancestry would thus be offset by the toilworn fingers of maternal inheritance. A sort of fatalistic feeling began to flow over him. His sister Emily talked strongly of her friendship with Sue and her wish·that he should not disappoint her, of what she assured him was her great devotion, and of how pleasant it would be if he did marry her good friend.

He said he had never offered himself in marriage to Sue, or anybody else, and when the day of his wedding actually dawned he felt far more as if he were going on to his hanging than to a supposable happy bridegroom's fate.

And very soon he found that the bride of former meek feelings changed utterly. As for children she would have none; she began that loftiness of demeanor which characterized her ever after. Many months elapsed before she would allow "the low practices" of married couples to approach her citadel. The possible ameliorations he had promised himself faded into thin air, and he had to make up his mind to live his own life untouched by any understanding or wish to aid in any of the large thoughts with which he had come back to his native village.

It was certainly a very unwise attitude which Sue assumed as soon as she had a fine husband safely secured from Amherst's best family, that of unutterable superiority to old friends and neighbors, and all new comers in the village. It caused such indignation among the simpler order of persons in town that they continued to repeat every story, real or fancied about her beginnings, and prevented any lapsing of tales of her childhood and girlhood—tales which under a different management of her manner might have been allowed to die a natural death. But her scorn of most of her neighbors kept alive the distressing stories, added to and enlarged as the narrators' imagination might suggest. They even told of her flirtations with delightful Sam Bowles, and of how she sent her husband off for a few hours occasionally in order that she might pursue her foolishness with him, untrammelled. Mr. Bowles was a man full of magnetic personality, and his relations with all his friends were full of this quality of responsiveness and appreciation. A pretty little aunt of mine [in margin: Colette Loomis], who had died shortly after I was born, had felt his affectionate interest in her poems until she had become one of the chief contributors of verse to the well-loved *Republican,* Mr. Bowles's splendid monument. Her friendship with the famous editor and proprietor had formed a bright spot in her short and promising life, which ended before she had passed her twentieth birthday.

A relative who came to the town to make a short visit to Austin, in leaving congratulated him on his most beautiful place, "a real Paradise," said the old man, and then, hesitating a bit "But why, Austin, *why* have you introduced the serpent already?"

Austin's father, the Hon Edward Dickinson, was an old-fashioned gentleman who used to answer the door bell in the evenings carrying a lighted lamp in his hand. In his own newly established home a fine hall lamp was always lighted. "Oh! Yes", said Austin to me in one of his early and heart-broken confessions, "Yes, everything was conducted on modern lines in my establishment. At first it pleased me, of course. The outward adherence to accepted kinds of life was just along my own thought, only I did not want to be so absorbed in the attempts to have the outward seeming

[ *281*

instead of the real thing that I should ever forget the real thing." He never could, of course.

For years before I came to Amherst Emily had not had any affectionate relations with the Sue once so loved, and it was years since Vinnie had frequented her brother's house with any freedom. But he loved both his sisters, and his loyalty was always theirs. Of course his genuine love was Emily's, and his half humourous admiration for Vinnie was hardly in the category of real love. Every day he visited them, and it was really a genuine refreshment of spirit to him.

The whole situation was another illustration of the impossibility of a marriage between different grades of society ever becoming a perfect fusion. Sue's father was a "tavern keeper" of decidedly convivial habits, and Austin's father was a dignified gentleman, a lawyer of the old school. The two could hardly have known of each other's existence, mentally, at least. In those early days the democratic mixing of upper and lower classes was, to be sure, much more easily accomplished than in these later and stricter days of preserving family and training carefully. And Sue always made a point of associating principally with daughters of the better class. She was a bright girl, who knew how to put herself on confidential terms with daughters of the upper class in Amherst, and for some years she and Lavinia and Emily were trusting friends.

Town gossip said that Sue inherited all her father's fondness for strong drink. He, poor man, had died in the poor house after his experiences in keeping a tavern; "or in the gutter," said Vinnie, as she first told me Sue's history, with a certain grim satisfaction. One of his sons [Dwight] came to the rescue of the old man's name, and paid back to the town all that had been spent. [Both Todds assumed the worst about Thomas Gilbert. The Greenfield, Mass., records, of which Mrs. Bingham had a search made in the summer of 1930, give a different impression. Gilbert had a good military record in the War of 1812. He was elected to many positions of trust in the town. The titles "Esquire" and "gentleman" recur in the records. The researcher (Lucy Cutler Kellogg) concludes: "I have failed to find anything anywhere that was of an adverse nature to an upright character"—letter to Mrs. Bingham, August 4, 1930.]

Austin's attachment to Emily was a serious matter. She to him was the embodiment of family devotion. Her curious leaving of outer life never seemed unnatural to him. He told me about her girlhood and her normal blossoming and gradual retirement, and her few love affairs; her life was perfectly natural. All the village gossip merely amused him.

For Vinnie he seemed to have a half humorous, half absurd feeling not to be compared to his real feeling for Emily.

Sue had taken me up as her intimate friend at first and then, as usual, dropped me. Austin was, of course, deeply grieved by Sue's abandonment of me as her special friend. "Oh, well," he said almost resignedly, "It is only like other affairs of similar character. There are many persons of admirable qualities still in town, many of them, who have been as violently taken up and as violently dropped. But a great many have left town, grieved to the heart and sadly going elsewhere. Try not to have her defection cause you to leave."

"Indeed no," I replied with spirit, which kept me on my chosen path instead of weakly losing it and so leaving.

David had one or two delightful offers to go elsewhere, but he did not care, really, to leave Amherst before he should have had the happiness of establishing the new observatory, and leaving the astronomical interest of the College well advanced. He had also been appointed professor of astronomy at Smith College, and was just building in Northampton a fine little observatory of which he was to be director for the next year or two, until he could train some member of the Smith faculty to assume that position; so our interests were for the time concentrated in the vicinity [region] of Amherst. President Seelye no longer talked of "the new observatory", but my husband did not give up hope, and my own pleasure was to remain in the beautiful old town [nor did I care to depart yet from the charming place], albeit my chief happiness [delight] was blurred by the changed attitude of Sue. I had to choose newer friends owing to that development. Yet her very abandoning me was the cause of many more friends flocking toward me than had come before.

Lavinia once said to me "Oh, I have seen many hearts broken in Sue's house—many!" and she went on with names of half the town who had been ardently liked at first, and then dropped or neglected or worse. It was Sue's genius to make each former friend feel that she or he or they were too despicable to be retained on the list of respectable people. Alas, I could never feel that way.

One lady, wife of an older professor, had come to me in very friendly fashion [way] during my first year in Amherst, and begged me to consider how really dangerous to my future peace of mind would be [was] my blindly following Sue and her prejudices [likes and dislikes]. This lady was respected in town [Amherst] despite her lack of taste in furnishing her home [house]. On that occasion, later in the conversation, she told me, as I was about to furnish [starting my own housekeeping in] the noble D K E mansion, that my bill for shades would amount to almost more than a young professor could stand [too high for a young professor to stand].

"But I am not going to have any shades," I replied, with mischief intent. The good lady evidently thinking me crazy, looked with amazement at me for a moment, while I explained that the thin silk curtains I was getting were quite as opaque as shades, and far prettier. Evidently a completely new idea to her, and one requiring profound [quite an expenditure of] thought. But at all events, she meant well and kindly, and I was grateful.

The daily life of Emily Dickinson would be a very innocent story of making cake and cream puffs, bread and all sorts of pretty sweets, largely to please the numerous friends who frequented the house, partly, doubtless, in the vain hope of seeing her, and perhaps as much to hear her sister Lavinia break into her familiar diatribes against those who, sometimes only temporarily, had excited her verbal wrath. This virulence could be matched only by Emily's own ability in the use of words—in her case simply used as a literary vehicle for the conveyance of intimate ideas. Her "lexicon" was her most intimate companion. Lavinia's only talent lay in this use of violent words to describe those, once friends, now withdrawn from that pleasant state and transformed into enemies who never by any chance could begin to use words as their present virulent enemy would describe them. People generally told all sorts of curious facts or supposable facts to her, perhaps only to hear her characterization. Town gossip penetrated to the quiet house under the pines in carefully expressed sentences, subsequently transformed into vituperative descriptions told as fact by the mistress of the closed [rooms] and silent halls of the big house. Once or twice Lavinia almost got herself into decided trouble by her frequently baseless tales told with dramatic realism to some enemy of the person described. It was averted however, as the Dickinson family was too important to be lightly accused of anything, especially in the person of its representative, the "old maid" resident of the dignified mansion. Probably she was well aware of this immunity; at all events she never learned to suppress her tongue of its well loved activities.

During all the years when I was working on Emily's poems, after that dearly loved character had passed beyond praise or blame, Lavinia, coming always late at night to our home across the meadow, used to enliven us with scandalous tales of well known persons in town. After she left I used to remark to my husband, who quietly listened to Lavinia's outpourings, that if I only chose I could make the town ring with scandal beyond anything imagined in its scholarly shades. But of course I never did!

When I first arrived in Amherst I was greeted with scores of tales from one and another about persons I had come to know; perhaps no more than any other small town might show to a new comer, but certainly spicy and interesting. Absorbed as I was in the details of my husband's profession, these bits of information came as a sort of high relief from the assistance I was giving to astronomical research, and I do not remember now that I ever asked my informers not to retail to me their tales. At all events they never did forbear. One of the first series of stories naturally related to the Dickinson family, apparently the target of many small and critical tongues. Possibly it was a normal subject for talk, and principally it dealt with "Sue" the handsome wife of the Treasurer of Amherst College, successor of his father in that office as well as leading lawyer of that part of Massachusetts. A man loved and respected by friends as well as by enemies if he had any, in their strong sense of pity for his noble reticence.

Sue was a person full of certain kinds of ability, never, however, used in any noble manner as help or affection for her fellow townsman, but practically always in their detriment. For many years before my coming to Amherst there had been no communication between the Dickinson homes. The two sisters lived their own life entirely independent of the "other house," and Austin was the only link between them. He went to see his sisters every day. [They] loved and revered him all the more since his profound unhappiness in his marriage had left him few satisfactions in his own home. The story of his disenchantment with Sue was told me, first by indifferent persons in town, and later more in detail by Lavinia, with a few comments by Emily in her curiously interrogative voice from the next room.

From the beginning Austin had formed an odd fondness for my husband which grew with the years into genuine love and respect on both sides. While never saying anything unjust of his family, Austin told us gradually the entire tale of his life's utter disappointment, not only in the affected [pretentious] Sue, who very unwisely had assumed an attitude of vast superiority. to all her surroundings, but of her having caused her son Ned and his daughter Mattie [especially] to assume the attitude of utter superiority to the town and all his neighbors which they preserved through life, and which caused not only profound anger in many persons quite as good both in family and attainments as the two young people. Their mother had so instructed them that neither could act naturally or honestly toward the world. He also told us both the real cause of Ned's delicacy of body—which cannot be repeated here. He was an epileptic with frequent attacks. Mr. Dickinson had had a third child, little Gilbert, who received his unutterable devotion. He often said this child would make up to him for his great disappointment in both the others. He was trying as carefully as any parent possibly could to train the boy to right ways of looking at life, and of regarding his acquaintances with affection, or at least appreciation. But the dear child died. Henceforth Austin was distinctly alone in the world.

[More than ever before] his attention was given even more than before to his love for the trees and shrubs of the region, preferably those which grew naturally there. The College grounds blossomed more beautifully than ever in their wealth of fine oaks, pines, hemlocks, ashes and the barberries and wigelia which made the paths radiant.

Few college grounds of institutions starting as many years in the past as Amherst College did—over a hundred years ago—can show as cultivated a development of their outdoor surroundings as the Hampshire County college. And this is virtually owing to the work and effort of one man, whose poetic taste was developed in as practical ways as if it were merely buildings or museum collections. And few institutions have any official as painstaking and generous as Amherst's treasurer.

Knowing how constantly I was working on Emily's somewhat confused and difficult manuscripts, he decided that my husband and I ought to build our own home, having lived as we did after the first three months with our ducal host in a large and beautiful house since being made over into the home for the D K E fraternity. So he gave us toward that home a lot in his "meadow" and we built a little house of thirteen rooms, in which we lived for ten years. Here it was that Vinnie used to come across the meadow to talk to us about the poems, to hurry me in my work upon them, and to spice these requests with tremendous "facts" about her neighbors.

The meadow had belonged to Austin's father, rich farming land, and where an immense number of hay cocks appeared every summer, later with almost as many monuments of "rowan," and to me it became a fairy land of sweet scents and the constant labours of many men. Unfortunately at one side, below the meadow itself, was erected the massive brick building of one of the two hat "factories," only industries of the village, making some little smooth rolling of machinery, heard to be sure only when all our windows were open, but showing its massive walls despite the high hedge of hemlock and pine which were at once planted below our artistic house. This meadow which Austin loved intensely contained many acres, and he always expected that other houses would appear in its fine precincts. But none came, and when we moved afterward to the big "Observatory House" given us by my cousin Mr. Wilder of Boston, it was still only the "meadow". But it was dear to me always.

It was very soon apparent to me at least that Austin Dickinson was quite as much a poet as his sister Emily. Only the poetry in his nature took the form not only of his love of fine pictures, but no less of the views to be seen all about Amherst and its environs. His love for nature was exact and cultivated, and his joy over the lovely scenes to be seen from every hill-top was passionate and never failing. The multitude of trees and of blossoming shrubs surrounding us on every hand formed his poems—and the grounds of Amherst College show a beautiful procession of growing things which could have been arranged only by a genuine lover of all outdoor beauty, and of one who could command necessary assistance to consummate so harmonious a picture. For years this beautification went on, and when the practical-minded Trustees deprecated any more money being "wasted" just for trees, then workmen of his own choosing and paid from his own willing pocket would complete his plans. The College grounds today bear lovely witness to his taste and wise expenditure; and not they only, but the private grounds of many of the earlier faculty too, of people who wished for beauty perhaps in a vague sort of way, but who did not know just what to plant, or how to preserve exotic growths through the long and cold winters. Flowers he left to themselves, devoting himself to native trees, or blossoming shrubs which kept decorative red berries during the winter, or remained evergreen through the cold and icy months. This community of interest deepened his friendship with Emily, whose poetry was expressed not only in writing verse, but in care for the rare flowers which bloomed so lavishly for her, at first in her garden, and when she no longer stepped outside, in her conservatory off the dining room.

When Lavinia brought the mass of manuscript to me with her request that I get it "printed" as soon as possible, I objected at first, feeling that Sue should have the first right to give the poems out, if she wanted it. Vinnie's repudiation of any effort on Sue's part was really terrific. She told me again of her treatment of Austin, of her ruining her two children, and lastly, probably most damning description of all, her procrastination in any literary work whatever. She went over again the weeks when she left the poems with Sue to look over, and when the only result had been her leisurely reading them to her callers, and subsequent description of them to those presumably interested. Finally her announcement that she doubted if any printing would be wise, for various reasons adduced; chiefly that one could not expect any public to be really interested, until Vinnie, who had left them there with a mistaken idea that it would be "decent" knowing Sue's reputation for literary interest, was utterly discouraged and had come to me with renewed zeal. So I finally consented, and began on them at once.

She must have had some kind of desire for outward friendship with Sue, notwithstanding that no real conversations or any intimate connection had existed for many years, between them, for knowing that by this time Sue's once devotion to me had changed as most of her enthusiastic likings had done, and that her hatred only equalled her former love of me, she tried, futilely as it happened, to keep the knowledge of my work on the poems from persons in the town lest, I suppose, Sue should learn of it; she also sent a request to T. W. Higginson not to let my name be used in connection with the poems, and this at the same time that she was supposedly most anxious that I should proceed as rapidly as possible with the editing. Her handwriting was an impossible kind of scrawl, which dear Mr. Higginson could by no means read. Several times he had sent me notes from Lavinia, asking me to assist him in making out their meaning, which usually I could do, but without their containing anything definitely to be answered. About the time that I was almost through with the actual copying and editing, she wrote again to him, this time evidently with the intention of keeping me completely out of the region of the poems at all; and as usual the good friend sent the note to me, with the request that if I possibly could make anything out of it, would I do so, adding that he supposed there would be nothing of any importance in it. After a few days, meantime being most busily at work on the last of the poems, I took up the note. It was even more unintelligible than her writings usually were, and I gave up, returning to the poems with zeal overflowing. Some time after I took it up once more making out the impossible word to be "co-worker". The whole line read "I dare say you are aware our 'co-worker' is to be 'sub rosa,' for reasons you may understand."

That was a species of treachery beyond my imagining, and I asked Mr. Higginson what we should do about it. Meantime the title-page had been set up, and the printing was going on. He tossed it off airily. "Nothing is going to be done about so foolish a request", he answered; "It does not amount to anything." I was well contented to let it remain as he had arranged it already, and the book proceeded merrily on its way.

My earliest years in Amherst had been passed in increasing intimacy with Sue. Every one tried, I see now, to make me cautious in my relations with her, and even the best people in Amherst, not by any means gossips, had tried in vain to make me see the unreliability of Sue and the danger to a young and somewhat trusting woman of a friendship with her, pointing out her having quarreled with every one once friendly to her, and most notorious of all her break with Lavinia and Emily. Thinking no evil I see that I tried, innocently enough, to find excuses in my own mind for her, not regarding the public estimates [the friendly advice I received].

During the years 1881–1886 I was very often in the ancestral mansion, where Emily begged me to come repeatedly, enjoying to a great degree my singing and playing, both of which I had pursued ardently for many years. As Sue grew farther from me Emily came closer, and her notes and messages grew more frequent and more intimate. After the recitals of this single [singular?] artist were over, would come in to her the usual silver tray, always with a different dainty, expressive of Emily's appreciation and affection.

Their mother, quiet, gentle little lady, died during the middle of November 1882, without causing a perceptible ripple on the surface of any one's life, or giving concern to any of her family. Austin told us that her chief claim to attention had been her constant attempts to bring something to any caller which he or she could possibly require, and continual questionings had almost exhausted their patience. "Won't you have this or that to make you more comfortable?" or "Can't I bring you another chair?" had been the basis of her poor little attempts to make anyone within her circle happier, which failed sadly, as she never seemed to realize. Well, she departed this life with little ostentation, and life flowed on as before.

Emily had become a very dear and intimate friend to me, and Vinnie conveyed to me quite constantly Emily's loving feeling. Her little notes were the acme of each day. My housekeeping had become alluring, and much company was flowing all about me. My whist parties, with a little water-colour for each guest, became quite an institution, and my musicales were celebrated. We did not hear any more about "the new observatory," but we still hoped. Day after day brought me joy.

Emily formed the brightest spots in my day. I painted several panels for her, the indian pipes, fantastic witch hazel, a great mass of brilliant orange trumpet vine which she called "the Soudan", and several tall stalks of mullein; her notes of appreciation and thanks made epochs in the day. The quaint tales told me by Vinnie of Emily's vagaries in attempting to elude the family routine were curiously amusing yet somewhat pathetic to me as showing the lack of understanding of Emily by her nearest and most devoted friends. On one Sunday in particular the dignified lawyer had assembled his family for divine worship in the village church and Emily was summoned with the rest of the group. But she had disappeared, nor could search reveal her hiding place. Late in the afternoon Vinnie discovered her rocking away peacefully in the cellar bulkhead, reading a favourite book. "Oh yes," she replied calmly, to exclamations of wonder at her chosen place of immolation, "Why should I argue? I did not wish to go to church." Edward Dickinson had not yielded and joined the church as soon as most of his acquaintances in the village, and his rather late giving in to the town habit had resulted as usual in a somewhat tighter rein on his family than was generally held.

We had taken an absurd little house for the intervening time before our artistic one in "the Dell" should be ready for us, but even there life in the village flowed on happily, and my numerous activities progressed [normally]. One summer I went abroad. That really seemed to bring real grief to Emily. Despite her many poems upon the great world, "Teneriffe, receding mountain," Tunis, "an easy morning's ride", "Dneiper wrestlers run" and other far-away [remote] regions [but nearby beauties] [still] she seemed to feel always that a European summer was always a danger to her dear friends. The great world after all was far-off and not "easy" to Emily. She had once written [Writing] to Mr. Bowles under similar [like] disquieting circumstances, "My friends are my estate. . . . Good night, dear friend. You go away, and where you go we cannot come. You sleep so far, how can I know you hear?" "I tell you Mr. Bowles, it is a suffering to have a sea—no care how blue—between your soul and you." "I am taking lessons in prayer, so to coax God to keep you safe." "How sweet it must be to come home, whose home is in so many houses, and every heart a 'best room!' I mean you, Mr. Bowles."

All the far-fetched and imaginative reasons for Emily having become a recluse, a white-draped and spectacular household ghost, are as unnecessary as they are false. It was merely a normal blossoming of her own untouched spirit. The revelations of the hundreds of her letters show this exactly, to those who can read between the lines and feel the trend of her inner movement. As long ago as while she was studying at Mount Holyoke Seminary, in writing of some school gayety which she did not attend, she says "Almost all the girls went; and I enjoyed the solitude finely."

Mrs. Ford seemed to think other explanations possible when she writes "I think in spite of her seclusion she was longing for poetic sympathy, and that some of her later habits of life originated in this suppressed and ungratified desire. As a prophetic hint she once asked me if it did not make me shiver to hear a great many people talk—they took all the clothes off their souls." Emily herself writes of the boarding place in Cambridgeport where she stayed with her cousins while her eyes were receiving special treatment in Boston, "A. N. lives here since Saturday, and two new people more, a person and his wife, so I do little but fly, yet always find a nest." Always disliking to have "new" people about her person, she [could] say anent the leaving her of an old servant, "I winced at her loss, because I was in the habit of her, and even a new rolling pin has an embarrassing element."

To her cousin Louisa Norcross, she wrote as long ago as 1859,—"For you remember, dear, you are one of the ones from whom I do not run away." "Odd that I, who say 'no' so much, cannot bear it from others. Odd, that I, who run from so many, cannot brook that one turn from me." Other intimations quite as definite could be adduced of her own inclinations, from Emily's own letters—which form the only prose available to us now. This is shown by a letter to her brother, which says, "I sat in Professor Tyler's woods and saw the train move off, and then came home again, for fear somebody would see me or ask me how I did." And when Edward Dickinson asked his son Austin to bring his mother and Vinnie to Washington, while he was a member of Congress, he added, "And Emily too, if she will, but that I will not insist upon her coming." Her disinclination was already manifest. She did, however accompany her family to Washington that spring [1855] for three weeks, and after the Washington experience two weeks more were spent in Philadelphia, in all five weeks, which was the longest time she stayed from home during her life, except her sojourns in Boston to have her eyes treated. Several of the "lives" of poor Emily speak of her as visiting whole seasons, in Washington, perhaps, or other centres of fashion, giving the impression of her as quite a young lady of the world, who might have had a dozen love affairs to change the current of her life; but those ideas are not borne out by fact. Emily did enjoy her few weeks in both Washington and Philadelphia, and it is quite certain that in the latter city she met the clergyman who felt her unusual character and to whom she turned for years afterward.

That she felt distinctly the urge of genuine love, that her love-poems were by no means theoretical outpourings, but actual experiences of her own, we must admit, however contrary they may be to a preconceived notion of her heavenly remoteness from earthly happenings. She knew perfect love, however she may have retreated from its more practical manifestations. And this was her inspiration for many of her exquisite lines.

When I had finally decided to yield to the popular demand that Emily's letters should be published, and Vinnie and I had begun the collection of some remote notes to almost forgotten friends, I had to deal constantly with the wide-spread notion that Emily was "irreverent." To me that seemed a really cruel animadversion. Full of the opposite idea of Emily's almost uncanny intimacy with the great father, and of her reverence for the infinitely glorious creator of the wonderful universe, I could hardly understand the questions which came to me in hundreds of letters, and verbal questions as well which assailed me after every one of the hundreds of talks which I gave for eight or ten years after the poems and letters were issued. Constantly I had to deal with the, sometimes intelligent, often quite the reverse, demands to know all about her interior life, her most intimate thoughts. People quoted to me line after line which would almost seem to prove their contentions. I argued on the other side and occasionally succeeded in convincing doubting readers of the truth of my belief that Emily was far from being irreverent.

"God is a distant, stately lover," was one poem invariably quoted to me as proof positive. That poem I had sent to *The Christian Register* and it was joyfully accepted by the editor, Samuel J. Barrows. But alas, my good friend the Reverend Brooke Herford, then pastor of the Arlington Street church, spoke most slightingly of that poem, calling it "One of the offensive pieces of insistent unitarianism ever published."

"Why, Mrs. Todd," he asked me in real friendliness, "Oh, *why* did you give that to any magazine to publish?" The editor, Mr. Barrows, was much hurt at this estimate, and wrote me that it was far less objectionable than many other utterances of well-known persons. Vinnie and I had considered it together for a considerable time before I sent it away, and she was mischievously happy to have it published.

This poem, I am told, is included in "Further Poems" of Emily, heretofore supposedly unpublished; a note says that "Mattie" printed its opening stanza somewhere, but it really saw the light first on April 2d, 1891, in the magazine mentioned above.

This subject, Emily's irreverence, seemed to worry many worthy persons, and all my numerous talks for several years had to deal with the subject, at least in passing to other aspects of her curiosity-provoking personality. I always told my deeply interested audiences that she was *not* irreverent, that she lived in retirement not at all from any love-disappointment, and that she was not an invalid. Those simple, self-evident facts seemed to fill any audience with surprise, and I have no doubt with some lingering suspicions that I did not probe to the bottom of Emily's mysteriously engaging self. But such were the facts. And no less today while the world is busily searching industriously for the supposed lover, and the story of the "break" which left her a disappointed maiden on the verge of ignominious insanity. The world cannot accept any story which does not gratify its love of the spectacular.

"Mattie," as she was known to the village, was not yet fifteen years old when I reached the town, and she had had no real communication with her aunt at that time, nor since six or seven years before, which was the time about which MacGregor Jenkins wrote his winning little sketch entitled "Emily Dickinson; friend and Neighbor." The children at that happy year were Mattie and her brother Ned, the invalid boy, and the two Jenkins children, "Mac" and his pretty little sister "Did"; their father was pastor of the village church until 1877, when he resigned. Two little Mathers, across the street, children of the professor of Greek, were occasional additions to the quartette of children, for whom Emily used mysteriously to lower baskets of delectable eatables out of her window, as told by Mr. Jenkins in his article. Mattie was receiving instruction about this time from one of the professors in College, her Latin being very good, so much so that the professor said he only wished poor Ned was half as good as his young sister in the Latin tongue. Ned kept on bravely enough with the class of 1884 in College, but he could not graduate, and only studied enough to make the friendships of the class a background in his life. Mattie was given after this time a year in Miss Porter's well-known school at Farmington, by one of her relatives.

These were the years when she was often asked to join in the students' merry makings, and her mother tried vainly, we must admit, to keep her back to her normal years of life. Ned's friends, much older than she, became her own especial friends, and their life her *metier*. If she could have been taken then, during her formative years, and instructed in right ways of looking at life, she was bright enough to have gained inestimable benefit from a saner outlook than her mother's prejudiced point of view. I have always regretted her not having been entrusted then to some woman of fine character and noble aspirations as well as brilliant characteristics.

Ned was a fine horseback rider, and he and Mattie—never a "sport" where physical attainments were concerned—used to go out, she riding a bicycle beside the gallant charger of her brother. Bicycles were very much the fashion in those years. But my grandmother, a handsome old lady of vast experience who looked at life with the sane calmness of long years of efficiency behind her, used to say with the indulgence of old age, "Why doesn't Mattie *do* something? Why does she always play only? Is there nothing she could get interested in?" And that was the trouble. It was Sue's trouble as well. Supposedly a judge of matters literary, she yet never did anything to prove that interest. And the Dickinson house was synonymous with gay junketings morning noon and night, poor Austin working also all the days through to keep pace with the luxurious living imposed on him. We admired him all the years through, when his sad face haunted us, as we knew how much he desired to live quietly.

After Emily's poems were finally published, and when they were tremendously appreciated, when my mail was filled with admiring and interrogative letters about the mysterious author, when scores of talks were demanded everywhere, some one said to Mattie how proud she must be to have her aunt so much admired, but she, her nose in the air, said she had never been interested in those poems; indeed had never even read many of them, turning away with scorn from their conversation. And so she remained until she decided to publish the early poems sent years before to her mother, during the affectionate days when Emily trusted Sue and admired her—long before the later poems were even written.

Always I had been more than well—carrying out long pieces of work without even fatigue; but in the spring of 1913 Susan Huntington Dickinson had died. She was my most bitter enemy, no one in the world except possibly her daughter Mattie held such unchanging hatred toward me as she. After a fashion I felt a bit relieved, and freer in my mind and occupations for her departure. For several days, even weeks, I was much more completely myself than before.

Then suddenly I started up the College Hill one intensely hot morning in order to take a swim in the College pool now that the students were away, and ladies were admitted. On my way up the hill I felt the hot sun supposedly on the back of my neck, though never before had sun or winter winds affected me even slightly. It was distinctly an unfriendly push or hand laying-on which startled me. I got into the pool feeling more and more under the hatred of some near-by influence, and I swam up to the end of the pool, ninety feet away, becoming there very helpless—very different feelings from any other I had ever felt. I managed to swim back to the point of entering the pool, when I got out and tipped over, completely in the power of any unfriendly influence being exercised against me. Becoming unconscious then, I must have lain there for half an hour before any one noticed my predicament. Finally David was sent for, and he brought Doctor Herbert Rockwell and his automobile up to rescue me.

During my severe illness from "heat stroke" as I lay for weeks in bed and afterward when I was taken to a veranda outside, I frequently thought of "Sue" and her possible power to injure me, and although I knew for certain that she had no further power to hurt me, as she had exercised her power against me in one fierce stroke not again available, I could not help feeling certain she had stricken me in her pleasure to be able to work her will upon me. I felt equally certain that Austin, who had died many years before, had just learned of Sue's cruel "getting even" with me, and during six or eight months, while I was slowly recuperating, determined to walk and be myself so far as possible, when I could scarcely stand without falling, many times when I did fall, some kind hand prevented me from injuring myself, and many times I knew of his neverceasing watchfulness.


5


Notes taken by Millicent Todd Bingham in an interview with her father, David Peck Todd, at Hector, New York, September 29–October 3, 1933.

This document contains the fullest account we have of David Todd's part in the Austin-Mabel-Sue situation and his attitude toward it. At the time of the interview, long after his first breakdown in 1917, Todd was seventy-eight years old and in the care of an attendant, William Field, in the home of a relative of Field's in Hector, near Elmira, N.Y. Todd was by no means a well man mentally, although physically he was very vigorous. To his visitors (Field told Mrs. Bingham) he appeared entirely normal; but he was subject to occasional irrational outbursts, several of which occurred during his daughter's visit. The jottings below are Mrs. Bingham's notes on his answers to her questions about the people and events in Amherst in the 1880s and 1890s. The jottings show how digressive and sometimes bitter Todd was. (For coherence, I have arranged them under headings and eliminated a few irrelevancies.) His judgments, though often cruel and of course undocumented, are at least rational and allow for some redeeming ambiguities. Thus, Sue may have been a "drunkard" and a "superhypocrite," but she was an "exquisite housekeeper." Lavinia was "snappy" and "had rows" but "she must have been an enchanting young woman." Austin was a "wonderful" man but "very unmoral." Some of Todd's remarks (worked into formal prose by Mrs. Bingham) on his part in the publication of the poems appear in *Ancestors' Brocades*, pp. 31, 51, 52, 134. (The parentheses below are Mrs. Bingham's; the material in brackets are additions of my own.)

# "War between the Houses": Documents

## Sue, Austin, Mabel, and the "War between the Houses"

"Little Dud Todd" Sue's name for me.

Sue drunkard.

Sue's father an inn-keeper in Greenfield.

Never knew whether two houses were friendly or not when I went over.

L[avinia] brilliant, witty, snappy—rows all the time between her and Sue. A[ustin]. He was very unmoral.

[To MTB's suggestion that DPT might have been attracted to her:] They (DPT and Sue) didn't like each other. What help could that have been? She never attracted me. Because an adultery has been[,] cancels it to have another? Well, it (adultery) ruined my life.

He (WAD) was [a] lawyer. Doubtless she (Lavinia) did make will. [On the Todds' return from Japan in 1896:] Town buzzing with gossip [about the quarrel with Vinnie over the strip of land]. "Todds can't live in Amherst." I said, "We'll see about it. Came here to build observatory and I'll build it."

Did not inquire (about gossip). Facts were so staggering to me didn't want to inquire.

Sue jealous because (mamma) succeeded. Nobody in Amherst who had a name outside.

Sue always making fun of A[ustin]'s going to church. She was a super-hypocrite. But an exquisite housekeeper. Began to wipe my feet on the grass all the way up from the gate, before I went into house.

With regard to adultery, "That's the trouble. Austin wonderful man, loved him more than any man I ever knew."

"I shall know why when time is over". DPT quotes it [Poem #193] and weeps.

Burst out: "Don't know what it all means—sometimes like a ghastly dream."

## Preparing the poems for publication

Lav. says "What shall I do." I said, "Don't burn 'em. Don't burn anything."

Used to spend hours and hours looking at poems. Vin used to bring over bushel basket of poems and dump it on floor in front of fireplace in back parlor. After she (MLT) had finished I compared with original and she did it all over again.

Some poems L[avinia] wouldn't let out of house. Mamita [Mabel Todd] had to copy them there. L. would sit there and watch and if Sue was coming the poems all hustled out of sight. This all distasteful to me as it seemed so underhanded but Mamita wanted me to and that was enough.

Typewriter made no speed then (for copying ED's poems).

TWH [Higginson] recommended them to H[oughton] Mifflin. They said "Too queer—rhymes are wrong." Thought H[igginson] must be getting out of his mind to recommend such stuff. "H-M will be very sorry some day," I said. TWH thought so too. "But what can I do." I went to see Niles. TWH too ashamed to go, reader for H-M couldn't go to another publisher.

[ 293 ]

On [Arlo] Bates [reader for Niles]: "Didn't amount to 3 tail puffs in a gale of wind."

Niles accustomed to using his own judgement in literary matters. Suggested hectograph 50 copies. Blue ink. Niles scared to death about printing a *printed* edition. Said he'd pay for 500 copies on hectograph. I walked out. They would either be published in best dress possible or nothing. Came to my way of thinking. (Went in May [1890], first.)

We used to sit up all night to read proofs.

Made ABC lists [of poems, for Higginson's consideration] independently.

[In answer to question about financial remuneration for work on poems:] That was the satisfaction of doing it, great poetry, and great leader [Emily Dickinson] without caring whether they followed her or not.

## On the Dickinsons

Austin had more power than all trustees put together. Never mentioned (my) salary. He raised it from time to time as he thought appropriate. I never asked him to.

His (WAD's) office—little building opposite Foster Cook's when I was in college. I paid my term bill [there]. Ed Dickinson a grim old fellow, never allowed you to see him smile.

Ned a weak minded fellow. Can't imagine the treasurership of the college could ever have been offered Ned.

6

THERE IS MUCH EVIDENCE in the Todd-Bingham Archive that Millicent Todd Bingham intended a full-length autobiography. There are many fragmentary beginnings in the archive, mostly reminiscences and impressions of her early days in Amherst. A recurrent theme is the oppressive air of the feud between the houses, her dimly felt sense of her mother's guilt, and the hatred that exuded from "the other house." The following excerpts come from one of the preliminary, incomplete chapters. It appears in the archive in two forms: (1) A penciled draft of fifty-three pages of 5″ x 8″ stenographer's copybook paper, sixteen 6″ x 9″ brown sheets, and five pages of yellow half sheets. The dates on these sections span the period between February 27 and August 30, 1927. (2) The same, typed, dated "August 1962," with frequent but minor stylistic changes and an occasional marginal note indicating a change of heart or attitude during the thirty-five-year interval.

The first excerpt is as good a near-contemporary view of the Dickinson houses and grounds as we have, while giving the child's reaction to the aura of tension and hate that surrounded them. The second is a composite view of Emily—part, perhaps, from actual experience but part, as the marginal comment admits, secondhand—a good example of how legends gain currency. The sketch of Vinnie is in startling contrast to the "tender, soft-lipped" girl Joseph Lyman knew; it is a measure, in part, of the toll the feud had taken. Austin's aristocratic, contemptuous bearing, as it impressed—or intimidated—young Millicent, bears out the legend of Dickinson snobbery. Mrs. Bingham's account of its effect on her mother is but one of her devastating criticisms of her mother: the shame of Mabel's behavior with Austin; her apparent insensitivity to the attitudes of the town or the effect of her behavior on her husband and her daughter; her vanity and love of applause. (A detached scrap in the archive reads, "Mamma's tendency to exaggeration & overstatement." Millicent's unquestioning loyalty during her childhood grew into a highly ambivalent attitude.) Another document in the archive (eleven pages, typed, headed "Mitchells, Stamford, Conn. December 14–15, 1935") contains this passage: "When mamma chose her course of action, she chose along with it the ignominy which such a New England community heaps upon that sort of behavior. I must not enter into any mother-defense like Mattie. . . ." Again: "Austin and Mamma. What could they have done? Crisp condemnation of one side with blanket approval of the other side is impossible. This also applies to the feud. How were they conditioned? What forces made the thing happen? This can be done better than you can pass judgment." Finally, David Todd's position in the affair is given a blunt and unequivocal statement, as is his "weakness" or "sin" with women. In Mabel's journal for November 26, 1911, she wrote: "I have even allowed misrepresentations and reproach to attach to myself, to be thought the gay and flirtatious one of the two; and never a word, written or spoken, has come from me to show I had the faintest justification for anything I have been supposed to do. David is innocently unmoral. . . ." (The next ten pages, probably containing incidents, have been cut from the journal.) Millicent's implied rejection of any such argument is notable, although she could not bring herself to remind her mother of her part in David Todd's tragedy.

## The Dickinson Enclave on Main Street

The two great Dickinson houses stand under tall trees between dense hedges confined by a fence, both before and behind, on a narrow strip of land along Main Street. There are clumps of rhododendron and other exotic shrubs which blossom gorgeously at certain seasons. The ground behind this strip of property slopes up to a great oak grove and a street which crosses its top. On the Dickinson side of that street there was throughout its length but one house of the early 1800s, a large affair, known as the Owen house at one time used as a girls' school, and for long periods of time unoccupied, or rented in the summer to Dr. E. W. Donald, an opulent and elegant Episcopal clergyman from New York (later Rector of Trinity, Boston).

There is a front gate to both mansions, also a carriage gate, which swings together behind the service wagon which has made its exit, or the light buggy and high stepping sorrel horse named "Ned," the Squire's [Austin's] pride when they are safely lodged in the barn. Through them [the gates] one catches a glimpse of a gravel walk bordered by hollyhocks joining the two houses, otherwise invisible.

The Squire's own house, a gaunt, smooth, wooden, tan-colored structure of the black-walnut mid-Victorian era, has all the forbidding solemnity of that era. It had a square tower. A walk of granite slabs leads up a few granite steps and again up a few more to the mansion portal.

I can say no more of that house as I never really looked at it. If I walked along Main Street, which I always avoided if possible, because I might meet a member of the Squire's family if I did; so I kept my eyes straight to the front and walked as steadily as possible till I was safely past. To be sure, they always walked up town on their side of the street, although it was only a gravel walk. On the other side it was a tar walk where the common herd walked.

But the other house, the older of the two, had been built at a more genial epoch in the early 1800s. It was of brick, near Georgian, and painted a warm yellow with white trimmings and green blinds. On either side of the swinging gate stood a giant pine whose great roots spread out under the hedge and under the gravel walk. Here they abruptly reached the light and air, where the street had been cut down ten feet or so long after the house was built to temper the grade of the hill. A flight of solid granite blocks spanned this distance up from the highway to the front gate. But I never used that gate. There was another, a few feet distant to the right, whose granite walks led past the Conservatory around to the back. The carriage gate was off toward the left. The fenced-in hedge led on toward the right a few hundred yards concealing from passersby the garden which was said to exist behind it. As there were no houses very close behind the property, only a grove of giant oaks, on the higher ground, one could not see within.

On the opposite side of the street, throughout the entire length of the Dickinson property, there were but three buildings. Across from the Squire's house, with the parsonage behind it, stood the granite-built village church whose construction he had supervised. To the east of it, two village houses, and then a wide flowery open meadow leading down to a little brook into the dell at the lower end. Across this open field, filled with daisies in June before haying time, the Dickinsons might, through closed blinds, look across to the blue hills of Belchertown, where Pelham and Holyoke hills blend in a dip in the horizon. Half way across his meadow (for the Squire owned it all), he cut through a street, crossing it from east to west, in the middle eighties; but it remained a private road, with square stone posts at the further entrance to mark it as a private road. It was called "Fowler Place," named in honor of his grandfather. Not until much later did it become an extension of Spring Street, the commonplace name of the public part of the thoroughfare leading from the center of town. This street was cut through in order to enable my father and mother to build a house upon it, which they did in the late eighties. . . .

*Emily*

In the old homestead there were two occupants, Lavinia Dickinson and Maggie. Emily had died just before we built our house. I was just six when they carried her back across the fields to the village cemetery. Though she saw no one grown, a small child might sometimes step inside the doorway to receive a cookie fresh from the oven, or a flower to hold in his hand. My only remembrance of her, as I was but six when she died, is of a brown silk net in which her auburn hair was held, with a brown silk tassel behind each ear. Once, from behind a closed blind, she lowered a cream-puff at the end of a string. [Mrs. Bingham's marginal note: "Some one told me this. No!"] The taste lingers today. But sweet Emily, who had inherited from some remote ancestor her love of beauty, was only a legend to me. The harsh qualities of her forebears which had passed her by had been incorporated in Lavinia. . . .

### Vinnie

There she sat in her apple-green kitchen or on the back porch, a trim little figure in a black cashmere dress of the style of the '60s. The knife pleatings which decorated it were always a marvel to me. Her sour, shrivelled face with its long nose was wrinkled like a witch of the fairy tale, her hands gnarled and knotted like the faggots in the wood-box. But her hair—her marvellous dark luxuriant hair streaked with grey!—it seemed to concentrate all the juices of her wizened body, the focus of interest in her person. Sometimes it was tied in a sort of bow-knot at the back of her head, held fast by two great pins thrust from each side. But usually she sat there with it hanging, while, with her knotty hands, outspread fingers rigidly extended, she thrust them through it, slowly lingering along from root to farthest tip. Pussy sat near by washing her face, fat Maggie billowed about the kitchen, as Miss Vinnie sat slowly combing her hair with her knotty fingers.

Sometimes she would open the door into the dining-room, windows closed, shades drawn so that the pattern of the dark-blue china on the sideboard could hardly be seen. (It was the Landing of Lafayette.) If I tip-toed in, it was sometimes to receive an apple which I might consume behind the closed door—for Miss Vinnie could not bear the sound of crunching. One other sound she could not bear—the rustling of a newspaper.

### Austin

But oftener, when the door was opened, there sat my mother and Mr. Dickinson. I cannot remember that I ever stayed—nor can I ever remember that he addressed a word to me. He referred to me, if ever he did refer to me, as "child," but that was to Miss Vinnie. What a figure! A tall lean man, sitting rigidly erect in his chair. His clean-shaven face, except for red side-whiskers, was without a smile. I could not have imagined how he would look if he should smile. It would never have occurred to me to try to imagine. But his hair! A great shock of coppery fine silken hair, standing out like a halo in a soft aureole about his austere face. Squire Austin Dickinson, spare form faultlessly dressed, about his neck a long gold chain of olden days, and long slender feet in soft kid shoes of curious ancient cut. Aristocratic, contemptuous, yes, but to me just the somewhat terrible center of the universe, though why he was such I could not have said. He was. No human being ever mentioned his name to me, nor did I ever mention his. I doubt whether he would have acknowledged my presence by so much as a nod had I met him on the street. But I never did. . . .

Through the long winter days in the little red house a fire was always burning on the hearth. Usually when I came home from school Mr. Dickinson was sitting there beside the fire with my mother. He wore a brown velvet cap which we kept in our music case in the back parlor. He knew all about a fire—just how a bright coal upon the top of two smouldering logs would pull the flame up through. One did not venture to touch the fire in his presence—but one might brush the hearth.

A presence he was, an awful omni-presence, whether upstairs behind closed doors or sitting in plain view. I cannot remember that I ever voluntarily stayed in a room in which he was sitting. He was there, a core of the scheme of things. I cannot remember that I ever consciously questioned myself why he was the center of my universe. But I felt the weight of him and carried it throughout my childhood, and until, when I was fifteen, he died. . . .

### Austin and Mabel

I watched him and my mother walking in the meadow when the haycocks gave off their sweet smell. When I was very small, I remember a certain stretch of road on the top of the Pelham Hills, with fragrant pine woods on one side and a blueberry pasture on the other. The beginning and end of that drive is lost in memory. But that little stretch of road is as vivid today as it was then. Each tree, each stone in the wall, the position of each bush and each cloud in the sky is etched in my remembrance. We were driving along in the shiny buggy, Ned stepping along with head and ears erect, aware of all that passed. I was sitting between mamma and Mr. Dickinson. I felt them lean together behind me. What transpired I do not know. I could have been borne rigid to a burning pyre before I would have turned my eyes from the tip of Ned's quivering ears. Unaware they thought me! . . .

One day I was starting down the stairs when I heard his voice in the lower hall. As usual, I stopped and waited. I did not go where he was, especially if mamma was there, if I could help it. And to his low voice I heard her reply, "My King"—and I tiptoed back to my room and shut the door. It was disloyal to even think about it—I would not—and yet—how strange! . . .

In the last few years I have been speculating somewhat upon the course of events and why things have turned out as they have. There was but one repugnant thing which did positively unnerve me. It was a sore which never healed and which got me in the middle like solar plexus nausea each time I looked at it. That was a diamond engagement ring and wedding ring which mamma wore on her left hand—her others, almost identical, which had preceded the union resulting in my birth, were now worn upon her right. The feeling never became a resentment, it was never even so much as speculation. Though as I think back upon it, I felt numbly degraded by the sight of those rings, and in a way disinherited. . . .

I say there was no visible result in childhood. There was: the disapproval and concern expressed themselves in trying to protect mamma. Of course I didn't know what from. Nor did I ever try to find out. But she needed someone to take care of her. I assumed the burden. It was an almost unbearable one, because there was so little sphere for action. I could not tell her not to sit in Miss Vinnie's parlor with Mr. Dickinson by the hour, not tell her not to go riding with him alone by the hour, nor to stay by the upstairs fire alone behind locked doors by the hour. No one of course knew of that but me. I never thought of my father. I never thought of him in that connection nor in any other. Nor did I think of that possibility—speaking to her, I mean. Usually it was not my own sensibilities that were offended. It was fear that those of the Amherst public would be, and my responsibility for making them see that it was all right, making them understand, that was all I needed to do. But, that locked door upstairs. That was hard to explain, or rather, no, I came up against it with a bang, if I thought of trying to make them understand. For I couldn't understand that myself. That formed a very substantial part of the weight I was carrying. . . .

My father did not mystify me. About him I then felt little concern. So it comes back again to my mother. What had been the result of her intimacy with the spare old Squire who despised the common herd? What was his influence on the tender, beautiful, talented young woman, who had been capable, under wise and generous care, of being a power of goodness and beauty not only in her community but throughout the land? Worse than the blight of hate which fell upon me from unknown sources, was the blight which came upon me from him by way of mamma as a medium. I just asked her a few moments ago what Mrs. Brown would think of something or other. Her reply was to stick out her tongue and simulate nausea at the mere mention of a good, simple woman who is her friend. And that is the essence of Mr. Dickinson's influence. He with his preeminence in the small world in which he lived, a survival of the days when men were not considered equal, enabled him to carry off his snobbery to the end, and yet be taken seriously by the community. Anything he chose to do was right by virtue of the fact that he did it. To the last, he and his gold-headed cane were looked up to in awe by every child in town, though secretly they laughed at his red wig, and imitated his important stride—Not in my presence, however! I also was his protector!

*Mabel*

My attitude toward her [my mother] has always been one of concern— ever since I was conscious of any attitude, and long before—why was she the object of the disapproval of the town? If I try to analyze those childish unacknowledged anxieties, they are thereby given a rational form, which they never had. They were dumb, inarticulate concern—concern—always concern. What could I do about it? Nothing, but be concerned, never allow her dashing, brilliant beauty to get far from my enveloping concern, but confine myself to that. Never speak to anyone about it, least of all to her, nor allow anyone to speak to me—though the possibility of *that* never could have been entertained by me for one instant. I recall the abhorrence with which I heard my grandmother refer, once or twice, to her disapproval of mamma and her sorrow because of it, though this merely referred to external things, such as love of dress. . . .

But her life and her talents? What became of them after their nurture in such a nursery? Her industry always and still is prodigious. From a young girl when she devoted herself with such zeal to painting and playing and singing and the theoretical study of music, her industry never flagged. But to what end was it all, and were all her talents directed? Alice Freeman Palmer, mamma's dear friend, with a fraction of her talent, is a national patron saint of the college girl. Artistically she was not gifted at all. In speaking and writing mamma was her superior. Mamma held audiences of thousands spell-bound for as long as she chose to wield her brilliant, picturesque tongue. But the loftiest motive that could be ascribed to her talks was the desire for self-expression and the sense of power she felt in holding the world at her feet. Her love of beauty was her only religion, and to that sum-total of beauty she has largely contributed. But the good of mankind, or village improvement, or the advance of knowledge—were farthest from her scintillating thoughts. The blight of self-interest and self-glorification had fallen upon her, which left her efforts worthy of oblivion instead of endearing her to half a nation. With all her energy and industry, what throwing away of talents—what prodigal waste of them because the scope of their use did not reach beyond herself! [In 1962, Mrs. Bingham inserted a marginal note at this point: "Not true."]

## The War between the Houses

What about his [Austin's] household? The family in the forbidding house behind the hedge? I tremble as I think of it. To meet one of them in the street was a sufficient shock for the day. That they could be human beings, made of flesh and blood, never occurred to me. They were a race apart. They walked about the village streets scattering venom as they walked. It fell upon and withered me, dropping down from their haughty gaze above my head as I passed by. Could anybody be more humble and more negligible than I? Especially since half the town seemed to agree with the Dickinsons. But that atmosphere was the one I breathed, my environment to which my small life was to be adjusted.

Out of the miasma of their presence which filled their house and extended its pestiferous aura across the street and as far as the eye could reach toward it, it was hard for me to pick out individuals. But that there were individuals I knew, because they could be met separately and could separately exhale their poison.

Mrs. Dickinson, known as Sue, though I never heard that word mentioned more than twice in my life, was a low being, the daughter of a stable keeper [elsewhere, "inn keeper"] whom the Squire had married by mistake. These facts I knew, but to me she was only a nebulous figure overshadowed by her virulent daughter. That individual, tall and spare like her father, contemptuous like him, intensified all his exaggerations and embodied the terror of the family; for her brother [Ned], though with all of the snobbery, had none of the power of his father, not enough indeed to carry it off. There had been a younger son, "Gildud" [Gilbert], I called him as a baby, who had died. The other son [Ned], also, died early. Instead of mother's milk, I was nourished on the hate of Martha Dickinson —"Mattie D." as she was derisively known by the townsfolk. To make the connection between the brown-velvet capped man sitting by our fire, or in Miss Vinnie's dining-room with mamma, and the blight which fell from that unyielding proud dame, was beyond my power or wish to do. I accepted it. If I had been questioned, unthinkable though that is to this day, I should have replied, "Why should he not talk with my mother?"—if the breath with which to reply had not been stricken from me by the question. A bolt from heaven would have been no surprise to me if a living mortal had dared to address me on the subject.

# "War between the Houses": Documents

## David Todd

I didn't think much about my father, in fact chiefly I can remember helping at night to thaw out his hands as he came back from observing the stars, or walking with him up to Vespers, when he told me to lift my feet, not scuffle, or his hiding my hat and coat, which made me late to school, in order to teach me to put them where they belonged. Yes, and once or twice he took me to skate on a frog pond on the outskirts of the town and often up to the great cow barns of the Agricultural College or the orchards and vineyards. But usually, I didn't think much about him, except as he glanced at me—doubtless without seeing me at all, but I didn't know that—each time he put fork or spoon into his mouth. . . .

And it was not until after I was married [1920] and papa was in Bloomingdale Insane Asylum that it ever occurred to me to think of what his [Austin's] influence on papa might have been. He, the youthful, serious young scientist—how could he have accepted the situation—an old aristocrat twice his age, who looked down upon him as a plebeian, and preempted his wife as by the divine right of his august preference?

Only last year, for the first time, did mamma refer to papa's attitude toward women. It is his fundamental weakness, it seems. They had hardly been married three years when he began to make love to anybody that would accept his advances. He had most of the women guests who came to our house, even beginning on my friends when I grew up. As mamma expatiated upon this inherent weakness of his, I saw him sitting behind his barred windows. And again the legacy of Mr. Dickinson closed down upon me like a vacuum bell shutting out the air which would be for me life to breathe. And all I could do was to sit and listen, while she, unconscious of any shortcoming of her own, revealed to me my father's sin. It would have taken a harder heart than my own to suggest to her that she perhaps was not without fault—and that her scathing denunciation of him was unbecoming, considering, perhaps, the part she played in staging the tragedy.

\*   \*   \*

After these long and often anguished documents—all-too-human in their mixture of indignation, bitterness, venom, and confession—the reader may well ask, "Why?" Ambience? atmosphere? the harsh realities of a situation long varnished over? Perhaps the best short, if incomplete, answer is an entry in Millicent Todd Bingham's diary for March 27, 1951:

The effect on Emily? She was glad that Austin had found some comfort after his all but ruined life. In my mother's words, "Emily always respected real emotion."

To right the balance, we have only to remember how much Emily respected Sue's emotion, too—Sue, her "torrid" sister-in-law, she who "fronts on the Gulf Stream."

References for

VOLUME ONE

PAGE

19 "Without some understanding . . ." Perry Miller, *The American Puritans: Their Prose and Poetry* (1956), p. ix.

19 If Hawthorne . . . Allen Tate, "Emily Dickinson," from *Collected Essays*, 1932, reprinted in *Emily Dickinson: A Collection of Critical Essays*, ed. R. B. Sewall (1963), pp. 16–27.

19 "I do not respect 'doctrines'" *L* II, 346 (to Mrs. Joseph Haven, February 13, 1859).

19 "While the Clergyman . . ." *L* II, 508 (to Mrs. J. G. Holland, early summer 1873).

19 "Ancestors' Brocades" *L* II, 491 (to Higginson, November 1871).

19 the ideal time for a poet Tate, "Emily Dickinson," pp. 21, 23.

20 ". . . the community was . . ." Theodora Ward, *The Capsule of the Mind*, pp. 4, 9.

21 "thin dry & speechless" *L* II, 475 (Higginson to his wife, August 17, 1870).

22 "She did not reason . . ." Tate, "Emily Dickinson," p. 25.

22 "Man is put . . ." Miller, *The American Puritans*, pp. 171–72.

23 "ecstasy in living" *L* II, 474 (Higginson's letter to his wife, August 16, 1870).

23 "'Consider the Lilies'" *L* III, 825 (to Mrs. Frederick Tuckerman, June 1884).

23–24 "Almost every Puritan . . ." Miller, *The American Puritans*, pp. 225–26.

24 Miller on Edwards and Stoddard Ibid., pp. 221, 222.

25 "The shore is safer . . ." *L* I, 104 (to Abiah Root, late 1850).

26 "the Flood subject" *L* II, 454 (to Higginson, June 9, 1866).

26 "The final direction . . ." Charles R. Anderson, *Emily Dickinson's Poetry: Stairway of Surprise*, p. 283.

26 "My dear Mr. Higginson . . ." Millicent Todd Bingham, *Ancestors' Brocades*, pp. 169–70.

26 "the most remarkable criticism . . ." Ibid.

26 "Unlike her contemporaries . . ." Tate, "Emily Dickinson," pp. 23, 25.

27 "Vesuvius at Home," *P* #1705, undated.

27 Erik Erikson on origins Cf. "Identity and Uprootedness in Our Time," in *Insight and Responsibility* (1964), p. 95.

CHAPTER 3

28 Carpenter and Morehouse on Samuel Fowler Dickinson *History of Amherst*, p. 187.

29 "He was trained . . ." *Reunion of the Dickinson Family at Amherst, Mass., 1883* (1884), pp. 172–74. The article is signed "The loving daughter," pretty clearly Elisabeth Dickinson [Currier].

31 "holds – so – " *L* II, 406 (to Mrs. Samuel Bowles, spring 1862).

31 "To see the little Tippler . . ." *P* #214, about 1860.

31 "these stirring words . . ." *Home*, p. 7, n.

33 "disillusioned, neglected . . ." H. F. West, "Forgotten Dartmouth Men," *Dartmouth Alumni Magazine*, XXVII (February 1935), p. 62.

34 the "original object . . ." Article 13 of the constitution of the "Collegiate Charity Fund" (see W. S. Tyler, *History of Amherst College*, 1895 ed., p. 9).

PAGE

35 Edward Hitchcock's description of Fowler *Reminiscences of Amherst College*, pp. 5, 6. Hitchcock adds, "From all that I can learn, I have no doubt that Samuel F. Dickinson and Col. Graves had more to do in forming and executing plans for the founding of Amherst College than any other men."

35 "urged by the command . . ." Preamble to the constitution of the Charitable Fund.

35 William S. Tyler on Fowler—"head"; "hand"; "one of the most . . ." *History of Amherst College* (1873 ed.), pp. 49, 120–21.

36 The *Hampshire Gazette* on Fowler *YH* I, 7.

36–37 The *New-England Inquirer* on Fowler *YH* I, 6.

37 Fowler on female education *YH* I, 17–18 (October 27).

37 Fowler at Western Reserve Frederick Clayton Waite, *Western Reserve University, the Hudson Era, 1826–1882* (1943), p. 315; quoted in *Home*, pp. 17–18.

37–38 Catherine Dickinson on Fowler's last years *YH* I, 28; *Home*, pp. 21–22.

38 "Everything looks beautifully . . ." *Home*, pp. 16–17.

38–39 Edward Dickinson on home *YH* I, 14 (May 20, 1830), 29 (September 7, 1835).

39–40 ED on travel
"The world is full . . ." *L* I, 137 (October 1).
"rich in disdain . . ." *L*, I, 141 (October 5).
"all is jostle . . ." *L* II, 317 (to Susan Gilbert, February 28).
a "Wilderness" *L* II, 433 (to Lavinia, July 1864).
"to see the Grass . . ." *L* II, 434 (to Susan Dickinson, September 1864).
"I never thought . . ." *L* II, 474 (Higginson to his wife, August 16, 1870).
"I don't care . . ." *L* II, 551 (spring 1876).
"I do not go away . . ." *L* III, 716 (about 1881).
"To shut our eyes . . ." *L* II, 482 (to Mrs. J. G. Holland; early October 1870).

40 "Back to myself" *Journals*, ed. Edward Emerson & W. E. Forbes (Boston, 1909–14), III, 199.

40 "fiery mist" *L* II, 461 (Higginson to ED, May 11, 1869).

41 "our rye field . . ." *L* I, 48 (October 21, 1847).

41 Austin on his grandfather "Representative Men of the Parish, Church Buildings and Finances, an Address delivered at the one hundred and fiftieth anniversary of the First Church of Christ in Amherst, November 7, 1889," published with other proceedings on that occasion, Amherst, 1890, p. 63.

41 *"Si monumentum requiris . . ."* *Reunion*, p. 173.

42 a "Beautiful Incident" *YH* II, 175.

42 "outran his capacity . . ." *YH* I, xxxvii.


CHAPTER 4


44ff. Early correspondence of Edward Dickinson The Dickinson Papers, Houghton Library, Harvard University. Letters not dated in the text are as follows:

44 "rational happiness" March 19, 1828.

46 "Don't let your natural liveliness . . ." November 16, 1822.
46 "I know well enough . . ." April 24, 1824. Baker's quotation is from *An Essay on Man*. Edward used it years later in an address to the House of Representatives in Washington. See note 4, p. 53.
47 "I suppose that you are applying . . ." June 9, 1824.
47 "My life must be . . ." June 4, 1826.
47 "as far as in our power . . ." August 9, 1827.
47 "in having assisted . . ." November 30, 1827.
47 "Let us prepare . . ." March 19, 1828.
48 "Females, also . . ." April 10, 1826.
48 a "new novel" July 10, 1827.
48 "the dwelling place . . ." November 27, 1826.
48 Edward on deaths of ex-Presidents July 12, 1826.
48 "It is very late . . ." September 26, 1827.
48 "the wind whistles . . ." December 10, 1827.
48 "and let our prayers . . ." January 27, 1828.
49 "the subject, as I always . . ." October 22, 1826.
49 "Judge Howe . . ." June 4, 1826.
49 "industry, frugality . . ." October 29, 1826.
49 "a warning to all young men . . ." March 19, 1828.
49–50 "Continue in the path . . ." October 17, 1827.
50 "I will plainly tell you . . ." March 2, 1828.
50 "after the business of the day . . ." August 9, 1827.
51 "And now, My Dear . . ." September 24, 1827.
51 "I have already waited a year . . ." January 21, 1828.
49 "Father [is] . . ." L II, 404 (to Higginson, April 26, 1862).
52 "The best financier . . ." Tyler, *History of Amherst College*, 1873 ed., p. 540.
52 "unbending firmness . . ." Ibid., p. 539.
53 "Father and Mr. Frink . . ." L I, 128 (July 27, 1851).
53 northern lights *Home*, pp. 172–73.
54 "Gen. and Mrs. . . ." *YH* II, 139.
54 "both were our royal guests" *YH* I, 351.
55 "At the age . . ." Tyler, *History of Amherst College*, p. 540.
55 The *Boston Journal* on Edward *YH* II, 209–10 (entry of November 8, 1873). The *Republican*, then under the editorship of Dickinson's friend and trustee of Amherst College, Samuel Bowles, captioned the article:

TRIBUTE TO A VETERAN
ONE OF THE OLD "RIVER GODS."

55 "remote" L II, 475 (Higginson to his wife, August 17, 1870); *LL*, pp. 70–71, ED to Joseph Lyman.
55 "the low, enjoying power" *Moby-Dick*, Chapter 37.
55ff. ED on Edward
55 ". . . he never played . . ." L II, 486 (to Louisa Norcross, spring 1871).
55 "I am not . . ." *YH* II, 482 (as reported by Ellen E. Dickinson, wife of ED's cousin Willie, in an article in the *Boston Evening Transcript*, October 12, 1895).
55 "among men . . ." L I, 213 (to Austin, June 20, 1852).
56 "Father is really *sober* . . ." L I, 173 (February 6, 1852).
56 "marching around the town . . ." L I, 254 (to Austin, June 13, 1853).

PAGE

56 "his pantaloons tucked . . ." *L* I, 148 (October 17, 1851).
56 "Father steps like Cromwell . . ." *L* II, 470 (early spring 1870).
56 "the Barn . . ." *L* II, 464 (to Susan Gilbert Dickinson, autumn 1869).
56 "Father looks very grand . . ." *L* I, 188 (March 7, 1852).
56 "we young ones . . ." *L* I, 119 (June 29, 1851).
56–57 "When I know of anything funny . . ." *L* I, 161 (December 15, 1851).
57 "He buys me many Books . . ." *L* II, 404 (to Higginson, April 25, 1862).
57 "We're rejoiced . . ." *L* I, 190 (March 24, 1852).
57 "world of parental tyrannies . . ." Clark Griffith, *The Long Shadow*, p. 279.
57 "No one openly . . ." *Home*, p. 3.
57 "Tutor Howland . . ." *L* I, 111.
58 "Mat came home . . ." *L* I, 190 (to Austin, March 24, 1852).
58 "like friendly and absolute . . ." *Home*, p. 413.
58 "where each member . . ." *L* II, 473 (Higginson to his wife, August 16, 1870).
58 "We have no statutes . . ." *L* II, 606 (to Mrs. Edward Tuckerman, about March 1878?).
58 "that charming second home . . ." *LL*, p. 1.
58 "Now you have got . . ." *LL*, p. 12.
59ff. ED on home
59 my "very dear home" *L* I, 53 (to Abiah Root, November 6, 1847).
59 "my *own* DEAR HOME" *L* I, 58 (to Abiah Root, January 17, 1848).
59 "We rode . . ." *L* I, 58 (to Abiah Root, January 17, 1848).
59 come back "to freedom . . ." *L* I, 146 (October 10, 1851).
59 "I am so sorry . . ." *L* I, 162 (December 24, 1851).
59 "I'm afraid . . ." *L* I, 197 (about April 1852).
59 "Home is the definition of God" *L* II, 483 (to Perez Cowan, late October 1870).
59 "Home is a holy thing . . ." *L* I, 150–51 (to Austin, October 25, 1851).
59 "Infinite power of Home" *L* III, 782 (to Mrs. J. Howard Sweetser, summer 1883).
60 "Went to Vinnie's . . ." from Mrs. Todd's diary for August 26, 1893 (reprinted in *AB*, p. 231).
61 "The father was terrific . . ." *AB*, pp. 232–33.
61 "Miss Vinnie told me . . ." *YH* II, 231 (letter from M. L. Hall to M. T. Bingham, December 29, 1938).
61 "There, father . . ." *AB*, p. 233 (letter from M. L. Hall to M. T. Bingham, August 5, 1933).
61 "I have never *before* . . ." *YH* I, 315 (early September? 1854).
62 "You know home . . ." *Home*, p. 305.
62 "very funny indeed . . ." *L* I, 230–31 (March 18, 1853).
62 "an Eclipse" *L* II, 404 (to Higginson, April 25, 1862).
62 "standard of good workmanship" *Home*, p. 112.
62 "One day . . ." Ibid.
63 "Oh! dear! . . ." Ibid., p. 235.
63 "Father was the only one . . ." *Home*, p. 413.

PAGE

63 "quite a hand . . ." *L* I, 66 (to Abiah Root, May 16, 1848).
63 "as gentle . . ." *L* II, 439 (to Louisa Norcross, early 1865).
63 "Father was *thoughtful* . . ." *Home,* pp. 312–13.
63 "in the habit of me" *L* II, 450 (to Higginson, early 1866).
64 "this is a lonely house . . ." *L* I, 233 (to Austin, March 24, 1853).
64 "the letters of suspected . . ." *L* II, 346 (to Mrs. Joseph Haven, February 13, 1859).
64 "such papers only . . ." *L* I, 157 (to Austin, November 16, 1851).
64 "militant Accent" *L* II, 537 (to Mrs. Holland, late January 1875).
64 "Father sat all the evening . . ." *L* I, 121 (July 6, 1851).
65 "Her father was not severe . . ." *L* II, 475 (Higginson to his wife, August 17, 1870).
65 "We are having a pleasant . . ." *L* I, 125 (July 20).
65 "the Mail of Anguish" *P* #165, about 1860.
65 "I dont love to read . . ." *L* I, 243 (to Austin, April 16, 1853).
66 "My father seems . . ." *LL,* pp. 70–71.
66 "While Hon. E.D. . . ." *YH* I, 178 (entry of early August 1850).
66 "I am standing alone . . ." *L* I, 94 (to Jane Humphrey, April 3).
66 "the ark of safety" *L* I, 60 (to Abiah Root, January 17, 1848).
67 "Old Neighbor – . . ." *P* #623, about 1862.
67 "lasts a Solid Year – " *P* #569, about 1862.
67 Edward's death *YH* II, 224 (entry for June 16, 1874) gives Mabel Loomis Todd's account of the event. "These facts," she concluded (in a letter to Higginson), "have just been re-told me by Mr. Austin Dickinson, so I am sure of their accuracy."
67 "even more respected . . ." *YH* II, 224.
67 "He was, indeed . . ." *YH* II, 224–25.
67 "It is a condition . . ." *YH* II, 226–27.
69 "Memorial service . . ." *YH* II, 227 (J. L. Skinner to his wife).
69ff. ED on Edward's death
    69 "I cannot recall . . ." *L* II, 526 (summer 1874).
    69 "The last Afternoon . . ." *L* II, 528 (July 1874).
    69 "I dream . . ." *L* II, 559 (August 1876).
    69 "accustomed . . ." *L* II, 591 and n. (to Harriet and Martha Dickinson, about 1877?).
    69 ED refers to "the mighty dying" of her father in *L* III, 716 (to Higginson, about 1881).
    71 "When I think . . ." *L* II, 551 (to Higginson, spring 1876).
71 "beautiful Hymn" *L* II, 528 (to Higginson, July 1874).
72 "She wrote it . . ." Higginson to Mrs. Todd, *AB,* p. 130.
73 "*My* business . . ." *L* II, 413 (to Dr. and Mrs. Holland, summer 1862?).


CHAPTER 5


74 "I never had . . ." *L* II, 475 (Higginson to his wife, August 17, 1870).
74 "I always ran . . ." *L* II, 517–18 (January 1874).
75 Austin on ED's "posing" *AB,* p. 167.
75 "I have been in a savage . . ." *YH* II, 77 (April 18?, 1863).
76 Emily Norcross's letter to her sister *Home,* p. 25.

76ff. The courtship letters are in the Dickinson Papers, Houghton Library, Harvard. The dates of letters not included in the text are given below.

  76 "amiable disposition," etc.  April 10, 1826.
  76–77 "I suppose you are now . . ."  January 27, 1828.
  77 "invitations without number"  February 8, 1828.
  77 "I find that . . ."  Ibid.
  77 "All I wish . . ."  April 29, 1828.
  77 "I think it best . . ."  Ibid.
  77–78 "I was much pleased . . ."  January 10, 1828.
  78 "A woman, you know . . ."  January 27, 1828.
  78 "May we be virtuous . . ."  April 29, 1828.
  78 "My Dear, my heart . . ."  April 18, 1828.
  78 "I have many friends . . ."  April 25, 1828.
  78 "The time is short . . ."  May 2, 1828.

79 "situated pleasantly"  *YH* I, 6 (May 21, 1828).
79 "The Hon. Mr. Bliss . . ."  *YH* I, 7 (September 23, 1828).
79 "It is enough . . ."  *YH* I, 9 (February 12, 1829).
79 "I have retired . . ."  *YH* I, 17 (June 1, 1831).
79 "grieved life"  *L* II, 578 (to Mrs. William A. Stearns, early 1877 ?).
79 "tremulous fear of death"  *Home,* p. 4.
81 "I have only a moment . . ."  *L* III, 675 (about September 1880).
81 "a holier demand"  *L* III, 716 (to Higginson, about 1881).
81 "Only the night . . ."  *L* III, 748 (to Mrs. J. Howard Sweetser, November 1882). The reference is to Dick Matthews, the Dickinson stableman.
81 "The habit that grew . . ."  Theodora Ward, *The Capsule of the Mind,* p. 7.
82 "Mother drives . . ."  *L* II, 476 (to the Norcrosses, late summer 1870?).
82 apples to Samuel Bowles  *L* II, 426 (to Bowles, autumn 1863).
82 bouquet to President Stearns  *YH* II, 81 (July 12, 1863).
82 the parties  *L* I, 59 (to Abiah Root, January 17, 1848); 288 (to Austin, March 16, 1854).
82 "Mother pines for you . . ."  *L* II, 593 (to Mrs. Holland, September 1877).
82 "There are a great variety . . ."  October 27, 1827.
82 Mrs. Dickinson's committee work and commendations
  In 1852 she was on the Fruit Committee; 1853, the Fine Arts Committee; in 1859, the Flowers Committee (*YH* I, 255, 282, 373). On September 2, 1853, the *Hampshire and Franklin Express* printed the following acknowledgment (*YH* I, 282): "We have received from Mrs. Edward Dickinson, a choice sample of Figs, grown under her cultivation. Also, from the same lady, a sample of apples, of the Russet variety, grown last season, looking as fresh as when gathered in the field."
83 ED on her mother's intellect  *L* I, 287 (to Austin, March 14, 1854); 180 (February 18, 1852); 11, 404 (April 25, 1862).
83 Mrs. Dickinson's books  *YH* I, 4 (May 6, 1828); 330 (March 3, 1855).
83 Mrs. Dickinson's reading  *L* I, 157 (to Austin, November 16, 1851); *L* II, 604 (to Mrs. Holland, early 1878).
83 Mrs. Dickinson as a letter writer
  "write her *name* . . ."  *YH* I, 31 (January 16).
  "Mother was much amused . . ."  *L* I, 257 (June 19, 1853).
  "to put you in mind . . ."  *L* I, 124 (July 13, 1851).

Her excuse for not writing  *L* I, 240 (April 8, 1853), and cf. Cody, pp. 155–56.

84 "making most desperate efforts . . ."  *L* I, 185 (to Austin, March 2, 1852).

84 Mrs. Dickinson quoted
"Mother had a nice time . . ."  *Home,* p. 249 (July 15, 1852).
"Mother says it seems . . ."  Ibid., p. 282.
"Mother tells how gently . . ."  *L* II, 421 (to the Norcrosses, late January 1863).
"Jennie Hitchcock's mother . . ."  *L* II, 425 (late May 1863).
"– and mother – oh she thought . . ."  *L* I, 274 (December 13, 1853).
"Mother feels quite troubled . . ."  *L* I, 151 (October 25, 1851).
"would be a very good Boy"  *L* II, 454 (to Susan Gilbert Dickinson, about August 1866).
"Mother wants . . ."  *L* I, 116 (June 22, 1851).
"The horse . . ."  *L* I, 137–38 (to Austin, October 1, 1851).

85 "Mother is warming . . ."  *L* I, 111.

85 ED's later remarks on her mother
"Mother went rambling . . ."  *L* II, 470.
"She has no Father and Mother . . ."  *L* II, 508 (early summer 1873).
"I ask Mother 'what message' . . ."  *L* III, 689.
"Had he a tenderer eulogy?"  *L* III, 713 (October 1881).

85–86 Mrs. Dickinson's understanding of family's complexity
"a mystery . . ."  Clara Newman Turner, as quoted in *Home,* p. 5. Later (p. 265), Mrs. Bingham refers to the source of her reference, Mrs. Turner's "My Personal Acquaintance with Emily Dickinson," referred to in Chapter 4, note 6.

86 "Austin and I were talking . . ."  *L* III, 667.

86 Mrs. Dickinson as loving and attentive mother
"Mother makes nicer pies . . ."  *L* I, 127 (July 27, 1851).
"– what with fruit . . ."  *L* I, 133 (to Austin, September 23, 1851).
"Mother and Margaret . . ."  *L* II, 439 (to Louisa Norcross, early 1865).

87 ED's baking  *L* II, 474 (to his wife, August 17, 1870).

87 "Vinnie's mother . . ."  *LL,* p. 14.

88 Mrs. Dickinson's lessons
"Soon the carriage . . ."  *L* I, 58 (to Abiah Root, January 17, 1848).
"Mother got a great dinner . . ."  *L* I, 270 (November 14, 1853).
"Two things I have lost . . ."  *L* III, 928–29 (Prose Fragment #117; in the MS, Emily crossed out the last sentence).

88–89 ED on her mother's death
"I hoped to write . . ."  *L* III, 749–50.
"Blow has followed blow . . ."  *L* III, 754 (to Mrs. Holland, mid-December 1882). The repeated blows probably include the death of Samuel Bowles in 1878, Dr. Holland in 1881, and Charles Wadsworth in 1882.
"Her dying feels to me . . ."  *L* III, 752 (to James D. Clark, late 1882).
"We were never intimate . . ."  *L* III, 754–55 (to Mrs. Holland, mid-December 1882).
"To have *had* a Mother . . ."  *L* III, 892 (to Mrs. James C. Greenough, late October 1885).
"All is faint . . ."  *L* III, 771 (to Maria Whitney, spring 1883).

89 "As Freezing persons . . ."  *P* #341, early 1862.

89-90 Lavinia on her mother
"The days are beautiful . . ." *YH* II, 397 (to Mabel Loomis Todd, April 30, 1883).
"and mother loved" *Home,* p. 414.

C H A P T E R  6

91 Mrs. Dickinson as "carrier of Dickinson traits" *Home,* p. 4.
92 Austin's friends
Henry Hills *YH* II, 295 (July 17, 1878).
Mrs. Todd Journal, January 6, 1885; Todd-Bingham Archive, Yale.
92 Skinner on Austin *YH* II, 228-29, 172 (March 31, 1871). The first incident occurred on August 2, 1874—as Leyda remarks, only six weeks after Austin's father's death and hence a period of great strain for him.
93 Austin and art
"in a feverish excitement . . ." *YH* II, 41 (to Samuel Bowles, December 25, 1861).
"bought a water color . . ." *YH* II, 425. The diary, now in the Todd-Bingham Archive, Yale, is for the years 1880, 1882, 1883, 1884, 1886, 1888, 1889, 1890.
95 "that Campaign inscrutable" *P* #1188, about 1871.
95-96 Austin's "Hurrah" *L* I, 3 (April 18, 1842); 123 (July 13, 1851); 83 (January 23, 1850); 174 (February 6, 1852); 276 (December 20, 1853).
96 Aunt Elisabeth on Austin *YH* I, 75 (April 21, 1842).
96 ED's and Austin's long talks *L* I, 245 (April 21, 1853).
96-97 Austin's drafted note *Home,* pp. 82-83.
97 the *"imaginative* note" *L* I, 68.
97 ED on the Dickinson difference *L* I, 239; 245 (April 21, 1853).
97 Joseph Lyman on "the ring" *LL,* p. 48. Vinnie was Joseph's sweetheart as Emily was not; but Emily was in the small elite group of those who "understood," as Vinnie was not.
98-99 Austin to Susan Gilbert *YH* I, 182 (November 9, 1850).
99 ED to Austin *L* I, 113 (June 15, 1851); 151 (October 25, 1851); 160 (December 15, 1851).
99 Lavinia to Austin *YH* I, 217 (October 10, 1851).
99 "Queen Recluse" *YH* II, 76 (Samuel Bowles to Austin, March? 1863).
100 "School masters . . ." *L* I, 101 (October 27, 1850).
100 "those useless boys" *L* I, 162 (to Austin; December 24, 1851).
101 ED's concern for Austin *L* I, 289 (March 16, 1854); 239 (April 2, 1853); 248 (May 7, 1853).
101 Austin to Susan Gilbert *YH* I, 184-85 (December 11, 1850).
101-2 "To know Emily's brother . . ." *Home,* p. xiv.
102 Mr. Gilbert's "convivial habits" *AB,* p. 219.
103-4 ED on Martha Gilbert *L* I, 205; 135 (September 23, 1851).
104 Samuel Learned on the Gilbert sisters *YH* I, 280 (July 27, 1853).
104 Emily's "clandestiny" *L* I, 228-29 (to Susan Gilbert; March 12, 1853).
104-6 Austin to Martha Gilbert *Home,* pp. 240-42 (May 11, 1852).
105 ED on her talk with Martha *L* I, 205 (May 13, 1852).
105 "I love the danger!" *L* I, 104 (late 1850, to Abiah Root).
108-9 "wade grief" *P* #252, about 1861.
109 "Susan fronts . . ." *L* III, 895 (to Susan; early 1886).

PAGE
109–10  Austin to Susan  *YH* I, 268, 269–70.
112  Austin to Martha  *YH* I, 266 (March 27, 1853).
113  Susan Gilbert to her brothers  *YH* I, 293–94 (January 6, 1854); 315 (September 4).
113–14  Susan Gilbert to the Bartletts  *YH* I, 342 (May 19, 1856).
114  Austin to Gordon Ford  *YH* I, 343.
114  Jane Hitchcock on the Dickinson houses  *YH* I, 344 (September 24).
115  "So Marm D – . . ."  *YH* II, 143 (Mrs. Samuel Bowles to her son; October 29, 1869).
115  "my crowd"  *L* II, 358 (to Mrs. Samuel Bowles; December 10).
115–16  Samuel Bowles to Sue  *YH* II, 276 (June 29).
116  John W. Burgess on Sue  *Reminiscences of an American Scholar* (1934), pp. 60–61.
116  Mrs. Todd on Susan  Letter to her parents, *YH* II, 353 (October 2, 1881).
116  "We almost forget . . ."  *L* III, 765 (to James D. Clark, mid-March 1883).
117  "crept out one evening . . ."  *YH* II, 133.
117  "filled to overflowing"  *YH* II, 132.
117  Austin's overwork  Mrs. Todd's letter to Austin, April 20, 1890; Austin to Mrs. Todd, March 6, 1890 (Todd-Bingham Archive, Yale).
  Austin on ED's "genius"  See Chapter 12, pp. 222–25.
118  "Brother Pegasus"  *L* I, 235.
118  Austin's "poem"  *YH* I, xxxix; II, 380.
118–22  "Representative Men . . ."  In *An Historical Review: One Hundred and Fiftieth Anniversary of the First Church of Christ in Amherst, Massachusetts, November 7, 1889.* Amherst, Mass.: Press of the Amherst Record, 1890, pp. 50–66.
121  "Women . . ."  Postscript in a letter to William Hayes Ward, who sent it to Mabel Loomis Todd, March 3, 1897.
122  "I wouldn't give . . ."  Austin to Mrs. Todd, November 16, 1887 (Todd-Bingham Archive). Other recorded trips by Austin: to Washington, D.C., 1854; to the Centennial Exposition, Philadelphia, 1876; to the Chicago World's Fair, 1893.
123  Austin to James Clark  Todd-Bingham Archive.
124  to "regulate"  *P* #1100; about 1866.
  ED on Austin  *L* II, 398 (to Louise and Frances Norcross, late March 1862); 399 (late March 1862).
124  Austin at his father's death  *YH* II, 226 (J. L. Skinner to his wife, June 22, 1874).
124  Vinnie's letter  MS, University of Virginia Library. (See Chapter 7, note 8.)
124  Mrs. Todd on Austin  Diary, October 6, 1883; Journal, November 11, 1883. Todd-Bingham Archive.
125  ED on "the Dyings"  *L* III, 843 (to Mrs. Samuel E. Mack, autumn 1884).
126  ED on eternity  *L* III, 750 (to Louise and Frances Norcross, late November 1882).

CHAPTER 7

128  "she had to think – . . ."  *Home,* p. 414.
129  "Area – no test of depth"  *L* III, 767 (to Mrs. Jonathan L. Jenkins, date unknown).

PAGE

129  "narrow, probing, Eyes" *P* #561, about 1862.
129  "instilling many a lesson . . ." *L* I, 66 (to Abiah Root, May 16, 1848).
129  "I think Emilie . . ." *Home*, p. 174 (October 1, 1851).
129–30  "Emilie tells storys . . ." Ibid., p. 203 (December 1851).
130  "inside the ring" *LL*, p. 48.
130  "very pious and very pretty" *LL*, p. 54.
130  Daniel Bonbright to Joseph Lyman  *LL*, p. 59.
130  "Vinnie says . . ." *L* I, 174 (February 6, 1852).
130  ED on Vinnie and practical matters  *L* I, 213 (June 20, 1852); 310 (November 27–December 3, 1854); 297 (early June 1854).
130  "the folks . . ." *Home*, p. 234 (March 24, 1852).
131  "more beautiful . . ." *YH* I, 274 (draft of a letter to Susan Gilbert, May 10?, 1853).
131  "happy with her duties . . ." *L* III, 862 (to Maria Whitney, early 1885?).
131  "Soldier and Angel . . ." *L* III, 794 (to Harriet Austin Dickinson, mid-August 1883).
131  "Your bond . . ." *L* III, 779 (to Charles Clark, mid-June 1883).
131  Chickering's eulogy  *Home*, pp. 490–91 (from the *Springfield Republican*, November 30, 1899).
131  "went East" *L* II, 377 (to Mrs. Samuel Bowles, about August 1861).
132  "*perter* and *more* pert . . ." *L* I, 127 (July 27, 1851).
132  "lively, brisk, smart . . ." Noah Webster, *An American Dictionary of the English Language*, Springfield, 1851.
132  Jane Hitchcock to Austin  *Home*, p. 90 (January 11, 1850). (I have not followed the order of the sentences in the letter.) Jane Hitchcock was the daughter of Professor Edward Hitchcock, at that time president of the college.
132  Lavinia in Washington  *YH* I, 302 (from the *Springfield Republican*, November 29, 1899).
132  "There was a pleasant . . ." *Home*, p. 211 (January 26, 1852).
132  "I will send you . . ." Ibid., p. 237 (April?, 1852).
133  Vinnie's letters  Ibid., pp. 249 (July 8, 1852); 214 (January 28, 1852).
133  "Received offer of *marriage*" *YH* I, 216 (October 8, 1851).
133  Vinnie as head of the committee . . ." *Home*, p. 303.
134  "Vinnie's sainted Garden" *L* III, 812 (to Mrs. Henry Hills, February 1884?).
134  "I feel unusually hurried . . ." *Home*, p. 283 (May 6, 1853).
134  "I fear you are . . ." *L* II, 397 (March 1862?).
134  "Vinnie is still subsoiling . . ." *L* III, 880 (August 1885).
134  "Vinnie is far more hurried . . ." *L* III, 676 (about September).
134  "Vinnie is under terrific headway . . ." *L* III, 693 (spring 1881).
134  who "was only sighing . . ." *L* III, 695 (1881?).
134  "when *we* are *all* gone" *Home*, p. 313 (to Austin, November 9).
134  "was only a happen" See p. 153.
135  Vinnie to Lyman  *LL*, p. 34 (December 29, 1856).
135  "that charming second home . . ."; "spooney" *LL*, pp. 1, 59.
135  " 'sweeter, sweeter . . .' " *LL*, p. 35.
136  "O Joseph I havn't seen . . ." *LL*, p. 18.
136  Vinnie's diary entry  *YH* I, 196.
136  "Poor little . . ." *LL*, p. 21 (November 25, 1852).
136  "garden of roses" *LL*, p. 42.
136  "her little fat hands" *LL*, p. 14.
136  "central strenuous life" *LL*, p. 43.
137  Lyman on Vinnie  *LL*, pp. 50–51 (mid-March 1858); 21, 22, 42–43.

PAGE

138   Lyman on ED  *LL*, p. 60.

138   Lyman on ED and Araminta Wharton  "one of those . . ."  *LL*, p. 66. permission to write  *LL*, pp. 58, 66. "My friendships . . ."  *LL*, p. 67.

138   "had been with Emily . . ."  *LL*, p. 18.

139–40   Lyman on ED's and Vinnie's epistolary styles  *LL*, pp. 1, 51–53 (June 13, 1858; the ellipses are Joseph's).

140   Lyman on Vinnie  *LL*, p. 53.

140   Vinnie "cruises about . . ."  *L* I, 311 (to Sue, November 27–December 3, 1854).

141–42   Vinnie vs. Mrs. Sweetser  *Home*, pp. 358, 359.

142   ED on Vinnie's belligerence  *L* II, 612 (to Mrs. Holland, June 1878); 592 (to the Rev. and Mrs. Jonathan L. Jenkins, September 1877).

143   ED on her dependence on Vinnie  *L* II, 346 (to Mrs. Joseph Haven, February 13, 1859); 348 (to Mrs. Holland, about February 20, 1859); 508 (to Mrs. Holland, early summer 1873).

143   "friendly and absolute . . ."  *Home*, p. 413.

143   ED's return from Cambridge  *L* II, 435 (early November 1864); 436 (November 13, 1864); 430 (about May 1864).

144   "Did you know . . ."  *L* II, 643–44.

144   "All men say . . ."  *L* II, 415 (to Higginson, August 1862).

145   "And Vinnie, Joseph . . ."  *LL*, pp. 70–71.

145   "Vinnie is sick to-night . . ."  *L* II, 353 (September 1859).

146   Martha Dickinson Bianchi on Vinnie  *Emily Dickinson Face to Face*, p. 13.

146   Skinner on Vinnie  *YH* II, 226 (June 22, 1874).

146   Vinnie on Gilbert's death  The MS of the letter, heretofore unpublished, is in the Library of the University of Virginia and is reproduced here by permission. (For acknowledgment, see note 8.) The recipients are as yet unidentified.

146–47   Mrs. Jameson on Gilbert's death  *YH* II, 406 (October 14, 1883).

147   Reunion with Mrs. Holland  *L* III, 814, 816.

147   "'Tom' whirls us . . ."  *YH* II, 416 (to Mrs. Todd, February 5, 1884).

147; 150   Vinnie to Mrs. Todd  *YH* II, 397 (April 30, 1883); 413 (December 27, 1883); 416 (February 5, 1884).

151   "Went to call . . ."  *YH* II, 402 (July 23, 1883).

152   "partially cracked poetess"  *L* II, 570 (Higginson to his sister Anna, December 28, 1876).

152   Eliza Coleman to John Graves  *YH* I, 319 (October 4, 1854).

154   Sue's obituary of ED  *Springfield Republican*, May 18, 1886 (*YH* II, pp. 472–73).

155; 156   ED to Higginson  *L* II, 412; 474 (August 17, 1870).

155   "auctioning the mind"  *P* #709, about 1863.

155   *"at the White Heat"*  *P* #365, about 1862.

156   "blossoming"  Mabel Loomis Todd, preface to *Poems*, second series (1891), p. 8.

157   "War between the Houses"  This phrase first appears in Mary Lee Hall's letter to Mrs. Bingham, August 5, 1933 (Todd-Bingham Archive, Yale), which is quoted in *AB*, p. 371. For selections from this correspondence, see Appendix II, 1.

CHAPTER 8

PAGE
161 "a family quarrel . . ." From the document "Scurrilous but True" (see Appendix II, 4).
163 we "please ourselves . . ." *L* I, 144 (October 9, 1851).
163–65 *Kavanagh* (1849), pp. 36–37, 77–78, 39.
165 "Sue – you can go or stay – . . ." *L* I, 305-7.
Leyda (*YH* I, 317) suggests the date of *late* September.
166 "I was foolish . . ." *L* I, 304.
167 "Mother sends . . ." *L* I, 203.
167–68 Lavinia to Austin *Home*, pp. 268, 282.
168 Mrs. Hills on the Dickinsons *YH* II, 119 (December 9).
168 Mrs. Todd on Vinnie and Sue *AB*, p. 61.
168 "I miss you . . ." *L* II, 315. A third letter written from Washington that February is addressed to *both* Sue and Mattie and concerns mostly her trip.

CHAPTER 9

170–71 Jay Leyda on Mrs. Todd *YH* I, lxxiii–lxxiv.
171 "among distinguished scientists . . ." *AB*, p. 4.
172 "Amherst is alive . . ." *L* I, 80 (to Joel Norcross, January 11, 1850).
172 "even the Cynic Austin" *L* III, 690 (to Mrs. Holland, early spring 1881).
173 "aunts" Mabel Loomis Todd, *The Thoreau Family Two Generations Ago*, Thoreau Society Booklet #13 (1938), p. 11 and passim.
173 "the preferred flower of life" *L* III, 740 (late September 1882).
173 "I cannot make . . ." *L* III, 740 (October 1882).
176 "I never should have left her" As told me by Millicent Todd Bingham.
178 Austin "married – " *L* II, 377 (to Mrs. Samuel Bowles, about August 1861).
178 "My Brother is – " *L* III, 765 (to James D. Clark, mid-March 1883).
181 "Dimity Convictions" *P* #401, about 1862.

CHAPTER 10

189 "cruel treatment" *AB*, p. 374 (letter of Mary Lee Hall to Millicent Todd Bingham).
191 [Austin] is overcharged . . ." *L* II, 575 (to Mrs. Holland).
191 "If after all his years . . ." Todd-Bingham Family Papers.
191 "Never have I lived . . ." Letter to Mrs. Bingham, August 5, 1933.
192 "in a lighted bay window . . ." This is Clara Newman Pearl's comment in a document entitled "My Personal Acquaintance with Emily Dickinson, by Clara Newman Turner, edited by Clara Newman Pearl." A

PAGE

    copy is in the Todd-Bingham Archive, Yale. See *Home,* p. 265, and Appendix II, 3.

192   "disgusted . . ."   *YH* II, 257.

192   "very sorry for Miss Vinny . . ."   *YH* II, 294.

192   "a little too aggressive . . ."   *YH* II, 124.

192   "In my boyhood . . ."   Alfred E. Stearns, *An Amherst Boyhood* (1946), pp. 72, 76.

192   "I carry very many burdens . . ."   *YH* II, 438.

192–93   Austin's will   Copy in the Todd-Bingham Archive; and see *AB,* p. 338.

193   "If there is any . . ."   *YH* II, 445.

193   "Ned told us . . ."   *AB,* p. 372 (September 14, 1930).

193   "I have wondered . . ."   Letter of August 5, 1933.

193   "had always admired . . ."   Letter of October 12, 1930, to Mabel Loomis Todd.

CHAPTER 11

197   ED on Sue   *L* III, 895 (to Sue; early 1886), 791 (to Sue; about 1883).

198   Mrs. Jameson's report   *YH* II, 406 (letter to her son, October 14, 1883).

199   "Gimblets . . ."   *P* #244, about 1861.

199   "my crowd"   *L* II, 358 (to Mrs. Samuel Bowles; December 10, 1859).

199   ED to Sue at Geneva   *L* II, 339–40 (September 26, 1858).

200   Edward at midnight   *YH* I, 367.

201   "the clandestine Mind"   *L* III, 790 (to Sue; about 1883).

201   "In a Life . . ."   *L* II, 632 (to Sue; about 1878).

201   "Safe in their Alabaster Chambers"   *P* #216. The episode is described in full, with the exchange of letters, in *P* I, 151–55.

201   "Balm for Susan's . . ."   *L* III, 700 (about 1881).

201   "Your impregnable . . ."   *L* III, 707 (late summer 1881).

202   "Only Woman . . ."   *L* II, 546 (about 1875).

202   "That Susan lives . . ."   *L* III, 659 (spring 1880).

202   "To thank one . . ."   *L* III, 699 (about 1881).

202   "vast"   *L* III, 672 (about 1880).

202   "great"   *L* III, 791 (about 1883).

202   "I must wait . . ."   *L* II, 631 (about 1878).

202   "Susan's Idolator . . ."   *L* II, 458.

202   "To miss you . . ."   *L* II, 489 (September 1871).

202   "To see you . . ."   *L* II, 477 (about 1870).

202   "Susan breaks . . ."   *L* II, 652.

202   "Thank her dear power . . ."   *L* III, 733 (about 1882).

202   " 'Egypt . . .' "   *L* II, 533.

202   "Tell the Susan . . ."   *L* III, 831.

202   "Susan knows . . ."   *L* II, 612.

202   "Dont do . . ."   *L* II, 465.

202   "pseudo Sister"   *L* III, 716.

202–3   Sue's gifts to Emily   *YH* II, 263, 336.

203   "The tie . . ."   *L* III, 893.

203   Mary Lee Hall on Sue and Emily   *YH* II, 440 (to Genevieve Taggard; December 8, 1932).

PAGE

203 "Could *I* – then . . ." *P* #220, and *L* II, 381 and n.: "The tension which developed between ED and Sue, when the infant Ned began to absorb Sue's attention, is hinted at in this note, which is in the handwriting of about 1861."
203 *"Private . . ."* *YH* II, 38.
204 "I had a terror . . ." *L* II, 404.
204–5 ED to Sue *L* III, 799 (early October 1883), 800, 800–1 (and *P* #1584).
206 "If it is finished . . ." *L* II, 315.


CHAPTER 12


219 "fierce insistence" Mrs. Todd's journal, November 30, 1890.
220 "palsy here, – . . ." *L* II, 408 (to Higginson, June 7, 1862).
221 "queer – . . ." *AB*, p. 51 n.
221 "It has always seemed . . ." *AB*, p. 53.
221 "colossal," "the real stuff . . ." Ibid.
221 "Miss [Lavinia] Dickinson . . ." *AB*, p. 67.
221 "no one left . . ." *AB*, p. 33.
221–22 "he died . . ." *Home*, p. 374.
222 "It struck me" *AB*, p. 66.
223 "we happen to *know* . . ." *YH* II, 295 ff.
224 "So I conclude . . ." *LL*, p. 71 (ED to Joseph Lyman, about 1865?).
227 "horrible . . . 'innocent . . .'" *AB*, p. 166.


CHAPTER 13


229 "What means . . ." Alfred E. Stearns, *An Amherst Boyhood*, p. 76.
229 "curiously in fear" Mabel Loomis Todd's journal, November 30, 1890.
229 "a bit ashamed" *An Amherst Boyhood*, p. 72.
230 "Sue was relentlessly . . ." Mary Lee Hall to Millicent Todd Bingham, February 20, 1935.
230 "Sue was a jealous . . ." Letter to Mrs. Bingham, August 5, 1933.
230 "Sue did everything . . ." Letter of April 10, 1934.
230 "During your Mother's absence . . ." Letter of February 20, 1935.
230–31 "I can remember . . ." Letter of April 15, 1945.
231 "I think Sue inherited . . ." Letter of September 14, 1930, to Mabel Loomis Todd.
231 "the Old Scratch" *AB*, p. 59.
231 " . . . you never will know . . ." Letter of February 20, 1935, to Mrs. Bingham.
231 "To me Sue . . ." Letter of August 5, 1933, to Mrs. Bingham.
231 "Vinnie told me . . ." Ibid.
232 "immorality," "in the arms of a man" *YH* II, pp. 375–76.
232 "So successful . . ." *Emily Dickinson: A Revelation* (1954), p. 61.
232 "Vinnie's special aversion" Ibid., p. 60.
232 "little hussy . . ." Ibid., p. 23.

PAGE

232 "deceptions," "falsehoods," *"stabbed . . ."* Mary Lee Hall to Mrs. Bingham (August 5, 1933).

232 "I do hope . . ." *AB,* p. 374 (Mary Lee Hall to Mabel Loomis Todd, July 29, 1930).

233 Gethsemane "but a Province . . ." *P* #553, about 1862.


C H A P T E R  1 4


236 "meditating majestically . . ." *YH* I, p. xx.

236 "It is hard to steer . . ." Cf. *AB,* p. 62.

236 "saved [her] Life" *L* II, 460 (June 1869) and *L* II, 649 (about 1879).

236 "but one or two" poems *L* II, 404 (April 25, 1862).

237 "the ancient people" *LL,* p. 12.

238 "the only male relative . . ." *L* II, 561 (to Mrs. Holland, August 1876).

238 "to spare expense . . ." *L* II, 427 (to Louise and Frances Norcross, October 7, 1863).

238 "raise an *awful* breeze" *Home,* p. 359.

239 "I don't pretend . . ." *Lord Jim,* Sun Dial ed., p. 76.

239 "how incomprehensible . . ." Ibid., p. 180.

239 "My eyes were . . ." Ibid., p. 241.

240 "When I try to organize . . ." *L* II, 414 (to Higginson, August 1862).

240 "short sharp probings . . ." Melville on Shakespeare, in "Hawthorne and His Mosses," *The Literary World,* August 17 and 24, 1850.

240 "Circumference" *L* II, 412 (to Higginson, July 1862).

241 "I wept a tear . . ." *L* I, 143 (October 9, 1851),

243 "She had to think . . ." *Home,* p. 414.

LIBRARY
FLORISSANT VALLEY COMMUNITY COLLEGE
ST. LOUIS, MO

INVENTORY 1983